VARIORUM COLLECTED STUDIES SERIES

Figures in the Landscape

Grace before Meat. Painted in England by Egbert van Heemskerck.
© Ursula van Edelman and with permission of the Städelsches Kunstinstitut, Frankfurt.

Margaret Spufford

# Figures in the Landscape

## Rural Society in England,
## 1500–1700

VARIORUM

Aldershot · Burlington USA · Singapore · Sydney

**Published in the Variorum Collected Studies Series by**

Ashgate Publishing Limited
Gower House, Croft Road,
Aldershot, Hampshire GU11 3HR
Great Britain

Ashgate Publishing Company
131 Main Street,
Burlington, Vermont 05401–5600
USA

Ashgate website: http://www.ashgate.com

ISBN 0–86078–804–0


**British Library CIP Data**
Spufford, Margaret
    Figures in the Landscape: Rural Society in England, 1500–1750 — (Variorum Collected
    Studies Series: CS666).
    1. Reformation—England. 2. Peasantry—England—History. 3. England—Rural conditions.
    I. Title.
    305.5'633'0942

**US Library of Congress CIP Data**
Spufford, Margaret
    Figures in the Landscape: Rural Society in England, 1500–1700 / Margaret Spufford.
       p.  cm. — (Variorum Collected Studies Series: CS666). Includes bibliographical references
    and indexes; hb; alk. paper.
    1. England—Rural conditions. 2. Villages—England—History—16th century. 3. Villages—
    England—History—17th century. I. Title. II. Series: Variorum Collected Studies; CS666.
    HN388.E53S68    1999                                    99–16490
    307.72'0942–dc21                                         CIP


The paper used in this publication meets the minimum requirements of the American National
    Standard for Information Sciences – Permanence of Paper for Printed Library Materials, ANSI
    Z39.48–1984.        ∞   ™

Printed by St Edmundsbury Press, Bury St Edmunds, Suffolk

VARIORUM COLLECTED STUDIES SERIES CS666

# CONTENTS

vii

This volume contains x + 364 pages

# ACKNOWLEDGEMENTS

Grateful acknowledgement is made to the following persons, institutions and publishers for kindly permitting the reproduction of the studies in this volume: Dr Kevin Schürer, editor of *Local Population Studies* (II); the Syndics of the Cambridge University Press (III, XIII); the Cambridge Antiquarian Society (IV, XII); The Past and Present Society, Oxford and *Past and Present* Publications, Cambridge University Press (VII); editors of *Albion* and Dr Takahashi (VIII); the Folklore Society, London (IX); International Thomson Publishing Services Ltd and Janet Blackman and Keith Nield, editors of *Social History* (X); Routledge (XI); Dr Martin Brett and Professor Diarmid MacCulloch, editors of *Journal of Ecclesiastical History* (XIV); and Dr Clyde Binfield, editor of *Journal of the United Reformed Church History Society* (XV).

I am grateful to the Master and Fellows of Magdalene College, Cambridge; the Department of Prints and Drawings, British Museum; the Library of Congress, Washington; Mr Dennis Jeeps; and Eyre and Spottiswood (Reed Books) for their kind permission to use original or copyright material in this book. I owe the frontispiece, Egbert van Heemskerk's 'Grace before Meat', described by Dr Henry Mount as one of a group 'representing specifically English scenes', now in the Städelsches Kunstinstitut, Frankfurt, to that body, and to Ursula Edelmann, the photographer.

# PREFACE

It seemed to me, on reflection, that the appearance of a collection of essays forms a very suitable moment to thank the great men and women who have trained and nurtured and taught me: so I wish to seize this moment to do so. Not for nothing did I write in the 'Preface' to *Contrasting Communities* in 1974, the book of which I am most proud, of Professor Herbert Finberg, who was my research supervisor and Head of the Department of English Local History at Leicester in my time, that he taught me all the craftsmanship I knew, and that I wished I had a better thank-offering to make. For integrity may be the virtue I value most, but craftsmanship is the skill I value most. Whatever he was doing, designing the layout of a book, printing it, translating the Latin of the Mass, or private prayers, drinking a glass of wine and savouring it, or writing prose in the brown ink especially made for his beautiful calligraphic hand, Herbert was a craftsman. It was not always pleasant, or an easy ride, to be his pupil. I remember the triumphant delight with which I finished, as I thought, my first monograph for press the day before our first child was due to be born: I remember with equal ease, and photographic recall, the letter in his perfect brown-inked hand that accompanied the returned manuscript, impeccably timed, six weeks later. The key sentence ran, 'This is a work of reputable and thorough scholarship, such as I should have expected from your pen', and continued, the brown script now italicised, '*it remains only to turn it into a work of art*'. He made me re-write, re-balance, and re-shape every single sentence, and it took me a whole year, new mother as I was. I was not then always thankful: but I have been ever since.

I am also deeply indebted to Dr Esther Moir, who first pointed me in the direction of the Department of English Local History at Leicester and made my work seem of value.

The years of Hoskins, Finberg, Hurst, Beresford, St Joseph and Maurice Barley, in which I served my apprenticeship, were great years. They were years in which we all learned to get 'mud on our boots'. Sometimes, as I discovered rather ruefully after making a necessary exit from a field on one occasion by crawling through a drain, under a hedge, we acquired mud in our hair, too. There were indeed 'giants in the earth in those days'. When I looked that sentiment up, I found it as far back as the *Book of Genesis* (I have had some difficulty dating this text, but reference works tell me that the 'J' version of it is 'generally dated to the tenth century BC'). Even half-a-generation before me, there were still giants. It was not always easy to be a junior research student in a department when the young Dr Thirsk was coming up to her prime. There was quite a long period when I wondered if I would ever have an idea that Joan Thirsk either had not had, or formulated, better, first. Joan cast then, and thankfully still casts, a long shadow. There are still giants about. But the rest of us may feel forgiven for feeling, as apparently we have felt ever since the author of *Genesis*, somewhat like pygmies, in their shade. Never mind, we have to do our best, while thanking those who taught us, with a generosity with their time which we scarcely deserved.

MARGARET SPUFFORD

*Whittlesford*
*Maundy Thursday 1999*

# ILLUSTRATIONS

# I

# The Scope of the Enquiry

All local historians used, at least before demography and social history adopted the microcosmic approach, and social anthropology climbed into bed too, to have to justify working on the mere local community, the villages, the Chippenhams and the Whickhams, the microcosms of this world.[1]

As microcosmic historians, we resemble, at first glance, the students in Rembrandt's 'Anatomy Lesson'. They are engaged on minute, concentrated dissection of a body, in my own case a body of people living, and interacting with each other in a village, parish or small town. They shared the economics of their daily lives within their parish communities, where they ran, or failed to run, the fields and the commons, and had some responsibility for the parish church, and perhaps the dissenting chapel, or chapels, too. This microcosm was made up of its component microcosms, the individual households of the parish, each with its own structure. They again were composed of single individuals, our predecessors, each just as complex and intricate as we are ourselves. Which of us will claim truly to comprehend, to 'know' in all reality, another human being, or even fully to 'know' ourselves? So this concentrated dissection of a village community, like a dead body, leads us further and further, deeper and deeper, until we reach the individual cells. These, as historians working on the 'common sort' of people of the past, whom John Brand described in 1776 as *'little ones,*[2] who occupy the lowest Place in the Political Arrangement of Human Beings' we can hardly ever put under our microscopes. We are, by definition, bound to fail. We do not have enough evidence. Yet we still, as micro-historians, have this vocation, or, if you prefer, this obsession.

Yet the analogy of Rembrandt's 'Anatomy Lesson' is false. Unlike the students he paints, we are not seeking to dissect a whole fresh dead body. On the contrary, our documents present us with only dusty fragments of a very old corpse. What we seek to do, when we examine a community in the past, is

---

[1]  H.P.R. Finberg, *The Local Historian and his Theme: An Introductory Lecture*, Department of English Local History, Occasional Paper 1, 1st series (Leicester, 1952). See also Charles Phythian-Adams (ed.), 'Editorial Foreword', *Societies, Cultures and Kinship, 1580–1850, Collected Papers in English Local History* (Leicester, 1993), pp.xi–xv.

[2]  His italics. Introduction to his amended edition of Henry Bourne, *Antiquitates Vulgares* (1776, earliest work on English popular custom published 1725).

scrupulously to re-assemble these fragments, to re-animate an organic entity, until we have reconstructed something as near the living organism as we can, given our exceedingly limited materials. We are the resurrectors: we seek to make the past live, as accurately as we can. But the dry bones that are given us, unlike the prophet Ezekiel, only come in small splinters.

My own contribution to this process of reconstituting communities of relatively powerless rural people in the past in England has been to expand the scope of the enquiry. When I went to Leicester as a research student in 1960, Professor Hoskins' great classic, *The Midland Peasant*,[3] was the last, complete, word and my starting-point. But, as all our words inevitably are, it was, in fact, incomplete. The earliest of the papers printed here, *A Cambridgeshire Community: Chippenham from Settlement to Enclosure* (chapter V, below) was very much in this orthodox mould. I have pointed out some of the ways in which I would now look at Chippenham in a *Postscript*, based on new material. Dr Esther Moir reviewed *The Midland Peasant* very favourably. I owe a great deal to her review, for it focused my own dissatisfaction. She ended it 'if one might be allowed to venture one criticism, it is that Dr Hoskins seems to equate peasant culture and peasant economy … One is left with the impression that Wigston Magna was peopled with that abstraction, economic man'. I became determined to turn those abstractions, economic men and women, into real human beings.

Demography I left severely alone: it was safely moving into the hands of more appropriate scholars than I.[4] The whole business of 'peasant' shelter had already done so. More was known in the 1960s in England than anywhere else in Europe, I believe, of small farmhouses and cottages.[5] But no-one knew, or had asked, how their inhabitants reacted to the Reformation, or to the

[3]     W.G. Hoskins, *The Midland Peasant: The Economic & Social History of a Leicestershire Village* (London, 1957). Esther Moir, 'Review of *The Midland Peasant*', *The Cambridge Review* (1957), pp.148–149.

[4]     Peter Laslett, *The World We Have Lost* was not published until 1965 (London) when I had already been working for five years. The Cambridge Group for the History of Population and Social Structure celebrated the thirtieth year of its foundation in 1994. For its main productions, see n.27 and also E.A. Wrigley, *Population and History* (London, 1969) and with R.S. Davies, J.E. Oeppen and R.S. Schofield, *English Population History from Family Reconstitution, 1580–1837* (Cambridge, 1997).

[5]     A summary of what was then known, and the bibliography, will be found in Joan Thirsk (ed.), *The Agrarian History of England and Wales, IV, 1500–1640* (Cambridge, 1967), chapters X and XI and select bibliography. The Vernacular Architecture Group has published three volumes of bibliography: R. de Zouche Hall (ed.), *A Bibliography on Vernacular Architecture* (1972); D.J.H. Michelmore (ed.), *A Current Bibliography of Vernacular Architecture* (1979), I.R. Pattison, D.S. Pattison and N.W. Alcock (eds), *A Bibliography of Vernacular Architecture 3, for 1977–89* (1992); vol. 4 is in preparation.

successive changes in their parish churches in the sixteenth and seventeenth centuries: were they passive, or active participants? Could they read, or were they dependent on what they were told from pulpit and manor house? Did they themselves found the dissenting church of the seventeenth century? Were the poorest of them, and the women, involved too? Was any cheap print available which they could afford? Was it distributed so that they could get it, if it existed, either at market or in their own villages? This, I decided, was my agenda. I did not know I was sentencing myself for life: but even if I had, I am not, as Professor Patrick Collinson once wrote of himself, in, I hope, a moment of flippancy rather than despair 'a failed escapologist'. I have enjoyed myself. My whole work was percipiently summarised long ago on a train back from a supervision in Leicester, with a fellow mature student and beloved friend, Dr Jack Ravensdale, who was working, like me, on Cambridgeshire.[6] He said 'Well Margaret, it is quite simple: I'll do the landscape, you paint the figures'. So that is what we did: although the contrast between his work and mine was perhaps excessively heightened when I cut the whole chapter on 'The Cambridgeshire Landscape' which should have opened my *Contrasting Communities* in order to reduce the typescript by 10 per cent for Cambridge University Press.[7] Ever since, I have been working on those figures which people the landscape, trying to get at their beliefs, thoughts, education, reading-matter, opinions and even feelings.

I have tried, however, not to neglect the landscape itself, which formed the essential background for my figures. Rural people cannot be separated from their agricultural and economic situations and constraints, and I have tried to bear these constantly in mind. In my work on cheap print, for instance, my cut-off point for consideration of any 'small book' was the upper selling price of 6d, since I reckoned this was the absolute maximum an agricultural labourer on wages of 12d a day could save from his wages for a luxury like this.

Because I have tried, in the last 40 years, to work onwards from the landholdings of 'the common sort', to their taxable capacity and economic status, the number of hearths in their houses, and the significance of this number, their household possessions, the accessibility of schooling to them, and hence their reading ability, the cheap print within reach of their pockets and its distribution, the knotty problem of whether their religious opinions could be discovered at all and what importance, if any, these had in their lives, and their religious networks, the contents of this volume are necessary extraordinarily

---

[6]　J.R. Ravensdale, *Liable to Floods. Village Landscape on the Edge of the Fens AD 450–1850* (Cambridge, 1974).

[7]　This is now forthcoming in the *Proceedings of the Cambridge Antiquarian Society*, over twenty-five years later.

various. I have only omitted popular politics and crime from my agenda, along with demography and vernacular architecture. My papers, therefore, cover a wide field, particularly since some of my enquiries necessarily involved a scrupulous examination of the biases of the source material I was trying to use. There are therefore early papers here on, for instance, the reliability of the Hearth Tax as a social and economic indicator, as well as on the scribes of villagers' wills. Some of these, like the scribal paper, were very influential in their time, and have formed the foundation of much later work.[8] It still seemed worth reprinting a paper which had started a new line of enquiry, and on which so many productive hours had been spent. I vividly remember asking the Archivist of the University of Keele to come and check my findings on scribal hands, made from some six or seven hundred xerox copies of original wills, now sorted into separate heaps in a seminar room at Keele. He flung up his hands after inspecting the evidence, and said, 'You don't want me, you want the Metropolitan Police!' It was neither the first, nor the last, time my faith in 'experts' was debunked, and I found I was really on my own.

The width of my enquiry explains, then, the diversity of the contents of my articles written along the way, and reprinted here. There is a fundamental integrity to my questioning, but it will only be discovered in this light.

One benefit of pursuing a line of questioning through so many diverse areas has been that it brings together classes and types of documentary reference which are not normally thought of together. In the early 1990s a group of research students and I solved the problem of establishing the social and economic status of various dissenting groups, for example, by matching entries for those prosecuted in the ecclesiastical courts with those in various taxation records. This is an obvious exercise for a local historian, but not so obvious to ecclesiastical historians. I am proud of the way my former research students have transformed, for instance, our knowledge of women's effective economic functioning in the seventeenth century, of the socio-economic spread of different types of religious dissenters and even conformists as well as of cheap print and its distribution.[9] They have all tended to use categories of records not normally found in conjunction.

---

[8]     See, for instance, Christopher Marsh, 'In the Name of God? Will Making and Faith in Early Modern England', *The Records of the Nation*, G.H. Martin and P. Spufford (eds) (Woodbridge, 1990). This, with Eric Carlson, 'The Historical Value of the Ely Consistory Probate Records', *Index of the Probate Records of the Consistory Court of Ely, 1449–1858*, Part I, Elizabeth Leedham-Green and Rosemary Rodd (eds) (British Record Society, 1994) pp. xvii–lix, looks likely to be the last word for some time.

[9]     All these matters are summarised in Margaret Spufford (ed.), *The World of Rural Dissenters, 1520–1725* (Cambridge, 1995) except womens' management in the seventeenth century. This can be found in Amy Louise Erickson, *Women and Property in Early Modern*

Only one more concern remains on my private agenda now: I have not yet fully covered these people with clothes.[10] This, indeed, takes me back to man as an economic animal; but no-one else has covered 'clothing' for the 'common sort' in the seventeenth century, as apart from the 'dress' of the fashionable. And, fatal last words for an historian, I have found a source. So I am not yet through my life-sentence, even though I laid down the terms of it over twenty-five years ago. Moreover, because tides turn, and fashions swing, I am becoming as alarmed now in the 1990s as I was in the 1960s and 1970s. Then, we only had 'economic man', sheltered, reproducing, and tilling his fields. We knew about his acreages. Now, there is an increasing tendency for us only to have 'social history man', reading, writing, responding to social control, deferential to his superiors, or sometimes exploding in the odd riot. But we quite often don't know what he farmed, any more. Our farmers and farm-labourers have become divorced from their farms. Just as in the 1970s I thought it was time to enlarge the scope of local history by asking questions about religion, literacy and cheap print, now I think it is time to re-anchor the balloon of social history to its foundations in the ground, and re-plant the men and women of the rural past with their feet firmly in the land they tilled.[11] If we do not, we shall be losing grip on *their* own reality. Their own reality and truth must be our prime consideration.

My first, and probably most important, book was *Contrasting Communities*, a study of three Cambridgeshire villages slotted into their backgrounds, in which different landscapes produced three different versions of social life. I spent what seemed a long time in the 1960s, as I wrote this book, immobilised

---

*England* (London, 1993). The work on cheap print and one group of dissenters and conformists will be found more fully set out in Tessa Watt, *Cheap Print and Popular Piety, 1550–1640* (Cambridge, 1991); David Harrison, *Ancestral Subject Catalogue of Chapbook Themes*, 4 vols, unpublished Ph.D. thesis (Roehampton Institute and University of Surrey, 1996); Christopher W. Marsh, *The Family of Love in English Society, 1550–1630* (Cambridge, 1994); Judith D. Maltby, *Prayer Book and People: Religious Conformity before the Civil War* (Cambridge, 1998) has added something on conformists. Mathew Storey has also made a contribution to conformist history with his edition of the diary of the sin-beset, hard-drinking, post-Restoration yeoman of Mildenhall, William Coe, whose faith meant so much to him, see Mathew Storey (ed.), *Two East Anglian Diaries, 1642–1729: Isaac Archer and William Coe*, Suffolk Record Society XXXVI (Woodbridge, 1994).

[10] I have made a start in *The Great Reclothing of Rural England* (London, 1984). I am grateful to the Leverhulme Trust and the Pasold Fund, which are supporting further work. The first fruits will be found in 'The costs of apparel in 17th-century England and the accuracy of Gregory King', *Economic History Review* (2000).

[11] One of the most recent pieces in this volume, 'Families, Will Witnesses and Economic Structure in the Fens and on the Chalk', written with Dr Takahashi, is a renewed plea for such an approach. I greatly look forward to Dr Keith Wrightson's sixteenth- and seventeenth-century volume in the new *Penguin Economic History of Britain*.

in a plaster cast with two very small children in Staffordshire. This immobilisation had one entirely negative effect: it meant that I was working in near-total isolation, unaware of current debate and discussion, without time even to read the most recent books. It also had the very positive effect, though, that the thoughts I came up with and the lines of enquiry I pursued were original and very much my own, apart, that is, from the mysterious alchemy which means that individuals working even in different countries on similar problems at the same time tend to come up with similar solutions. Not for nothing did I use a quotation from Emmanuel Le Roy Ladurie's book on Languedoc at the beginning of the 'Introduction' to *Contrasting Communities* because it was so apposite. Yet I only came to *The Peasants of Languedoc* after I had submitted my own text to the publisher. My work ever since has been both handicapped and enriched in the same ways. When I wrote *Contrasting Communities* I made two major errors. The first was to treat my three communities of study as if they were isolated from the macrocosm of England, subsisting in a vacuum. We are all now familiar with Professor John Chartres' work on the carriers[12] who worked a regularly weekly service or services out from the inns of London, recorded from the 1630s and surely existing long before. No-one can yet be familiar with Dr Frearson's work on the newsbooks of the 1620s. It has a splendid chapter on the dissemination of the newsbooks, which adds greatly to our knowledge of the distribution networks under the early Stuarts.[13] He has also mapped the roads of England, using the stages given in the Elizabethan roadbooks.[14] One of his quotations is from John Earle, who, when he wrote in 1627, likened the character of a carrier to 'the vault in Gloucester church, that converses whispers at a distance: for he takes the sound out of your mouth at York and makes it be heard as far as London'.[15]

But Dr Frearson's newsbooks are, to me, possibly upmarket print. They only cost 2d each, but he argues the regular purchase of weekly copies was necessary to follow the news (Plate I).[16] My own work on the mainly poverty-

---

[12]     J.A. Chartres, 'The Capital's Provincial Eyes: London's Inns in the Early Eighteenth Century', *London Journal* 1 (1977), pp.24–39; and 'Road Carrying in the Seventeenth Century: Myth and Reality', *Economic History Review* 33, 2nd series (1977), pp.73–94.

[13]     Michael Frearson, *The English Corantos of the 1620s*, unpublished Ph.D. thesis (Cambridge, 1993), to appear in the series edited by David McKitterick, under the title 'The History of the Book in Britain', Cambridge University Press.

[14]     This road system appears as part of an integral map, Map 1, in Spufford, *World of Rural Dissenters*, pp.38–39, reproduced below in this chapter.

[15]     Frearson, *English Corantos*, p.19.

[16]     Frearson, *English Corantos*, pp.278–279.

stricken pedlars who distributed cheaper print,[17] along with their other goods, as well as the specialist ballad salesmen, and women, and the almanac and mercury saleswomen, to relatively very poor readers opened my eyes to the way our microcosms are interconnected, and cannot be treated in isolation from each other. My work on the huge semi-pastoral parish of Eccleshall in Staffordshire,[18] which lay astride the arterial highway from London to Chester (Map 1), has shown me how wrong I was to think of even the very poor, at a great distance from the metropolis, living in total ignorance of current events, the latest news, jokes and songs. For Eccleshall had a large number of readers, avid for news, and was a paradise for pedlars, who found havens in its numerous very disreputable ale-houses. Our microcosms were not unaware of the macrocosm they formed.[19]

My ignorance of this awareness of interconnection was one major error. The other, even more massive, was this. After *Contrasting Communities* was published, I failed to take up the invitations that came my way, to discuss my methodology. I thought it would be boring for my audiences. I have regretted this error ever since, and increasingly so as individual village studies have come out which have not been set in a regional context, in which the 'typicality' or '*a*-typicality', the 'normality' or 'abnormality' of that particular settlement, for its own agricultural type, has not been established. Increasingly, this issue of *typicality or a-typicality for an agricultural type seems to me the central problem with which microhistorians have to wrestle.* We all fall into the same trap. It takes so long to re-articulate the bones, organs and muscles of a settlement in the past, and clothe it in at least some flesh, to re-create some features of some of the inhabitants, that when we have done it, we look, exhausted, at our own re-creation, and say to ourselves, subconsciously at least, 'So *this* is what "the English village" was like before industrialisation'. But, of course, it is not. It is what one *type* of English village was like, perhaps. So a part of what I want to do in this introduction to my work is to seize that opportunity I missed over twenty-five years ago, and at least sketch out my fundamental methodology, which attempted to find a method for distinguishing the typical from the a-typical example, by region. This I believed, and still believe, is essential before embarking on any individual case study.

---

[17] Margaret Spufford, 'The Pedlar, the Historian, and the Folklorist: Seventeenth-Century Communications', see chapter IX below.

[18] Margaret Spufford, *Poverty Portrayed: Gregory King and Eccleshall, Staffordshire* (Staffordshire Studies, 1995).

[19] My own new awareness of this seventeenth-century awareness of 'news' was itself partly responsible for my more recent suggestions of the reasons for the partial correlations between protoindustrial areas, and more numerous proportions of dissenters. See below, pp.16–17.

8

In 1960, while I was working on my MA dissertation, on the old county of Cambridgeshire, excluding the Isle of Ely, in the sixteenth and seventeenth centuries, I became aware that individual case studies in depth from villages with abnormally rich records, were throwing up widely varying results. Any individual example was, I discovered, unsafe. This was before the fundamental *Agrarian History of England and Wales, IV*, edited by Dr Thirsk, setting out the basic tenets, and areas, of agricultural regionalism, was published in 1967.[20] Those regions delineated in *The Agrarian History* were based on a wholesale study of the different agricultural practices demonstrated by probate inventories. But this biblical tome was not available to me. What I discovered was that there was apparently a pattern in the different developments in my own county of study. I also discovered a code for cracking this pattern. It was based on the taxation returns.

I discovered that if I took the returns of the *relatively* thorough 'Great Subsidy' of 1524/5, which purported to list the names of all the adult males of each settlement, down to and including, the wage-earners paying on wages of £1 a year, and divided these into economic bands across the taxpaying spectrum, and then mapped the proportional results, I got very different patterns for different types of agricultural economy. I had three main regions in Cambridgeshire besides the river-valleys: the upland chalk, one of the great champagne, barley-growing, malting areas; the fen-edge, where there was relatively little arable compared to the wet pasture, fen-commons; and the heavy clay uplands, more suitable for grass than for barley.

On the chalk, a very high proportion of agricultural labourers, so necessary in all arable regions, were taxed. There were fewer in the middle bands, and a greater proportion of the yeomen farmers who ran these chalk farms. In the fens, the picture was quite different: fewer wage-labourers, fewer of the most prosperous, and many more in the middle bands of the taxable spectrum. The clay was less strongly distinguished, but tended to follow the pattern of prosperity and poverty on the chalk.[21]

---

[20]     Thirsk, *Agrarian History*, IV, p.4, fig. I. This was elaborated in Joan Thirsk, *The Agrarian History of England and Wales, VI, 1640–1750* (Cambridge, 1984), p.xx.

[21]     Great caution is necessary, of course, in treating these returns of 1524/5. Professor Richard Hoyle has shown that in the Craven area of the West Riding of Yorkshire the 'assessments were engineered: the number assessed and their individual valuations rose and fell in accordance with political exigencies and local circumstances'. He also showed the completely different expectations of the likely range of assessments which an historian of the North and an East Anglian historian would have. So much lower are the expectations of the northern historian, and, no doubt, the taxable capacity of the North, that Professor Hoyle finds the group of young men between puberty and marriage seriously under-recorded since 'only' 14.6 per cent of those recorded in one of the fullest of his sources are taxed on less than 6/8d. R.W. Hoyle (ed.), 'Early Tudor Craven: Subsidies and Assessments, 1510–1547', *Yorkshire*

I next went on to carry out a similar exercise with one of the Hearth Taxes of the 1660s, which purported to include most heads of household, down to, and including, those exempt from taxation on the grounds of poverty. I got a similar, but more highly accented, picture. The Fens were distinguished by a higher proportion of taxpayers of moderate means, taxed on 2 and 3 hearths, from their chalk-upland counterparts, where the prosperous seemed to live in grander houses with more hearths. There was a higher proportion of those paying on only one hearth, or altogether exempt, on the chalk, too. Another feature distinguished fen from chalk: the fen settlements had grown, radically, with the influx of incomers seeking to make a living on the fen commons, or as sub-tenants in the great population rise of the sixteenth and seventeenth centuries. The picture of prosperity on the clays was different again, but more nearly akin to the chalk. It also had one noticeable variation: only on the pastures of the heavy clays did population shrink somewhat, in this period of demographic growth.

It is very important to stress that some taxation levels in different agricultural regions could, and did, mean different levels of prosperity. A man taxed on two hearths in the Fens was probably a half-yardlander, a man with 15 acres or so of arable. But he had his fen-common, and his substantial house had 'cheese chambers' in its cross-wings (Plate 2). He could be, and often was, a prosperous man. His counterpart on the chalk, with only 15 acres of arable and no common, was hanging on desperately in the face of engrossing yeomen attempting to acquire his farm, trying, and often failing, to prevent the foreclosure of the mortgage on his land he had had to take out after a bad harvest.

But these fundamental differences in the economic status of those taxed on the same sum, or the same number of hearths, in different agricultural regions,

---

*Archaeological Society Records Series* 145 (1987), pp.xv, xviii–xix and fig. 3. No less than 58 per cent of people in the townships in the loan book of 1522, which is one of the fullest of his sources, were assessed on *less* than £1 in goods. Despite this he concludes the return 'seriously underestimates the number on the lowest margins of society'. Such a conclusion would be unthinkable further south and east, as my own surprise at finding as many as 53 per cent of wage earners taxed on £1 or 30s. in Cambridgeshire shows. This was a much higher proportion than comparable figures obtainable for other counties at the time of writing. Margaret Spufford, *Contrasting Communities* (Cambridge, 1972), pp.31, 33. Dr John Sheail's irreplaceable article 'The Distribution of Taxable Population and Wealth in England during the Early Sixteenth Century', *Transactions of the Institute of British Geographers* 55 (1977) has to be used to set these different levels of assessment in a national context. We still do not know what criteria the township or village jurors used as a rule-of-thumb guide to base their assessments on, since their bills do not apparently survive (Hoyle, 'Early Tudor Craven', p.xiii). The rare exceptions are discussed in R.W. Hoyle, *Tudor Taxation Records: A Guide for Users* (P.R.O. Publications, 1994) pp.17–20. They still do not give the basis of assessment.

*The Scope of the Enquiry*

did not, and this is a very important point indeed, affect the fact that these different regions, and their consequently different economic and social structures, could be picked up from the quite different proportions and distribution of those taxed in the different bands. If you normally had as much as 40–50 per cent of your taxable population assessed on two hearths in the 1660s in the fens, and under 20 per cent with two hearths assessed on this middle band on the chalk downland and the clays, you know you are dealing with a different type of society.[22] Therefore, when I came to write *Contrasting Communities*, in which I took as case studies, Chippenham on the chalk, Willingham in the fens, and Orwell on the clay, the choice of these particular richly-documented villages was very firmly rooted in those analyses of the taxation records of the 140-odd villages which made up the whole county, in the 1520s and the 1660s. The essential ledger of analysis of taxation behind it all is known to my husband as 'Margaret's Domesday' – and without establishing typicality, or a-typicality, by these means, and setting a new case study firmly in context, I will not, metaphorically speaking, stir a step. Serendipity, the lucky find, is indispensable: but it is *not* the basis of my methodology. Similarly, before looking at religious practice in any individual parish, I first created an 'ecclesiastical domesday' based on cross-sections of the visitation records for the whole of the old county of Cambridgeshire.

There is a profound irony in this discussion. All my life, the regular criticism of my work has been that it focused on the qualitative, not the quantitative. (The 'bon mot' made by myself at my own expense, at one of my seminar talks, that 'my methodology was serendipity' was thought so apt that it crossed the Atlantic, and appeared almost immediately, as a genuine criticism, in a review published in California.) I have, in fact, always tried for a quantitative skeleton to my work, to which I attach my qualitative work securely. I have tried to encourage my doctoral pupils to follow this method. But good skeletons should be invisible, or at least, the bones should barely show. Now I am revealing the skeleton.

Behind my qualitative history there does lie a basic, quantitative frame. This introduction to the scope of my enquiry is therefore in part the discussion of an underpinning methodology, which is always meant to be almost invisible, but which underlies my work: and which I feel might also be useful as underpinning in the work of other people.

---

[22]    My unpublished analysis of the 1664 Hearth Tax for the old county of Cambridgeshire, excluding the Isle of Ely. Mrs Nesta Evans's volume on *The Cambridgeshire Hearth Tax, Michaelmas 1664*, the first of the British Record Society volumes on the Hearth Tax, will supplement this (1999). Also my MA dissertation, 'Rural Cambridgeshire, 1520–1680' (Leicester, 1962), pp.80–82, and 'The Significance of the Cambridgeshire Hearth Tax', *Proceedings of the Cambridgeshire Antiquarian Society* 55 (1962), pp.53–64, see chapter IV below.

Map: Roads, Industry and Dissenting Connections, c. 1600.
*The World of Rural Dissenters, 1520–1725*, Margaret Spufford (ed.),
Cambridge University Press, 1995, pp. 38–39.

12

Plate 1: Men in Tavern by Egbert van Heemskerck.

Plate 2: A Reader of the *London Gazette* by Francis Le Piper.

A Merry new Song
Les Chanteurs de Chansons
Cantarine ẜ Strada

Plate 3: Ballard Sellers by Marcellus Laroon from
*The Cryes of the City of London Drawne after Life*, 1687.
Lilly Library, Indiana University, Bloomington, Indiana.

Buy a new Almanack
*Almanachs Nouveaux*
*Lunarij dell Anno Nueus*

_ Maureen delin·                                    P.Tempest exc:
                                                    Cum Privilegio

Plate 4: Almanac Seller by Marcellus Laroon from
*The Cryes of the City of London Drawne after Life*, 1687.
Lilly Library, Indiana University, Bloomington, Indiana.

16

Plate 5: The House of Thomas Greaves of Willingham, a Willwriting Yeoman.
Private collection of 19th-century photographs of Mr Dennis Jeeps.

My work on the Hearth Tax of Michaelmas 1664 for Cambridgeshire gave me the essential frame of similarity and differences which enabled me to pick case studies of villages which seemed to be typical of their agricultural regions. I have wanted to extend the possibility of using the Hearth Taxes in a similar way elsewhere. When I moved to the Research Chair of Social and Local History at Roehampton Institute, University of Surrey, in 1994, it seemed an appropriate moment to try and do something about this ambition. My department has nobly aided and abetted me. The analysis of the main taxation returns for England has itself a long history. In 1952 Professor Darby published his *Domesday Geography of Eastern England*, the first of his area studies which came to make up, by 1977, *Domesday England.*[23] This *Geography* was the Domesday returns, analysed and mapped. He was a notable charioteer, and out of his stable came equally notable horses. In 1975, the British Academy published the next great medieval return which permits examination of the distribution of population and wealth for the whole country, the subsidy-returns of 1334.[24] The first volume of the analysis of the Poll Taxes of the fourteenth century has been published by Dr Carolyn Fenwick.[25] Dr John Sheail mapped the numbers taxed, and the wealth of each settlement in the Great Subsidy of 1524/5, as long ago as 1968.[26]

The great hole comes next.[27] Between 1541 and 1650, the population of England almost doubled from two and three quarter millions to five and a quarter millions.[28] This huge rise in population has made, until now, the wholesale analysis of the next great taxation-returns, the Hearth Taxes of the 1660s and the 1670s, beyond the scope of the most enterprising research student. Dr Wrightson has recently used the Hearth Taxes for as many types of settlement as possible to establish the abnormality, in terms of extreme poverty,

---

[23]     Darby, *Domesday England* (Cambridge, 1997). See Appendix 21 to the volume for his discussion of the history of the project.

[24]     Robin E. Glasscock (ed.), 'The Lay Subsidy of 1334', *Records of Social and Economic History*, new series 2 (British Academy, 1975).

[25]     Carolyn C. Fenwick (ed.), 'The Poll Taxes of 1377, 1379 and 1381, Part I, Bedfordshire-Leicestershire', *Records of Social and Economic History* 27, new series (Oxford, 1998).

[26]     John Sheail, *The Regional Distribution of Wealth in England as indicated by the 1524/5 Lay Subsidy Returns* (London, 1968), now published by the List and Index Society.

[27]     Professor Palliser is doing something to fill this hole, since he is compiling a volume for the British Academy on the figures of households in 1563 and communicants in 1603. But these cannot be used for the analysis of wealth, although they will do much to enlighten us on the distribution of population.

[28]     E.A. Wrigley and R.S. Schofield, *The Population History of England, 1541–1871: A Reconstruction* (London, 1981), pp.207–211.

of his coal-mining *Whickham*,[29] but this is still not an easy thing to do. After the pioneering work of Mr Meekings, Mr Arkell has done most to make the tax accessible to us.[30] So has Dr Husbands, who wrote in 1987 'alone amongst mid and late seventeenth-century taxes, the Hearth Tax allows historians to draw general, comparative conclusions about local economies', and himself undertook an analysis of the tax for 859 randomly-sampled communities. But as he wrote in 1992, 'much of the potential of the Hearth Tax to provide a general framework for the socio-economic history of the later seventeenth century still remains to be exploited at both local and national levels'.[31]

Analysis on a grand scale is impossible without both computer-technology and a whole co-ordinated team of researchers, guided of course by a computer-specialist. Since my appointment to Roehampton Institute, my department has developed a departmental project of great ambition, made possible by the appointment of Dr Rose as a computer historian. We are attempting to analyse the population densities of those taxed, and exempt from taxation, and produce maps for the 1660s or 70s for the whole country. With the British Record Society, we are trying to transcribe and print at least one Hearth Tax return for every county that has not yet got one in print. Where did this huge expansion of population since Dr Sheail's tax of 1524/5 settle? Was the steepest rise in density in just those areas of marginal cultivation with common land, like the fens, and the Staffordshire forest areas, where one would expect it? Furthermore, we want, crudely at least, to analyse poverty and wealth. Were those same forest and fen areas also refuges for the highest proportion of the poor, exempt from taxation? Where were the richest in rural society? And were the great sweeps of corn-growing chalk always the sustainers of both

---

[29]     David Levine and Keith Wrightson, *The Making of an Industrial Society: Whickham, 1560–1765* (Oxford, 1991), pp.156–165.

[30]     Kevin Schürer and Tom Arkell (eds), *Surveying the People: The Interpretation and Use of Document Sources for the Study of Population in the Later Seventeenth Century*, Local Population Studies (Oxford, 1992), contains chapters by both Mr Arkell and Dr Husbands, and a bibliography of their relevant work, pp.279 and 285. There is a masterly unpublished article by Mr Arkell which summarises the state of debate on the Hearth Taxes 'The Problem of Establishing Regional Variations in England's Hearth Tax Household Structure in the Later Seventeenth Century'. See also, Tom Arkell, 'Introduction', with Kevin Schürer, 'Printed Instructions for Administering the Hearth Tax', and bibliographical entry in Schürer and Arkell, *Surveying the People*, pp.1–5, 38–64 and 279.

[31]     Christopher Husbands, 'Hearths, Wealth and Occupations: An Exploration of the Hearth Tax in the Later Seventeenth Century', and bibliographical entry, idem, pp.65–77 and 285. The quotations are to be found on p.76 (from his 'Regional Change in a Pre-Industrial Economy') and p.77.

capitalist yeomen farmers, Professor Ladurie's 'coqs du village'[32] and a high density of the wage-labourers they employed?

There are now (2000) four volumes of returns for Cambridgeshire, Kent, Durham and Northumberland almost ready to go to press. When possible, the introductions will include some material on the surviving buildings themselves. We do not wish only to count hearths without awareness of the houses that contained them. Another nine county volumes are in various stages of preparation. We have deliberately chosen counties which are likely to show strong contrasts for our first county volumes. The wealth, and surviving affluent buildings for Kent and Essex should give very different analyses of hearth numbers and prosperity from the poverty of Westmoreland and Cumberland, and the pastoral and coal-mining areas of Durham and Northumberland. We hope that this series will provide professional historians interested in wealth and density of population, and local historians wishing to establish the 'typicality' of an example, as well as family historians searching for surnames and ancestors, all with fresh material. In the end, we should be able to provide maps of the Hearth Tax analyses for the whole of England and Wales.

We have, then, embarked on a wholesale analysis of the Hearth Taxes, to compare these with Dr Thirsk's farming regions and see whether the economic structures revealed in the two taxations really did correlate, in a rough and ready way, as I have postulated, with agricultural regions. This is a hypothesis that needs careful testing.

So far, I have been discussing the ways that microcosmic history might be fitted into a typology based on taxation, reflecting agricultural regions, which might be supposed to be of interest and great importance only to economic and agricultural historians. Until it is done, my hypothesis that different agricultural regions throw up different taxation patterns, cannot even be tested properly. Examples of 'typical' and 'a-typical' settlement by agricultural region cannot be established. Nor can we look at the relative densities of population and poverty in the regions which were soon to industrialise.

There is a further axiom that also needs careful testing. There has been a belief amongst some social and ecclesiastical historians, that protestant 'godly' beliefs appealed mainly to the 'middling sort' amongst local communities in Tudor, and especially Stuart, England. My research students and I began to investigate this proposition in *The World of Rural Dissenters*. Dr Derek Plumb matched up a sufficiently large sample of the late Lollards in the Thames Valley with their appropriate taxation records in 1524/5 to demonstrate that

---

[32]     Emmanuel Le Roy Ladurie, *The Peasants of Languedoc* (1966), trs. John Day (Illinois, 1974), pp.122-125.

20

they spread across the whole taxable spectrum.  What is more, they did so approximately in proportion to each taxable group in society at large; so Lollards spread roughly evenly across the whole of rural society, from wage-labourers to substantial yeomen.  All social or economic groups had the potential to be Lollards.

Dr Bill Stevenson found a huge group of over 700 individual post-Restoration dissenters belonging to all the sects, whose sectarian careers he could match with their Hearth Tax records.[33]  Well over a third of them, 38 per cent, of all these dissenters were either exempt from the tax on the grounds of poverty, or paid on only one hearth.  It may well be that this proportion, high though it was, was not, unlike Dr Plumb's poor Lollards, in proportion to that section of society at large.  It is still extremely significant that in chapel, conventicle and meeting-house this substantial poor third, the 'meaner' sort, sat alongside the other two-thirds, significant numbers indeed of the 'middling' and 'chiefer' sorts.  For the total comparative analysis of the proportion of these groups in society at large we must again await the results of the Roehampton investigation. But the investigation of the Hearth Taxes should throw light on problems in religious and ecclesiastical history, too.

Furthermore, a correlation has been made, again, between different types of agricultural region, and higher proportions of dissenters. The first person to suggest there was a correlation between forest or pastoral areas and time for reading, leading to dissent, or 'fanatic', opinions was John Aubrey, writing in the 1680s about the contrast between the 'cheese and butter' country of north Wiltshire, and the great chalklands of the south.  He wrote:

> In North Wiltshire, and like the vale of Gloucester (a dirty clayey country) ... hereabout is but little tillage or hard labour, they only milk the cowes and make cheese ... These circumstances make them melancholy, contemplative and malicious ... And by the same reason they are generally more apt to be fanatiques ...
> On the downes ... the south part, where 'tis all upon tillage, and where the shepherds[34] labour hard, their flesh is hard, their bodies strong: being weary after hard labour, they have not leisure to read and contemplate of religion, but goe to bed to their rest, to rise betime the next morning to their labour.[35]

---

[33]    Bill Stevenson, 'The Social and Economic Status of Post-Restoration Dissenters, 1660–1725', in Spufford, *The World*, pp.332–359, especially pp.333–336, and p.19.

[34]    'Shepherds' may sound as if they belong in pastoral areas, but in fact the fertility of chalk arable areas was kept up by sheep-flocks.

[35]    John Aubrey, *The Natural History of Wiltshire*, ed. John Britton (London, 1847), p.11. I am particularly indebted to Adam Fox for this reference.

Among contemporary historians, the first to notice the correlation between forest, pastoral, fen areas and dissent later amplified by Dr Hill, was Dr Joan Thirsk.[36] Professor Everitt later went on to write on seventeenth-century dissent in Kent:

> Dissenters were everywhere most numerous in the forest parishes, and in the Wealden area of Mid-Kent they comprised as much as 17 per cent of the population ...

He went on to say:

> In the past, the predominance of Dissent in rural areas like the Weald has usually been attributed to the cloth industry. Quite why there should be this apparent association between sectarian Christianity and cloth has always seemed, to one student of history at least, something of a mystery.

But he qualified this:

> When one looks more closely into the distribution of rural Dissent, however, it becomes clear that it also flourished in many districts where there was no cloth manufacture to speak of. The truth rather seems to be that the link was only an indirect one, and that cloth-making and Nonconformity were probably fostered independently by certain local characteristics peculiar to the society and settlement pattern of these areas. What were these characteristics so far as Dissent is concerned?[37]

he asked.

There is a very high correlation indeed between the lists of areas where early industry flourished, made by agrarian and economic historians, and that made by Dr Christopher Hill of areas in which there might have been linear continuity between radical dissenters (Map I). 'Both Lollardy and later heresy are found especially in clothing counties, and in pastoral, forest, and fen areas', he wrote. He stressed large parishes, weaker ecclesiastical and manorial control and resources for the poor and vagrants, as the best conditions for radicals.[38]

---

[36]　Thirsk, *Agrarian History*, IV, p.112.

[37]　Alan Everitt, 'Non-Conformity in Country Parishes', *Land, Church and People: Essays Presented to Professor H.P.R. Finberg*, Joan Thirsk (ed.) (Reading, 1970), pp.188–189. Joanna Mackinder's work (see below, p.17 n.44) shows that in some groups of coterminous parishes in the Weald, the proportion was much higher than 17 per cent.

[38]　Christopher Hill, 'Lollards to Levellers', originally 1978, reprinted in *The Collected Essays of Christopher Hill*, ii, *Religion and Politics in Seventeenth Century England* (Brighton,

If there is indeed a strong correlation between areas of handicraft industries and areas where there is a tradition of questioning, radical religious belief, the question we have to ask is 'Why?'. Why should regions with early industry, or by-employment, also produce more dissenters? Is this economic determinism?

My growing awareness of current events and religious discussion and debate up and down the arterial roads, and the settlements near them, made me stress, in the *World of Rural Dissenters* the way radical beliefs seemed to travel along the highways and road networks, as well as being imported from reformed areas of Europe overseas, along with the goods traded by merchants, and the workmen who moved from area to area seeking and supplying work. It is not sufficiently stressed that England's main trade connections were with Reformed areas of northern and central Europe.[39]   Trade connections and religious beliefs went together. We sought to show this linkage on Map I by showing the places, widely diverse, yet on, or near, an arterial main road, where the inhabitants made use of the preamble to the radical Protestant will of William Tracy, who was dug up and posthumously burnt after his will had been declared heretical in 1532. The will was in print by 1535.[40] The so-called 'protoindustrialised' areas[41] which are also shown on the map, were in frequent contact with each other through exchange of their products and the travels of their merchants and their workmen, who frequently moved from area to area. They exchanged ideas, as well as products. The Tracy will preamble was used in a suggestive number of these places. Nothing more subtle or complex seems to lie behind the correlation between areas of early industry and manufacture, and early dissent and radicalism puzzled over by many historians led by Christopher Hill,[42] than this degree of interconnection brought about by trade.

But once again, we are stuck, for lack of maps. We cannot compare the distribution of nonconformists, recorded in the Compton Census of 1676, so

---

1986), pp.89–116. The whole of this discussion is to be found in Spufford, *The World*, chapter I, 'The Importance of Religion in the Sixteenth and Seventeenth Centuries', especially pp.1–5, Part Two, 'The Distribution of Dissent, By-employment, and Communications', pp.42–45, Derek Plumb, chapter II, and Bill Stevenson, chapter VIII. I have listed Dr Hill's 'likely' areas of continuity of radical beliefs on p.6 and the 'proto-industrial' areas on p.41, n.128. They are mapped on Map 1, pp.38–39.

[39]     Spufford, *The World*, pp.52, 56–57, 58.

[40]     John Craig and Caroline Litzenberger, 'Wills as Religious Propaganda: The Testament of William Tracy', *Journal of Ecclesiastical History* 44 (1993), pp.415–431.

[41]     Donald Coleman, 'Proto-Industrialization: A Concept too Many', *Economic History Review* 36, 2nd series (1983), pp.435–442. See also L.A. Clarkson, 'The Leather Trades in Tudor and Stuart England', *Agricultural History Review* 14 (1966), pp.25–39, since the areas where the leather crafts were extremely important show a high degree of coincidence with the areas of 'industrial' production discussed by Professor Coleman.

[42]     See above, n.37.

handily near the Hearth Taxes, with Dr Thirsk's agricultural regions and thereby test this correlation with any exactitude. The Compton Census figures are indeed in print, in that mighty volume of Miss Whiteman's, but they have not been mapped until very recently. Only the unmapped text was available until 1998.[43] The maps which had been made of these returns before 1998, together with those of the licences for protestant nonconformists issued in 1672 are suggestive, but not conclusive, since they are organised only by diocese,[44] and diocesan boundaries do not correlate with those of farming regions. We desperately need the Compton Census figures of 1676 properly mapped to show us the distribution and concentration of nonconformists then.[45] They therefore need to be mapped with more subtle determinants than dioceses in mind. We will begin to see whether there really were greater concentrations of dissenters in the pastoral, fen and forest areas, which may also have contained many more of those exempt from the Hearth Taxes on the grounds of poverty.

Some insight has also been given by the very simple realisation that pastures and by-employment areas gave more time for reading. My study of pastoral Eccleshall showed a noticeably higher number of readers among the poor.[46] Richard Baxter actually described how his carpet-weavers in Kidderminster could, and did, prop a book open upon their looms, and read as they worked.[47] Again, as these handicraft areas were also in touch with each other, print, and workmen, could, and did, flow between them.

Yet despite my eager curiosity, and this whole discussion, I would like to enter a strong *caveat* to it. I do not myself believe in any economic determinism for religious conviction or dissent, although there may be conditions that foster it. The scattered information now at our disposal, together with my own examination of seventeenth-century nonconformity in south Cambridgeshire, that great corn and malt area so despised by Defoe because it had no by-

---

[43]     The unmapped text is available in Anne Whiteman (ed.), *The Compton Census of 1676: A Critical Edition*, Records of Social and Economic History 10, new series (Oxford, 1986).

[44]     Andrew Browning (ed.), *English Historical Documents*, vol. VIII: 1660–1714 (London, 1966), pp.415 and 425. These should be compared with the simplified map of farming regions in Thirsk, *Agrarian History*, V, p.xx. The patterns produced by the ecclesiastical returns have been examined by Professor Bossy in his splendid piece (n.49 below).

[45]     Joanna MacKinder now has this mapping in hand, and her first results show that there were conditions, as in the Weald, which fostered dissent, but that, as one would expect, these conditions were by no means deterministic. Cranbrook in the Weald of Kent was, for instance, one of a group of coterminous parishes with very high percentages of dissenters, but the Sussex Weald did not foster dissent in the same way. I am very grateful to Miss MacKinder for allowing me to quote her preliminary results here.

[46]     Spufford, *Poverty Portrayed*, pp.50–52.

[47]     Spufford, *The World*, p.46.

employment at all and Dr Stevenson's new examination of dissenters in areas of his counties, which were mainly arable,[48] show very plainly that dissenters were to be found everywhere. This must never be forgotten. Not all John Bunyan's poverty-stricken Open Baptists in open-field Bedfordshire were lace makers.

Whatever the results of this enquiry show, we must still avoid the temptation to reduce the great range of human motives to economic reflexes. The man I know who was most sublimely untouched by historians' models, and even by the seventeenth-century opinions of John Aubrey, was Stephen Duck, a day-labourer working on Salisbury Plain early in the eighteenth century, who wrote the elegant verses of *The Thresher's Labour* after borrowing copies of Shakespeare, Dryden, Virgil, Seneca, Ovid, *The Spectator*, *Paradise Lost* (which he had to read twice with the aid of a dictionary), and Pope's *Essay on Criticism* from a friend who had been in service in London. He knew all about sweat, muscle-fatigue, and arable routine. Indeed, he vividly portrayed in this poem the social polarisation of the great chalk uplands. None of this stopped his passion for both reading and writing.[49] *The Thresher's Labour* is well worth reading. Such men were too important, in the corn-growing regions they represent, ever to subsume into the handy generalisations that make our lives more convenient. As Professor Bossy writes, 'The closer we get to the creativity of real life, the larger such individuals will loom, putting their clumsy feet into the shapely machinery of the model'.[50]

Most of this introduction to my papers has been devoted to demonstrating that it might be possible to establish a typology of the microcosms of rural England before 1700, and suggesting a way to do this which will complement Dr Thirsk's huge analysis based on probate inventories. It, too, will be based on agricultural type, which depends on soil type, which to some extent dictates the type of society which evolved. These societies in turn, I postulate, throw up different patterns of taxability. Only further analysis will show if I am right. You must not take chalk Chippenham, or any other village either, extrapolate out from your particular microcosm, and call the results 'England' – or the 'world', either! The Whickhams and the Eccleshalls are quite different from the Chippenhams and the Terlings.[51] Each village study has to be set in context.

---

[48]    Bill Stevenson, 'Social and Economic Status', *passim*.

[49]    Stephen Duck can be found in my 'First Steps in Literacy', *Social History* 4 (1979), pp.424–425. See chapter X below, pp.236–237.

[50]    John Bossy, 'The Map of Christianity in Early-Modern England', *Regional Studies in the History of Religion since the Later Middle Ages*, Edward Royle (ed.) (Conference of Regional and Local Historians, 1984).

[51]    Keith Wrightson and David Levine, *Poverty and Piety in an English Village: Terling, 1525–1700* (New York and London, 1979).

But they are *not* quite different from other villages in the same sort of region. This is where my typology, which taxation returns can help establish, comes in. So far, I differ from Professor Patrick Collinson, who wrote sadly in 1988, 'The difficulty with local or regional history is that *everywhere is different* [my italics], so the subject by its very nature courts particularism and resists treatment on a general, or national scale'.[52]

I hope I have shown a way forward from this pessimism. Yet I would now like to turn my argument upside-down, for I also, paradoxically, agree with Professor Collinson. All I would wish to assert is that the differences are not without pattern. I am very far from being an economic and geographical determinist, but these economic and geographical backgrounds do much to influence patterns. Yet even if you take a group of settlements in similar geographical settings, with similar economies, if the records survive for an adequate reconstruction of one of them, and the historian ends up with an organism which at least partly lives under her hands and in the work of her pen, it will be unique. For all places, and all communities, are unique, as their inhabitants are. This uniqueness is not only a facet of the reconstructor's mind. No psychologist, as far as I know, has suggested that the art of biography should be dead, because studies of one individual do not rest on statistics. The personality reconstructed by a biographer does not create a model transferable to other human beings, though there may, of course, be general insight to be obtained from it into other human beings from the same sex, period and social and economic background. Yet we need these reconstructions of individual figures from the past.[53] Sidney Painter wrote at the beginning of his preface to his life of *William Marshall*[54]

> biography is an essential part of historical literature. It cuts across the
> fields of history, political, social and economic, and shows how an
> individual lived in his world. Without the aid of biographies, one cannot
> fully comprehend the life of any age.

It is a long step from the life of a regent of England in the late twelfth and early thirteenth centuries to our microcosms of rural settlements in the sixteenth and seventeenth centuries, but just as we needed the life of William

---

[52]     Patrick Collinson, *Birthpangs of Protestant England: Religious and Cultural Changes in the Sixteenth and Seventeenth Centuries* (New York, 1988), p.49.

[53]     See, for instance, the outstanding study of a very obscure gentleman of Suffolk, and his social circle.  Colin Richmond, *John Hopton: A Fifteenth Century Suffolk Gentleman* (Cambridge, 1981), chapters 3 and 4.

[54]     Sidney Painter, *William Marshall, Knight Errant, Baron and Regent of England* (Baltimore, 1933) p. vii.

Marshall, we need our Forncetts[55] and our Wigston Magnas,[56] our Kibworth Harcourts,[57] our Chippenhams, our Balshams[58] and our Terlings, our Willinghams, our Sheffields[59] and our developing Birminghams,[60] our Whickhams, and our Eccleshalls. Without them, we will not fully comprehend the infinite variety and complexity of the very various microcosms, aware of each other, and heavily interconnected with each other by central legislation, government and news, an established road network, the carriers' carts and the pedlars, which together made up the macrocosm of England. Without these microcosmic studies, which also cut across political, social, economic and ecclesiastical fields of history just as biography does, we cannot fully comprehend the richness, the variety, and the entirety of the life of the world in pre-industrial England.

---

[55]     Frances Davenport, *The Economic Development of a Norfolk Manor, 1086–1565* (first ed. 1906, reprinted 1967). This classic is too often forgotten.

[56]     Hoskins, *The Midland Peasant*.

[57]     Cecily Howell, *Land, Family and Inheritance in Transition: Kibworth Harcourt 1280–1700* (Cambridge, 1983).

[58]     Marsh, *Family of Love*.

[59]     David Hey, *The Fiery Blades of Hallamshire* (Leicester, 1990).

[60]     Victor Skipp, *Crisis and Development. An Ecological Case Study of the Forest of Arden, 1570–1674* (Cambridge, 1978). Particular attention should be paid to Mr Skipp's n.7, p.118, for the original studies are in many cases more vivid than the composite work. Also see Marie B. Rowlands, *Masters and Men in the West Midland Metalware trades before the Industrial Revolution* (Manchester, 1975).

# II

The Scribes of Villagers' Wills in the Sixteenth
and Seventeenth Centuries and their Influence

## The Background

Wills have been used by historians interested in life at the village
level perhaps less than any other single class of document.   This is
strange, considering the vogue of the probate inventory, which, ideally,
should accompany the will.   It is also strange considering the rich
mine of general information on social affairs, the way the kinship
network worked, inheritance customs, retirement, provision for widows,
and so on, which can be worked from wills.   This information goes
far beyond the narrower and more immediate purposes for which
genealogists frequently use wills.   The normal will may be expected,
in this period, to surrender any copyhold held by the testator into the
hands of the lord, and to express a wish as to its disposal.   Any
freehold will be carefully bequeathed.   If land is not left to younger
sons, cash sums will be, probably with directions as to how they
should be raised.   Doweries in cash will be left to daughters, and a
minimum age will be laid down at which they should be handed over.
If there is a defective child, provision may be made for its upkeep.
If a widow survives, extraordinarily detailed instructions will be made,
giving her a certain amount of houseroom, and a certain amount of
land and stock.   Often directions will be given to the inheritor of
the main holding to keep this land up, plough it and sow it for her.
The moveable goods, down to the last blanket, sheet, copper pot and
brass pan, and in the case of a widow, the last neckchief, will be
divided up.

There is just one way in which historians have used wills more
commonly and that is to establish, if possible, the religious convictions

of the ordinary villager, be he yeoman, husbandman, craftsman, or labourer, who once in his life, and once only, at the beginning of his will, made a statement which bore on his religious beliefs. The first bequest in a will was of the soul. This may appear strange to modern eyes, but the reasoning behind it is made plain in the will of a maltster of Orwell in Cambridge, Thomas Brocke, in 1597, the body of whose will began 'First as thing most precyous,[1] I Commend my soule to God the father my Creator'. So a testator with Catholic beliefs may well leave his soul to 'Almighty God, the Blessed Virgin Mary, and the whole company of Heaven', or some equivalent phrase, and a testator of puritan or Calvinistic beliefs may well leave his soul to 'Almighty God and his only Son our Lord Jesus Christ, by whose precious death and passion I hope only to be saved' or some other similar phrase. Any will which mentions the Virgin, the saints, or the angels may be suspected of Catholic tendencies. Any which stresses salvation through Christ's death and passion alone, or the company of the elect, may be though of as Protestant. In between, lie a vast number of indeterminate neutral wills, which simply leave the soul to 'Almighty God, my Creator', or in which the stress on salvation through Christ appears so minimal, that they cannot be classified. The spectrum of these clauses is very wide; but because of their existence, historians seeking to penetrate the iron curtain which hides the religious opinion of the really humble laity, below the social level of parish priest or minister, in the upheavals of Reformation or Counter Reformation, sometimes analyse them in an attempt to establish what was going on at the parochial level. [2]

Unfortunately there is one major technical difficulty, which has not been given attention in doing this. For most purposes, the content of the will itself is all that matters; the identity of the scribe who wrote it is irrelevant. For this particular purpose, the identity of the scribe might be all-important. A very high proportion of villagers wills were made in the testator's last illness, on his death bed.[3] It is almost common form to get, at the beginning of a will, a statement that the testator is 'sick in body but thanks be to God of good sound understanding and memory' and extremely rare to get the opposite statement, which headed the will of William Griggs, a yeoman, of Orwell in 1649, that he made his will

'beinge in good healthe of body (but) considering the frailty of this life, although there is nothinge more certaine than death, yett there is nothing more uncertaine than the tyme of the coming thereof ... now intending the disposition of landes ... in this tyme of my good health and memory for the better quieting and satisffying my mynd and conscience whensoever it shall please God to visit me with sickness'.

A man lying on his death bed must have been much in the hands of the scribe writing his will.   He must have been asked specific questions about his temporal bequests, but unless he had strong religious convictions, the clause bequeathing the soul may well have reflected the opinion of the scribe or the formulary book the latter was using, rather than those of the testator.

I have therefore considered the whole question of the identity of the scribes who wrote villagers' wills in relation to the historical points to which the identity of the scribe may have been crucial.   When old Leonard Woolward of Balsham died in 1578, he wished to leave an acre or so of his free land away from his son and daughter-in-law, to each of his three daughters.   His son's death followed soon on his own, and his daughter-in-law's indignation induced her to bring a case to the ecclesiastical court. [4]   The details set forth in the depositions made there bring home, with extraordinary clarity, the conditions under which wills could be made in the sixteenth century. Leonard Woolward had retired;   he was living in the 'low chamber' off the hall in the house of his son and daughter-in-law.   He feared that his desire to provide land for his daughters would bring him discomfort, if not maltreatment in his last illness, and that 'he shoulde not be well-tended and have that he woulde have, and yf enye of his friends or aquintances .. should write his sayd will, his sayd sonne yonge Leonard ... woulde knowe of yt, and so laye on him that he shoulde not or coulde not make his wyll accordinge to his own mynde'.   He therefore asked the young barber surgeon, Henry Spender, who came from Little Wilbraham several miles away and not from Balsham at all, who was trying to bring him some relief from pain in his last illness, to write his will for him 'as pryvelye as mighte be'.   The barber surgeon was ill-prepared for such a task, and, as he said, 'went to the house of John Allen of Balsham and desyred (him) to bestowe him a penne, yncke and paper'. After writing the will alone in the room 'leaning uppon the sayd testators bedd' and reading it aloud to him after he had attempted and failed to read it to himself, Henry Spencer took the will back to John Allen's house, and read it aloud to him and to his wife, and declared it to be Leaonard Woolward's true will.   The will itself is duly witnessed by Henry Spencer and John Allen.

It is immediately evident from this that the circle of people who could be asked to draw up a will was wide.   Quite obviously

Leonard Woolward had a number of 'friends and acquaintances' whom he could have asked to write his will and he thought first of them, not instinctively of the minister, curate, or parish clerk.   The implication is that as early as the 1570's, there were in a village several members of the community who could write a document at need, even in a village like Balsham, where there were only isolated references to school-masters at work. [5]   Since he desired secrecy, his choice fell on the doctor, who came from another village altogether.   There is a modern case, which shows how traditional methods of making a will persisted, although in this case, the testator's instinctive first choice was for a gentleman.   Leonard Woolf [6] writes of a time in about 1918 when the farm carter of Rodmell in Sussex

'came to me and asked me to make his will for him.  He had several sons and one daughter and he wanted me to write out on a sheet of paper a statement, which he would sign in the presence of his children and of me, saying that he left every-thing to his daughter.   I told him that this would not be a legal will and that he ought to go to a solicitor and sign a proper legal will.   He refused to do this and said that if I would do what he asked, his sons would carry it out after his death.   So I did what he asked.  I wrote out the statement and took it round to his cottage one Sunday morning.  He, his sons, and his daughter were all there in their best clothes. I read aloud the document and he signed it and they all thanked me and we shook hands.   When he died, everything went to the daughter without difficulty.'

It is obvious therefore that in the search to identify scribes, not only the incumbent or his curate, who may seem the obvious choice, but the local gentry and acquaintances of the testator, must be considered.

## The scribes

There is an obvious, major difficulty in identifying the hand of the scribe who wrote a particular will, for the local historian, who is not a highly trained paleographer.   Any hand of the late 16th and 17 centuries, once educated beyond a certain point to write a reasonably formalised hand, has so many features in common with any other, that the non-specialist may well pause.   There is one redeeming feature.   A local historian working on a particular community, and on all the surviving wills for that community, is limiting himself so strictly by date and by place that only a small number of scribes are likely to be at work at any one time.

The smaller the community, for a pilot study, in some ways the
better.    Orwell is a small village on the clay uplands of Cambridgeshire.
When it was mapped in the 1670's, there were only 55 houses there,
so the Hearth Tax was not far out in taxing 52 of them. [7]    Between
1543 and 1700, 99 wills of which the originals survive, were proved in
the Consistory Court although until the 1580's, the 'originals' were
mostly office copies, [8] and therefore useless for these purposes.

It is possible to make at least a reasonable guess at the identity of
the scribes who were responsible for a surprisingly large number of
these wills.    Sometimes the scribe was the only witness of one or
more wills who could actually sign his name;   sometimes his hand
was the only one even approximately of the same type in a run of
wills, and he was also a witness to all of them.    In order to tell
whether or not the clause bequeathing a soul to Almighty God was
dictated by the testator's opinions, or by the scribe's, at least two
wills in the same hand are necessary, and obviously, a much longer
run is desirable.

The Orwell wills include half a dozen each written by an identifiable scribe,
who only appears to have written one will.    They are therefore
useless for comparative purposes.    Often the scribe's name is
unfamiliar to the historian of the parish, and he may therefore have
been an outsider, and possibly a notary or ecclesiastical official.
There were four pairs of wills by the same scribe, one series of
three, by George Holder, a villager who held at least an acre of freehold in the defective survey of Orwell made in 1607, and two very
interesting series of four.    One of these was by John Martin, about
whom nothing is known, and the other by Neville Butler.    He had
been educated at the Perse School and Christ's College, and was the
grandson of a yeoman.    He ended up by buying the lands of the
dissolved Priory of Barnwell, becoming a gentleman, and disappearing
from the Orwell scene.    There were also, most usefully for
comparative purposes, two longer series, overlapping in date.    One
of six wills was written by Nicholas Johnson between 1614 and 1626.
He was one of Neville Butler's father's first cousins, was frequently
a churchwarden, and was tenant of fourteen acres of copyhold land.
William Barnard, M.A., Rector of Orwell from 1609 to 1644, who
held a licence to teach there, wrote twelve surviving wills during his
incumbency, between 1615 and 1642.

Nicholas Johnson, who was described as the 'well beloved in Christ'
of Catherine Rutt of Orwell when she made him the supervisor of

her will in 1614, probably had his own religious convictions.    Not only Catherine Rutt's testimony, but his career as a churchwarden bears this out.    In all six of the wills he wrote, the clause concerning the soul is so nearly identical, that if there were any doubt that the scribe's hand had been identified correctly, it would be disposed of. Every one read 'I commend my soul into the hands of almighty God that gave it me ... when it shall please God to take me out of this present world'.    Whatever the opinions of the testator, they did not influence Nicholas Johnson, who started off each will in his accustomed fashion, which unfortunately did not reveal much of his doctrinal position.

Each of the four men who wrote a pair of wills apiece in the seventeenth century, as well as George Holder, who wrote three at the beginning of the century, also used his own common form.    Laurence Johnson one of the numerous literate Johnson clan, wrote in his horrible hand and entirely neutral phrase at the end of the 1640's 'I bequeath my soul to Almighty God'.    George Holder wrote with slightly more protestant emphasis in each of his three wills 'I commend my soul to God the Father my Creator, and his son, Jesus Christ my Redeemer'. John Wicks took up a slightly stronger position again in 1640, and wrote 'I bequeath my soul to God my Maker expecting (or believing) to be saved by and through the merits of Christ Jesus my Saviour and Redeemer'.    Matthew East, at about the same date, wrote more strongly still.    Both his wills contain the phrase 'I commend my soul into the hands of Almighty God who gave it to me assuredly trusting through the death and passion of his son Jesus Christ to be saved'. Ambrose Benning, who appears as 'Mr. Benning' in a rental of the 1670's, and was probably a freeholder and a gentleman, again adopted his own formula.    Again, if there was any doubt of the correct identification of a hand which only occurs twice, six years apart, it would be resolved by the identical wording.    'I commend my soule into the hands of god my maker, redeemer and preserver, in an assured hope of a joyful resurrection through the meritts of Jesus Christ my saviour'.

It appeared quite clearly then that each of these half dozen men adopted his own formula, and that the religious conviction of the scribe, not the testator, is apparent in the will.

This provisional conclusion can be taken further, by looking at the series of twelve wills written by the Rector, William Barnard, between 1615 and 1642.    William Barnard's phraseology was not much more striking than that of his churchwarden, Nicholas Johnson.

Eight of his twelve wills bequeath the soul of the testator to 'the hands
of God Almighty my Creator, (Saviour) and Redeemer ... whenever it
shall please the Lord to take me to his mercy'.   They were all
written before 1636.   In 1637, he added a new phrase which appeared
in three of the remaining wills and strengthened his formula by the
expectation of a 'joyful resurrection to life eternall'.   But in the will
of Richard Flatt, made in 1636, a strongly individual piece of
phraseology was inserted within William Barnard's formula.   Richard
Flatt commended his soul

'Into the hands of God Almighty, my maker, my Saviour and
Redeemer, trusting to be saved by the only sufficient merits
of Jesus Christ my Saviour ... when it shall please the lord
in mercy to take me out of this world, being fully assured
that this my mortal body shall one day put on immortality,
and being raised again by the virtue of Christ's resurrection,
I shall live forever with him'.

Here is a piece of Pauline theological thinking, which is so far outside
the scribe's usual formula that it seems for the first time that a
testator feels sufficiently strongly for his opinions to come through
clearly into his will.   In any long series of wills for any one village,
there are a large number of individual formulae which occur, and
some deviants, which fit into no pattern.   It looks, from the example
of Richard Flatt, as if these deviants can be taken to reflect the
genuine convictions of the testator; the rest reflect the opinions of
the scribe, who may, of course, have been a villager also.

This suggestion is strengthened by examination of the four wills
John Martin appears to have written.   Two of the testators Mary
Barton and Elizabeth Adams, were members of families who were
strongly nonconformist. [9]   Their wills were witnessed by Simon Grey
who was also a nonconformist [10] as well as by John Martin.   The
other two wills were written for men who do not appear on the
dissenting church lists, or as absentees from church in the episcopal
records.   Simon Grey witnessed one of the latter as well as those of
the dissenters; but it had a purely neutral clause commending the
soul of the testator into the hands of Almighty God, its maker,
despite being drawn up and witnessed by dissenters.   The last of the
four was also neutral.   The wills of Mary Barton and Elizabeth
Adams were highly individual, however.   Mary Barton bequeathed
her soul into the hands of Almighty God her maker, 'hoping through
the meritorious death and passion of Jesus Christ my only saviour

and redeemer to receive free pardon and forgiveness of all my sins'.
She also spoke of the temporal estate that 'God in his infinite mercy
has lent me in this world'. So did Elizabeth Adams, though she felt
that her temporal estate had pleased 'God far above my deserts to
bestow upon me'. The clause in which Elizabeth Adams bequeathed
her soul had the same sense as Mary Barton's, but it was not phrased
in the scribe's identical wording. She ended her will with an injunction
to her son and principal heir that related worldly prosperity to prudence,
which I have not seen duplicated anywhere else. As Solomon said
to his son 'My son fear thou the Lord and the king, and beware that
you live not above your living especially in the beginning for that will
bring you to wanton necessity, both in the midst and the ending'.

This scribe then, wrote dissenters' wills, which expressed the testators'
strong sense of justification by faith, but did not dictate the form
when a more neutral phrase was required. Neville Butler likewise,
wrote two wills which were neutral and simply bequeathed the soul to
God that gave it [11] but also two in identical wording when more
appeared to be called for. Richard Johnson and Robert Bird both
left their souls

> 'With a right good will .. to god that gave it whensoever it
> shall please him to take it out of this transitory life hoping
> by his infinite mercy and the only merryt of my saviour
> Jesus Christ that it shall again put on this my corruptible
> body of flesh and that they (sic) shallbe made partakers of
> everlasting life'. [12]

One further interesting point emerges from the Orwell wills.
The vicar, when he was present as a witness, and not as a scribe,
was not necessarily deferred to over the form of the clause bequeathing
the soul. Roger Davis, clerk, wrote his own will in 1580 [13] and
appears to have been a protestant, for he bequeathed his soul to
'Jesus Christ in faith in whom I hope undoubtedly to be saved'. He
witnessed a will couched in similar terms for John Adam, yeoman, in
1569, but the two others he witnessed for John Johnson, husbandman,
in 1568, and Edmund Barnard, another husbandman, in 1595, both had
neutral clauses bequeathing the soul. John Money, the vicar in 1595,
witnessed Katherine Ingry's will in that year, and she also simply
bequeathed her soul to Almighty God. Nicholas Butler, who had the
same faith in the resurrection of his temporal body that was later
expressed by his grandson Neville, as a scribe, both witnessed
Katherine Ingry's will along with the vicar, and had his own will

witnessed by the vicar; but his faith in the resurrection of his earthly
body seems to have been entirely his own, and was not dictated by
John Money.

Willingham, on the edge of the fens, was three times the size of
Orwell. It differed from Orwell, which had no school permanently
established before the eighteenth century, in having a school founded
by public subscription in 1593. This seems to have been based on the
work of the first known schoolmaster, Laurence Milford [14] and had
a continuous life thereafter. The same features found amongst the
Orwell wills are also found amongst the much more numerous surviving
wills from Willingham. There are nearly two hundred and fifty wills
written between the 1570's and 1700 by an identifiable scribe, although
fifteen of these are the only ones by that particular scribe, and are
therefore useless for comparative purposes. Amongst the scribes,
there are a considerable number of series by the same men.
Laurence Milford himself wrote fifty wills between 1570 and 1602,
beginning before he was first licenced as a schoolmaster to 'teach young
children' in 1580, and continuing after William Norton, the curate, was
licenced to teach grammar in 1596. After experimenting with various
formulae hoping to 'obtain everlasting joys and felicitie' for the soul
in the 1570's and 80's, he went through a neutral phase before settling
down in 1590 to the constant usage of one of his early experimental
formulae, 'I bequeath my soul into the hands of God the father, and
to Jesus Christ my saviour, by whose merits I hope to enjoy his
everlasting rest'. William Norton only wrote four wills, and
bequeathed the soul in an unusual Trinitarian form to 'God Almight,
Father, Son, and Holy Ghost'. This was obviously entirely his own.

Laurence Milford was succeeded as the principle Willingham scribe,
not by Norton's successor as schoolmaster, John Nixon, who taught
and was curate in Willingham from 1608, but by John Hammond, a
local gentleman who was lessee of the sub-manor of Bourne in
Willingham. He, with a relation of his, Edward, wrote over thirty
wills between 1609 and 1639. He also acted as a scribe when a
petition against the charges of fen drainage was drawn up. [15] His
phraseology was again almost identical throughout the wills that he
wrote, and he had been very heavily influenced by Milford. He
strengthened the protestant element and added 'by whose only merits and
mercies' to Milford's formula. Otherwise he duplicated it. There were
only three wills in the Hammond series which varied from the standard
opening in any way, and none of them, with the possible exception of his
own, was of importance. John Gill, a labourer, who died in 1623 hoped
to enjoy everlasting rest 'after this transitory life ended'. Philip Fromant,

a husbandman, trusted to obtain 'remission of all my sins'.    When
John Hammond himself wrote his will in 1637, it became evident that
a genuine faith lay behind his standard protestant formula, for he left
his soul to

> 'Almighty God my creator, and to Jesus Christ my redeemer,
> by whose only mercies and merits (Sealed unto me by their
> blessed Spirit) I trust to obtain forgiveness of all my sins and
> to enjoy their everlasting rest'.

The laity of Willingham, are known from other sources to have been
particularly zealous protestants.    They probably had secret conventicle
meetings in Mary's time, and were anti-episcopal in the late 1630's.
From these beginnings, a strong and lasting congregational church
developed under the Commonwealth.    Quakerism was present there
too. (16)    Laurence Milford, either in his work as teacher or as
scribe, unfortunately seems to have made such an impact on the people
of Willingham, that their individual convictions, which were undoubtedly
strong in very many cases, are masked, in their wills, by his
phraseology.

The early wills of the 17th century do provide ample evidence that old
Leonard Woolward of Balsham was right to feel he could depend on
'friends and acquaintances' to write his will, if not to keep it secret,
for enough villagers acted as scribes in Willingham to prove the point.
Four men from the Greaves family, who were half-yardlanders with
twenty acres or so at the turn of the century, and therefore in this
fenland village were substantial yeoman, wrote twenty-two wills
between 1609 and 1647.    Fifteen of them were by Thomas Greaves.
With the exception of one neutral one by Robert Greaves which simply
bequeathed the soul to 'the hands of Almighty God', they all made use
of the Milford formula, or the variant on it employed by Hammond.
Henry Halliwell, who was a representative of another family which
had held arable of between nine and twenty two acres in 1603, wrote
five wills between 1614 and 1619.    They were all neutral, and
unrevealing, except for a single one which adopted Milford's terminology.
John Pitts, who was described in his own will as a 'woolwinder'
wrote three wills between 1617 and 1626, all using the Milford
phraseology.    His own will, made in 1631, was couched in stronger
terms.    His soul was left to the 'hands of Almighty God my Creator
hoping for remission of my sins by the death and passion of Jesus
Christ my redeemer'.    Unfortunately John Pitts own will was an
isolated one, written by Thomas Ambler, so it is impossible to tell

whether John Pitts made a fuller and more revealing assertion of his
faith on his own death bed, or whether Thomas Ambler was asserting
his own beliefs.   Henry Bissell who wrote two wills in 1630 and 1631,
was another villager who was descended from the tenant of nine and
a half acres in 1603.   He also used the Milford terminology.   So did
another six villagers in the first part of the seventeenth century, who
only wrote one will apiece, but all used the Milford formula or the
Hammond variant of it.   There was a further series of six wills by
Edward Allen, written between 1625 and 1630, and one series of
fourteen by Robert Stocker between 1631 and 1639, using exactly the
same wording.   Neither family appears in the land survey of 1603,
but both wrote distinctly village hands.   The school obviously
produced a large number of fully literate villagers.

The strength of protestant feeling in Willingham, combined with
Laurence Milford's influence, makes the wills of the villagers so
consistently Protestant, that as in any orthodox group it is impossible
to tell how far individual feeling is involved, even when minor variants
in the phraseology do occur, since the sense is so uniform.
Occasionally individual testators do stand out, just as Robert Flatt did
in Orwell.   Robert Shilborn wrote the will of Thomas Lambert, who
was a husbandman, in 1625, and that of Thomas Bowles, who was a
fisherman in 1632.   There was no doubt at all of the strength of
the convictions of Thomas Lambert.   Shilborn wrote for him

'I bequeath my soul to God that gave it trusting in the only
merits of Jesus Christ my saviour and redeemer for the
forgiveness of my sins, and that death shall be an entrance
for me into a better life'.

The will ended with the desire that

'The Lord out of his never decaying or failing mercy be a
husband to my wife and a father to all my children'.

Thomas Bowles' will began with an orthodox phrase, but contained the
tell-tale bequest 'To my eldest son William Bowles ... my bible
wishing him to use it to God's glory.

Although the influence of Laurence Milford at last declined, the
Willingham scribes continued each to write their own standard formula.
There was one important change.   From the 1650's, the testators
customary bequest of his body to the churchyard for burial, which

followed that of the soul, was replaced by a phrase leaving the burial of the body to the discretion of the executor or to 'Christian' burial. This may well reflect the growth of the nonconformist element in Willingham. But congregationalist or quaker wills cannot be picked out as such from the phraseology. They can sometimes be identified by virtue of local knowledge. Two Henry Orions wrote thirteen wills between 1634 and 1648, and 1659 to 1667. They were probably father and son, and of humble stock. There had been no Orions in Willingham in 1603, but the family held twelve acres of arable there in the 1720's. Both men wrote a roughly standardized form of will, bequeathing the soul to 'God that gave it men, and to Jesus Christ my redeemer by whose mercies and merits I hope to have forgiveness of all my sins and to have a Joyful Resurrection at the Last Day'. The emphasis on the resurrection was typical of them; the formula was their own, but some of the testators obviously had religious convictions, which were hidden behind the devout but customary formula of the scribes. John Carter, a chandler, whose will was made in 1648, left both his son and his daughter bibles. Mary Marshall, the widow whose will Henry Orion wrote in 1669 left Francis Duckins a bequest of £2. She did not appear to be related to him, and he was a leading congregationalist in whose house the conventicle met in 1669.[17] This is not proof that the Orions were writing for congregationalists, particularly since the very last will in the series, in 1667, expressed the, by now, unusual desire to be buried in the churchyard; but there is a suspicion. It is partially confirmed because the Henry Orion alive in the 1720's had his house licenced as an independent meeting place. (18)

The same suspicion applies to Edward Negus even more strongly. He wrote forty three wills in an educated hand between 1661 and 1693, mostly with a brief clause bequeathing the soul into the hand of God and the body to the ground in Christian burial. Until 1670 he usually wrote, when he came to the disposal of the testator's goods 'touching such wordly estate as God in his Mercy far above my estates has been pleased to bestow upon me'; after 1670 he dropped this additional clause also. But there was no doubt that he was writing the wills of convinced Protestants. In 1669, the will of Edward Hammond, 'yeoman' who was one of the sons of John Hammond who had acted as a scribe earlier in the century, contained the clause 'I give unto Edward Negus my book of martyrs'. Deborah Frohock, a congregationalist widow, left her son Samuel three books, incidentally bibles in 1672. Neither of the inventories of the testators concerned mentioned the four of the twelve men who were known to be congregationalists in Willingham in 1675 [19] had their wills written by Negus; A Suspiciously large number of the witnesses appeared charged with absence from church in an ecclesiastical court of 1673. But despite this, individual conviction did not come through Edward Negus' accustomed phraseology, except in the case of two men, William Bowles, a yeoman in 1673, and John Allen a maltster, in 1686, both of whom trusted in a joyful resurrection at the last day. Neither was known from other sources to belong to a particular sect. Negus himself held the lease of a shop in 1665, and does not appear to have been involved in agriculture at all.

Robert Osborne wrote eleven wills between 1665 and 1693 in a village hand, and wrote a much more vivid clause, but one which was still in a common form peculiar to himself, bequeathing the soul 'Unto the hands of God that gave it to me trusting through the merits of Jesus Christ my redeemer, to have a joyful resurrection at the Last Day'. One of the eleven wills was written for one of the Willingham Quakers, and a second was witnessed by another Quaker.

The clauses in wills bequeathing the soul of the testator to God are therefore mainly couched in whatever phrase the particular scribe was accustomed to use and taken alone tell little, or nothing, of the testator's opinions. But just as the strength of Robert Flatt of Orwell's convictions in 1636 broke through his rector's common formula, so also did a handful of the Willingham wills reflect, in the strength of their language, what must have been the strength of the dying man's faith. John Osborne, who only wrote one will in 1668, must have been closely related to Robert, because their hands were so alike. Even though the will cannot be compared with any others written by John, it is impossible to believe that anything but the feelings of Thomas Staploe, the testator, lie behind the last and only statement of faith which he ever made.

> 'I ... calling to remembrance the uncertain state of this
> Transitory life that all flesh must yield unto death when it
> shall please God to call ... first being penitent and sorry
> from the bottom of my heart for sins past most humbly desiring
> forgiveness for the same, I give and commit my soul unto
> Almighty God my Saviour and Redeemer in whom and by the
> merits of Jesus Christ, I trust assuredly to be saved, and to
> have full remission and forgiveness of all my sins and that my
> soul with my body at the General Day of resurrection shall rise
> again with joy and receive that which Christ hath prepared
> for his elect and chosen'.

## Conclusion

It seems from this analysis, as if, for any village there will often be two or three scribes writing wills at any one time, and a large number over a period of a hundred years. They will range from the Lord or lessee of the manor, to the vicar, curate, church clerk or churchwarden, to the schoolmaster, a shopkeeper, or any one of the literate yeoman or even husbandmen in a village who could be called in to perform this last neighbourly office for a dying man. If the village lay near a county town, it was possible for a public notary to be called in, although this I have less evidence for.[20] Most of these scribes evolved their own slightly different formulae for bequeathing the soul, which can be traced through most or all of the wills they were responsible for. If the scribe was an identifiable villager, as he often was, of course, one is still getting irreplaceable information on the doctrinal convictions of the peasantry, since the scribe came himself of humble stock, like the Greaves, or Thomas Pitts, or Edward Negus of Willingham, or Nicholas Johnson or George Holder of Willingham. Even when the rector, like William Barnard of Orwell, or the schoolmaster, like Laurence Milford of Willingham, is the scribe, one is still getting information on whatever doctrine is generally accepted at the village level. It is a great mistake to assume the docility of the normal parishioner. If the Rector of Cottenham, which was a radically nonconformist village in the seventeenth century felt unable to let his children out to play after one of them had been attacked and scarred for life with a fork in the school yard by a 'sone to an adversary', [21] it is scarcely likely that such an 'adversary' would call on the Rector to make his will, while the choice of potential scribes was, as I have shown, wide. It is therefore safe to assume that however near death the testator was, he still exercised a choice over his scribe, as Leonard Woolward did. He probably did not influence the form of the preamble the scribe normally used, unless he had abnormally strong convictions, but he is highly unlikely to have chosen a man who did not hold the same general opinions as himself.

Wills can, therefore, be used as Professor Dickens used them, to show a swing away from the cult of the Virgin and the Saints in the 1540's continued into the 1550's, but he was entirely right when he wrote 'The results should not be presented in any spirit of statistical pedantry'. The evidence is not statistical. It is wrong for the historian to assume that if he takes a cross-section of four hundred and forty wills proved over a particular period, he is getting four hundred and forty different testators' religious opinions reflected,

unless of course the wills also come from four hundred and
forty different places. One is still getting evidence on the
attitudes of the peasantry to whatever ecclesiastical settlement was in fashion, but it would take much more stringent
analysis to show how much evidence one is getting, and to elim-
inate more than one of a series of wills written by the same
scribe. On the other hand, when a testator had strong religious
convictions of his or her own, this may come through, expressed
in a varient of the formula usually used by the scribe concerned. If any local historian wishes to study the religious
opinions of the peasantry, he should look for these strongly-
worded individualistic clauses which occur in any run of wills
for a parish, which alone record the authentic voice of the
dying man.

## NOTES

1. This phrase is not common form. I have come across it nowhere else. The original wills of the Consistory Court of Ely, which I have used for this study, are bundled under years, by date of probate, in The Cambridge University Archives. They have no reference numbers. Wherever italics appear in this paper, they are mine.

2. The clause leaving the soul to Almighty God is never as elaborate and lengthy, in a villager's will, as those of the puritan clergy (See, for instance, the wills printed by R.A. Marchant, The Puritans and the Church Courts in the Diocese of York, 1560-1642 (1960), pp. 212-15). They none the less contain significant differences. Professor Dickens has used these differences effectively in Nottinghamshire and Yorkshire wills to illustrate the progress of the Reformation amongst the Laity. A.G. Dickens, Lollards and Protestants in the Diocese of York, 1509-1538 (1959) particularly pp. 171-2 and 215-17.

3. A comparison of the date the will was written, and the usually close, date of probate, shows this.

4. Cambridge University Library, Ely Diocesan Records, D/2/11, ff. 259-61. I am very grateful to Mrs. Owen, Ely Diocesan Archivist, who drew this revealing case to my attention.

5. Margaret Spufford, 'The Schooling of the Peasantry in Cambridgeshire, 1575-1700', Ag.Hist.Rev. 18 (1970), supplement, Map I, p. 124.

6. Leonard Woolf, Beginning Again, p. 68. Mrs. Elizabeth Key noticed this case.

7. Public Record Office E.179/244/23.

8. When the 'original' wills of the Consistory Court of Ely are indeed the originals, and not office copies kept by the court, while the true originals, signed or marked by the testator, were returned to the testators' executors. At some point in the latter 16th century, this custom changed, and the original document was retained, for registration, and presumably an office copy given to the executors.

9. G. Lyon Turner, <u>Original Records of Early Nonconformity under Persecution and Indulgence</u> (1911), I p. 36.

10. C.U.L. Ely Diocesan Records, B/2/6 f.51-52v.

11. Wills of Richard Kettle and Robert Adam.

12. This example is a confusing one, because the phraseology Neville Butler uses, and his emphasis on the resurrection of the body echoes almost exactly that of his grandfather Nicholas, in 1601 (P.C.C. 74, Woodhall) and his great uncle Henry in 1594 (P.C.C. 32, Dixy) although his own father, Thomas, wrote a neutral clause bequeathing his soul in 1622 (P.C.C. 18, Saville) and his own will 'all written with my own hand' only expressed his belief in justification by faith, not in the resurrection of the body (P.C.C. 1675, f.42). We may here be getting an example of the scribe's own religious beliefs, rather than the testator's, but it is interesting that he only applies it when it is called for, and does not automatically write a phrase expressing his own opinions.

13. It ends 'per me Rogerum Davys'.

14. Margaret Spufford, <u>art.cit</u>, pp. 139-140 and pp. 131-3.

15. B.M. Add. Ms 33466 f.190. I am indebted to Mr. Dennis Jeeps, of Willingham, for lending me his photostat of this.

16. Margaret Spufford 'The Dissenting Churches in Cambridgeshire from 1660 to 1700' <u>Proc.Camb.Ant.Soc.</u> LXI (1968), pp.70, 76-7.

17. G. Lyon-Turner, <u>op.cit.</u>, p. 38.

18. This information also comes from Mr. Dennis Jeeps, who likewise kindly provided me with additional information on Negus.

19. See my forthcoming paper in <u>Studies in Church History,</u> 8, 197, on 'The Social Status of Some Seventeenth Century Rural Dissenters'.

20. Samuel Newton, a public notary, wrote and signed, as such, the will of Edward Daintry the elder, a husbandman of Milton, in 1665; likewise John Brayshaw, a public notary wrote the will of John Foot a husbandman of Milton in 1628.

21. Taken from an abstract by W.N. Palmer of a letter from the daughter of the Rector of Cottenham, who was ejected under the Commonwealth, in the Walker MS., Bodleian Library, C.S. fo.17.

# III

# The limitations of the probate inventory

In 1895, Mr J. H. Round published his collected essays under the title *Feudal England*.[1] The index entry for 'Freeman, Professor' is justifiably famous. It runs to two columns: some of the entries run as they are set out below.

*Freeman, Professor*:
his 'certain' history . . . his 'undoubted history' . . . his 'facts' . . . underrates feudal influence . . . overlooks the Worcester relief . . . influenced by words and names . . . his bias . . . confuses individuals . . . his assumptions . . . his pedantry . . . misconstrues his Latin . . . imagines facts . . . his supposed accuracy . . . his guesses . . . his confused views . . . evades difficulties . . . his treatment of authorities . . . misunderstands tactics . . . his special weakness . . . necessity of criticising his work . . .

This index entry seemed likely to remain unique in the annals of criticism. However, it has recently been equalled if not surpassed, by an even longer entry in a biography of Scott.[2] This runs, in part

*Scott, Robert Falcon*:
early flirtations . . . runs aground . . . unimpressed by other Polar explorers . . . endangers ship through ignorance of ice . . . failure of first attempt at sledge travel . . . belated study of Polar literature . . . inadequate preparation . . . ignorance of snowcraft . . . risks comrades' lives in determination to achieve southern record . . . Admiralty mistrust of his ability . . . his scientific knowledge criticised . . . quarrels and tension with companions . . . collapses as leader . . . last camp and immolation in

[1]  J. H. Round, *Feudal England* (London, 1895), pp. 580–1.
[2]  Roland Huntford, *Scott & Amundsen* (London, 1979), pp. 658–60.

140

tent . . . farewell letters . . .
self-justifying message to
public . . . creation of
legend . . . as heroic bungler
. . .

*Characteristics*: absent-
mindedness . . . agnosticism
. . . command, unsuitability
for . . . criticism, refused
to accept . . . depression,
bouts of . . . emotionalism
. . . impatience . . . improvi-

sation, belief in . . . inade-
quacy, sense of . . . insecu-
rity . . . insight, lack of . . .
irrationality . . . isolation
. . . jealousy . . . judgment,
defective . . . leadership,
failure in . . . literary
gifts . . . panic, readiness
to . . . recklessness . . . responsibility, instinct to
evade . . . sentimentality . . .
vacillation.

These index entries, which appear to have nothing whatever to do with the subject in hand, came to mind simply because I was considering the bland and pallid prose of my own index to a book on pedlars and their goods.[3] It runs, in part

*Inventories, probate*:
dowries omitted from:
goods omitted from: mis-
leading nature of . . .

The limitations of the probate inventory have been much in my mind since the work on pedlars, which largely rested on them, was completed. I was led to crystallize my doubts by a day conference on the probate inventories as a source, run by the ESRC in London in the autumn of 1984. Professor Cole of Swansea was then launching a project to 'explore the possibilities of using probate inventories as a source for the study of long-term economic growth in England and Wales'. The immediate objective was 'to identify a representative sample of areas in England and Wales from which long-running series of inventories have survived in sufficient abundance to form the basis of a . . . project designed to produce and analyse series illustrating the occupational distribution of the labour force, the level and consumption of household wealth, and changes in the pattern of consumption in the period from about 1529 to the mid or late eighteenth century'. In the discussion on the project, it appeared that Professor Cole's pilot study was confined to the values of household goods in inventories. These values are free

---

[3] *The Great Reclothing of Rural England: Petty Chapmen and their Wares in the Seventeenth Century* (London, 1984) (henceforward, *The Great Reclothing*).

from most, but not all, of the dangers of the source that most worry me.[4] But this chapter is the fruit of general reflection on probate inventories as a source, and further work which I have been led to carry out as a result, to see if some of the limitations of inventories could be corrected from other documents.

If this chapter concentrates on the limitations of the source, it only does so because the English can be regarded as an expert audience. English economic, social, and local historians probably know more about probate inventories as a source than any other Europeans. Ever since William Hoskins pioneered the use of inventories in 1950[5] and Joan Thirsk followed him up with her essay 'Fenland Farming in the Sixteenth Century' in 1953, inventories have been familiar. Dr Thirsk followed up her work on the Fens by her much more major study of Lincolnshire, in which for the first time she attempted to delineate agricultural regions by the analysis of inventories. They must be one of the most used sources for the *Agrarian History of England and Wales*, IV, *1500–1640* (1967). Its companion volume, V, laid the regional farming boundaries of England firmly on the map, using the same analytical techniques. The trickle of work based on the probate inventory has become a flood, demanding its own bibliography.[6] English work on agrarian history, and on vernacular architecture, also based on probate inventories, has led the field. It is astonishing that the probate inventory has only recently been 'discovered' as a new source on the continent.[7] Because the use of inventories has been pioneered in England, and they are known to be both valuable and irreplaceable, largely thanks to Dr Thirsk's work, it seems appropriate also that their disadvantages should be stressed in England, to an audience already fully aware of their potential. It is a good moment to do so, for if anything the fashion for using these convenient documents, which are so readily susceptible to analysis, is growing. This paper concentrates on one disadvantage, the omission of debts owing by the dead

---

[4] See below, pp. 144–5, for reservations.

[5] W. G. Hoskins, *Essays in Leicestershire History* (Liverpool, 1950).

[6] Mark Overton, *A Bibliography of British Probate Inventories* (Dept. of Geography, Newcastle upon Tyne, 1983). Dr Overton's own work is probably the best introduction to recent developments in the field.

[7] A. G. Bijdragen, *23, Probate Inventories: A New Source for the Historical Studies of Wealth, Material Culture and Agricultural Development*, ed. A. Van der Woude and A. Schuurman (Wageningen, 1980). The 'newness' of the source is stressed not only in the title, but in the Introduction, pp. 2–3.

142

person from the inventory, but it seems convenient to itemize other disadvantages, before concentrating on the omission of debt.

## I

Every economic historian knows that real estate is not included in an inventory. The inventory only legally listed goods belonging to the administrator, or executrix, of an estate.[8] These included movable goods and leasehold land, but not real property. Real property included copyhold land, which would descend according to the custom of the manor if it was not bequeathed in a will, and freehold land, which descended according to common law, if it, similarly, was not bequeathed. Some of the omissions of an inventory can therefore be repaired if a will survives. Even so, only two-thirds of freehold land could be willed, although all leasehold and copyhold could. There was no necessity to bequeath any property at all if the testator desired it to go to the executrix or executor. In this case, it would not appear in either will or inventory. However, the two documents together do give a much more balanced picture. It is often one which is much at variance with the picture of a man's prosperity drawn from the inventory alone.

The will, which may accompany the inventory, is not nearly so readily broken down, nor does it lend itself to computer analysis, yet the total, brutal, differences between the individuals who look so alike from an analysis of their inventories can only be demonstrated from these documents taken in conjunction with each other. The most striking example among the group of inventories on which I have recently been working, those of the petty chapmen, or pedlars, also happened to be that of a man who appeared from his inventory to be the most outstandingly successful of them all. Charles Yarwood of Macclesfield had money and goods worth, according to his inventory, a total of £9,226 4s 8d. This included 'shop goods' valued at £497 8s. He had in the house and 'att London' at his death, the colossal sum of £3,454, and was also owed over £5,000 in good and bad debts. However, Charles Yarwood's will told a very different story. It laid down that his debts owing at his

---

[8] Both nouns have appropriate feminine forms. I have not wished to use four nouns to replace two, and cover all the variables, and have therefore deliberately used the masculine version of one and the feminine of the other here.

death to Francis Dashwood of the City of London should be paid out of the 'monies which I have Lodged in his hands, and such as there shall bee found in my owne custody soe farr as itt will Extend'. If, on the other hand, 'these monies shall fall short to discharge the said debt . . . the residue thereof to be paid out of my Personal Estate'. If, in turn, 'that bee not sufficient for that purpose' then his debts were to be paid out of the sale of the burgage in Macclesfield he lived in, and the messuage of which he had a lease in Upholland, Lancashire.

Patently, his financial affairs were not in the straightforwardly healthy state the inventory would give the reader to suppose. He was himself a worried man, because the provision for payment of his debts 'if what I have before appointed for payment to my debts shall fall short to discharge them all' is repeated three times in different wording in the will.

Charles Yarwood may have provided the most dramatic, but he did not provide by any means the only example of the way inventories can mislead. For instance, when they died in 1663, 1712, and 1714, Thomas Large of Foulsham in Norfolk, Walter Martin of York, and John Young of Brasted in Kent left gross estates which from their inventories were worth £73, £65, and £71 respectively. Thomas Large, from his inventory, had a well-furnished house, and was totally dependent on his chapman's trade. He had a good stock, worth £49, and presumably travelled to sell it. However, his will left his widow all his goods, land, tenements, and 'shoppes' in Foulsham on the condition that she was 'to be Carefull in the paying of my debts, according to the trust I have reposed in her'. Walter Martin of York had selling goods worth £62, more than those of Thomas Large, listed in his inventory of 1712, and his gross estate was worth £65. There was no indication of indebtedness at all. His will, unlike that of Thomas Large, not only failed to reveal the existence of any real property, but also stated 'I am indebted to Mr. John Dickinson of the City of York, Linen Draper for a Considerable Sum of money.' It left all the goods to him in at least part-payment. The selling wares of John Young were worth £50 a couple of years later. He looked at first sight much less prosperous than Walter Martin, except for his hopeful debts. This will revealed not only that he was not, like Thomas Large and even more, Walter Martin, heavily indebted, but also that he was in a position to bequeath 'messuages, lands and appurtenances' lying both in Leigh and in Tonbridge, as

144

well as the residue which presumably included his shop and house at Brasted. Yet both the selling wares and the gross estates of Martin and Young look very comparable.[9]

Here, then, are examples of estates in which comparison of the will with the inventory reveals something of the real estate omitted by the inventory, and demonstrates that the financial standing of men who from their inventories look extremely similar is, in fact, very different indeed. The inventory alone is a seriously misleading document.

Its most major defect may be in the omission of the freehold or copyhold land, the real property, which may appear in part in the wills. But the inventories also mislead in other ways. They do not reveal occupations properly. We are becoming more and more conscious of the importance both of dual occupations and of the family budget. The probate inventory throws no direct light on a man's second occupation, unless by inference from his tools. It also frequently reveals a difference of opinion about a man's social status made by his neighbours in the inventory and his own opiniion, or his scribe's opinion, revealed in his will.

The legal scope of an inventory, which included only movable goods, that is those which belonged to the administrator or executrix, explains two other possible omissions in the inventory, both of which could be serious to historians using household goods as an index of spending power and consumption. The bequests made in a will were sometimes not included in the inventory. These were often the testator's most precious possessions. Edward Chew of Lancashire, for instance, left his 'Clock and Chimbs' to a son in 1697. A clock is one of the really significant possessions in the late seventeenth century, but the possession of this one could only be deduced by the wary historian from the existence of a room called 'the Clock Chamber' in the house. The clock itself, separately bequeathed, had been removed by the time the inventory was made.

John Uttinge of Great Yarmouth appears to have worried about the possible abstraction of goods not specifically bequeathed by him from his inventory. He was a linen-draper-cum-chapman, who left over £65 in bequests 'in goods out of my shop' when his will was made on 20 February 1627. He appointed four appraisers in the will,

---

[9] *The Great Reclothing*, pp. 37–9.

and said his goods were to be appraised within seven days after his death. After the appraisal, the key of the shop was to be delivered to his supervisor: the goods bequeathed were to be handed over at the shop within two months. However, although three of the four men Uttinge wanted as appraisers did in fact act for him, they did not make their inventory until 9 April. The whereabouts of the key meanwhile has to be borne in mind. It is almost certain that £65 worth of goods bequeathed in the will were not included in the total of £100 worth of goods the appraisers did list. Omission on this scale, if it was common, would seriously distort conclusions drawn from the household goods remaining within an inventory, since there is no reason to suppose that the habits of testators were uniform.

Yet another possible omission affecting the household goods and consumables in an inventory concerned the widow's property. My work on the pedlars drew my attention to peculiar examples of men who appeared from their inventories to be itinerant pedlars with nothing but their selling wares and the clothes they stood up in, who appeared from their wills or administrations to be married. There were also cases in which the wife's original dowry was separately listed in the inventory.[10] There is no indication of how often her possessions, or portion, were excluded altogether, if she was not the executrix.[11] Without her goods, the house would appear very scantily furnished indeed.[12]

Despite these disadvantages, the household goods in inventories do provide an index of domestic comfort and consumption which

---

[10] Amy Louise Erickson, of Corpus Christi College, Cambridge, tells me she has found examples of widows' inventories including goods which were not in the earlier inventory of the husband.

[11] The inclusion of goods originally belonging to the wife seems to have been debatable. Her apparel, her bed, and any personal ornaments, later called *paraphernalia*, were, according to Burn, to be omitted from the husband's inventory by law. Different authorities disputed this, but, he eventually summarized, 'if we shall respect what hath been used and observed . . . widows have been tolerated to reserve to their own use, not only their apparel and a convenient bed, but a coffer with divers things therein necessary for their own persons; which things have usually been omitted out of the inventory of the dead husband's goods . . . '. Richard Burn, *Ecclesiastical Law* (1st edition, London, 1763), pp. 649–51. Individual appraisers may well have been confused, or cajoled.

[12] *The Great Reclothing*, pp. 40–1, for Chew, Uttinge, and omission or separate listing of the wife's property.

146

show change over time, just as the crops on the ground or in the barn, and the stock in the yard, provide information on farming practices. Mrs Rachel Garrard's work comparing interior furnishings in Suffolk between the late sixteenth and the late seventeenth centuries[13] and Dr Lorna Weatherill's work[14] examining the distribution of certain key household goods by period, region, and social status both show inventories providing the material for broad brush-strokes to draw outlines.

But there are maddening omissions of goods by the appraisers, either for legal reasons or because of the low value of the items. These goods omitted for legal reasons could be extremely significant. 'Corn growing upon the ground, ought to be put into the inventory; seeing it belongeth to the executor: but not the grass or trees so growing; which belong to the heir, and not to the executor', ran the legal direction.[15] In the same way, grass ready to be cut for hay, apples, pears and other fruit on the trees, shall not go to the executors because they come 'merely from the soil, without the industry or manurance of man'. The protagonists of arboriculture and the orchard growers of the seventeenth century[16] were therefore engaged in labours not yet recognized as such by the law in the eighteenth century. As a result the spread of orchards and their fruit cannot be traced in inventories, which listed only the 'executors'' goods. Hops, saffron, and hemp came in a different category 'because sown; shall go to the executors', said the law. These therefore should, and often did, appear in inventories. However, the logic applied by legal maxim is bewildering to the modern mind. The 'new' root crops were also sown, yet one judgement was recorded that 'roots in gardens, as carrots, parsnips, turneps [sic] . . . and such like, shall not go to the executor, but to the heir', since they could 'not be taken without digging and breaking the soil'. Of roots in the open fields nothing was said, but the same judgement

---

[13] Rachel P. Garrard, 'Patterns of Conspicuous Consumption and Spending on the Domestic Environment in England, 1560–1700', Cambridge Ph.D. thesis in progress, 1982. See her paper 'English Probate Inventories and their Use in Studying the Significance of the Domestic Interior, 1570–1700', A. G. Bijdragen 23, pp. 55–82.

[14] L. M. Weatherill, *Consumer Behaviour and Material Culture in Britain, 1660–1760* (London, 1988).

[15] All quotations from Burn, *Ecclesiastical Law*, pp. 646–7; Wills, ch. 5, para. 10.

[16] Joan Thirsk (ed.), *Agrarian History of England and Wales*, V (Cambridge, 1985), pp. 309–11.

may have applied. They might therefore not be found in an inventory. It seems highly likely that the historian might search as hopefully, but quite as vainly, for root crops in inventories as for fruit, egged on by mentions of saffron, hops, and hemp. Awareness of the legal distinctions involved, which are by no means self-evident, is very necessary. Moreover, the law was, in some ways, attempting to bring itself up to date, and was, therefore, even more confused. There was nominal awareness that improved grassland did involve the 'industry and manurance of man', even if arboriculture was as yet unrecognizable as the fruit of human industry. According to the textbook, for '*clover, sain foin* and the like, the reason of manurance, labour and cultivation is the same as for corn; but no case hath occurred, wherein these matters have come in question; this kind of husbandry having been in use only of late years'. It seems that, at least in theory, clover, sainfoin, and lucerne should have appeared in inventories along with hops, saffron, and hemp, whereas fruit could never, and roots very rarely, be found there. Here, however, yet another set of disadvantages comes into play, on top of the legal ones. The appraisers, as well as not necessarily being informed of the exact detail of the law, were extremely unlikely to bother to list goods which were insignificant in value. But goods of small size and trifling value can be extremely significant to the historian looking for clues in all sorts of areas, from agriculture, to literacy, to the 'growth of the consumer society'. Such goods could well be covered by the frequent use of 'etc.' or 'and other things', or 'other lumber'. Seed for improved seventeenth-century grassland, for instance, is usually missing, although it was of vital agricultural importance. Dr Thirsk discusses the spread of ideas and information amongst the gentry after 1649 on the cultivation of clover, sainfoin, and lucerne, but it is not possible to underpin this discussion with the spread of these seeds amongst non-gentle society, because their possession cannot be demonstrated from the inventories.[17] Only if a man had an unusually large quantity of seed would it appear in an inventory. Michael Havinden's elegant and convincing demonstration of improvement in the open fields of Oxfordshire, which showed the median sheepflock in the inventories there increasing fourfold in size from fourteen between 1580 and 1640, to sixty between 1660

---

[17] Joan Thirsk, 'Agricultural Innovations and their Diffusion', in *Agrarian History*, V, pp. 553–6.

148

and 1730, rested on the spread of improved grassland within the open fields to support these extra animals.[18] It is fortuitous but remarkably useful that Robert Plot, with his maddening fixation for only describing the unusual and the abnormal, wrote in 1677 in his *History of Oxfordshire* of the new grasses that they were grown everywhere, 'so nothing of it'. Mr Havinden's discussion did not, and could not, rest on direct evidence from inventories. As he wrote on another new crop, 'the earliest reference to turnips which I have come across in examining thousands of probate inventories from Oxfordshire is in 1727, when John Deane, a cordwainer of Brize Norton, had twenty bushels of turnip seed worth 10s. a bushel'.[19] He deduced from this an absence of turnip husbandry in Oxfordshire. However, in view of the legal attitude to roots, at least in gardens, as part of the freehold, we can probably draw no conclusions at all about the presence, or absence, of the turnip and its like from the open fields of Oxfordshire, or anywhere else either. The additional unwillingness of the appraisers to list goods of small value meant that seed in stock, rather than crops in the ground, would only appear in an inventory if, like John Deane's turnip seed, it was present in usually large quantities. Therefore, although the 'seedsmen' who appear in the fifth volume of the *Agrarian History* as such important figures as the source of supplies for these new crops are frequently discussed, they, and their customers, remain shadowy figures, because the possession of such seeds cannot be demonstrated. Amongst the itemized goods of the petty chapmen whose surviving inventories were collected by me only two mention seeds specifically. Roger Carrington of Lincoln had 'onion seed' which must have been a large enough quantity to bother with, because it was worth 20s in 1613. John Bibbie of Manchester had 'garden seed' lumped together with worsted yarn and other selling goods in 1661. Inventories cannot be used either for evidence of the cultivation, or diffusion, of many of the new crops: yet the absence of these from them has sometimes been taken as evidence. Indeed, the sneaking suspicion arises that the relative lengths of the sections devoted to various new crops in works of agricultural history may in

[18] M. A. Havinden, 'Agricultural Progress in Open Field Oxfordshire', *Agric. Hist. Rev.*, 9, part 2 (1961), 73–83. See also M. A. Havinden (ed.), *Household and Farm Inventories in Oxfordshire, 1550–90* (Oxfordshire Record Society, 1965).
[19] Havinden, 'Agricultural Progress', 77.

some way relate not to the relative importance of these crops, but their legal status, as well as their relative overall value, in the minds of the appraisers who drew up the inventories on which such works to some extent depend.

In a completely different area of interest, the historian of literacy likewise finds it impossible to trace the spread of cheap print from the probate inventory. Almanacs, chapbooks and ballads, items worth 1d to 3d when new in the seventeenth century, stood no chance of being listed as old, whereas a family's expensive bound bible might. So the spread of reading habits amongst the barely literate, those who could read but not write, is untraceable.[20]

The historian working on the 'growth of the consumer society' finds it is equally impossible to trace the spread of the humble shirt, or indeed any other clothing, since items of clothing are so rarely separately appraised in England. A shirt would be a particularly useful index of domestic comfort and consumption.[21] Yet 349 Suffolk inventories made between 1570 and 1599 yield thirty-seven references to shirts and none to shifts. Three hundred and ninety-seven inventories made between 1680 and 1700 yield only thirteen references to shirts and three to shifts. It is inconceivable that shirts and shifts were becoming less common, in the light of a set of Suffolk overseers' accounts for the 1630s, as well as the accounts of detailed expenditure on children's clothes discussed below.[22] The overseers' accounts list the clothing made for children for whom the parish was responsible. They were fitted up with one 'suit' of outer clothing, or a petticoat and waistcoat, one or two canvas bodices for girls, one pair of hose knitted of grey yarn, and one pair of shoes apiece. But they all had two shifts, made of two yards of linen each, or two linen shirts. The girls had two coifs each. The linen, in this

---

[20] Margaret Spufford, *Small Books and Pleasant Histories* (paperback edition, Cambridge, 1985), pp. 48–9.

[21] For what follows, and the limited appearances of clothing in inventories, see *The Great Reclothing*, pp. 125–9. Dr Weatherill did what could be done on the lump sums given by appraisers in a paper given to the Pasold Conference on the Economic and Social History of Dress in September 1985, 'Consumer Behaviour, Textiles and Dress: The Evidence from Probate Papers and Household Accounts, 1670–1730'. She then stated that clothing was not mentioned at all in about a fifth of her sample of 2,902 inventories. It was as likely to be omitted in the inventories of the rich as in those of the poor. Moreover, only half of the inventories valued clothes separately from cash and other personal possessions like saddles, watches, and jewellery. Details of individual items were very rare.

[22] See below, p. 171.

150

case, was lockram. If even 'parish' children had a change of shifts or shirts by the 1630s in Suffolk, the probate inventories have to be misleading here. Moreover, Gregory King's unpublished table of the 'Annual Consumption of Apparell' of 1688 includes no fewer than ten million shirts and smocks, at 2s 6d or 2s each. This figure was only equalled by that for stockings, and exceeded by that for shoes. It indicates that every family in the kingdom was acquiring over seven new shirts or smocks a year. Such garments were, then, commonplace. It seems much more likely that the increasing cheapness and spread of the garments made them objects for appraisers to ignore. An increased rarity of comment thus perversely argues a spread of usage. The paradox is that as an article becomes commoner and cheaper, it appears less often in inventories, once it has fallen below a certain value. A new, or still unusual, object would attract attention, however. Window curtains were another very useful index of increasing comfort. They were also cheap. Yet the proportion of inventories in which window curtains were recorded grew rapidly from 7 to 21 per cent from 1675 to 1725.[23] Some labourers had them.[24] It seems therefore quite possible logically to claim that the disappearance of the shirt from Suffolk inventories has nothing to do with the disappearance of the garment from Suffolk backs, but on the contrary, argues its increasing ubiquity.

## II

Lastly, I come to the second most important drawback of inventories after the omission of real estate, and the one on which this chapter focusses. In 1974 I wrote of the way English rural society, like the French rural society of the Beauvaisis, was underpinned by a complex system of debt and credit, and the powerful motive to learn reading that the ubiquity of the bill or bond must have provided.[25] In the following year, Dr Holderness's first article drawing attention to inventories as a source for credit appeared.[26] 'Infor-

[23] Weatherill, *Consumer Behaviour*.

[24] *The Great Reclothing*, pp. 115–16, especially nn. 26 and 27.

[25] Margaret Spufford, *Contrasting Communities* (paperback edition, Cambridge, 1979), pp. 78–82, 212–13. The 'forthcoming article' cited as n. 48, p. 80, was made redundant by Dr Holderness's work. See also below, p. 173.

[26] B. A. Holderness, 'Credit in a Rural Community, 1600–1800: Some Neglected Aspects of Probate Inventories', *Midland History*, III (1975–6), 94–115.

mation about debts which they reveal has so far been neglected', he wrote. But inventories, although they draw our attention to debt, only do so by revealing good, or bad, debts due to the dead man. Only a minority record his debts to others. Indeed, they should not have done so. 'Debts, which the deceased owed to others, ought not to be put in the inventory, because they are not the goods of the deceased, but of other persons', wrote Burn.[27] Dr Holderness said tentatively in 1975 'One must assume that a proportion of the "credits" revealed would have been offset by "debits" if only a balanced account existed . . . the inventories reveal neither the real extent of borrowing within particular communities nor the complex network of credit amongst various social groups in the country-side . . . '[28]

The magnitude of the problem and the way in which probate inventories can mask the actual state of a man's finances, even excluding the most major item, real estate, was brought home to me by the study of a tiny group of citizen-stationers of London. The aim was to establish the profitability of their businesses. This tiny group of people provided two extreme examples.[29] Josiah Blare and Charles Bates were men whose total movables, the value of which could be established in their inventories, were worth £341 and £400 in 1707 and 1716. They looked extremely similar in financial standing. But they left real net estates, the value of which could be established from the Orphans' Accounts of the Freemen of the City of London, of £3,274 and £236 respectively. The difference was accounted for by Josiah Blare's very considerable investments. My sense of caution, and of moving on quicksand in the use of inventories to establish net wealth, even excluding real property, was increased by these two men. The prospect of documents like this being treated even as 'semi-complete' indices of a person's net movable estate alone is an alarming one. There seems to be no reason why there should be any consistent pattern in habits of indebtedness or in savings, which should cancel each other out.

Alarm was not allayed by work on the pedlars. A total of 127 probate inventories for petty chapmen were found, but it was only possible to establish a net estate for 23 of these after their debts had

---

[27] Burn, *op. cit.*, p. 646.    [28] Holderness, 94, 95, 108.
[29] See Spufford, *Small Books and Pleasant Histories*, pp. 85–90, for a full discussion of Josiah Blare and Charles Bates, and the misleading nature of their inventories.

Table 1. *Gross and net values of chapmen's movables in the sixteenth and seventeenth centuries*

| Rank order (gross) | Total inventory value | Value of goods | Debts owed to him | Name | Place | Date | Debts owed by him | Net value | Rank order (net) |
|---|---|---|---|---|---|---|---|---|---|
| 1 | £411 | £13 | £398 | Richard Trendall | Norfolk | ?1595 | £396 | £16 | 9 |
| 2 | £402 | | | Thomas Teisdale | Lincoln | 1619 | £236 | £166 | 2 |
| 3 | £282 | £260 | £22 | James Pilkington | Lincs. | 1635 | £35 | £247 | 1 |
| 4 | £161 | £104 | £57 | Thomas Walker | Lancs. | 1662 | £15 | £147 | 4 |
| 5 | £160 | £93 | £67 | Robert Marler | Lancs. | 1558 | c. £10 | c. £150 | 3 |
| 6 | £117 | £10 | £107 | John Crosby | Bristol | 1674 | £58 | £60 | 5 |
| 7 | £86 | £83 | £3 | Robert Wilkinson | Lincoln | 1678 | £115 | -£29 | 20 |
| 8 | £83 | £18 | £65 | Robert Chadwick | Rochdale | 1661 | £47 | £37 | 7 |
| 9 | £65 | £65 | nil | Walter Martin | York | 1712 | More than estate | Negative | 16? |
| 10 | £65 | £65 | nil | John Tomkins | Bristol | 1661 | £23 | £42 | 6 |
| 11 | £61 | £43 | £10 | William Wilson | Boston | 1666 | £73 | -£12 | 19 |
| 12 | £53 | | | John Poynton | Notts. | 1658 | £80+ | -£37+ | 23 |
| 13 | £39 | £21 | £14 | Reece Barratt | Salop | 1675 | £32 | £7 | 11 |
| 14 | £35 | £33 | nil | William Davies | Bucks. | 1588 | £68 | -£33 | 22 |
| 15 | £33 | £25 | £6 | John Smith | Herts. | 1615 | £26 | £7 | 12 |
| 16 | £31 | £28 | | Roland Johnson | Penrith | 1683 | £28 | £3 | 14 |
| 17 | £28 | £12 | £16 | John Hollinshead | Macclesfield | 1688 | £29 | -3s | 17 |
| 18 | £28 | £19 | £8 | Samuel Dewhurst | Rochdale | 1680 | £3 | £26 | 8 |
| 19 | £27 | £18 | | Anne Hall | Cumberland | 1670 | £18 | £10 | 10 |
| 20 | £18 | | nil | Christopher Dalton | Holderness | 1695 | £50+ | -£32+ | 21 |
| 21 | £18 | £7 | £11 | William Davidson | Tweedmouth | 1663 | £18 | 12s | 15 |
| 22 | £11 | | £15+ | Charles Cutliffe | Lincs. | 1625 | £15+ | -£4+ | 18 |
| 23 | £11 | £8 | £3 | Oliver Jones | Hereford | 1665 | £7 | £5 | 13 |

All figures are rounded to the nearest pound.

been collected, and above all, their creditors paid. Even this 'net estate' was, of course, the value of movable goods and cash only, excluding any real estate. These twenty-three were listed in rank order of the total assessed value of their movables downwards (see Table 1). Then, after calculating the net estate after collection, and payment, of debts had been made, a new rank order of their estates in terms of movable goods was established. This new rank order was frequently very different from the first one.[30] Furthermore, whereas the median gross wealth of all 127 chapmen, excluding debts, was £28, the median net estate of the 23 for whom a net estate could be established after their creditors were paid off was only £6 19s 8d, though the group included some of the more substantial men.[31]

It could well be objected that the changes in rank order of financial status among the pedlars are too small to be of any significance, especially since the group were almost all worth under £100 gross. However, the fact that no reliable economic hierarchy could be established amongst them from the inventories alone suggested that there might well be equally misleading examples over a much wider economic span of people. Indeed, the nasty warning provided by Josiah Blare and Charles Bates, worth £341 and £400 from their inventoried wealth, but £3,274 and £236 in reality, showed the real adjustments to be made are very great indeed. These adjustments might mean not only that an inventory cannot be trusted to establish the true net economic worth of any individual's estate, but also the standing of whole social groups within the population for which inventories were made might be affected. An essay for Joan Thirsk seemed a very suitable place to explore not only the disadvantages of the inventory, but any documentary source which might redress these disadvantages.

Such a source does indeed exist, in the form of the barely known and little exploited[32] final document in the probate series required by the ecclesiastical courts, the probate, or administrator's account. These listed all the expenses paid out of the deceased's estate, usually a year after death, but sometimes more. The account began by stating the amount recorded at the foot of the inventory as 'the

---

[30] See, for instance, nos. 5, 9, 14 and 18.
[31] *The Great Reclothing*, pp. 43, 69–70.
[32] As far as I know, these documents have been used exclusively by Clare Gittings, *Death, Burial and the Individual in Early Modern England* (London, 1984).

154

charge' or money at the disposal of the executor or administrator.
So whether or not the inventory survives, its total is still known. The
account continued by listing all payments outwards by the executor
or executrix, from the physic and funeral expenses, through those of
raising minor children or paying bequests to those who had attained
their majority, the payment of back debts, rent, parish expenses,
and the court costs. They finish by recording the sum left in the
hands of the executor or administrator, or possibly the amount by
which he or she was overspent, by deducting this expenditure from
the credit sum in the inventory. Directions are sometimes recorded
by the court on the way this final remaining sum is to be divided to
support the widow and heirs. The probate accounts do, in fact, meet
the need expressed by Dr Holderness in 1975, when he lamented the
lack of 'a balanced account'. Moreover, they most certainly do
'reveal the real extent of borrowing within particular communities',
as well as 'the complex network of credit amongst various social
groups in the countryside'.[33]

Although the probate accounts are rare, they are not as rare as
has been supposed.[34] At least 27,000 of them survived. Happily, one
of the largest groups is in Lincoln. For reasons of *pietas*, this was the
most suitable county to work on, since Dr Thirsk's own work on
inventories was based there. Moreover, Dr Holderness's work on
credit was also, felicitously, based on Lincolnshire.

An investigation of the probate accounts for Lincolnshire to
explore the relationship between inventoried wealth and the final
probate account wealth further therefore seemed the ideal subject
for this chapter. Groups of seventeenth-century probate accounts
for Lincolnshire labourers, husbandmen, and yeomen were

[33] See above, p. 151.
[34] I became interested in probate accounts during my work on chapmen, and
suggested they might form a fruitful source to Amy Louise Erickson for her
thesis, 'Property Ownership and the Financial Obligations of Women in Early
Modern England' (Cambridge PhD. thesis, submitted 1989). Erickson's
preliminary survey of surviving accounts shows there are at least 27,000 in various
record offices in England, mostly concentrated from the mid sixteenth to the late
seventeenth centuries. My husband, Dr Peter Spufford, and I have submitted
(autumn 1986) a joint proposal to the ESRC which, if it is accepted, will enable
us to produce an index to these survivors in the *British Record Society* series. We
hope if the proposal is accepted that the volume may appear in 1993. Meanwhile,
I would like to thank Amy Erickson very warmly for her help with this project so
far, and for collecting the sample of probate accounts for Lincolnshire which form
the basis of the following discussion.

examined. Twenty-nine accounts were found for labourers, thirty-five for husbandmen, and thirty-five for yeomen.[35]

The immediate aims were firstly, to discover whether the final credit sum given in the probate inventory bore any predictable relationship to the final net estate of the dead man given at the end of the probate account. Secondly, I wanted to know whether the initial financial status of individuals in each social group, in relation to each other, gave any reliable guide to the final size of their estates and their ultimate financial standing, or whether the inventoried sums were as wildly misleading for other social groups in the countryside as they had been for the migrant chapmen. That is, did the degree of indebtedness of individuals vary so much that their relative prosperity within the group changed violently in relation to each other, and was it very different from that which the reader would deduce from the inventory? Thirdly, even if the rank order of individuals within each group in relation to each other did change wildly, did the financial relationship of each group to other groups remain constant, or did that also change? In other words, just how much ultimate economic difference was there between rural groups labelled by themselves, or described by their neighbours as 'yeomen', 'husbandmen', and 'labourers'?

The twenty-nine labourers' accounts showed that from the assets included on their probate inventories at their deaths, they were worth from £12 to £89. The lower quartile ran from £12 to £20 and the upper from £42 to £89. The median inventory wealth was £29. The accounts themselves showed a very different picture. After funeral and sickness expenses, the court expenses, the debts, rent, and necessary charges for the upkeep of minor children had been deducted from the inventory values, the administrators of these

---

[35] The ninety-nine inventories and accounts examined came from the early 1630s, and from 1660 to the mid 1680s. There were thirteen from the 1630s, nearly forty from the 1660s, thirty from the 1670s, and just over a dozen from the 1680s. Despite the disparity in dates, it seemed fair to compare the values of the probate inventories given in each, since a graph of decennial averages of agricultural products from the 1590s to the 1740s, taken from the statistical Appendices to the *Agrarian History*, IV (1967) and V (1985), shows rough comparability between the beginning of the decade of the 1660s and the end of the 1680s, despite a drop of five index points to the mid 1670s. The figures obtained from table XIII of the *Agrarian History*, IV, p. 862 were reduced to the same level as table XII of *Agrarian History*, V, p. 856. Agricultural prices were obtained by multiplying all figures by 104/644, and industrial prices by multiplying by 97/306.

Table 2. *Gross and net value of labourers' estates in Lincolnshire in the seventeenth century from probate inventories and probate accounts*

| Order (gross) | Gross wealth: inventory total | Name | Place | Date (inventory or account) | Net wealth: account total | Order (net) |
|---|---|---|---|---|---|---|
| 1 | £89 5s 0d | Jo. Hanson | Burgh-in-Marsh | 1680 | £60 17s 7d | 2 |
| 2 | £79 2s 2d | Ric. Charles | Asklackby | 1669 | £64 17s 1d | 1 |
| 3 | £73 19s 4d | Will. Anthony | Helprioryhorn | 1665 | £50 4s 1d | 3 |
| 4 | £68 11s 8d | Hammond Craven | Boothion | 1678 | -£2 15s 0d | 25 |
| 5 | £62 4s 8d | Steph. Drust | Wrawby | 1662 | £29 17s 0d | 5 |
| 6 | £44 4s 6d | Wm Walton | Gainsborough | 1676 | £21 3s 0d | 6 |
| 7 | £42 9s 6d | Chris. Picklington | Cumberworth | 1669 | £38 19s 4d | 4 |
| 8 | £36 16s 8d | Ed. Mason | Scremby | 1669 | £20 2s 0d | 7 |
| 9 | £34 7s ?d | Fra. Martin | Little Panton | 1670 | £20 0s 1d | 8 |
| 10 | £34 3s 4d | Thos Roweth | Swineshead | 1670 | £17 ?s ?d | 10 |
| 11 | £33 13s 6d | Jo. Chapman | Poynton | 1670 | £4 5s 6d | 22 |
| 12 | £33 6s 8d | Thos Lyson | Ashby cum Fenby | 1680 | £17 3s 0d | 12 |
| 13 | £32 10s 4d | Nic. Collingwood | Lincoln | 1669 | 12s 7d | 24 |
| 14 | £31 16s ?d | Jo. Froth | Croft | 1672 | -£7 3s 0d | 28 |
| 15 | £29 7s 6d | Matth. Burtoft | Burringham | 1666 | £5 16s 8d | 21 |
| 16 | £28 2s 0d | Thos Brown | Horncastle | 1670 | £12 19s 4d | 14 |
| 17 | £27 3s 8d | Chas Johnson | Swineshead | 1670 | £15 6s 2d | 13 |
| 18 | £25 0s 2d | Will. Reader | Flixborough | 1667/8 | £17 3s ?d | 11 |
| 19 | £23 9s 10d | Geo. Martin | Awborne | 1669 | £9 8s 0d | 16 |
| 20 | £23 0s 0d | Dan. Hardell | Coulsterworth | 1631 | £17 12s 0d | 9 |
| 21 | £21 4s 8d | Robt Hall | Skirbeck | 1630/1 | £7 10s 4d | 19 |
| 22 | £21 1s 0d | Walt. Jebb | Deeping St James | 1667 | £7 9s 0d | 20 |
| 23 | £20 0s 0d | Jo. Morgan | Saleby | 1678 | £11 1s 2d | 15 |
| 24 | £19 8s 0d | Will. Townend | Haxey | 1671 | -£3 8s 1d | 27 |
| 25 | £17 7s 6d | Hen. Bauger | Brigend, Horbling | 1632 | £8 3s 10d | 18 |
| 26 | £16 6s 4d | Tobias Chapman | Croxby | 1632 | £8 19s 2d | 17 |
| 27 | £15 8s 8d | Will. Michaill | Wrangle | 1666 | -£3 2s 6d | 26 |
| 28 | £13 0s 0d | Will. Clapham | Weston | 1683 | -£10 14s 4d | 29 |
| 29 | £11 17s ?d | Godfrey Wood | Willoughton | 1678 | £3 15s 4d | 23 |

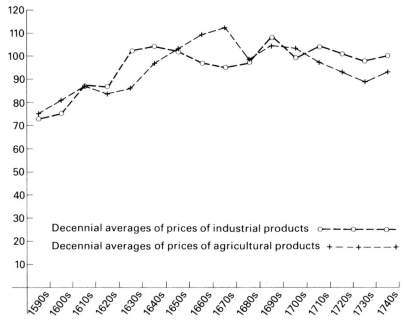

Figure 2 Decennial averages of prices of industrial and agricultural products (source: *The Agrarian History of England and Wales*, IV and V; 1640–1749 = 100)

labourers generally ended up at least £20 worse off then the totals in the inventories would have led the reader to expect. The labourers' estates ended up in a range, from the unfortunate administrator who was £11 out of pocket after paying all the charges, to the man who still had a net credit of £65 after all debts were paid. The lower quartile now ran from −£11 to £4 in credit, and the upper from £20 to £65. But there was no predictable relationship between the total value of the labourer's probate inventory and the net value at the end of his account. The labourers' degrees of indebtedness and their family and demographic circumstances varied so much that it was quite impossible to tell from the figures at the end of the inventory how any individual estate would end up. Just under a third of the twenty-nine labourers' estates moved six places or more either up, or down, in order of value between the first, probate inventory, value, and the final probate account value. The median value of the labourers' probate accounts was that of the estate of John Morgan of Saleby, £11 1s 2d (see Table 2 and Figure 3).

158

Substance is given to these rather bleak figures by considering further the situations of Matthew Burtoft, the labourer with the median inventoried wealth, and John Morgan, the labourer with the median net probate account wealth. Matthew Burtoft of Burringham, in the Lincolnshire fens, had had goods valued at £29 7s 6d in 1667. His inventory survived and showed him living in a two-roomed cottage with a 'parlour' for sleeping and a 'house' fulfilling all other functions. The place was in considerable domestic disorder, with a strike of rye and a straw skip as well as a wheel and yarn in the parlour, and the coulter and share of a plough in the 'house', which was meagrely furnished with essentials. There were only three pairs of sheets and a single blanket to go with the standing bed and the trundle bed in the parlour, although it did have bed curtains. The only modest signs of comfort were the three cushions in the 'house'. The stock in the yard suggested that Matthew had common rights, for he had seven cows, yearlings, and calves as well as two little pigs, geese, hens, and a cock. He also had two old horses and a cart and the gears. These, along with the ploughshare in the hall and 'hemp, hemp seed and wheat' in store suggested that he did hold an acre or two of land and did not depend only on wages. He also had a stock of peat in the yard and part of a 'small moore' valued at £3. But the number of his tools suggested employment as an agricultural labourer as well, for he possessed forks, spades, pruning hooks, and mole-catching equipment. All in all, then, the inventory indicated that Matthew and his household ploughed some land and cultivated wheat and rye, grew and spun hemp and yarn, dug and stacked peat, ran cattle on the common and raised calves, possibly with a little dairying on the side, kept pigs and poultry, and indulged in a multiplicity of skilled agricultural tasks.

The inventory was one of the very rare ones which give any indication of debts owed outwards: the appraisers made a list of sixteen debtors, including the landlord's rent of £4. The total debts, a little larger in the account, were £13 6s 4d, or nearly half the value of the inventory. Interestingly Matthew owed 1s as 'chimney money', so we know both that he had one hearth in his two-roomed house, and also that he was not exempt from the Hearth Tax on the grounds of poverty. Apart from the £4 he owed as rent, his other debts were all owed to Burringham men and women, except one to a relation of his landlord who lived in Gainsborough and one to a man who came, like his landlord, from Messingham. The account gave no idea of the reasons for his borrowing, except for the two forks and scythes he had bought, but not paid for. Matthew also had family problems which may have helped account for the indebtedness. His wife was dead, his administrator lived elsewhere, and the account included expenses for 'nursing' and clothing the children, 'looking to' the dead man's house and land, ploughing the land, and removing the goods by water to the administrator's village. These were all responsibilities the widow, as administratrix, would have undertaken. There were four children. The eldest, a thirteen-year-old boy, Thomas, had been bound apprentice since his father's death at a cost of £3. Mary, one of the three little girls, had died, and interestingly, more was spent on her funeral than on her father's, although both were meagre in the extreme, and cost only 6s 8d and 5s respectively. The surviving two girls, Anne and Sarah, were eleven and six when the account was drawn up, and received 13s 4d apiece as their children's portions. The reader wonders about the sleeping habits of this family. When their mother was still alive, did the 'standing bed' in the parlour serve as a sort of *letto matrimoniale* for the whole family, or did the trundle bed under it take more than the youngest of the four children? However the family slept, they had inadequate covers with only one blanket. The last group of expenses in the Burtoft account were the ecclesiastical court fees involved in obtaining letters of administration, and finishing off the business, including travelling and apparitors' fees. These were roughly standard in all probate accounts, whatever the size of the estate, or social status, of the dead man. However, they naturally represented a much greater proportional expense of the value of the inventory goods on a labourer's probate account than on a yeoman's. In Matthew Burtoft's case, they amounted to £3 19s 10d, or over an eighth of the inventory value. His administrator ended up with £5 16s 8d in his hands, and two little girls to look after. The estate was reduced to this both because of the dead man's indebtedness, and also because of the expenses of a young family left motherless. The final net value of a man's estate may, then, have been as much related to his stage in the family life-cycle, and his demographic situation, as to his degree of indebtedness. These may, of course, have been strongly connected. It is pure surmise to suggest that the wife of a labourer may usually have contributed considerably to the family budget, and it was the absence of his dead wife's earnings which led to Matthew's running up so many local debts, but it is still a potentially

160

useful suggestion for exploration. Certainly, the expenses of keeping a family between the date of the inventory and the date of the final account were the second major category of expenditure to influence the final net value of the account. Because of the combination of debts and family expenses since his death, Matthew Burtoft's estate ended up at only twenty-first place amongst the twenty-nine labourers.

The suggestion that indebtedness and the stage a man had reached in rearing his family may have been strongly interconnected is reinforced by considering the probate account of the man who emerged as holding the median net figure for labourers on the final values retrieved from the probate accounts. John Morgan of Saleby had only £20 worth of goods in his inventory of 1677, and stood twenty-third in order amongst the twenty-nine labourers. His inventory also survived, and showed him living in a five-roomed house. It had a hall, a parlour, and chamber, with two service rooms, a dairy, and a buttery as well. His furnishings were also adequate, but not luxurious, and he only had two pairs of sheets with the bed in the parlour. There were fewer beasts in the yard. The three cows and a calf there suggested both common rights and dairying. This time the suggestion was borne out by the cheese tub and nine bowls in the dairy indoors. The swine in the yard were for domestic consumption, judging from the flitch of bacon in the dairy. Nothing in the yard suggested that John Morgan had any land or grew his own flax or hemp. But the implication of spinning made by the 'two wheels' in his chamber is amply borne out by the two webs of cloth 'at the weaver's' worth £1 10s 0d. The probate account demonstrated John Morgan's carefulness, and his different family circumstances. His widow was his executrix, and he had no debts at all, apart from his rent of £4 15s 0d. After his funeral expenses and his mortuary were paid, the only charges on his estate were his widow's travelling to Louth twice on business connected with the court, getting letters of administration, and getting the account passed, as well as the court fees. Either his family was grown, or he had none. His wife's spinning was an asset, judging from the webs at the weaver's. Whether the lack of a family, or having a grown family, accounts for his lack of indebtedness must remain open. But it is not surprising that the final value of his estate from his account was over £11 and brought him up to fifteenth place.

III

The totals of inventory values recorded in the thirty-five husbandmen's accounts showed that, from their assets at their deaths, this
social label was applied to men who had movables valued at as little
as £9 to as much as £388 at their deaths. The lower quartile of inventoried value ran from £9 to £32, and the upper from £112 to £388.
The median of inventoried wealth was £62. Again, the probate
accounts themselves showed a very different picture. After all the
deductions were made, the husbandmen's administrators usually
ended up £60 worse off than the inventories had indicated. The final
range ran from those overspent by as much as £64 to those in final
credit of £319. The whole lower quartile of husbandmen's administrators varied from being out of pocket by £64 and just in credit by
£2. The upper quartile was very wide, from £38 in credit to £319 in
credit. So the median net estate for husbandmen was finally as low
as £13, only just over that of a labourer. The relationship between
inventoried wealth and net wealth was even less predictable for
'husbandmen' than for labourers. Nearly half the husbandmen's
estates moved more than six places up or down the rank order
between the value of goods when the inventory was drawn up, to the
time the final account was made. Examples of this movement, and
its reasons, may not come amiss (see Table 3).

The goods of William Presgrave of Steddington, for instance,
were appraised at £291. He was the second most prosperous
amongst the husbandmen from his inventory. But the account of
1674 included amongst his debts arrears of rent of over £140 to two
landlords, as well as an allowance for losses for one hundred sheep
which 'dyed the last Rott' and cattle and horses which died since the
taking out of letters of administration. He was a hirer of labour, but
he had not paid his wages either: he owed two maidservants, two
menservants, and a shepherd sums of money. When all was paid off,
the two sons who acted as his administrators ended up £12 out of
pocket, or so they claimed. The net value of the estate placed
William Presgrave only thirty-first amongst the thirty-five husbandmen. Here the cause of the trouble may have been the disease
amongst the livestock which may have caused the arrears of rent.
Yet the inventory indicated the scale of Presgrave's farming
activities accurately, although it was no guide at all to the ultimate
solvency of a man who was deeply financially embarrassed.

Table 3. *Gross and net value of husbandmen's estates in Lincolnshire in the seventeenth century from probate inventories and probate accounts*

| Order (gross) | Gross wealth: inventory total | Name | Place | Date (inventory or account) | Net wealth account total | Order (net) |
|---|---|---|---|---|---|---|
| 1 | £387 13s 10d | Thos Hudson | Melton Ross | 1679/80 | £318 1s 2d | 1 |
| 2 | £291 4s ?d | Will. Presgrave | Steddington | 1668 | –£11 14s 0d | 31 |
| 3 | £239 8s 6d | Hugh Dickinson | Billinghay | 1671 | –£12 9s 10d | 32 |
| 4 | £174 17s ?d | Robt Dance | Ryby | 1666 | £38 15s ?d | 9 |
| 5 | £150 10s 4d | Robt Bettison | Glenthorn | 1632 | £100 19s 8d | 3 |
| 6 | £133 0s 0d | Ric. Thornton | Arncotts | 1667/8 | £81 15s 8d | 5 |
| 7 | £122 0s10d | Thos Parrett | Hallington | 1678 | £26 19s ½d | 12 |
| 8 | £112 19s10d | Jo. Godsave | Fenton | 1680 | –£64 18s ?d | 35 |
| 9 | £112 8s 4d | Anthony Duke | Lutton | 1678 | £81 11s 4d | 6 |
| 10 | £111 0s 0d | Thos Waterland | Craisland | n.d. | £102 13s 2d | 2 |
| 11 | £101 12s 0d | Robt Chapman | E. Kirby | 1632 | £93 12s 0d | 4 |
| 12 | £92 1s 0d | Will. Turnard | Brothertoft | n.d. | £45 15s 0d | 8 |
| 13 | £82 15s 0d | Ric. Tenby | Foxhill | 1666 | £38 14s 2d | 10 |
| 14 | £78 6s 0d | Hen. Goodman | Fleet | 1666 | £6 4s 2d | 22 |
| 15 | £77 11s 4d | Wm Parkes | Norton Disney | 1673 | £13 2s 6d | 18 |
| 16 | £69 11s 4d | Ed. Cooke | Bicker | 1678 | –£48 0s 4d | 34 |
| 17 | £68 5s 10d | Peter Grainger | Harpswell | 1668 | £11 2s 4d | 20 |
| 18 | £62 6s 0d | Math. Wilkinson | Tottle | 1679 | £46 6s 8d | 7 |
| 19 | £61 0s 10d | Ric. Pepper | Pinchbeck | 1669 | £1 8s 0d | 24 |
| 20 | £59 1s 9d | Wm Tysedale | Tydd St Mary | 1683 | £11 1s 8d | 21 |
| 21 | £54 0s 0d | Wm Coopeland | Dogdike | 1664 | £24 18s 0d | 13 |
| 22 | £50 4s 4d | Thos Lawrence | Nether Toynton | 1678 | –£2 13s ?d | 27 |
| 23 | £38 3s 0d | Robt Lawrence | Froddingham | 1669 | £15 3s 6d | 16 |
| 24 | £36 13s 1d | Thos Stennet | Moulton | 1681 | –£8 19s 11d | 30 |

| | | | | | |
|---|---|---|---|---|---|
| 25 | £35 16s 2d | Will. Fox | Bottesford | 1673 | £27 15s 2d | 11 |
| 26 | £35 7s ?d | Jo. Taylor | Digby | 1673 | -£7 9s 0d | 29 |
| 27 | £31 15s 8d | Stephen Burd | Hallington | 1669 | £13 8s ?d | 17 |
| 28 | £29 3s 0d | Robt Doulton | Carlton-in-Moreland | n.d. | £6 12s 2d | 23 |
| 29 | £27 8s 11d | Will. Abraham | Leake | 1632 | £22 14s 7d | 14 |
| 30 | £26 0s 11d | Ric. Chatterton | Snitterby | 1673 | £22 2s 11d | 15 |
| 31 | £25 10s 0d | Fra. Charity | Dembleby | 1667 | £12 1s 2d | 19 |
| 32 | £21 8s 4d | Robt Smyth, Snr | E. Halton | 1666 | -£26 4s 0d | 33 |
| 33 | £16 16s 10d | Thos Hardy | Fishtoft | 1683 | -£7 6s 6d | 28 |
| 34 | £12 10s 0d | Jo. Whelston | Wainfleet | 1669 | -9s 4d | 25 |
| 35 | £8 10s 2d | Barth. Onn | Wigtoft | 1632 | -£2 0s 9d | 26 |

164

There were other examples, which were almost as dramatic, in the other direction. Richard Chatterton, husbandman, of Snitterby, had goods worth only £26 when his inventory was taken in 1673. His estate came thirtieth amongst the thirty-five husband-men. His hall and parlour were reasonably comfortable. He had more sheets, which usually seemed to provide a fair index of comfort and possibly surplus purchasing power,[36] than either of the labourers discussed above. From the inventory, the reader would guess at both the existence of a wife, and domestic by-employment. There was a woollen wheel and a spinning wheel in the chamber, with half a stone of hemp. The four yards of hempen cloth, and six yards of harden in the parlour, therefore could have been either bought or made. The stock and farm tools in his yard likewise indicated that he held more land than the labourers: he had three mares and a foal as well as his cattle, and two wains, three yokes, and a plough and harrows. There was a little grain in his barn with the hay. Yet his goods were still worth less than the inventoried value of the median labourer. The reader could not possibly guess that when his adult son, who was the administrator, came to the final accounting, there would not be a single charge on the estate apart from 13s 4d for the funeral, 6s 8d for a mortuary, and the inevitable court charges. There was not a single debt to be paid, no rent in arrears, no expense on other minor children, and no evidence of a widow. Despite the low value of Richard Chatterton's goods in the inventory, his frugal habits and domestic situation as someone unencumbered with any other person and yet still an active man, meant that the net value of his estate was as much as £22. It was fifteenth, not thirtieth, and came well above the median for husbandmen. His son, improbably, inherited more in terms of cash from his father than did the sons of William Presgrave.

Despite the wide range of inventory values for husbandmen, the median of £62 was significantly different from that of the labourers, as the scale of operations of the husbandman also seems significantly different. They quite frequently owed more than one rent in the accounts for land, and they also quite frequently owed wages.

[36] *Yeomen and Colliers in Telford*, ed. B. Trinder and J. Cox (Chichester, 1980), pp. 36–7. This study regards the capacity to change the bedlinen as 'one of the best indicators the inventory gives of steadily rising standards of comfort' in the 1680s. See also my discussion of the resources to change one's shirt, above, pp. 149–50.

Although there is no evidence of the acreages they farmed, the whole 'feel' of their enterprise is that of the tenant of half a yardland or a yardland in the seventeenth century. The 'median' husbandman from the inventories, Matthew Wilkinson of Tottle, owed £8 4s 0d in rent, double that for a labourer, and also owed wages to one man and one girl. He, like Richard Chatterton, owed no other debts and there were no minors to establish. His widow had remarried by the time she had put the account in. The estate ended up with a net value of £46, over triple the median value for the probate accounts for husbandmen. William Parkes of Norton Disney, whose estate in 1673 was worth the net median of £13, had had goods worth £78 originally on his inventory. He had owed two rents, house repairs and some wages, as well as payments for grazing. The main charges on his estate had been payments of £13 18s 0d to each of his three daughters, however. These were very much more substantial than the marriage portions payable by any labourer's estate and had actually been paid out before the account was drawn up. The scale of farming operations and provision for sons and daughters made by husbandmen who emerged as 'median' on the probate inventories and the probate accounts respectively was indeed much more considerable than in the case of the labourers, although the whole range of 'husbandmen' overlapped so heavily with that of the 'labourers', and the median account value was so little higher.

IV

In the same way, the thirty-five yeomen's probate accounts showed another leap in the scope of their operations. The totals of their inventory values brought forward to the probate accounts showed a range of movables valued at between £18 and £2,583. The lower quartile ran from £18 to £55, the upper from £287 to the very substantial £2,583 worth of goods and chattels left by John Forman of Bardney Dairies in 1673. The median of inventoried wealth was that of George Bartrum of Pickworth, whose goods were appraised at £149 in 1669. An increased scale of indebtedness and family obligation went with this increase of inventoried wealth. The probate accounts showed an overall drop between the inventory and account which varied between as little as £4 and as uch as £598. The median drop was £59. The final range of value of yeomen's

166

estates in their accounts varied from that on which the unfortunate administrators showed a loss of £188 to the £2,580 still left in the hands of John Forman's sisters and administratrixes. The lower quartile of yeomen's administrators ended up almost entirely over-spent: the top of the quartile was just in credit at £4. The upper quartile ranged from £114 to Forman's £2,580. But the median plummeted between inventory and account, from the £149 in George Bartrum's inventory to the £26 in the account of Stephen Trigot of Haburgh. Even though this was double the median of the husbandmen's accounts, it still demonstrated a really startling drop between inventory and net value. It was very noticeable that of the yeomen with really substantial farms above the median inventory value, also almost all indulged in transactions involving their credit very heavily. The median drop in value between inventory and account for yeomen with inventories worth over £161 was as much as £217, whereas for the yeomen below the median inventory value, who overlapped so heavily with the group of husbandmen, the median drop was only £29. Borrowing power was then immediately related to the size of the large-scale farmer's operations. The debts were likely to be to scale. The extent of the deductions meant the yeomen's final financial position in relation to each other was even less predictable than for any other group. Nineteen of the thirty-five, or over half of them, changed six places or more in relative order between inventory and account (see Table 4).

Individual examples again illustrate the scope of yeomen's farm-ing activities, their use of credit, and the scale of their endeavours to provide their daughters with portions at marriage or majority, and their sons with land or money to set up. The two yeomen who had the median inventory, and the median account wealth, George Bartrum and Stephen Trigot, also had disappointingly brief records. There was no surviving inventory for Bartrum in 1669, although the account of course recorded the inventory total of £149. The widow, the executrix, was recorded as 'having noe children'. There were no debts, as well as no portions to be paid, or expense for young children. George Bartrum was not even in arrears with his rent. So the widow's sole expenses after paying £3 for the funeral were the court fees. She was left with £142 in hand. The combined absence of debt and family charges meant that the estate ended up seventh, rather than eighteenth, in order of net value. In exactly the same way, Stephen Trigot, whose inventory of 1632 showed him in possession of merely £36 of goods, which only put him thirtieth in order amongst the thirty-five yeomen, had no family obligations and only minor debts. His widow, after paying these, his funeral expenses, and the court costs, was still left with £26 in hand, which astonishingly made the estate eighteenth in value and gave it the median final account value for the sample of yeomen. In both these cases, the childlessness and carefulness of the yeomen concerned seem to have been the overriding factors which put men farming in a relatively modest way disproportionately high amongst their fellows in the same social group.

The reader might suppose, from these yeomen, that childlessness was the overriding factor which brought the final value of the yeoman's estate in the probate account up in relation to that of his fellow yeomen. But this is not so. There are examples of childless yeomen who have plunged deeply into debt. There are also examples of yeomen with families who had managed to establish their heirs, or paid the expenses of their minor children, without running deeply into debt. Moreover, both these indebted childless yeomen and those who had successfully established families occurred at all economic levels in the wide range covered by the yeomen. Robert Holmes of Markby was worth £562 according to his inventory, which did not survive. His widow ended up out of pocket by £36 in 1683. Yet she had paid nothing to support any of his children, although there was admittedly a deduction of £100 left in his will to her five children by an earlier marriage. The back rents, at £40 a year at least, alone amounted to over £270. His 'servants'' wages at over £5 a quarter and 'labourers'' wages for threshing, hedging, sheep-washing, and shearing, and the mowing, cocking, and 'leading' of hay and corn were also unpaid, as was his bill to the smith and the carpenter. He owed poor rates, constables' charges, church lays, and assessments for the repairs to the old and the new sea banks at Sutton. The account was a mine of detail for farm and parish charges. There were small debts due for purchases of barley, pigs, and calves, as well as larger unspecified ones due upon bond. Robert Holmes was in arrears with everything, and the value of all his movables, which no doubt would have looked very substantial indeed in the inventory, was gobbled up by these numerous debts. The establishment of his own children, and even the £100 to his step-children, had nothing to do with this. His widow may have looked fifth most prosperous amongst the yeomen from the inventory, but

Table 4. *Gross and net value of yeomen's estates in Lincolnshire in the seventeenth century from probate inventories and probate accounts*

| Order (gross) | Gross wealth inventory total | Name | Place | Date (inventory or account) | Net wealth account total | Order (net) |
|---|---|---|---|---|---|---|
| 1 | £2,583 1s 10d | Jo. Forman | Bardney Dairies | 1673 | £2,579 10s 6d | 1 |
| 2 | £1,093 17s 0d | Hen. Boulton | Bardney | 1632 | £850 15s 2½d | 2 |
| 3 | £1,015 16s 4d | Thos Appleby | Thornton Curtis | 1664 | £435 1s 10d | 4 |
| 4 | £624 19s 2d | Thos Lockin | Laughton | 1666 | £448 16s ?d | 3 |
| 5 | £562 3s ?d | Robt Holmes | Markeby | 1683 | –£36 4s 8d | 32 |
| 6 | £426 6s 8d | Jo. Harrison | Canwicke | 1670 | £118 4s 0d | 8 |
| 7 | £290 12s 10d | Jas. Mabbut | Sutton St Ed. | 1684 | £145 15s 4d | 6 |
| 8 | £287 5s 7d | Thos Christian | Kitlington | 1686 | –£5 17s 9d | 28 |
| 9 | £253 18s 5d | Hen. Maltby | Crowland | 1679 | £226 12s 10d | 5 |
| 10 | £218 2s 0d | Will. Tebbutt | Gt Hale | 1666 | £6 15s 5d | 25 |
| 11 | £210 15s 0d | Thos Squire | Washingborough | 1666 | £97 1s 0d | 11 |
| 12 | £205 9s 2d | Simon Pennell | N. Kelsey | 1673 | –£7 15s 5d | 30 |
| 13 | £194 11s ?d | Chas Milnes | Normanton | 1690 | –£34 10s 10d | 31 |
| 14 | £193 7s 0d | Thos Pawling | Hindleby | 1666 | £114 15s 8d | 9 |
| 15 | £191 3s 4d | Vincent Russell | Bassingham | 1679 | –£71 7s 4d | 33 |
| 16 | £179 17s 4d | Jo. Creswell | Wragby | 1663 | £127 11s 4d | 10 |
| 17 | £161 4s 2d | Jo. Hodgson | Kirkton | 1683 | –£188 2s 10d | 35 |
| 18 | £149 1s 0d | Geo. Bartrum | Pickworth | 1669 | £142 9s 8d | 7 |
| 19 | £101 7s ?d | Fra. Short | Dunholm | 1676 | £72 13s 0d | 12 |
| 20 | £84 14s 4d | Geo. Deyne | Swineshead | 1632 | £26 4s 2d | 17 |
| 21 | £80 13s 0d | Will. Watkinson | Reepham | 1683 | £49 4s 0d | 13 |
| 22 | £79 10s 10d | Thos Crainton | Heckington | 1666 | £21 10s 8d | 19 |
| 23 | £78 7s 0d | Geo. King | Sereby | 1672 | –£7 15s 8d | 29 |
| 24 | £69 9s 0d | Wm Simpson | Gosbertowne | 1632 | £10 16s 2d | 22 |

| No. | Amount | Name | Place | Year | Amount | No. |
|---|---|---|---|---|---|---|
| 25 | £68 13s 0d | Nic. Leach | Raceby | 1683 | £48 ?s ?d | 14 |
| 26 | £61 8s 0d | Jo. Seamor | Caythorpe | 1664 | £8 7s 8d | 24 |
| 27 | £55 3s 0d | Will. Rodgers | Crowle | 1669 | £33 0s 8d | 15 |
| 28 | £46 8s 4d | Jas Harnson | Burnham | 1669 | £32 5s 0d | 16 |
| 29 | £38 8s 0d | Thos Johnson | Gedney | 1666 | £4 5s 0d | 26 |
| 30 | £36 0s 0d | Steph. Trigot | Haburgh | 1632 | £25 17s 10d | 18 |
| 31 | £29 12s 2d | Jo. Raven | Northwitham | 1631 | £20 10s 0d | 20 |
| 32 | £29 11s 0d | Arthur Wilkinson | Boston | 1666 | £4 3s 11d | 27 |
| 33 | £28 12s 10d | Will. Nichols | Hareby | 1669 | £15 6s 4d | 21 |
| 34 | £22 17s 0d | Thos Obbington | W. Keale | 1668 | -£73 11s 0d | 34 |
| 35 | £18 8s 0d | Ric. Hardy | Skidbrook | n.d. | £8 15s 0d | 23 |

170

she ended up thirty-second amongst the thirty-five on the accounts. There was no necessary causal connection between the indebtedness and the demographic circumstances or the family structure of the dead man.

Other yeomen's accounts also demonstrated this, from their proven ability to establish the next generation, or sustain the expenses of minor children between the time of their deaths and the final account. An example shows the way adult sons and daughters had been successfully established. Thomas Appleby of Thornton was the third most prosperous of the Lincolnshire yeomen when his inventory was taken in December 1664. The most substantial item in his inventory was 'corn in the barne and stackes in the yard' worth £467 10s 0d at this point immediately after harvest. There were three teams of plough horses in the stable, with their gears. He also had a flock of over 160 sheep and lambs, ten mares and colts and over thirty dairy cattle, calves, oxen, and three bulls. The possession of bulls was usually as certain a sign of economic prosperity in an inventory, as was the desire to be buried inside the church in a will an index of social status. There were two different sets of 'servants' beds'. The widow's disbursements in her account showed practically no indebtedness apart from the massive rent due of £250, which she had already paid. Apart from the court charges and the funeral, her only other expense had been even more massive, £300 'paid to Laurence Appleby, the deceaseds sonne being oweing to him . . . upon the Solemnization of a marriage betweene the said Laurence and one Mary Smyth, his now wife'. So we know that this yeoman's son had been financially established on his marriage, not with land but with cash, which was actually paid by his mother. Moreover, the notes made by the court official demonstrated much more fully just how successful this yeoman had been. There were four sons and a daughter, aged 33, 31, 29, 27, and 25 at the time of the account. Each of them received 5s as a token, since each of them had already had £150 in cash in his or her father's lifetime. Although she paid out £581 before the account was drawn up, the widow still ended up with £435 in hand, fourth most prosperous of the administrators. Her husband's provision for his grown children had been realistic, as well as lavish, and had not led to indebtedness. This widow was indeed in comfortable circumstances.

Two other yeomen's accounts in this sample give rare and invaluable examples of the expenses of bringing up minor children, and again demonstrate that these did not necessarily reduce an estate proportionately very much. The Thomas Lockin of Laughton, indeed, was fourth most prosperous amongst the yeomen, from his inventory. When all expenses were deducted, and the account drawn up, he ended up third most prosperous. The inventory, worth £625, showed Thomas Lockin lent money on a very considerable scale. Nearly £330 was due to him on 'specialty'. But he was still actively farming as well. His flock of over 350 sheep had no fewer than eight rams to serve it. From the account, he was, as one would expect, a respected local figure and parish official. A small sum was due to the town, outstanding from his accounts at the time of his church-wardenship. He owed a year's rent, and wages to a maidservant, a manservant, and two labourers. His executor paid out the family legacies in Thomas's will, and painstakingly accounted for the uncollectable debts amongst those due to Thomas. But the major expenses were for the 'diet, maintenance and other necessaries' laid out for the young, only son, William. These came to just over £100 for four years, and were broken down in minute and fascinating detail. From them, exact costs for food, clothing down to the price of broadcloth per yard and tailor's bills, individual bands (collars) and shoeties, hats, pocket money, and entertainment can all be worked out. But young Master Lockin, who was well dressed and well mounted, had his hair cut regularly, attended cock fights, and had a new knife in his pocket, along with his pocket money, was by no means too expensive for his father's estate. It seems he inherited it in good heart. The final account showed a surplus of £448.

In the same way, the two little daughters of Jonas Mabbut of Sutton St Edmunds, Sarah and Joan, were not too expensive for their father's estate. It was worth £291 according to the inventory. The administrator put in three years' accounts for all the expenses of the two children, ranging from board for them to minute details of their clothes, down to straw hats, stockings, and all the various types of linen to make them clothes, to medical expenses, a 'Testament' for Joan, and Sarah's schooling at 2d a week. Just as William Lockin had his pocket knife, so these girls had black whisks and ribbons, and Sarah obtained the dignity of a 'Mantua Gowne', as well as boarding in Wisbech for a year, possibly at school. The accounts finished £146 in credit in 1684, despite the educating of two girls who would have been extremely well treated and dressed.

78

172

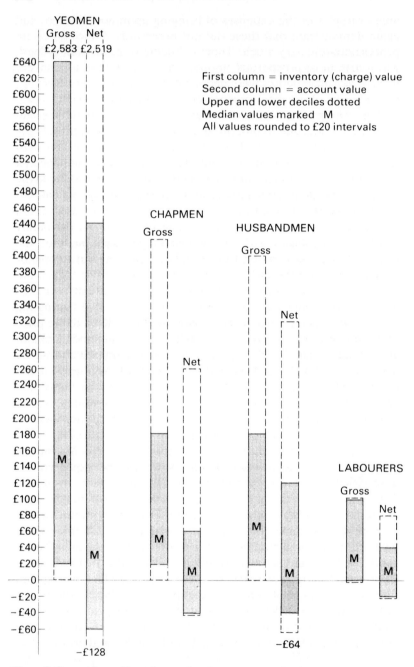

Figure 3 Comparison of inventory and probate account valuations

V

It seems from these examples that neither child-rearing nor the payment of portions to adult daughters, or cash sums to adult sons, were themselves the cause of indebtedness. There could be, but was not necessarily, a relationship. Such expenses were, however, one of the major categories of expenditure in many of the probate accounts, and certainly form one of the headings for future analysis, just as indebtedness formed another. This cursory survey of a small sample of probate accounts for Lincolnshire shows how much work needs to be done. It also shows how much new material there is in the accounts, from information on inheritance customs and settlements down to exact expenditure on servants' wages, and on the hitherto inaccessible subject of clothing below the gentry level. Most of all, the accounts demonstrated that the probate inventory alone is no guide to a man's relative financial standing within his own social group. Indeed, the net wealth of groups in relation to each other is very different from that which the relative values of the movables within each group would indicate.

The sum which appears at the foot of the probate inventory cannot be taken to indicate any individual's real net wealth, even in any approximate manner not only because it does not include, as we all knew, real estate, but because it carries no clue to the extent of his indebtedness. Rural credit underpins the whole of English rural society so completely that the humblest individuals above the levels of vagrants, and possibly even they, were involved in the network.

I argued much better than I knew in 1974 when I suggested the necessity to be able to read the bill or bond must have been as powerful an incentive to learning the skill of reading as any pressure to read the Holy Scriptures. Not only is the sum at the foot of the inventory no guide to the individual's net wealth, but it is no guide at all even to his relative financial standing within the same occupational or social group. We are all familiar with the nebulous nature of these same social groups, comprehending, as they do, wide extremes of inventoried wealth. Now this nebulous nature is stressed even more when the median net wealths of labourers, husbandmen, and yeomen are compared with their inventoried wealths. Certainly the 'median yeoman' from the Lincolnshire probate administrators' accounts, Stephen Trigot of Haburgh, was worth, with his £26, more than the 'median husbandman', William

174

Parkes of Norton Disney, with his £13. He, in turn, was worth a little more than his fellow 'median labourer', John Morgan of Saleby, with his £11. But such distinctions are so very much a matter of niceties, when compared with the glaring differences in the medians, £149, £62, and £29, taken from the probate inventories for these same social strata, that we are entitled to ask whether these groups do in fact have any economic reality at all. Do they lack economic cohesion to the point at which they are meaningless? Close reading of the inventories and administrators' accounts taken together suggests that although the former must be disbelieved as guides to wealth more strenuously than ever before, the groups called 'labourers', 'husbandmen', and 'yeomen', with all their huge economic overlaps and lack of distinction, probably still act as good guides to a man's scale of operations, his social pretensions, and possibly quite explicitly, his borrowing power. Labourers owed the rents of their cottages and were owed a year or in some cases half a year's wages. They borrowed within these limitations, and, in the manner of individual personalities at all times, some of them were much rasher than others. These men, or rather their widows, came out much worse than their more cautious brethren. Yeomen owed rents of land, possibly to many different landlords in many different parishes. They also owed wages to the labourers or servants they employed. Their scale of borrowing was explicitly adjusted to their scale of farming, and to their pretensions within the community. Indebtedness might therefore increase in direct proportion to the inventoried value of the yeoman concerned. Inventories must still be used, but their air of spurious exactitude, and their quantifiability, must be taken no longer with pinches of salt, but with whole salt-cellars of disbelief. Some of these inexactitudes can be corrected with the complementary probate account.

We owe to Dr Thirsk's work over the last thirty years the wholesale exploiting of the probate inventories as sources to draw the map on which the regional boundaries for the agrarian history of England can be laid out. The inventories have yet to be fully exploited for household interiors and domestic furnishings, to give us the guides to consumption that they could. But the next thirty years should partially be spent by social and economic historians exploiting the 'new' and complementary sources of the surviving probate accounts, which add so much new information on both social and economic customs.

# IV

# THE SIGNIFICANCE OF THE CAMBRIDGESHIRE HEARTH TAX

DR HOSKINS in his appendix on housing in *The Midland Peasant* was able to connect hearth-tax entries with certain probate inventories for Wigston Magna, and to suggest the number of hearths that might possibly go with the number of rooms. During the course of work on seventeenth-century Cambridgeshire it proved possible to follow this up, by relating a hundred probate inventories from the decade 1661–70 to the appropriate hearth-tax entries, thereby testing the extent to which the hearth tax may be used as a general social and economic guide.[1]

Hearth-tax entries are potentially useful in two ways. If it can be established that varying numbers of hearths do in fact indicate different wealth or social status, the tax provides a rough and ready guide to this, once the differentials have been established.[2] It can also be used as a guide to the state of rural housing in a county, as it was used by Dr Hoskins.

It must be emphasized that findings on the economic position or status that go with a certain number of hearths cannot be applied from one county to others unless they are in a region affected by the 'great rebuilding' at the same time.[3]

Results from the Cambridgeshire probate inventories for 1661–70, contrasted with a sample of 89 probate inventories from Lincolnshire for 1669, showed that Cambridgeshire had nearly twice as many people worth under £30 as Lincolnshire, and only two-thirds as many people worth between £30 and £60 (Table 1). In spite of this the rebuilding of small houses was much further advanced than in Lincolnshire, and both the inventories for the decade and those for 1669 itself showed that, even

---

[1] Information on the position of hearths, the number of rooms appropriate to different numbers of hearths, and the medians of wealth of those with one, two, three and four hearths is taken from this sample of 101. Information on house plans and their frequency, together with that on the proportions of different sizes of houses in Cambridgeshire, is taken from the whole group of 340 probate inventories of the Consistory Court which survive for the county for the decade 1661–70. They may be found in the Cambridge University Archives bundled under years. The hearth-tax assessments used were that for Michaelmas 1662 (P.R.O. E. 179/84/436), its revision made in Michaelmas 1664 (P.R.O. E. 179/84/437) and that for Lady Day 1666 (P.R.O. E. 179/244/22). Only those inventories were used for which the deceased, who had to be the only man of that name taxed in the village, was taxed on the same number of hearths in all three assessments if he died at the end of the decade, or in two assessments if he died in 1666. If he died in late 1662 the correlation between inventory and assessment in 1662 was accepted if the 1664 roll mentioned a change of tenure but still assessed the house on the same number of hearths as in 1662.

[2] The use which can then be made of the tax is shown in W. G. Hoskins, *Industry, Trade and People in Exeter, 1688–1800*, pp. 111–22.

[3] M. W. Barley, *The English Farmhouse and Cottage* (London, 1961), has shown the tremendous regional variations which existed in rural housing until the end of the seventeenth century.

54

in the fen-line region of the county, five-roomed houses formed the largest single group,[1] whereas three-roomed houses formed the largest single group in Lincolnshire (see Table 2).

From this example it can be seen how misleading it could be to apply an interpretation of the economic significance of the hearth tax in Cambridgeshire to a county not affected by the rebuilding at the same time.

The correlation of inventories and the hearth tax showed that a house with one hearth might have from one to six rooms, although two, three and four were most common[2] (see Table 3). It might be occupied by a person worth from under £10 to just under £200 (see Table 4 for the relationship between house-size and wealth), but 84 per cent of the occupiers of one-hearth houses had under £50, and the median wealth of such people was £24.[3]

Two-roomed cottages with no second floor were still numerous in Cambridgeshire, which in this respect differed from its prosperous neighbour Essex. They were inhabited mainly by people who left under £20, and were generally made up of hall and chamber, or parlour, although it was not very common for a chamber to be known as a parlour in as small a house as this, even if the use was identical. There was an interesting small group of two-roomed houses in which the hall had become demoted to a kitchen; examples of this were found more frequently in the fen-edge villages than anywhere else. Only one two-roomed house with hall and kitchen was found.

Three- and four-roomed houses were commonly occupied by those with goods worth under £30. Half the labourers who left inventories had three-roomed houses (see Table 5 for the relationship between status and house-size). By far the commonest design was of hall, chamber or parlour, and one service room. It appeared from the inventories that the chamber in a three-roomed house was usually a lower chamber;[4] one of the very few exceptions was the cottage of John Collis, a labourer of Harston, which had hall and dairy and a chamber over the hall. There were also examples of three-roomed cottages with hall and two service rooms and hall and two chambers.

Upper rooms were found commonly for the first time in four-roomed houses. The predominating plan was the simple one found in the East Midlands and Bedford-

[1] Secondary service rooms like brewhouses and boulting houses (flour-sieving houses), and malthouses and maltchambers are included as rooms in these figures, since the inventories show that they may sometimes, although not always, be in the main range. However, the inclusion of these rooms does not seriously affect the figures, since they only appear in houses with six or more rooms, and only appear in any numbers in houses with ten or more rooms.

[2] These findings should throughout be compared with those of Dr Hoskins in *The Midland Peasant* (pp. 299–300), which they almost completely confirm.

[3] The median wealth of the eighteen labourers whose inventories occur amongst those presented in the Consistory Court for the 1660's was £15. That of the twenty-four husbandmen was £30. That of the fifty-five craftsmen was £40, and that of the fifty-eight yeomen was £180. Analysis of all the inventories for the decade gave a median of £40.

[4] A 'chamber' in Cambridgeshire might be up- or downstairs. It was, therefore, impossible to be certain of the layout of any house containing a chamber not specifically described as upper or lower. This meant that exact figures showing the prevalence or rarity of any one design could not be given.

shire,[1] with hall, parlour or chamber, one service room and an upper chamber which was placed indiscriminately over the hall or parlour, and occasionally, although rarely, over the service room. There was a very rare variant of this with hall and two service rooms down, and an upper chamber. This type was common to a wide social range. Robert Caldecot of Barrington, who was known to his neighbours as a yeoman even if he only farmed three acres on the open fields, lived in such a house, and so did John Creede, a labourer of Thriplow. The second, smaller group, the exact proportion of which it was impossible to assess because of the difficulty of terminology, was that with four ground-floor rooms, hall, parlour or chamber, and two service rooms. Lastly, there was a very small class with hall and service room both chambered over, like the cottage of the labourer Thomas King of Hauxton.[2]

The hearth in a single-hearth house was obviously in the hall, or its variant, so that the hall was still used for cooking in spite of the fact that almost half the service rooms in three- and four-roomed houses were known as kitchens. The usual pattern was for spare utensils to be banished to the kitchen, which held, like the kitchen of William Tilbrook of West Wratting, kettles and pewter and dairy equipment. There were no utensils in his hall except those which belonged to the fireplace itself: the bellows, tongs, firepan and cob-irons.[3] There were however three very strange examples of houses with one hearth in which the inventory seems to suggest more or less clearly that the hearth might not have been in the hall. The inventory of Thomas Fordham, a husbandman of Cottenham, is not conclusive. He had hall, chamber, kitchen, and dairy. The curious thing about the inventory is that it shows him with a bed, two cupboards and chests, and a little table in the hall, but no provision for seating at all, while the kitchen contains hutches,[4] a table, three chairs, and—the only cooking utensils mentioned—an iron pot and an iron kettle. The fire-irons are not mentioned, so the position of the hearth is not known; but it does seem that Thomas Fordham has been caught in the act of gradually using his kitchen as a main living room more than his hall. It suggests that in another generation, the hall in that house would no longer be known as such.

The other two cases are quite clear. John Farrow, a carpenter of Thriplow, and John Harvey, a husbandman of Ickleton, both had the commonest four-roomed type of house with one hearth. In neither case does the connection of the inventory with the hearth-tax entry seem in any doubt. Both men used the hall as the main living room and kept their big table, chairs, forms, stools and cupboards there. But John Farrow's kitchen contained as well as all his kettles, pots and skillets, the iron pot and its hooks, which was the principal cooking vessel, the spit, the frying pan and all 'his Colls that was in the hod'. It seems incredible that in an untidy age tidiness

[1] M. W. Barley, *op. cit.* p. 151.
[2] Nowhere in Cambridgeshire did the type of cottage with hall and parlour both chambered over—which made up just under a quarter of the four-roomed houses on the Duchy of Lancashire estates in Lincolnshire in 1608—occur (M. W. Barley, *op. cit.* p. 85).
[3] Cob-irons were alternatives for andirons, or firedogs. For a fuller description, see F. W. Steer, *Farm and Cottage Inventories of Mid-Essex, 1635–1749* (Colchester, 1960), pp. 25–6.
[4] Hutches were small chests, used for storage. See F. W. Steer, *op. cit.* p. 19.

should be carried to the extreme of keeping the hod of coal in a room away from the hearth. John Harvey had no hod of coals, but he kept in his service room, which was a buttery not a kitchen, the spit, tongs, and firepan, as well as all the cooking vessels. These cases either throw doubt on the hearth-tax assessors' capacities, even in the careful 1664 revision, or show the extent to which the relationship between the kitchen and hall was changing in this period.

A house with two hearths might have from two to ten rooms, although two-thirds of those in the sample had four, five, or six rooms. Their occupiers had from under £10 to over £300 but three-quarters of them had between £10 and £100, and the median wealth of occupants of two-hearth houses was £60.

Five-roomed houses formed the largest single class in Cambridgeshire and were occupied by the biggest group of husbandmen, some craftsmen and some yeomen, who usually had anything from under £10 to £70. They were also occupied by a sprinkling of much more wealthy men, with from £100 to £200, and in one case over £400. Thirty per cent of the Cambridgeshire yeomen lived in five- and six-roomed houses.

Three main types of five-roomed houses emerge from the inventories. The commonest was that with hall, parlour or lower chamber, two service rooms, and one upper chamber. The upper chamber in these cases was usually over the hall, but sometimes over the parlour, leaving the two service rooms normally single-storeyed. Next came a group with two upper chambers, which normally had hall, parlour, and one service room downstairs. Thirdly came a very small group which possibly had all five rooms downstairs. The likelihood is that it was very rare.

The commonest type of six-roomed house was one with hall and parlour, two service rooms, and two upper chambers which were usually over the hall and the parlour. There were examples, however, both of the hall and parlour being apparently left open.

Secondly came a group of houses with only one upper chamber. It included a small number of houses with both lower chamber and parlour; but wherever this combination was found in six- or seven-roomed houses it had the effect of lessening the extent of chambering over. Only in houses with ten or more rooms was the existence of two parlours or their equivalent an indication of wealth rather than that of backwardness in the construction of a second storey. There was even one example of a six-roomed house with no upper chambers given at all. This may simply be indicative of the appraisers' failure to go upstairs; but it is symptomatic of one of the most striking features of Cambridgeshire housing as it emerges from the inventories—the rarity of symmetrical chambering over. The third and smallest group of six-roomed houses was that with three upper and three lower rooms, and it is typical that this should be the smallest group, for in houses with up to eight rooms, cases in which the upper storey had been extended as far as it could be were very rare.

When there was more than one hearth, probate inventories cannot be trusted to indicate the position of the additional ones, for they usually give only the main cooking hearth. In most two-hearth houses the cooking was done in the kitchen and so the kitchen hearth was given; occasionally it was still done in the hall, and so a hearth in the hall was given. Only in one two-hearth house did the inventory give both hearths, and they were in kitchen and hall. There is not a single example of a house with two hearths in which a heated parlour or chamber was indicated.

A house with three hearths might have from six to eleven rooms, but over three-quarters had six, seven, or eight rooms. They were occupied by people with personal wealth of from just under £30 to over £500, but the vast majority had from just under £30 to £200. The median was £141. The biggest single group of Cambridgeshire yeomen lived in eight-roomed houses.

The plans of seven- and eight-roomed houses become too difficult to interpret. The largest class of seven-roomed houses had two upper chambers, and the largest class of eight-roomed houses had only three. It is noticeable that half the very small group of eight-roomed houses, in which the position of every room is known, had no chamber over the hall. Service rooms in these more wealthy yeomen's houses began to multiply, and the majority of eight-roomed houses had three or four.

The position of the third hearth varied considerably according to the information given in the inventories. The hearth most commonly supplied with fire-irons was in the kitchen still, with the hall hearth mentioned next. But the parlour may be heated in a house of this size; Henry Sell, yeoman of Gamlingay, had a hearth in his 'chamber below' judging from the 'iron grate' listed there, although he does not seem to have one in his parlour. Richard Wootton of Ickleton had hearths in his parlour and hall. Moreover, one hearth may be upstairs in a three-hearth house. Thomas Alban, blacksmith of Shepreth, who had seven rooms and three hearths, had a hearth in his hall, which he used for cooking, having no kitchen, and another in the chamber over the parlour, for there were listed there with his bedstead, five chests and six chairs, a little pair of cob-irons and a fire-shovel. There were no fire-irons in his parlour, where the third hearth presumably was. Samuel Mortlock of Whittlesford had a hearth in his hall, and the only other implements connected with fires were in the chamber over his buttery, where he had two pairs of cob-irons.

A house with four hearths or more had from six to fourteen rooms, and might be occupied by a person with from £34 to £1132. Five-eighths had over £300, and the median value of their wealth was £360. Only very considerable yeomen or prosperous shopkeepers occupied such houses in general. The house of John Mickelly of West Wickham, who left £546. 12s. 2d., is a good example of these outstanding houses. It had thirteen rooms. Not all their positions are known, but downstairs he had a hall, and a parlour (which contained amongst other things a long table and eighteen leather chairs), kitchen, dairy, brewhouse and cellar. Upstairs he had chambers over the hall, the parlour, the dairy and the porch. The positions of his own bedchamber and of the chamber for storing cheese were not stated, nor was that of his 'round' chamber, which contained a bed with curtains, had hangings on the walls, and contained plate and linen which brought the value of the contents of the room up to

£25. The house had five hearths, and it is the only large house in which the inventory gives the position of all five. There were fire-irons, cob-irons and tongs in the hall, the parlour, the kitchen, the chamber over the parlour, and John Mickelly's own bedchamber.

The number of hearths that a house is assessed on in the hearth tax can then, within very broad limits, be used as a guide to the size it is most likely to be. But it is not a certain one. A three-roomed house with hall, lower chamber, and service room, or a four-roomed house with hall, upper and lower chambers, and service room, was most likely to have one hearth, but might possibly have two. A five-roomed house with hall, lower chamber or parlour, two service rooms and one upper chamber was most likely to have two hearths, but might only have one. A six-roomed house with hall, parlour, two service rooms, and two upper chambers, might have two or three hearths. There were examples of eight-roomed houses with hall, parlour, three service rooms, and three upper chambers, with two, three, four and even five hearths. In large houses of ten or more rooms individual preference played an immense part, and it becomes impossible to predict how many hearths there will be. William Folkes, yeoman of Westley Waterless, who died leaving £324. 7s. 4d., had ten rooms and only two hearths. William Amye, yeoman of Little Abington, who left £253. 13s. 4d., and Francis Nun, yeoman of Swaffham Prior, lived in ten-roomed houses which each had hall, parlour, four service rooms and four upper chambers. William Amye had four hearths and Francis Nun had eight.

The main fact which emerges from this work on the hearth tax is that it can be used as a general economic guide. The widely differing medians of wealth of those with differing numbers of hearths show this.[1] It can also be used as a social guide in the sense that all persons with three or more hearths were almost certain to be yeomen or extremely prosperous craftsmen of a similar status. It does not follow that those with fewer hearths were not yeomen. The extent of economic and social overlap, and the blurring of economic and social divisions caused by inheritance and personal preference, means that although the tax may be used as a guide to status and wealth in general, it may not safely be used in any individual example. The cases of Richard London, husbandman of Hinxton, who had eight rooms and five hearths and only £34 to his name, and, conversely, of Thomas Amey, husbandman of Harston, who had a two-roomed cottage and left £119. 15s. 6d., are instructive examples of the dangers of oversimplification.

An analysis of one of the hearth-tax returns for Cambridgeshire was made,[2] and its results showed when they were mapped that there was no clear regional pattern

[1] It is important to note that the medians of those with four, and more than four, hearths were taken together. The numbers of those with more than four hearths are too few, and the connection between wealth and house size so much looser at this end of the scale than at the other, that this must be done to get a fair picture.

[2] The return of Michaelmas 1664 was chosen for this purpose, since it is an extremely detailed revision of the 1662 return which includes frequent corrections of concealments, and comments which were obviously based on personal inspection, in some cases. For this reason it seemed likely to be the most accurate return of the series. It is also nearly as full as the return for Lady Day 1674 (see C. A. F. Meekings, *V.C.H. Cambs. and the Isle of Ely*, IV, p. 273).

of personal wealth in the county.[1] In general, 30–50 per cent of the houses in each parish had one hearth, 20–40 per cent had two hearths, less than 20 per cent had three hearths, and less than 20 per cent had four or more hearths (maps, Figs. 1–5). There were very numerous exceptions to this. Of the parishes with under 30 per cent of houses with one hearth, Willingham and Histon lay in the fen or on the fen-edge, Stapleford and Little Shelford in the river valley, and Hardwick, Toft and Gamlingay on the western upland. On the other hand, a noticeable block of parishes which all had more than 50 per cent of these small houses lay together on the south-eastern upland. Most of the parishes with over 40 per cent of houses with two hearths were grouped together in the fen or on the fen-edge to the north of Cambridge, but the fen parishes to the north-east were dissimilar. Of the parishes with 20–30 per cent of houses with three hearths, Burwell lay on the fen-edge, Babraham and Duxford in the river valleys and Croydon and Gamlingay on the western upland. Exceptional parishes with 30–40 per cent of houses with four or more hearths were similarly widely distributed.

This result is particularly interesting, since it conflicts in some ways with the results obtained from analysing the personal wealth of each Cambridgeshire region as it was shown in the probate inventories. Over eighty inventories survive from the upland, and over a hundred each from the valleys and the fen-edge, for the decade 1661–70. The median wealth of the testators from the upland was £47, and that from the river valleys £30, while that from the fen-edge lay between, at £40. Most of the upland inventories came from the villages above the 300-ft. contour to the south-east of the county. But it was just here that the hearth-tax returns showed a remarkable grouping of villages with over 50 per cent of houses with only one hearth. This conflict of evidence shows the dangers inherent in relying on even a large sample of inventories, for it is quite plain that in the south-east of the county the proportion of small men leaving a will must have been very low, and the results, in consequence, are extremely misleading.

The lack of any clear pattern of prosperity in the hearth-tax return for 1664 shows clearly that the individual history of tenure and farming, and indeed of particular local initiative and the lack of it, must be investigated in villages which stand out as exceptionally poor or exceptionally prosperous. No regional generalizations will supply this deficiency.

## ACKNOWLEDGEMENTS

I am indebted to Mr M. W. Barley, Dr J. Thirsk, Dr H. P. R. Finberg, and Dr P. Eden, for their help and advice with this work.

[1] For discussion of natural regions in Cambridgeshire, see J. J. Jones, *A Human Geography of Cambridgeshire* (1924), pp. 27–42 and 51–9, and *The Cambridge Region*, ed. H. C. Darby (1938), pp. 106–15.

60

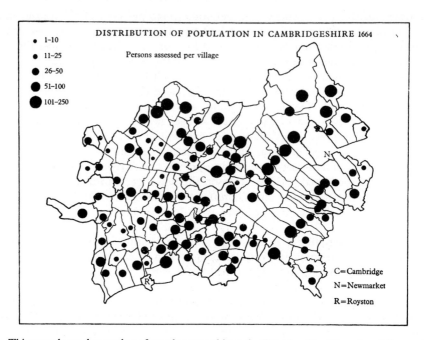

Fig. 1. This map shows the number of people assessed in each village in 1664. There is a difference in the numbers of people assessed in this return, and the number of houses in each village, since the former figure excludes empty houses, whereas the latter excludes additional inmates in houses which are divided. However, the difference between the two is usually very small, and only changes the numbers appearing on the map in the cases of Bassingbourn, East Hatley, Horseheath and Burwell. Subdivisions of houses at East Hatley, Horseheath and Burwell meant that while the number of people taxed fell within the '11–25', '51–100', and 'over 200' groups, the number of houses fell within the '1–10', '26–50' and '100–200' groups. At Bassingbourn, the number of empty houses brought the total number of houses to just over 100, while the number of people assessed fell just below that figure.

Pairs of semi-detached cottages of the seventeenth century have been found by the investigators of the Historical Monuments Commission in the county, which also has very early examples of rows of cottages (M. W. Barley, *The English Farmhouse and Cottage*, pp. 247–8). The hearth-tax return of 1664 shows that, although subdivision was not far advanced in the county, it was sufficiently common for over forty villages to have an example or two. There is of course no reason to suppose that many of these examples were of cottages built as semi-detached. The process of inheritance by which division could be brought about is shown very clearly in the court books of Linton for 1603–65 (Cambs. R.O., R.59.5.1). In 1617 William and Elizabeth Ridgewell were admitted to a tenement near 'le Bridgefoot' in Linton. In 1633 Ann Ridgewell was admitted to the same tenement on the death of her father William, Katherine Ridgewell was admitted to the 'end' of the same tenement on the death of her mother Elizabeth, and William and Elizabeth Byr were admitted to a tenement 'cald a kitchin', which was part of the same property. Finally, in 1651, Ann Ridgewell and Elizabeth Byr were admitted to the end of the tenement formerly in the tenancy of their sister, Katherine. Many divisions recorded in the hearth tax must have been brought about by similar means. In Chesterton and Linton, Swaffham Prior and its hamlet of Reach, Burwell and Cottenham, between ten and fifteen subdivisions each were recorded, however, and in those cases it seems quite probable that semi-detached cottages existed by 1664. The work of the Royal Commission on Historical Monuments will presumably decide this point.

*Note:* Numbers for Cambridge are omitted from this and the following four maps.

89

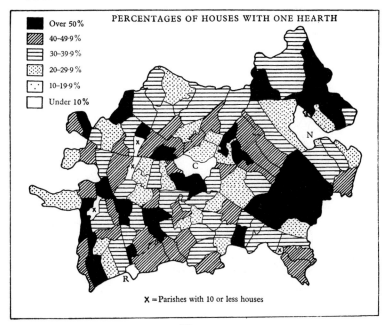

Fig. 2

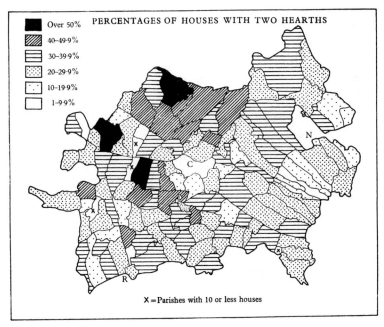

Fig. 3

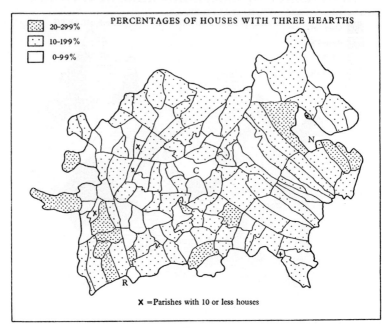

Fig. 4

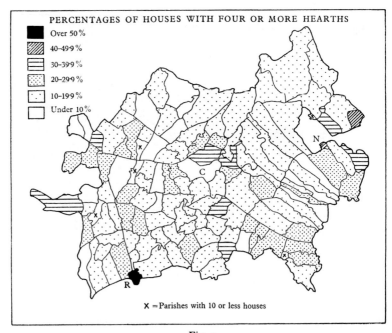

Fig. 5

## TABLE 1. *Distribution of wealth shown in probate inventories*

|  | Cambridgeshire 1661–70 | | Lincolnshire 1669 | |
|---|---|---|---|---|
|  | No. | % | No. | % |
| £1–£30 | 142 | 41·8 | 22 | 22·5 |
| £30–£60 | 63 | 18·5 | 28 | 28·8 |
| £60–£80 | 22 | 6·4 | 10 | 10·3 |
| £80–£100 | 20 | 5·8 | 9 | 9·2 |
| Over £100 | 93 | 27·4 | 28 | 29·0 |
|  | 340 | 99·9 | 97 | 99·8 |
|  | Median £40 | | Median £56. 16s. | |

The information on Lincolnshire in this and the following table is taken from M. W. Barley, *Econ. Hist. Rev.* VII (1955), pp. 293 and 294.

## TABLE 2. *Number of rooms shown in probate inventories*

|  | Lincolnshire 1669 | | Cambridgeshire 1669 | | Cambridgeshire 1661–70 | | Cambridgeshire Fen-line 1661–70 |
|---|---|---|---|---|---|---|---|
|  | No. | % | No. | % | No. | % | No. and % |
| Dubious | 6 | 7·3 | 10 | 11·6 | 34 | 10·5 | 15 |
| 2 | 15 | 18·4 | 6 | 7·0 | 33 | 10·1 | 9 |
| 3 | 16 | 19·4 | 10 | 11·6 | 44 | 13·5 | 14 |
| 4 | 13 | 15·8 | 11 | 12·8 | 36 | 11·0 | 7 |
| 5 | 8 | 9·7 | 12 | 14·0 | 53 | 16·4 | 17 |
| 6 | 8 | 9·7 | 11 | 12·8 | 39 | 12·0 | 16 |
| 7 | 9 | 11·0 | 5 | 5·8 | 21 | 6·5 | 8 |
| 8 | 2 | 2·4 | 9 | 10·3 | 27 | 8·3 | 6 |
| 9 and over | 5 | 6·1 | 13 | 15·0 | 38 | 11·7 | 9 |
| Total | 82 | 99·8 | 87 | 100·9 | 325 | 100·0 | 101 |

## TABLE 3. *The relationship between number of rooms and number of hearths*

| No. of hearths | No. of rooms | | | | | | | | | | | | | | Total |
|---|---|---|---|---|---|---|---|---|---|---|---|---|---|---|---|
|  | 1 | 2 | 3 | 4 | 5 | 6 | 7 | 8 | 9 | 10 | 11 | 12 | 13 | 14 |  |
| 1 | 5 | 8 | 8 | 12 | 3 | 2 | . | . | . | . | . | . | . | . | 38 |
| 2 | . | 1 | 2 | 6 | 12 | 5 | 2 | 3 | . | 1 | . | . | . | . | 32 |
| 3 | . | . | . | . | . | 4 | 3 | 4 | 1 | 1 | 1 | . | . | . | 14 |
| 4 | . | . | . | . | . | 1 | 3 | 1 | . | 1 | 2 | 1 | 1 | . | 10 |
| 5 | . | . | . | . | . | . | . | 1 | . | 1 | . | . | 1 | . | 3 |
| 6 | . | . | . | . | . | . | . | . | . | 1 | . | . | . | . | 1 |
| 7 | . | . | . | . | . | . | . | . | . | . | . | . | . | . | . |
| 8 | . | . | . | . | . | . | . | . | . | 1 | . | . | . | . | 1 |
| 9 | . | . | . | . | . | . | . | . | . | . | 1 | . | . | 1 | 2 |
|  | | | | | | | | | | | | | | | 101 |

TABLE 4. *Personal wealth and number of rooms—Cambridgeshire 1661–70*

No. of rooms

| Wealth | Dubious | 2 | 3 | 4 | 5 | 6 | 7 | 8 | 9 | 10 | 11 | 12 | 13 | 14 | Total |
|---|---|---|---|---|---|---|---|---|---|---|---|---|---|---|---|
| Under £10 | 8 | 10 | 11 | 1 | 5 | 1 | . | . | . | . | . | . | . | . | . | 36 |
| £10–£20 | 14 | 10 | 13 | 9 | 6 | 2 | 1 | . | . | . | . | . | . | . | . | 55 |
| £20–£30 | 4 | 3 | 9 | 12 | 7 | 6 | 3 | 1 | . | . | . | . | . | . | . | 45 |
| £30–£40 | 4 | 3 | 3 | 4 | 8 | 1 | 2 | . | 1 | . | . | . | . | . | . | 26 |
| £40–£50 | 1 | 1 | 2 | 1 | 7 | 4 | . | 2 | . | . | 1 | . | . | . | . | 19 |
| £50–£60 | 1 | 1 | 1 | . | 4 | 2 | 3 | . | 1 | . | . | . | . | . | . | 13 |
| £60–£70 | . | . | 1 | 1 | 3 | 5 | . | 1 | . | 1 | . | . | . | . | . | 12 |
| £70–£80 | 1 | . | 1 | 2 | 1 | 4 | . | 3 | . | . | . | . | . | . | . | 12 |
| £80–£90 | . | 1 | 1 | 1 | 1 | 2 | 1 | 1 | . | . | . | . | . | . | . | 8 |
| £90–£100 | . | 1 | 1 | 1 | 1 | 2 | 1 | 2 | . | . | . | . | . | . | . | 9 |
| £100–£150 | 1 | 1 | 1 | 1 | 5 | 4 | 1 | 4 | 1 | 1 | 1 | 2 | . | . | 23 |
| £150–£200 | . | 1 | . | 1 | 4 | . | . | 4 | 2 | . | 1 | . | . | 2 | 15 |
| £200–£250 | . | 1 | . | . | . | 2 | 1 | 3 | 1 | 1 | 1 | . | 2 | . | 12 |
| £250–£300 | . | . | . | 1 | . | 1 | 1 | 2 | . | 3 | 1 | 2 | . | . | 11 |
| £300–£350 | . | . | . | . | . | . | 3 | 1 | . | 1 | 1 | . | . | . | 6 |
| £350–£400 | . | . | . | 1 | . | 1 | 2 | 1 | 1 | . | . | . | . | . | 6 |
| £400–£450 | . | . | . | . | . | . | 1 | . | . | . | . | . | . | . | 1 |
| £450–£500 | . | . | . | . | . | . | 1 | . | . | . | . | . | 1 | 1 | 3 |
| £500–£550 | . | . | . | . | . | 1 | . | . | . | . | 1 | 1 | 1 | . | 4 |
| £550–£600 | . | . | . | . | . | . | . | . | . | . | . | . | . | . | — |
| £600–£650 | . | . | . | . | . | . | . | 1 | . | . | . | . | . | . | 1 |
| £650–£700 | . | . | . | . | 1 | . | . | . | . | . | . | . | . | . | 1 |
| Over £700 | . | . | . | . | . | 1 | . | 1 | 1 | 2 | 1 | . | . | 1 | 7 |
| Total | 34 | 33 | 44 | 36 | 53 | 39 | 21 | 27 | 8 | 9 | 8 | 5 | 4 | 4 | 325 |

TABLE 5. *The relationship between social status and house-size*

| No. of rooms | Labourers | | Husbandmen | | Craftsmen | | Yeomen | | Gentlemen | |
|---|---|---|---|---|---|---|---|---|---|---|
| | No. | % | No. | % | No. | % | No. | % | No | % |
| Dubious | 4 | 23.5 | — | — | 6 | 10.9 | — | — | — | — |
| 2 | 2 | 11.8 | 2 | 8.7 | 7 | 12.7 | 1 | 1.7 | — | — |
| 3 | 8 | 47.0 | 2 | 8.7 | 4 | 7.3 | 1 | 1.7 | — | — |
| 4 | 2 | 11.8 | 4 | 17.4 | 5 | 9.1 | 3 | 5.2 | — | — |
| 5 | 1 | 5.9 | 9 | 39.2 | 7 | 12.7 | 9 | 15.5 | 1 | 10 |
| 6 | — | — | 3 | 13.1 | 10 | 18.2 | 9 | 15.5 | — | — |
| 7 | — | — | — | — | 9 | 16.4 | 5 | 8.6 | 1 | 10 |
| 8 | — | — | 1 | 4.3 | 5 | 9.1 | 11 | 19.0 | 1 | 10 |
| 9 | — | — | 1 | 4.3 | 1 | 1.8 | 2 | 3.6 | 1 | 10 |
| 10 | — | — | — | — | 1 | 1.8 | 7 | 12.1 | — | — |
| 11 | — | — | — | — | — | — | 4 | 7.3 | 3 | 30 |
| 12 | — | — | — | — | — | — | 2 | 3.6 | — | — |
| 13 | — | — | 1 | 4.3 | — | — | 2 | 3.6 | 1 | 10 |
| 14 and over | — | — | — | — | — | — | 2 | 3.6 | 2 | 20 |
| Total | 17 | 100.0 | 23 | 100.0 | 55 | 100.0 | 58 | 101.0 | 10 | 100 |

TABLE 6. *The relationship between number of hearths and personal wealth*

*Number and percentage of hearths*

| Moveable Wealth | 1 | 2 | 3 | 4 | More | Totals |
|---|---|---|---|---|---|---|
| Under £10 | 7 | 2 | | | | 9 |
| £10-£20 | 10 | 3 | | | | 13 |
| £20-£30 | 8 | 4 | 1 | | | 13 |
| £30-£40 | 5 | 2 | | | 1 (5 hearths) | 8 |
| £40-£50 | 3 | 3 | 1 | | | 7 |
| £50-£60 | 1 | 2 | 2 | | | 5 |
| £60-£70 | | 4 | 1 | | | 5 |
| £70-£80 | | 2 | | | | 2 |
| £80-£90 | | 2 | | | | 2 |
| £90-£100 | 2 | 2 | 1 | | | 5 |
| £100-£150 | 2 | 2 | 2 | | | 6 |
| £150-£200 | | 3 | 2 | 2 | | 7 |
| £200-£250 | | 1 | | 1 | | 2 |
| £250-£300 | | | 1 | 1 | 2 (6 and 8 hearths) | 4 |
| £300-£350 | | 1 | 2 | 1 | | 4 |
| £350-£400 | | | | 1 | | 1 |
| £400-£450 | | | | | | |
| £450-£500 | | | | 1 | 1 (9 hearths) | 2 |
| £500-£550 | | | 1 | 1 | 1 (5 hearths) | 3 |
| £550-£600 | | | | | | |
| £600-£650 | | | | | | |
| £650-£700 | | | | | | |
| Over £750 | | | | 1 | 2 (5 and 9 hearths) | 3 |
| **Totals** | 38 | 33 | 14 | 9 | 7 | 101 |

Figures boxed to omit upper and lower quartiles

V

# A Cambridgeshire Community

## CHIPPENHAM FROM SETTLEMENT TO ENCLOSURE

## CONTENTS

# TABLES

# A CAMBRIDGESHIRE COMMUNITY

## INTRODUCTION

IN 1696 Edward Russell, First Lord of the Admiralty, and member of
parliament for Cambridgeshire, began a sweeping series of changes on
his estate of Chippenham, by which he intended to provide a suitably
grandiloquent setting for the victor of the Battle of La Hogue. By 1712 these
changes were completed to his satisfaction, and he therefore took pains to
have his improvements recorded in the magnificent map of Chippenham which
survives from that year. The village itself covered an entire sheet of the map
and was dominated by the Russell mansion. This was surrounded by its wooded
park, which was prettily ornamented with grazing deer, and contained a
landscaped lake. North of the manor lay the High Street, bordered with the
fifty odd houses of the tenantry and the church, together with the charming
charity school in the latest modern idiom. Chippenham in the early eighteenth
century, as today, was a model village.

It had, however, been radically altered. Close inspection of the map shows
that at least half the length of the High Street, still outlined in the trees, lay
within the new park, and that a further road, also blocked and emparked, had
once crossed it to the south. Along both these roads the outlines of former
crofts are still visible on the map, and right down to the south of the park two
cottages survived in isolation, well over half a mile from any other in the village.
All this suggests that eighteenth-century Chippenham was a shadow of its former self. Earlier sources immediately confirm the suspicions raised by the map.

The Hundred Rolls record that there were nearly a hundred and fifty
tenants on the Hospitallers' manor of Chippenham in 1279, probably representing as many households. The population explosion of the twelfth and
thirteenth centuries had more than quadrupled the size of the Domesday
village. A century later, in 1377, the village had shrunk by over a half. The
renewed rise in population beginning in the late fifteenth century did not
touch Chippenham. When the manor was surveyed in minute detail in 1544
for its new owner after the Dissolution, there were only sixty householders
there. The map of the model village of 1712 delineates the skeleton of a community which had once been three times the size.

The object of this essay is to trace the effect this steep early medieval rise
and equally steep late medieval fall in population had on landholding in
Chippenham, and so on the physical layout of the village and its fields. Dramatic changes in the availability of land, and so in the size of farms, involve
equally dramatic changes in the structure of the society farming the land. In

many ways these changes were entirely orthodox at Chippenham, which almost forms a textbook example of the effects of the expansion and contraction of medieval population. This is perhaps because the poverty of the soil made Chippenham highly sensitive and quick to reflect the consequences of general population trends. In the fifteenth century the rise of the yeoman farmer becomes the dominant theme in the history of Chippenham. How far the development of the social structure of this single village was typical of Cambridgeshire remains to be seen. Comparison with other fifteenth-century villages in this congested county suggests that the degree of shrinkage it suffered was by no means unusual, and therefore that the opportunities offered by the land market to the enterprising yeoman were no greater than elsewhere. The yeoman elsewhere, however, did not necessarily make the same use of his opportunities as he did at Chippenham. The engrossing of farms was carried so far during the sixteenth and seventeenth centuries that the fields themselves were transformed. Enclosure, which is so often thought to have been the death sentence of the smaller peasant, here came too late, for the smaller peasant had disappeared from Chippenham society even before Edward Russell undertook his improvements.

## I. SETTLEMENT AND ENVIRONMENT

CAMBRIDGESHIRE was reached early by the Saxons. The archaeological evidence points to considerable settlement before the end of the fifth century,[1] and in spite of the lack of obvious 'ingas' elements in the place-names of the county, the occurrence of rare and unusual elements supports the archaeological view.[2] Even before the eponymous Cippa founded his homestead a little west of the river Kennet, the place had been by no means unfrequented, for it lay on that great prehistoric traffic artery, the Icknield Way. The Saxons did not pioneer heavy clay soils here; the territory of the future parish lay on the barely sloping chalk ridge which carried the Way above the edge of the fen. Its soils were derived mainly from chalk and were therefore mostly light and freely drained. There were also patches both north and south of the Saxon village site, of poor sandy soils closely allied to those of the Breckland just across the Kennet, on which neolithic man found his most easily acceptable habitat.[3]

The heath and the fen were already the two outstanding physical features

[1] P. H. Reaney, *The Place-Names of Cambridgeshire and the Isle of Ely*, English Place Name Society, 1943, p. xvii.

[2] *Ibid.*, p. xviii. Badlingham, the hamlet next to Chippenham on the east, is one of the three village names in the county in which the element *-ingas* occurs.

[3] Soil Survey of England and Wales, Sheet 188, Cambridge, Ordnance Survey, 1963.

when the Saxons made their appearance. At the highest point of the parish, to the south, the 'heath', an area of downland grazing on the chalk, which was to dominate physical descriptions and maps of the parish until the eighteenth century, is likely to have been semi-cleared. Every Cambridgeshire parish on the line of the Way had an area of heath grazing on the waterless part of the chalk, and these grazing areas were to have a decisive effect on the village economies. The other dominant feature was the inlet of peat fen which today remains the largest remnant of fen vegetation in Cambridgeshire after that at Wicken. For many centuries it was to provide both fuel and common pasture.

The Icknield Way itself was to form the southern parish boundary, but two lower summer routes, the Ditch Way and the Street Way, ran parallel to it and nearer the fen.[1] The Street Way was later to be built up as the medieval South Street of Chippenham, and was to remain in use until Edward Russell blocked it in the seventeenth century. Numerous barrows testify to the amount of prehistoric traffic on these routes. Four of them, including two from the early Bronze Age, stand on the heath itself.[2] A thirteenth-century field name bears witness to the existence, west of the Saxon village site, of three others which have long since disappeared.[3] These stood on the line of the Street Way near which a late Bronze Age smith's foundry has also been discovered.[4] The main prehistoric settlement area in Chippenham lay well north of the Street Way, however, on a patch of the poorest, sandiest soil in the parish. Here, four more barrows showed evidence of use throughout the Bronze Age, and themselves overlay a mesolithic working floor and a neolithic settlement.[5] Near at hand gravel digging has brought to light an Iron Age village,[6] and Iron Age and Romano-British sherds in the barrows point to their continuing use. This part of Chippenham had thus been regarded with favour by many successive cultures before the Saxon advent, but its continuous use did not extend to the Saxon period. The Romano-British is the last identifiable ground surface below the present, implying that the ground was under cultivation by the

[1] Sir Cyril Fox, *The Archaeology of the Cambridge Region*, Cambridge, 1923, pp. 147–50, describes the course of the Street Way which is conjectural through Chippenham, since it was swept away by the emparking. The line of it is however shown on the map of 1712 and is fully described in the survey of 1544. Dr Reaney confused the Ditch Way in Chippenham with the Street Way, *op. cit.*, p. 30, but the two medieval cartularies, BM Cotton MS. Nero C. IX and MS. Harl. 3697, and the survey of 1544 make it plain that several furlongs lay between the two. The map of 1712 shows the Ditch Way as a furlong boundary for its whole length. See my forthcoming note, 'The Street and Ditch Ways in South East Cambridgeshire', *Proceedings of the Cambridge Antiquarian Society*, LX, 1966.

[2] C. S. Leaf in *Proceedings of the Cambridge Antiquarian Society*, XXXIX, 1940, pp. 29–33.

[3] See below p. 18.     [4] Fox, *op. cit.*, pp. 59–60.

[5] C. S. Leaf, *loc. cit.*, and 'Two Bronze Age Barrows at Chippenham', *Proceedings of the Cambridge Antiquarian Society*, XXXVI, 1936, pp. 132–55.

[6] *Council for British Archaeology Bulletin*, II, 1955.

Saxons. Cippa's people rejected this principal settlement area in favour of a site round the edge of the peat fen further south, and their ploughs gradually wore down the earthworks of their predecessors in the creation of what became North Field. Only their cemetery lay near those of earlier cultures. However, the shape of the parish boundary, which is a straight line to the west and east between Chippenham and its neighbours of Snailwell and Kennet, but an indented one to the north towards the village of Freckenham, suggests that the Saxon furlongs had reached the boundary there, not elsewhere, when it was drawn up. The Saxons may have avoided the actual house sites of their predecessors but were not averse from ploughing the easiest land where the bulk of the work had already been done for them.

In the ninth century the inhabitants of Chippenham were joined by later intruders. The Scandinavians did not leave such a deep impression on Cambridgeshire as on many of the eastern counties. Only six parish names incorporate Scandinavian elements,[1] and there is no indication in Domesday of the kind of 'double community' which occurs in Leicestershire, in which wealth was concentrated in the hands of the newcomers, and a physical division of the settlement was the result,[2] but the invasion was strong enough to have a lasting effect on the field names of the county.[3] Chippenham was not immune from this. South of the village the thirteenth-century name for the marsh at the head of the stream, *Flothowe* or *Flordhowe*, incorporated the Old Norse *flot* which described it as a piece of flat ground. The stream itself, the *bekkr* to the newcomers, gave its name to *Littlebek* field, and further east or *austr*, the meadow of *Esterbek* also bore witness to their presence. The three barrows in the field next to the Street Way gave it the Scandinavian name of *Tremhowe*.[4] In the thirteenth century this field still had alternative names derived from Saxon and Old Norse, both of which were in common use.[5]

## II. THE EARLIEST WRITTEN EVIDENCE

### A TENTH-CENTURY LAWSUIT

THE earliest evidence of the social organization of the little township near the Kennet emerges incidentally from the somewhat tedious details of one of the many transactions which Abbot Brihtnoth of Ely and Bishop Æthelwold of Winchester entered into in their efforts to provide the newly refounded abbey with an adequate territorial endowment in the tenth century.[6]

---

[1] Reaney, *op. cit.*, p. xix.    [2] W. G. Hoskins, *The Midland Peasant*, 1957, pp. 7–10.
[3] Reaney, *op. cit.*, pp. xix–xxi.    [4] *Ibid.*, pp. 312, 329.    [5] See below, pp. 17–18.
[6] E. Miller, *The Abbey and Bishopric of Ely*, Cambridge, 1951, pp. 16–17.

Some time between 970 and 984 Abbot Brihtnoth accepted the offer of a certain Ælfwold the Fat and his wife to sell three hides in Chippenham which the lady had inherited from her first husband.[1] When the parties met in Chippenham to conclude the bargain, two spokesmen claimed seventy-five acres of the woman's land and seven acres of land held by two villeins on behalf of one Ulf. A bystander then unnervingly remarked that even if this claim were discounted, there would not be three whole hides. The dissension which followed was settled by a party of men chosen from the abbot's people and the woman's going round the land and measuring it. It is apparent that whatever the original relationship between the hide as a fiscal unit and the actual acres in the field, in tenth-century Chippenham men thought of it as a measurable unit of a hundred and twenty acres. The surveying party showed that the woman held only a hundred and forty-four acres apart from the eighty-two claimed, successfully in the end, by Ulf. The latter immediately ordered his men to sow his own seventy-five acres. The abbot, however, intent on acquisition, persuaded Ulf to part with his claim for a consideration, and went on to add another holding of a hundred and ten acres built up by a certain Wine. Wine had bought land in Chippenham from three different men, two of them residents of other vills, to form this holding. Leofsige of Freckenham had sold him eighty acres and five "predia domibus constructa"; Ælfric of Wicken had sold him twenty acres and an "allodum domibus edificatum"; and Wulfhelm, brother of Wulfwine, sold him ten acres.

In all, then, three hundred and thirty-six acres passed into the abbot's hands with the five *predia* and the *allodum* of Wine, together with six and a half *predia* ... *nuda et vastata* of the woman's which are not mentioned before the summary of the bargain. The chronicle implies that the abbot ended up with three whole hides or three hundred and sixty acres in Chippenham.[2] He did not keep it, however, but exchanged it with Ælfric, son of Earl Hereric. Ælfric had inherited land in Chippenham from his mother, but had given it to his younger brother Leofwine in return for two hides in Downham. He now re-exchanged the two hides in Downham for the three acquired by the abbot of Ely in Chippenham. It is obvious that the soil of Chippenham was considered vastly inferior to the rich fen soil of Downham; not only were two hides exchanged for three, but the abbot threw in as well sheep worth twenty shillings, a palfrey worth ten shillings, and ten shillings in money. The whole transaction left the two sons of Earl Hereric in possession of what must have

[1] For what follows see *Liber Eliensis*, ed. E. O. Blake, Camden Society, 3rd series, xcii, London, 1962, pp. 87–91.

[2] It is by no means clear whether the acreage which must have been attached to the *predia* and the *allodum* was included within the total acreage of the land of Wine and the woman, or was separately reckoned and not stated in the *Liber*.

been at least five hides, made up of the original inheritance from their mother and the new acquisition from the abbot.

The very name of Chippenham indicates a settlement dominated from the beginning by a leader, who presumably had had some power and authority over the distribution of land, rather than the creation of a group of free peasants.[1] Whether this was so or not, the information given by the *Liber* shows that in the tenth century groups of subordinate peasants existed in the township. They held their land from others, like the two villeins cultivating seven of Ulf's acres, and the tenants Leofsige of Freckenham presumably had in the five *predia* which he sold to Wine. It seems likely that some of these peasants performed labour services; the men who sowed Ulf's land for him after he won his claim do not sound like slaves. They did not hold their land from a single lord, however, but from a multiplicity of small landowners.

The status of the landowners who sold to the abbot on this occasion presents some difficulty. The acreages concerned are far from being of thegnly dimensions, unless, of course, the participants had considerable property elsewhere.[2] It seems possible that they were the precursors of the two sokemen who, in 1066, held two, or three,[3] hides from the king in return for the provision of a horse for his service, or a payment in lieu of this. They were free to dispose of their land as they wished. If this identification of the participants in the transactions of 970–84 is correct, the *Liber* shows these men very actively exercising their right of disposal, and its corollary, the acquisition, of land. Moreover, it seems that they themselves had dependant tenantry performing labour services for them. The comparison is perhaps far-fetched, but the picture given by the *Liber* is in many ways somewhat like that given by the monastic cartularies of the activities of the free peasantry of Chippenham in the thirteenth century, buying and selling, before the creation of sub-manors was arrested by the Statute of *Quia Emptores* at the end of the century. On the other hand the tendency in the tenth century, under Ely's influence, was towards the consolidation, not the dispersal, of estates. By 984, land which had previously been in the occupation of five men had been added to the already considerable acreage in the hands of a sixth family.

---

[1] Cf. T. H. Aston, 'The Origins of the Manor in England', *Transactions of the Royal Historical Society*, 5th. Ser., VIII, 1958, p. 74.

[2] Ulf is known to have had two hides in Milton, which he exchanged with the abbot for the same amount in Fordham. He may also have been the man who witnessed as a *minister.—Liber*, pp. 90, 104, 78n. Wine may perhaps have been identical with the man in the abbot's service who rode errands for him, exchanged fifty-three acres and a weir with him, and was given a hide to provide himself with clothing.—*Liber*, pp. 90, 95, 96, 96 n. 2.

[3] Different amounts are given by the *Inquisitio Comitatus Cantabrigiensis* and Domesday Book, which are conveniently printed together in *English Historical Documents*, II, pp. 880–1.

DOMESDAY BOOK

By Domesday, all manorial subdivisions, if such there were, had been swept away, and Chippenham was one of the few Cambridgeshire manors which coincided with the vill. The sokemen had disappeared, like so many of their contemporaries in the county,[1] and nineteen villeins with thirteen bordars remained.[2] These thirty-two households, with the six slaves who worked the demesne ploughs, made one of the smaller but typical villages of the Cambridgeshire fen-edge. The most densely settled area of the county was the valley of the Cam, together with the valleys of its tributaries, where between ten and fifteen people are recorded to the square mile; next came the chalk ridge, the western upland and part of the fen edge, including Chippenham, with five to ten people per square mile.[3]

Between them the villeins and the bordars shared fourteen ploughs, and the demesne had three more. There was no discrepancy here, as there was in some other villages in the county, between the number of ploughlands available and the number of ploughs working. By 1086, therefore, the whole area which was reckoned to be suitable for arable cultivation was under the plough. Already the outline of land-use in the township is apparent. There was meadow for three plough-teams, presumably those of the demesne, which probably lay round the marsh, known later as Flordhowe Marsh. The "pasture for the livestock of the village" must have been the heath, which also supported fourteen beasts and three rounceys as well as 285 sheep. Chippenham then took its lesser place beside the other Cambridgeshire villages with a heath area, Wood Ditton with over 500, Carlton with over 600, and Weston Colville and West Wratting with over 700 sheep apiece,[4] where the considerable demesne flocks indicated the nascent 'sheep-corn husbandry'. Already a mill stood in the fields, although it is impossible to say on which of the two later mill sites. Finally a fishery rendered fifteen hundred eels.[5]

It is impossible to assess the relative wealth or average size of tenement of the peasantry in 1086, since the villeins and the bordars are lumped together in the sharing of the ploughs.[6] This is especially true since Cambridgeshire had one bordar with as many as fifteen acres and a fair number with ten acres, although the majority had from nothing up to five acres.[7] On the other hand,

[1] H. C. Darby, *Domesday Geography of Eastern England*, 1957, p. 290.
[2] The *I.C.C.* gives twenty-nine villeins.      [3] H. C. Darby, *op. cit.*, Figs. 79 and 80, pp. 288–9.
[4] R. V. Lennard, *Rural England 1086–1135*, Oxford, 1959, p. 263.
[5] If Mr Lennard is right that the existence of a *piscaria* usually implied a weir, it is possible that this fishery was not in Chippenham Fen. The Hospitallers' Cartulary records the de Mandeville grant of "Belwere" in Wicken, which may have been the fishery appurtenant to Domesday Chippenham.
[6] Lennard, *op. cit.*, pp. 349–50.      [7] *Ibid.*, p. 346.

only just over two families had to share to make up a plough-team in Chippenham, which indicates that the average size of the holding, though made up of poor soil, was relatively large.[1] It seems also that the ratio of demesne to tenant ploughs was lower than usual at Chippenham, which may indicate a small demesne. Alternatively the tenants' ploughing services may have been heavy, to compensate for the small number of demesne ploughs.

The value of the manor was comparatively high. It had risen steadily from £12 under King Edward to £16 when Geoffrey de Mandeville received it of the king, and to £20 by 1086. The first de Mandeville seems to have had some measure of skill in estate management, like his successors. Orgar the Sheriff, who had held the manor under Edward the Confessor, had got into financial difficulties and had had the assessment of *feorm* reduced from ten to five hides. In spite of this he had had to mortgage the estate, probably to Æsgar the Staller, whose man he became. From Æsgar the manor came, like the rest of his fee, to Geoffrey de Mandeville.[2]

### SOME TWELFTH-CENTURY CHARTERS

Chippenham remained entirely in the hands of the de Mandevilles for just under a century. In 1184 William de Mandeville, third earl of Essex, gave the township, and all rights over it, to the Hospitallers in free alms.[3] He excluded from the grant the parish church of St Margaret which had already been given to the abbey of Walden. The fifteenth-century cartulary of the Hospital also contains copies of the confirmations made by William and his elder brother Geoffrey of the grants of land in Chippenham which their mother Rohese, widow of the great Geoffrey, had made to her Gilbertine foundation of Chicksands in Bedfordshire. The identification of the topographical references[4] in these grants to Chicksands shows that the arable acreage of Chippenham was expanding considerably in the twelfth century and that many of the later major field divisions already existed.

Rohese apparently gave Chicksands the site for a grange "and all its compass," together with common pasture, common of turbary, and some meadow land. Between 1144 and 1146 her son Geoffrey confirmed her grant, and added to it a hundred and twenty acres in the "field east of the grange," all his

[1] Cf. R. H. Hilton, 'Medieval Agrarian History', *Victoria County History, Leicestershire*, II, pp. 152–4. Professor Hilton shows that the Leicestershire figures of the average number of families which had to share to make up a team was 4·8, whereas even if the *I.C.C.* figure for Chippenham population rather than the Domesday one is correct, the average there was only three families to the team.

[2] R. V. Lennard, *op. cit.*, p. 29.

[3] BM. Cotton MS. Nero C. IX (hereafter cited as A), fo. 29. I have throughout used the modern foliation of both this and the Walden cartulary.

[4] See map at end.

demesne in "Sund," seven acres in "Stanhull," and pasture for 500 sheep and lambs as for his own.[1] His brother William in turn confirmed the grant of the grange, the land east of it, common rights, pasture for sheep, and the meadow, but altered the rest.[2] He retracted the gift of the demesne in Sund and Stanhull and gave in exchange 116 acres in the "newly cleared land," and ten acres in "Blatherwyc." To all this he added a new grant, of forty acres of arable in Blatherwyc, and ten acres of sheep pasture south of the grange, and east of the newly cleared land.

The existence of a minutely full survey, listing every strip in the open fields, made in 1544, after the Dissolution had thrown the Hospitallers' estate of Chippenham into lay hands, makes it possible to locate practically all the medieval field-names scattered throughout the cartulary of the Hospitallers and that of Walden Abbey.

With the exception of the few acres in "Stanhull," Stonehill Field in 1544, to the east of the village, all the gifts to Chicksands were clustered together south of the village towards the heath. In 1544 the site of the grange itself was described as "grounde compassed w^th a diche conteyning bie estimac' iiij acres."[3] It lay in Sound Field, one of the three southern fields of Chippenham, on the road from Newmarket to Brandon, which in the sixteenth century formed the northern boundary of the heath. The boundary between Sound Field and Littlebeck Field ran immediately to the east of the grange, and the adjoining furlong in Littlebeck Field was made up of a block of sixty acres of "Chicksonde landes."[4] Littlebeck Field must then have been the "field east of the grange" which the twelfth-century charter distinguishes from the "Sund." Sound and Littlebeck Fields are thus proved to have existed in the twelfth century.

The only other land farmed as part of the possessions of the grange here was another twelve acres to the east of the "Chicksonde landes," but cut off from them by the road to Moulton,[5] which in 1544 formed the boundary between Littlebeck and Blackland Fields. It is evident that this land must represent the remainder of the original grant in the single "field east of the grange." Blackland Field did not therefore exist as a separate entity in the time of the de Mandevilles, although land that was later contained in it was under cultivation.

The work of clearance had by the mid-twelfth century spread to the limit of cultivated land in the sixteenth century. The identification of "Blatherwyc" and the "newly cleared land" shows that it had also gone beyond it.

[1] A fo. 144, printed in *Bedfordshire Historical Records Society*, I, 1913, pp. 112–13.     [2] A fo. 144v.
[3] Cambridgeshire Record Office (hereafter cited as C.R.O.), R.55.7.5.1(15), fo. 75.
[4] *Ibid.*, fo. 29.          [5] *Ibid.*, fo. 37v.

In 1544 "Blethewick," as it was then called, was an area of 200 acres at the western end of the heath "severall continually to the lord." Next to it on the east lay 100 acres of heath of the fee of Chicksands which was likewise non-commonable. Only half the heath was common to the tenants.[1] The hundred acres of Chicksands heath necessarily represent part of the newly cleared land of the twelfth century, and it is obvious that a portion of "Blatherwyc" further west was also then under arable cultivation. The de Mandevilles were engaged on assarting a considerable quantity of heath land.[2] For all that, William de Mandeville showed judgement in his own cause when he retrieved his demesne in Sound Field in exchange for a grant on the heath. The block demesne in Sound included all the meadow land around the head of the stream and was highly valued in the sixteenth century, whereas the western end of "Blather-wyc" lay on the same soil as Newmarket Heath. It might give good yields in the first year or two of cultivation, but they would drop rapidly thereafter.

As well as assarting, the de Mandevilles seem likely to have been increasing the number of sheep run in the parish. The 285 demesne sheep which appeared in Domesday must have been increased dramatically before the grant of pasturage for 500 sheep and their lambs to Chicksands, for it is difficult to believe that the de Mandevilles granted the right to fold more sheep than they kept themselves. The evidence is fragmentary, but is enough to show that the family made enterprising, if uncomfortable, landlords.

## III. OVERPOPULATION: CHIPPENHAM IN THE THIRTEENTH CENTURY

THE cartularies of the Hospital and Walden Abbey are the main sources of information on Chippenham in the thirteenth century. Most of the charters contained in them, although not precisely date-able, seem to fall in the period between 1225 and 1290, and they peter out almost completely after 1300.[3] Some of the families of free tenants whose doings are recorded in the cartularies also appear in the Hundred Rolls of 1279. The

[1] C.R.O., R.55.7.5.1(15), fo. 77v.

[2] It seems likely that this land remained in cultivation for more than a century. The figures for demesne acreage given in the description of the Hospitallers' estate in 1338 only make sense on the assumption that they include 300 acres on the heath. There is little indication of any clearance on the heath other than that of seignorial initiative; the evidence is indirect, but the acreage of villein and free land given in the Hundred Rolls (see below, p. 29) is almost exactly that of the acreage of customary and free tenants in 1544 which did not include any heath land.

[3] They are most numerous in the same period as were the *Carte Nativorum*. I have dated them mainly from internal evidence, but have also used the formal test of the changed wording after the Statute of Quia Emptores described by C. N. L. Brooke in *Carte Nativorum*, ed. C. N. L. Brooke and M. M. Postan, Northamptonshire Record Society, xx, 1960, p. xvii.

combination of these sources therefore provides both evidence of the activities of the free tenantry throughout the century and a convenient summary of the effects these activities had had by 1279.

The descriptions of land and its whereabouts contained in the charters also give, again with the help of the 1544 survey, a picture of the lay-out of the village and its fields.

By the end of the thirteenth century the recorded population of Chippenham was higher than at any other time in its history. There were 143 tenants in 1279,[1] which indicates perhaps between 650 and 700 inhabitants.[2] This is a minimum estimate, considering that the Hundred Rolls do not include details of any subtenants. The parish must have been bursting at the seams. It is sobering to consider that the land which at Domesday was supporting only thirty-two families was now supporting over four times that number. We can hardly avoid the conclusion that here, as elsewhere, at the end of the thirteenth century population pressure must have led to acute land hunger and the proportion of smaller holdings must have meant that a large proportion of the villagers were living at subsistence level and vulnerable to any failure of crop.[3]

This increase in population was reflected in the physical extension of the village, which had now reached its maximum. The housing had spread from the two main streets which crossed at the green, along the lane which ran above the edge of the fen to Snailwell, fording one of the streams. In the sixteenth century this lane was known as Fordbridge Lane or Newyards Lane. Thirteenth-century references to "Fordestrete" and to the "Newyards" suggest that it was built up and was in the process of acquiring its later names. The survey of 1544 which witnessed that there was here "severall grounde . . . wherein be conteined certein mease groundes . . . which hath ben occupied by the farmer without the memory of man," spoke the truth.[4] Cottages and crofts had stood here three hundred years before. The High Street which ran from the "head of the town" in North Field to the village green towards the south, passing the church and the site of the manor on the way, was itself badly congested, as charters subdividing closes indicate.[5] South of South Street, where again the houses were all "clere decaied" in 1544,[6] various free tenants lived in the thirteenth century.

---

[1] *Rotuli Hundredorum*, II, pp. 505–6.

[2] Assuming multipliers in the range 4·5 to 5.—J. Krause, 'The Medieval Household: Large or Small?', *Economic History Review*, 2nd series, IX, 1957, pp. 420–32.

[3] Cf. M. M. Postan and J. Titow, 'Heriots and Prices on Winchester Manors', *Economic History Review*, 2nd ser., XI, 1959, pp. 392–417.

[4] C.R.O., R.55.7.5.1(15), ff. 11v and 11.          [5] A fo. 37v.

[6] C.R.O., R.55.7.5.1(15), ff. 1v–2v.

THE LAY-OUT OF THE VILLAGE AND ITS FIELDS

The area round the Hospitallers' hall was one of the few parts of the township which was, naturally, not touched on by the charters. Chippenham was not merely one of the Hospital's many manors. It served, as the survey of the Hospitallers' possessions in 1338 shows,[1] as the infirmary for the whole of the English Priory. The hall and the infirmary buildings with their chapel were entirely separate, and were manned by a considerable staff. There were three brethren and two secular chaplains in the hall under the preceptor, and seven brethren in the infirmary, with provision for others "according to the number of cases of sickness in the priory."

The site of the manor house contained about five acres, according to the survey of 1544.[2] It fronted immediately on to the High Street, with the village houses continuing north and south. Behind it, beyond the "mote called the blacke ponde or drawebridge" and the "holte of wood called the great garden" lay the "holmes with the pondes."[3] The principal buildings which still survived in that year were "ij bayse courtes wth⁰ an yinner courte." A chapel still existed, for the lease of the manor bound the lessee to find a fitting chaplain to say divine service in it.[4] South of the manor the thirty-three acres of demesne arable and meadow called South Croft ran down to the back of the houses on South Street. It seems likely that all the medieval monastic buildings had been contained within the five-acre site of 1544, for the survey, which is meticulous in specifying land where buildings once stood, gives no suggestion that any part of South Croft had ever been built over.

To the west of South Croft in the sixteenth century lay the forty acres of the "Hallmore" and the "Townmore."[5] Beyond these again lay the open fields. The Town Moor was common all the year round and the Hall Moor was open to the tenants from Lammas to Crispinmas, and several to the farmer the rest of the time. The disposition of this whole area behind the manor was related to its soil and water supplies. It all lies on the only considerable area of ill-drained soil in the parish, a patch of fine clay loam by the fen. One of the Chippenham springs rose somewhere in the vicinity, and fed the "pondes" in the sixteenth century as it today feeds the ornamental waters laid out in the eighteenth. It also provided suitable conditions for "Monks Meadow" and "Parsons Meadow." The two commons lay on the poorer part of the soil, and part of the place which was once town common is today judged fit only for a coniferous plantation.

---

[1] *The Hospitallers' Inquest of 1338*, ed. P. Larking, Camden Society, LXV, 1857. The Chippenham entry is discussed in *V.C.H. Cambs. and the Isle of Ely*, II, pp. 264–5.

[2] See map at end throughout this section.     [3] C.R.O., R.55.7.5.1(15), ff. 8v–9.

[4] P.R.O., S.C.6/Hen. VIII/7268, m.7.     [5] C.R.O., R.55.7.5.1(15), ff. 21–21v.

A CAMBRIDGESHIRE COMMUNITY 17

The only information on the whole area in the thirteenth century is provided incidentally by one of the charters which describes a free tenement on the north side of South Street as backing on to the "moram."[1] From this it is safe to assume that part of it, in the thirteenth century as in the sixteenth, was common. For the rest, the very silence of the free tenants argues their lack of legitimate interest and so perhaps suggests that this part of the parish round the Hall was, in the thirteenth century, as in the fifteenth and sixteenth, demesne.

The other area not mentioned in the charters was that immediately east of the fen. In 1712 the closes there were one of the most prominent features on the map; but they were not new.[2] In 1544 there were seventy acres of demesne in the same position "severally enclosed" called North Croft and North Meadow.[3] The fifteenth-century court rolls and their presentations of trespass make it abundantly clear that this land was already enclosed, and the silence of the cartularies strengthens the conjecture that here lay part of the Hospitallers' meadow, estimated in 1338 at 109 acres in all and valued highly at £11 15s. 2d.[4]

The open fields surrounded the core of church, village streets, green, common, and the closes and headquarters of the preceptory of Chippenham. In 1544 there were eight of them, but the thirteenth-century position was even more complicated, particularly south of the town.[5] East, north, and west of it the thirteenth-century fields remained the same. North Field, one of the largest,[6] was bounded on the south by the road to Badlingham, and by the Lachmere common, which adjoined the fen. The main prehistoric settlement had lain in it, and it had been under continuous cultivation since the Anglo-Saxons drove their ploughshares over the Romano-British occupation layer. South of the fen were the two west fields: West Field itself, which abutted on the marsh, and its neighbour, divided off from it by the road to Snailwell, and abutting in its turn on the Sound Field. This area is variously described in the cartularies as Brech Field, or simply "The Brech," and "Tremhoue Field." The two names are at first sight difficult to account for. The field's proximity

[1] A fo. 50.    [2] C.R.O., R.58.16.1.    [3] C.R.O., R.55.7.5.1(15), fo. 39v.
[4] op. cit., ed. Larking, p. 78.
[5] H. L. Gray, *English Field Systems* (reprinted 1959), p. 458, gave Chippenham a three-field system on the basis of only the first of the fifty-nine Walden charters, BM. Harl. 3697, fo. 155. This lists the strips in a half-yardland. The names of three fields appear in the list, and Gray wrongly assumed that they formed headings under which the other strips described in the charter were entered. In fact the descriptions show that they lay in other fields, which are named but not described as "fields" in this particular charter.
[6] The sixteenth-century field acreages were Mill or North Field approximately 424 acres, Sound 392 acres, West 218 acres, Thremhoue 279 acres, Littlebeck 190 acres, Blackland 182 acres, Pudman-hill 133 acres, and Stone 93 acres.

to the village makes it appear highly unlikely that it had acquired its name of "Brech" as a 'breach' or recently broken-up area under temporary cultivation, since its soil was not inferior to that elsewhere. The solution is provided by a charter to Walden which describes a strip in the "Berw" field.[1] Here the name is derived not from 'breach', but from 'barrow'.[2] Since the alternative name Tremhowe means 'three barrows',[3] it seems that the two field names are simply translations in Saxon and old Norse of a description showing that the field contained noticeable earthworks. The Norse name proved stronger, and no trace of the earlier name appears in the sixteenth century, although the eighteenth-century estate map shows a Foxborough Furlong, and the name, in that form, survives today.

In the sixteenth century three fields lay south of the village, Sund or Sound Field, Littlebeck, and Blackland. The principal stream ran across the top of all of them, rising in "Flordhowe Marsh" in Sound Field, where the demesne was concentrated, continuing south of the block of demesne called Wyndmilbred and turning northwards through the demesne meadow called Esterbek in Blackland Field. All three fields were also crossed by the Ditch Way, which was a furlong boundary throughout its length. The charters describe a slightly different situation. The Sund, which derived its name from the sandy soil on which it partly lay, had existed in the twelfth century, as had the field boundary east of it, exactly where the boundary with Littlebeck later ran. In the thirteenth century the Sund is frequently mentioned, although in the Walden cartulary it is with few exceptions known as the "Suth" Field. Littlebeck Field was less commonly referred to, but did exist. Blackland Field, on the other hand, apparently did not exist.[4] The only reference is to three furlongs "called Blackland" which apparently had not acquired the status of a separate field at that time.

On the other hand, three other small field divisions which do not put in a later appearance are frequently mentioned. Flothowe or Flordhowe Marsh commonly lay in "Flordhowe Field;" Esterbeck Meadow likewise in "Esterbeck Field." and an unplaceable "Scote" Field ran as far down as the Ditch Way. Furthermore, there is a casual reference to the "Ditch Way Field," and on more than one occasion simply "the field south of the village" is used as a description. The field boundaries seem to have been in a state of flux throughout the area.

There are no medieval accounts for Chippenham, and there is therefore no means of telling whether these manifold fields existed because each served as

---

[1] Harl. MS. 3697, fo. 157.    [2] P. H. Reaney, *op. cit.*, p. 312.    [3] *Ibid.*, p. 329.
[4] This ties in with the twelfth-century evidence of Chicksand Furlong extending later into what was Blackland Field (see above, p. 13).

a separate cropping unit. The distribution of the free tenants' holdings among the eight or more fields was by no means equal, as it would have been in a classic three-field system, in which the fields do represent rotational units. Over half of the twenty-four acres granted by Richard de Camera to the Hospital, and later leased by them as a separate holding, lay in three of the southern fields. There were six acres in the North Field, four acres in the two western fields, and only one acre in the two eastern fields.[1] The eight-acre holding leased by Nicholas Clericus to a servant of the Hospital lay entirely in the southern fields, except for a single acre in the Pudmanhill Field.[2] This lack of balance argues that the fields of Chippenham were not cropping units. Despite this, some kind of controlled rotation did exist in the township, at least by the early fifteenth century, for in 1404–5 a tenant was fined for sowing a bond tenement unseasonably with barley instead of rye the year before he surrendered it. Common rights of pasture over the fallow, presupposing an organized crop rotation, also existed by the fifteenth century, for in 1468 a by-law was broken which dealt with the pasturing of horses on the stubble. The memoranda made by the jury in 1544 made it clear that all "great cattell" were included in these rights over the stubble.[3] The functions of the fields remain obscure, but despite the unequal distribution of individual holdings amongst them, they were obviously worked under communal discipline.

The fields may of course have been simply topographical units, perhaps representing the original areas of clearance. In that case their boundaries should have been so glaringly obvious to their cultivators that each field had an unmistakable physical identity. In most cases this was so, and the field boundaries were formed by roads and streams. However, the tortuous, and if the twelfth-century grants to Chicksands are to be believed,[4] ancient, boundary between Sound and Littlebeck Fields belies this interpretation, winding its way as it did round projecting furlong ends. Here the field division postdated the furlong divisions, and must have been drawn up with some definite purpose in mind. The late creation of Blackland field, out of land in cultivation long before, argues the same deliberate intent.[5] It seems likely from this that the fields were functional rather than purely topographical units, although the rotation worked in them was probably a highly complex one. It is even possible, for instance, that the southern fields nearest the heath were only in intermittent cultivation, even in the thirteenth century, judging from references to the field called "la leys" and to the Hospital land "que vocatur le leye."[6]

In the fold-course area of Norfolk, where each tenant's holding tended to

[1] A ff. 40 and 48.    [2] A ff. 36v and 40.    [3] C.R.O., R.55.7.5.1(15), f. 78v.
[4] See above, p. 13.    [5] See above, pp. 13 and 18.    [6] A ff. 144–144v and fo. 34v.

112

be grouped in one area of the fields, as at Chippenham, a tenant was compensated for the temporary loss of his land when it lay within a fallow season, or 'shift', by other land elsewhere.¹ Possibly this custom extended into Chippenham, which also depended on the folding of the demesne sheep on the fallow for the maintenance of its fertility. The heath provided them with summer feed. The size of the Hospitallers' flock in the thirteenth century is unknown, but the de Mandeville and Chicksands flocks together must have numbered at least a thousand in the twelfth century. The jurors of 1544 bore witness in that year that the previous farmers of the manor had never kept above 1140 sheep, presumably in addition to the Chicksands sheep.² They also noted that every tenant had previously kept a certain number of sheep, stinted according to his "Custimary hold."³ It seems likely that payment for this right of contribution to the manorial flock was made and that the entry of fifty shillings representing the profits of common for six hundred sheep at a penny each in the Hospitallers' survey of 1338 gives the size of the township's contribution to the flock. Various free tenants also had the right of free fold. John Cocus granted the Hospitallers his rights of free foldage over the fields of Chippenham in free alms in the late thirteenth century,⁴ and Henry de Lindfell sold his brother a tenement with free foldage in 1324.⁵ A tenement could carry a considerable number of sheep, as the quitclaim of half a yardland in the hamlet of Badlingham in 1306 showed. It carried with it the right of foldage for 140 sheep "for the reasonable manuring of the same" at the rate of five acres each year.⁶ Villein tenements could also carry sheep, at a price. In 1426 John Imayn of Chippenham was granted fifteen acres at farm for the high rent of 13s. 4d. a year, and the additional rent of 3s. 8d. an acre if he had a fold on the same land. Forty years later this tenement was in the hands of the lord for lack of tenants, and was granted to the farmer of the demesne, together with various small closes and the right to run three hundred sheep. There is no information on the organization of these folds, but judging from the constant presentments in the fifteenth-century court rolls of tenants for "setting up a fold" without proper title, the sheep were hurdled together on the strips of the man concerned.

The average size of the arable strips, scattered about these fields in the thirteenth century, was surprisingly high, judging from those of the free tenants alone. It varied little from the average size of strip three hundred years later. Then, as in 1544, the half-acre strip predominated, but it was followed

¹ K. J. Allison, 'The Sheep-Corn Husbandry of Norfolk in the Sixteenth and Seventeenth Centuries', *Agricultural History Review*, v, 1957, p. 20.
² C.R.O., R.55.7.5.1(15), fo. 78v.     ³ *Ibid.*, fo. 79.     ⁴ A fo. 34v.
⁵ MS. Harl. 3697, no. 54, fo. 162.     ⁶ *Ibid.*, no. 58, fo. 163.

TABLE I

FREEHOLDERS' STRIPS IN THE THIRTEENTH CENTURY

| Size a. r. | Walter Clericus | Gilbert de Berford | Richard de Camera | Nicholas Clericus | Ralph and Beatrice le Porter Richard Priest's son | Adam le Waleys, tenant 1279 | Jo. Cocus, tenant 1279 | Jo. s. Ric. Cocus, tenant 1279 | Elias le Wagger, tenant 1279 | Total |
|---|---|---|---|---|---|---|---|---|---|---|
| 4 0 |  |  | 1 |  |  |  |  |  |  | 1 |
| 3 1 |  | 1 |  |  |  |  |  |  |  | 1 |
| 3 0 |  | 1 | 1 | 1 |  |  |  |  |  | 3 |
| 2 1 | 1 | 1 |  |  |  |  |  |  |  | 2 |
| 2 0 | 1 | 1 | 7 | 2 | 2 |  |  |  |  | 13 |
| 1 3 |  | 1 |  |  |  |  |  |  |  | 1 |
| 1 2 | 2 | 1 | 3 | 1 |  |  |  |  |  | 7 |
| 1 0 | 5 | 2 | 16 | 10 | 11 |  |  |  |  | 44 |
| 0 3 | 3 | 1 | 3 | 4 | 6 |  | 1 | 1 | 2 | 21 |
| 0 2 | 1 | 1 | 18 | 13 | 21 | 1 | 3 | 6 |  | 64 |
| 0 1½ |  | 1 | 2 | 10 | 15 | 1 |  |  | 3 | 32 |
| 0 1 |  |  | 2 | 7 | 9 | 3 |  | 4 | 1 | 26 |
| 0 ½ |  |  |  | 1 | 1 | 1 |  |  |  | 3 |
| Total | 13 | 11 | 53 | 49 | 65 | 6 | 4 | 11 | 6 | 218 |

in frequency by the acre strip, not, as in 1544, by the rood strip (see Table V). Half-acre and acre strips together made up over half the total sample. Certainly the "typical one-rood strip" is a myth as far as Chippenham was concerned. On the other hand, the table shows some very striking variations. It covers the grants to the Hospital of nine freeholders, including two complete half-yardlands and a twenty-four-acre tenement later leased entire to another tenant. If each tenant's strips are separately analysed, the proportions of different sizes vary very markedly. The fifteen acres granted to Walter Clericus included no less than nine strips of an acre or more, out of thirteen;[1] eight of

[1] MS. Harl. 3697, no. i, fo. 155.

the eleven strips granted by Gilbert de Berford to Walden Abbey were a similar size. The grants of Richard de Camera and Nicholas Clericus included respectively over a half and over a quarter of strips of an acre or more. All these men were probably active in the first, rather than the second, half of the thirteenth century.[1] On the other hand, none of the four men who made grants to the Hospital, and also appeared as tenants in the Hundred Rolls in the last quarter of the thirteenth century, had a strip over three roods in size. It is impossible to date the grants sufficiently accurately to be certain, but it seems suspiciously likely that the size of strip was dropping during the century. The holding of Richard Priest's-son contained a high proportion of smaller strips, although it was probably granted away in the first, rather than the second, half of the century. Its history provides a possible reason for the diminishing areas of strips during the period. Richard had inherited his tenement from his father, also Richard Priest's-son, who had divided his land between his son and his daughter Beatrice, wife of Ralph le Porter. All three relations made grants to the Hospital, and in one case Beatrice granted three roods lying end to end, next to three roods granted by her brother, also lying end to end. It seems quite clear that the division of the father's holding had been accomplished by the physical division of strips longitudinally, which explains their small size. In the circumstances it is highly suggestive that nearly half the strips granted by Richard Priest's-son lay next to those of his brother-in-law, Ralph le Porter. This concrete example of the workings of inheritance means that caution must be employed in interpreting the fact that in many of the cases in which one man granted land away, a significant proportion of his strips had the same neighbour on one side. At first sight, this looks like a much battered survival from the original allotment of strips; in fact it may not be the product of co-aration, but of the division of holdings between heirs.[2]

The arable in the open fields seems to have reached its maximum limit in the thirteenth century; there is little sign that the tenants ever invaded the

[1] Walter Clericus was probably dead by 1253, see below, p. 25, n. 2. Gilbert de Berford witnessed the charter of Richard de Camera in 1236.—A fo. 41, and of Nicholas Clericus in 1253, *ibid.*, fo. 39v., and so these two men may also be placed early in the century. Nicholas Clericus, son of Walter, was certainly dead by 1275, see below, p. 26.

[2] I am indebted to Dr Joan Thirsk for letting me see in typescript her forthcoming paper on The Common Fields, since published in *Past and Present*, no. 29, 1964, pp. 3–25. Her suggestion that intermingled strip holdings were the result of inheritance and partition and that common rotations were later super-imposed over these and led to the emergence of the two- and three-field system in arable areas is in many ways extremely applicable to Chippenham. If this view is taken, the numerous fields and unevenly distributed holdings of the thirteenth century show the process of formation of the open fields in the stage before a common rotation was enforced. But in this entirely arable area the second stage, that of the resolution into two or three fields, never took place, although a common rotation and common rights of pasture over the fallow did apparently exist in the fifteenth century.

heath beyond the Newmarket to Brandon road, whatever the de Mandevilles and their successors as lords did. In 1544 there were 1276 acres of open field, excluding the heath area, in the tenants' hands, and in 1279 the freeholders and villeins held between them 1352 acres. It seems unlikely that the outer boundaries of the fields had changed. On the other hand, there was a definite diminution of the open-field area, probably before the time of the Hundred Rolls, with the construction of a rabbit warren by the Hospitallers in the southeast of the parish. In the later part of the century they bought out John Cocus' rights of common in the rabbit warren between its "fossata et limites."[1] In the time of William de Hanvilla, prior of the Hospital in 1284,[2] an acre of land in the field called "la leys" was exchanged by the Hospitallers for an acre of Chicksands land against the side of the warren. The latter was to be enclosed.[3]

The introduction of rabbit keeping in the parish must have had a disastrous effect on the growth of crops in the immediate area, since it is unlikely that the "fossata et limites" were sufficiently well maintained permanently to prevent the free passage of rabbits.[4]

Apart from the open fields and their management, and the heath and its contribution to the 'sheep-corn' economy of the parish, the fen provided the other significant natural area for exploitation. Peat digging had been known in the twelfth century, as the Countess Rohese's grant of common of turbary to Chicksands shows.[5] It was obviously from the Hundred Rolls a very important element in the economy. The 'works' of both villeins and cottars included the digging of one cartload of turves a year each. The Preceptory obviously relied on turf for fuel in the absence of wood. Rights of digging were also granted away by charter, as they were to Walter son of Richard of "hisham" who could dig eighteen loads of turves a year.[6] It seems possible that this digging resulted in the creation of 'broads' on a small scale. In 1544 two "lakes" were described in Chippenham Fen which had disappeared again by the eighteenth century. It is not impossible that these owed their existence to twelfth- and thirteenth-century activities.[7] Rights of digging for

---

[1] A fo. 34v.     [2] *British Museum Index to Charters and Rolls*, II, pp. 650–5.     [3] A ff. 144–144v.
[4] The Hospitallers were showing themselves fashionable and improving landlords in their introduction of the rabbit, which was still a rare delicacy in the late thirteenth century.—Elspeth M. Veale, 'The Rabbit in England', *Agricultural History Review*, V, 1957, pp. 85–90. The warren was still productive in the mid-sixteenth century, when it was let for 505 conies a year. Almost exactly 500 years after the rabbit was brought to Chippenham, the improving landlord of his own day was writing to his son that wild rabbits would "overrun and destroy my estate, if not timely checked."—C.R.O., R.55.7.22.1(a).
[5] See above, p. 12.     [6] A ff. 146–146v.
[7] C. T. Smith, 'Historical Evidence' in *The Making of the Broads*, Royal Geog. Soc. Research Series 3, 1960, pp. 64–82.

fuel in the fen were treasured by the very poor in Chippenham, and their abolition with enclosure at the end of the eighteenth century gave rise to a great deal of trouble.[1]

### THE APPEARANCE AND DISAPPEARANCE OF THE FREE TENANTS

The charters naturally give considerable insight into the doings of the free tenantry whose dealings they record. But the free tenants were never an important element in Chippenham. The largest freehold touched on by the cartularies was only ninety acres. By the end of the thirteenth century free land made up only ten per cent of the acreage of the manor, while demesne accounted for thirty-six per cent and villein land for as much as fifty-four per cent of the total.[2]

Since no sokemen survived in Chippenham at Domesday, it seems likely that this small quantity of free land had its origin in villein land enfranchised in the twelfth century, like much other Cambridgeshire free land.[3] The occasional instances in which the charters show that heriot was due from one or other of these free tenements support this view of its origin, and the surnames of many of the holders suggesting either clerical or 'service' antecedents give a clue to the reason for its creation.

In spite of the relative insignificance of the freeholders, the two cartularies show them busily buying and selling land. Sub-letting and sales were common amongst them, from those who held a yardland or more, to those who held very much less. Adam le Waleys, who had a tenement of 12a. 3r., received a halfpenny a year for an acre let out,[4] and Elias le Wagger, tenant of nine acres in 1279, let half an acre to "Fulcom son of Henry Milkesoppe of Multon" for nine shillings entry fine and a halfpenny a year rent.[5] The cartularies also show, however, that the existence of a flourishing land market, which appears to have been already fully operative in the first half of the thirteenth century,[6] and was associated with high purchase prices for land, does not seem to have greatly benefited the free tenants of Chippenham. In general, the charters show the rapid attrition, in numerous small grants to one or other of the religious houses concerned, of the freeholds of a few families.

The most striking example is that of Richard de Camera, who was by far the largest freeholder about whom any information survives from thirteenth-century Chippenham. Richard's father Geoffrey held three yardlands in Chippenham, which had previously been in the tenure of "Robertus miles."

[1] See below, pp. 53–4.        [2] See Table II, p. 29.
[3] E. Miller, *The Abbey and Bishopric of Ely*, Cambridge, 1951, pp. 121–3.
[4] A fo. 32.        [5] A fo. 43.
[6] E. Miller, *op. cit.*, p. 130, and M. M. Postan in *Carte Nativorum*, edited C. N. L. Brooke and M. M. Postan, Northamptonshire Record Society, xx, 1960, pp. xxxvii–xxxix.

Since Geoffrey's son Richard was himself putting through transactions by 1235 this earlier history of the holding must run back some way into the twelfth century. By 1235 Richard was granting away land. In that year he leased half a yardland, Esterbeck Meadow, and a croft and house, to the Hospital for twenty years, receiving in exchange £2 13s. 10d., three loads of corn, two tunics, and an over-tunic of russet. He was also granted the right to run one horse with the Hospitallers' stock, and one cow with their cows. He later gave the same holding to the Hospital outright, together with another five acres. Three more charters conveyed another thirty-five acres to the Hospital in free alms, and finally Richard recognized himself tenant of the Hospital of a messuage and thirty-four acres at a rent of ten shillings a year, and bound himself not to alienate it without their consent, on condition that the brothers would give him as good a price as he would obtain elsewhere if he sold.[1] In all, Richard's charters account for eighty-eight and a quarter of the ninety acres he started with. He does not even seem to have remained in possession of his last thirty-four acres and house. The only tenant to appear in the Hundred Rolls who might have been his heir is Richard "Chamun" who held a messuage and nine acres from another free tenant.

The Clericus family held very much less land than Richard de Camera. Walter Clericus, son of Richard of Chippenham, was granted fifteen acres, or exactly half a yardland, and a croft, by Walden, probably early in the thirteenth century.[2] There is of course no means of knowing whether he also held land of the Hospitallers, as his son did. Walter's interests extended outside the parish, for he leased the fishery of "Belwere" in Wicken, and sublet it to a Wicken man, before eventually selling it to the Hospitallers.[3] He added to his holding by renting three acres from Richard de Camera for tenpence a year, and only diminished it by the grant of an acre in free alms to the Hospital.[4]

His son Nicholas, on the other hand, was involved in a mass of transactions, mainly granting the Hospitallers his interest in land he had sold or sublet. His two sisters held closes of him by charter, and he had also subdivided his own close and let a piece of land on it with a house, thus affording good evidence of the effects of population pressure in Chippenham. The rent of these three closes he granted to the Hospital in return for a diminution of his own rent by six shillings a year.[5] Another seven charters granted six acres and his croft and house to the Hospital. Five more charters to the monks of Walden disposed of just over twenty acres of land, including a small part of the original

---

[1] A ff. 44v, 45, 147v, 40–42v.
[2] Walter's son Nicholas was drawing up charters by 1253.—A fo. 39v.
[3] A ff. 31–31v.    [4] A ff. 42, 38v.    [5] A fo. 37v.

half yardland his father had held,[1] and in 1253 Nicholas leased three acres of meadow to the Hospital in return for a daily livery to himself and his wife of two wheaten loaves, a fantastic quantity of ale, and a portion of flesh or fish "sicut fratres."[2] His son Thomas gave the meadow outright to the Hospital in 1275–6, by which time Nicholas was presumably dead. The Thomas "cleric" who appears in the Hundred Rolls as a free tenant held one messuage only from the Hospitallers at a rent of fourpence a year.

The same process of attrition can be seen at work in the Walden cartulary, in the charters of the Priest family.[3] Richard, son of Richard the Priest, early in the century alienated six acres of his land, half directly to Walden, half to Walter de Bradwell. He then left his land divided between his son Richard and his daughter Beatrice, wife of Ralph le Porter.[4] These three, in a series of seventeen charters, granted twenty acres half a rood of land, and half a messuage, of the "fee" of their father to the abbot and convent of Walden, all in small amounts, and all before 1278.[5] Such examples can be multiplied, and all show the same tendency towards the resignation into the hands of one or other of the religious houses concerned, of freeholds which would not, by midland standards, be thought large originally, mainly in a series of small grants adding acre to acre and rood to rood. Even the more shadowy figures of those leasing land from the free tenants seem curiously unsuccessful; Walter de Bradwell, who appears as a purchaser or lessee from at least three free tenants, himself granted away his acquisitions.

One serious drawback to the evidence of the cartularies is its negative nature. In essence they record only the doings of those who failed, not those who succeeded. From the Hundred Roll entries it appears that one of the only two free tenants in the village who still held a full yardland, William de Twamhille, himself had four sub-tenants, holding four messuages and eighteen acres from him. The only appearances of the Twamhille family in the charters show them as witnesses, granting a messuage and two acres to Walden before 1278, and gaining exemptions from the two suits of court they owed for their yardland in 1298.[6] They thus increased their independence, but nothing else throws light on their comparative success.

---

[1] MS. Harl. 3697, ff. 156v–157.

[2] A ff. 39v, 40. This was presumably the granting of a corrody. There were five corrodians in Chippenham in 1338, receiving various sums of money, and the right to eat at the servants' table.— *Victoria County History, Cambridgeshire and the Isle of Ely*, i, p. 265.

[3] It is probably not without significance that the three holdings chosen for illustration are those of men bearing surnames suggestive of an administrative or clerical capacity. Other examples can be found, like the "Cocus" family who alienated land round about and after the date of the Hundred Rolls, although it is not true to say that all free tenants bore such names.

[4] MS. Harl. 3697, ff. 156 and 158v.          [5] *Ibid.*, ff. 156, 157–159v.

[6] *Ibid.*, fo. 160, and A fo. 45v.

The other major difficulty in assessing the evidence is in judging how often this acquired land was regranted by the two corporations, and how often retained. The Hospitallers regranted more frequently than Walden, but a distinct impression is created, perhaps simply because grants were not so carefully registered in the cartularies, that much more free land was coming in than was going out again. This was certainly true of Walden. In 1278 the prior of the Hospital confirmed the grants made by free tenants to Walden Abbey before that date, amounting to 102 acres.[1] In 1279 the abbey's five tenants held only fifty-two acres in all. The forty-five acres which the abbey held to its "own use" with the church are said in the Hundred Rolls to have been the gift of William de Mandeville, but when the de Mandeville charter granted Chippenham to the Hospital in its entirety, with the sole exception of the church, which had already been given to Walden, it made no mention of any land passing with the church. It is difficult to escape the conclusion that the glebe had, in 1279, recently been formed from the grants made by the free tenants to Walden, since the acreage of the glebe, together with that of the abbey's free tenants' holdings, amounted almost exactly to that of the grants.

The decline of the free peasants at a time when some at least of them might be expected to be profiting from the expanding corn and land markets is difficult to account for, except on the supposition that the two religious foundations had a deliberate policy of buying up the freeholds. Certainly both the abbey and the Hospital showed anxiety and attempted to prevent alienation by the freeholders, with varied success. Equally obviously, the Hospitallers were encouraging sales by preferential treatment: the grants of stock-grazing rights and corrodies show this. But it is evident, from Richard de Camera's reservation when he bound himself not to alienate "unless the brothers shall pay me as much as I shall get elsewhere," that the freeholders to some extent retained their independence and bargaining power in face of the squeeze.

The appearance of free tenancies in Chippenham between Domesday and the beginning of the thirteenth century and their disappearance again up to the passing of the Statute of Mortmain in 1279,[2] fits well with the general pattern of the reduction of demesne in the twelfth century and its re-expansion in the thirteenth.[3] The deliberate purchasing policy of the Hospital and Walden and the formation of the glebe land by the latter coincided with the building

---

[1] MS. Harl. 3697, fo. 160v.

[2] T. A. M. Bishop, 'Monastic Demesnes and The Statute of Mortmain', *English Historical Review*, XLIX, 1934, pp. 303–6.

[3] M. M. Postan, 'The Chronology of Labour Services', *Transactions of the Royal Historical Society*, 4th ser., xx, pp. 169–93.

up of monastic estates elsewhere,[1] and prevented the free tenants of Chippenham from consolidating their holdings while the land market was in their favour, although it seems that the existence of the market gave them the power to exact a good price for their land under the threat of taking it elsewhere.

## THE COMMUNITY IN THE HUNDRED ROLLS

In 1279 the abbey had five free tenants in Chippenham and the priory had nine, including William de Twamhille, who had four tenants of his own. Of these eighteen, only two held full yardlands, and three more between half a yardland and a yardland. Eight held a messuage only, or a messuage and one or two acres. The 'rural aristocracy' here was thin indeed. The history of Chippenham is not therefore primarily concerned with the free tenants, but with the changing fortunes and sizes of holdings of the villeins.

At the end of the thirteenth century the Hospital had 70 villeins in Chippenham holding half a yardland or 15 acres each.[2] No villein held a full yardland, and this predominance of fifteen-acre holdings was typical of Cambridgeshire at the time.[3] Each half-yardlander paid 2s. 6d. rent and two hens yearly. Besides this, he was liable for 30½ 'works' annually, carrying services, brewing two and a half quarters of barley, ploughing eight and a half acres, and digging one cartload of turves from the fen. The four villeins holding seven or nine acres, typically,[4] paid much higher rents of seven and ten shillings apiece, and performed negligible labour services, at most reaping one acre and digging a cartload of turves.

Week-work had therefore disappeared on the holdings of the majority of the Chippenham villeins, although the outright commutation of nearly all services found amongst the quarter-yardlanders was rare. The absence of accounts means that there is no evidence to show whether the 30½ 'works' which remained attached to the half-yardland holdings were in fact exacted. No money values are given for them in the Hundred Rolls, but in 1338 a value of £27 7s. 1d. was set on the work and customs of the tenants against money rents of £20 8s. 10d.[5] Kemble assumed that the services were com-

[1] T. A. M. Bishop, 'Monastic Granges in Yorkshire', *English Historical Review*, LI, 1936, pp. 193–214.

[2] These round figures may have concealed subletting, and there may therefore have been even more holdings below the subsistence level. For the same reason, the population figure given for Chippenham is the minimum, not the maximum. Cf. *Carte Nativorum*, pp. xli, lix; and E. A. Kosminsky, *Studies in the Agrarian History of England in the Thirteenth Century*, Oxford, 1956, pp. 211–14.

[3] E. A. Kosminsky, *op. cit.*, p. 216.     [4] *Ibid.*, pp. 168–9.

[5] *The Hospitallers' Inquest of 1338*, p. 78. It is probably fair to apply these proportions to a period forty years earlier; in 1279 the money rents of free tenants holding directly from the Hospital and of the unfree tenants amounted to £21 14s. 0d., as against £20 8s. 10d. in 1338. This suggests that there can have been little change in the intervening period. Only £2 12s. 0d. of the 1279 total was made up of free rents; the drop in the whole rental before 1338 may well have been accounted for by the continued attrition of these freeholds between 1279 and 1290.

# A CAMBRIDGESHIRE COMMUNITY 29

## TABLE II

### LAND TENURE IN 1279

| | Demesne and Chicksands* (arable and meadow) Acreage | Free | | Unfree | | Total | |
|---|---|---|---|---|---|---|---|
| | | No. | Acreage | No. | Acreage | No. | Acreage |
| Abbot of Walden | 769 | | | | | | 769 |
| 30a. and | | | 45 | | | | 45 |
| over | | 2 | 62 | | | 2 | 62 |
| 20a. | | 2 | 40 | | | 2 | 40 |
| 12–15a. | | 3 | 39 | 70 | 1050 | 73 | 1089 |
| 7–9a. | | 3 | 27 | 4 | 34 | 7 | 61 |
| 1–2a. | | 3 | 4 | 51 | 51 | 54 | 55 |
| Messuage only | | 5 | — | — | — | 5 | — |
| Total | 769a. 36% | 18 | 217a. 10% | 125 | 1135a. 54% | 143 | 2121a. |

* The Hundred Rolls do not give the demesne acreage for this township; I have taken the figures of the acres of the Hospitallers' estate here in 1338. I have also assumed that the land of Chicksands, which was leased to the Hospital, was in the hands of the Preceptory at this time, although the rent of 20s. a year for it was not included in the debit side of the account.

The accuracy of the picture of land-holding in Chippenham which is given by the Hundred Rolls can be roughly checked by comparing the 'customary' acreages of land described there with the acreages given by the survey made in 1544 (Table IV, p. 40).

In 1279 the abbot of Walden held 45 acres of land, and also had five free tenants holding 52 acres among them, giving a total for the abbey of 97 acres. In 1544 the area of the parsonage and vicarage farms together amounted to 100 acres. This very close correspondence in size between the two dates is also to be found in the freeholds and copyholds taken together.

The unfree tenants of the Hospital in 1279 held in all 1135 acres, compared with a total of 1276 acres of copyhold and 'seized holdings' in 1544. In between the two dates, however, most of the remaining freehold land disappeared, to be found amongst the seized holdings of the sixteenth century. If the figures are adjusted accordingly, the difference in arable acreages farmed by the tenants in 1279 and 1544 is under fifty acres. It therefore seems quite clear that the estimates given in the Hundred Rolls are sufficiently accurate for this township to be used with confidence (E. A. Kosminsky, op. cit., pp. 40–2), and that in spite of the suspiciously round sizes given to the villein tenements in 1279 the vast majority of the Hospitallers' villeins really did hold approximately 15 acres each or half a yard-land, whether or not any of it was sublet.

30    A CAMBRIDGESHIRE COMMUNITY

muted since their value was entered as available income.[1] Perhaps in reality they were exacted only in time of special pressure.

Well over a third of the unfree tenants of Chippenham were cottars with only an acre of land, paying 3s. 4d. apiece for their holdings and digging one cartload of turves. The proportion of villeins with insufficient holdings was higher in Cambridgeshire than in any other county covered by the Hundred Rolls,[2] and it seems likely that this fragmentation was related to the density of settlement in the county. These men, with their utterly inadequate land, must have been dependent for their livelihood on wage-labour, and they were presumably indispensable to the running of the demesne.

The almost total absence of information on the demesne farm is the chief weakness in the documentary material.[3] Even the survey of 1338 is ambiguous; the profit side of the balance sheet records the price per acre of the demesne arable, meadow, and pasture, and the profit from stock. The debit side records expenditure on foodstuffs for the inmates of the house, including various grains and their prices per quarter. Kemble assumed from the necessity of purchasing foodstuffs that the price per acre given to the demesne land represented its rent, and that the estates of the Hospital were largely leased in the early fourteenth century.[4] It is difficult to see why, if this were so, the profit of any stock should be entered on the credit side of the sheet;[5] and Professor Hilton reaches the conclusion that the Hospitallers were actively farming their lands in Leicestershire in 1338, with the exception of one or two small properties where there was no monastic house, which were specifically said to be "dimittuntur ad firmam."[6] If the Hospitallers were farming their Chippenham estate themselves, it is remarkable that there was no wage bill on the debit side of the account. Its absence certainly suggests that they must have been making use of the labour services of their tenants.

In 1334 the subsidies levied on local communities were adjusted to new and supposedly realistic figures. Population had ceased to rise by this date, but the plagues of the fourteenth century had not yet had their devastating effect.

[1] *The Hospitallers' Inquest*, introduction by J. Kemble, p. xxviii.

[2] E. A. Kosminsky, *op. cit.*, pp. 216–17.

[3] When the demesne was leased, it was leased as a block, and so entries concerning it, with very rare exceptions, do not even reach the late fourteenth- and fifteenth-century court rolls.

[4] *The Hospitallers' Inquest*, p. xviii.

[5] Although the £1 profit of stock at Chippenham is a very small sum if the Hospitallers were keeping sheep on the scale of the de Mandevilles; elsewhere in the survey, £1 represented the profit from only 100 sheep.—*Ibid.*, pp. xxv–vi.

[6] R. H. Hilton, *The Economic Development of Some Leicestershire Estates in the XIV & XV Century*, 1947, p. 7. For an example of lands which were definitely farmed in Leicestershire see *The Hospitallers' Inquest*, p. 178.

The community taxed in 1334 was still in essence the community of the Hundred Rolls, and the return permits a last look at Chippenham before the Black Death. The village was assessed at eight pounds. This was a fairly high sum and was typical of the large villages on the edge of the Cambridgeshire fen, which tended to be assessed at between seven and eleven pounds.[1] It was in no way remarkable, however. The choked conditions in the village of the late thirteenth century were representative of Cambridgeshire, for the density of settlement in the county gave it the greatest taxable capacity for its area in England at this date.[2]

## IV. UNDERPOPULATION: CHIPPENHAM IN THE FIFTEENTH CENTURY

WHEN the surviving series of court rolls begins in 1381, Chippenham was a changed place, and its fifteenth-century history is a reflection of its altered fortunes. The overpeopled village of 1279 had disappeared. The Poll Tax records only 204 adults over the age of fourteen.[3] There cannot have been more than three hundred inhabitants in the village, at the most.[4] Even at a conservative estimate the population must have fallen by over a half in the century between 1279 and 1377. The extent of late medieval population fall is well known, so that such figures tend to be taken for granted; but when, as at Chippenham, a later source exists describing whole streets as "clere decaied" and every other house as missing, they renew their power to shock. When the jury went its rounds surveying the manor in 1544, sixty village houses were still standing, together with the manor, parsonage, and vicarage. The jurors were able to describe another sixty-four crofts as sites where houses had once stood, thus accounting for all but about twenty of the households in the village in 1279.[5] Over half the village was still missing

[1] I have taken these figures from P.R.O. E.179/81/23 (25 Ed. III) since E.179/81/8 (8 Ed. III) is in bad condition.

[2] W. G. Hoskins and H. P. R. Finberg, *Devonshire Studies*, 1952, p. 217.

[3] I have taken the figures from W. M. Palmer, *Cambridgeshire Subsidy Rolls, 1250–1695*, Norwich, 1912.

[4] If a very rough adjustment is made for children under fourteen.—M. W. Beresford, 'The Poll Taxes of 1377, 1379, and 1381', *The Amateur Historian*, III, 1958, p. 275.

[5] Most of these missing house sites must have been in the twelve acres of Newyardes Close, which was identified as an unknown number of "mease grounds" by the jury. They only fumbled once or twice in their knowledge of past land use, as they did over the Drove Close, where it is recorded "whether it be a mese ground or not the said tenantes are uncerteyne." "Mease ground" was used throughout the survey for the land on which a house had previously stood: "M that upon all the said mease groundes there was sometime ten'tes and cotageis and nowe clere decaied."—C.R.O., R.55.7.1 (15), fo. 2. Miss Davenport found the same usage at Forncett. The villagers' ability to pinpoint nearly all the thirteenth-century house sites was a remarkable feat of communal memory, considering

in 1544. The empty crofts and shrunken streets all emphasized the severity of the decline and make it appear catastrophic to a reader of the survey. It is all the more striking that the fifteenth-century tax reliefs for poverty treat Chippenham as if it had not suffered at all badly. In 1432–3 Chippenham was relieved only of ten shillings, or six per cent, of its assessment of 1334.[1] In 1489–90, even after a fire sufficiently disastrous to linger on in folk memory, the relief rose only to fifteen shillings or nine per cent.[2] These percentages are low by Cambridgeshire standards. Reliefs of twenty per cent were reasonably common and in some parishes they rose to over thirty per cent. The hamlet of Badlingham, under half a mile away, was relieved of nineteen per cent of its tax burden in 1432–3 and twenty-eight per cent in 1489–90. If the judgement of the assessors of the reliefs is to be trusted, the disappearance of half a village was so commonplace an affair in an area as thickly populated as Cambridgeshire had been in the thirteenth century, that it called for no special action and indeed earned only a low relief. If the 'normal' village had shrunken to half its medieval size,[3] this is to be borne in mind when the fifteenth-century reliefs are used to judge the effects of depopulation. In them, a village which would appear from a full description as catastrophically reduced as Chippenham would scarcely appear affected at all, and even less as a candidate for 'lost village' status.

### LAND TENURE

The court rolls from 1381 onwards illustrate the effect this dramatic, but normal, shrinkage was having on land tenure.[4] The survival of the rolls also makes it possible to examine the demand for land and the price it was fetching in the fifteenth century.

The fall in population had the general effect of swinging the economic balance in favour of the tenants and against the landlords, since the vacant holdings would be taken up only on favourable terms. It therefore frequently became impossible for landlords to continue to exact customary services. As a result, a conversion from customary to leasehold tenancy was a common effect of the population fall either after, or even before, the Black Death.[5] Chippen-

that many of the sites must have been vacant for nearly two centuries. It is all the more striking since no recollection exists in the village today of the disappearance of half of it during emparking at the very end of the seventeenth century. There is no reason for communal memory without communal responsibility for the organization of the community and its fields.

[1] P.R.O., E.179/81/80.     [2] P.R.O., E.179/81/120.

[3] Miss Davenport's sixteenth-century evidence on Forncett seems to point to a similar degree of shrinkage.

[4] I have not referred to the individual membranes of the rolls since they are unnumbered. The rolls I have chiefly used are: C.R.O., R.55.7.1 a. 1381–94; b. 1399–1413; c. 1417–20; d. 1423–60 and 1471–2; e. 1461–84; f. 1509–47.

[5] See for instance: R. H. Hilton, *The Economic Development of some Leicestershire Estates in the XIV &*

ham was no exception, apart from cottage tenancies which always remained on a customary basis. From 1381 to 1446 the majority of holdings of seven or more acres which passed through the court were leased for a term of years. Between 1381 and 1394, for instance, there were approximately forty-five farms involving any considerable amount of land, against seven surrenders and admissions to copyhold. The first roll shows customary land being converted to leasehold. Alice Baker held two customary holdings of about fifteen acres each in 1388, which had been her father's and her husband's. One was surrendered to John Scot "in bondagium" for work and customs; the other to Thomas Curtis for ten years at ten shillings per year. It is only fair to add that there were occasional examples of the reverse process; in 1383 John Thatcher surrendered his last year in the tenement called Pekocces and it was taken on customary terms.

Farms were most commonly for ten years in the late fourteenth century, and showed no signs of lengthening in the fifteenth, for between 1423 and 1446 ten-year terms only just predominated over seven-year terms, although there were a couple of isolated examples of leases of fifteen-acre holdings for life.[1] Presumably the advantage to tenants of holding farms free of customary service was enough to offset the disadvantage of relatively short leases, although it is difficult to sort out the real conditions of tenure from the confused terminology of the rolls. In general, until 1433 a tenement held "at farm" was simply said to be held for a certain term of years at a money rent, while a customary holding was taken by a man and his heirs for the service due. After a gap in the rolls from 1429 to 1433 the distinction between customary and leasehold was softened, to the scribe at least, for land held at farm was frequently held for customary service as well as rent. At the same time a stated money rent was added to the few customary holdings which came into the court. The practical difference, if any, these changes of phraseology made to the tenants is impossible to judge. Leaseholds must have been free from the disadvantages of labour services before 1433, or there would have been no inducement to the tenants to take land on a short-term basis, and it is difficult to believe services could have been re-imposed, in the renewed depression of the 1430's. On the other hand, the services due from customary land before 1433 must have included at least the half-crown rent due from any villein holding in the thirteenth century, although this is not stated in the rolls.

*XV Centuries*, Oxford, 1947, pp. 95, 122–4; F. M. Page, *The Estates of Crowland Abbey*, Cambridge, 1934, pp. 113–14, 126–9; and F. G. Davenport, *The Economic Development of a Norfolk Manor, 1085–1565*, Cambridge, 1906, pp. 52, 57–8.

[1] This contrasts with the development of tenures at Forncett, where there was a similar conversion to leasehold by 1406. There, leases lengthened throughout the fifteenth century and turned into fee farm.—F. G. Davenport, *op. cit.*, pp. 57–8, 77.

However, it seems probable that the rents of seven to ten shillings for a customary holding given in the rolls from 1433 onwards, which were at the same level as those for leaseholds, represented a real commutation of service. If this was so, the short leasehold tenancies must at the same time have become less attractive, shorn of their previous merit.

Some service was actually exacted, however, and continued to be exacted until the sixteenth century, although trouble over getting it performed is recorded from the beginning of the rolls. It at no time approached the $30\frac{1}{2}$ 'works' which the villeins of the Hundred Rolls were liable to be called on to perform for their fifteen-acre holdings.

In 1390 Nicholas Benet was amerced for not performing the services of reaping an acre and ploughing an acre which were due from the messuage he held and which had been performed, or so the roll stated, by the tenants of the same messuage for the previous forty years. Cottages were frequently let for a rent and a stated service in the fifteenth century, and there seems to have been a tendency for messuages without land to be let for rent and service also. In 1481 Elizabeth Taillieur surrendered three half-yardlands with crofts, and a messuage. The rents, separately given, were all money, except for that of the messuage which was held for three shillings a year and reaping and binding nine roods of rye in the autumn. In 1529 the homage inquired into services, and found that fifteen customary tenants were liable for them. In each case they consisted of the service which later appeared in a rental of 1560 as "wedeth one day and shereth three roods," except for one tenement which carried triple this amount. It seems likely that services had usually disappeared from all but cottages, and possibly tofts which had become divorced from the land during the period when leasehold tenure predominated in Chippenham.

Between the 1380's and the 1420's rents in Chippenham dropped from the already low figure of $7\frac{1}{4}$d. an acre (excluding fines) to $6\frac{1}{2}$d. an acre, or from the normal rent of 10s. a half-yardland to 8s.[1] They were competitive, as the admittedly dramatic example of the farm of fifteen acres called "Puttockland" showed. In 1381 Thomas Spencer took it to farm for ten years at 12s. a year and a 6s. fine. In 1390 he took it again for nine years at 7s. "que solebat reddere per annum xijs et ulterius sic non potest dimitti." The fine dropped to 1s. The market in land was slackening, and must already have slackened by the beginning of the first roll. Between 1381 and 1394 there was a yearly average of under four transactions involving an acreage of any magnitude; between 1424 and 1433 the average was down to one, and it rose only fractionally between then and 1446. Tenements were already coming into the hands of the lord for

---

[1] I have throughout used yardland for a 30-acre holding.

A CAMBRIDGESHIRE COMMUNITY

TABLE III

RENT, 1381–1523

| Date | No. of acres* in sample | Type of Tenure | Average rent per acre† | Range of rent per 15a. holding | Median rent per holding | No. of holdings‡ in sample |
|---|---|---|---|---|---|---|
| 1381–94 | 412 | leases | 7¼d. | 6s. to 12s. | 10s. | 29 |
| 1424–29 | 150 | leases and copy-hold | 6½d. | 6s. to 10s. | 8s. | 9 |
| 1434–46 | 69 | leases and copy-holds | 6¾d. | 6s. to 10s. | 8s. | 16 |
| 1457–71§ | — | — | — | — | — | — |
| 1471–83 | 21 | copyhold | 5d. | 5s. to 8s. | 6s. 8d. | 17 |
| 1509–23 | 199 | copyhold | 6½d. | 6s. to 10s. 7d. | 8s. | 29 |

* Total acreage of those holdings for which a specific acreage is given.     † Excluding fines.
‡ Holdings presumed to be of standard 15-acre size.     § Inadequate sample.

lack of tenants by 1381.[1] From 1428 proclamations for the heirs of customary tenements were frequent, and were often completed by the entry "nullus venit," although a new tenant was usually found. On the other hand, the rolls also record the appropriation of land without licence, and so show a continued demand for it. Even in 1429 one John Baker thought it worth his while to appropriate two acres at the unpromising-sounding "Waryndore."

In 1446 part of Chippenham was burnt, and a local disaster was added to the already existing economic stagnation. The fire was sufficiently consider-able to pass into folk-legend as the source of all the village woes, for in 1533 the homage, recording the obligation of the farmer of the manor to pay three-quarters of the common fine, as he had done since 1461, added to the usual explanation "causa paupertatis tenentium" the rider "et maxime causa combustionis maioris partis predicte villate." Certainly the church was partly destroyed, and an indulgence was granted for its rebuilding in 1447.[2]

[1] This is a little before the first difficulty in filling the holdings on the Cambridgeshire estates of Crowland.—F. M. Page, op. cit., pp. 123, 152–3.
[2] D. and S. Lysons, Magna Britannia, ii, London, 1808, p. 167.

It is probable that when in 1481 the homage inspected the farm buildings of the manor "devastated" at the time of a certain Wade, formerly farmer of the manor, they were investigating the effects of the fire. They then found the "Chepen" fallen to the ground, and the barley barn, wheat barn, great and little stables, dove-house, bake-house, and hog-sty, all lacking plaster, roofing, and timber work.[1] Naturally the village houses must have suffered even more, although it is impossible to judge the extent of the damage. Two tenants admitted to copyholds after 1446 took them on condition that they would each build the "mansionem" on the toft; and one of them lay very near the church in the devastated area. It is likely that when William Porter was admitted to a vacant croft and its appurtenant land in 1478 on condition that he would build "de novo" a house 30 feet long and 16 feet wide in the next fourteen years, the Hospital was still attempting to repair the loss. But the tenants were wrongly seizing on the simplest, and most obvious, cause when they ascribed the poverty of Chippenham to the fire. There is plenty of evidence from the beginning of the court rolls that the decay of houses was already far advanced, as one would expect from the magnitude of the drop in population between 1279 and 1377.[2] It was indeed a direct result of consolidation of holdings.[3] In 1381 itself tenants were presented for holding "domos ruinosas," and by 1419 a clause adding repairs at the tenant's own cost to the admission to copyholds was creeping in. By 1426 it was normal.[4] The attempt to arrest the decay of houses was fruitless, as various items show. Richard atte Moor took a toft and 15 acres in the "Forth Strete" in 1391; by 1417, when the tenement called "Richard-atte-Moors" was next taken, it was "non edificatum."

The fire may not have been responsible for the decline of prosperity in Chippenham, as the tenants thought, but its effects were still drastic enough. Few courts were held until 1457. In that year the tenants were ordered to display their copies of court roll, in an endeavour to sort out the resulting confusion. There were then twenty-five copyhold tenants in Chippenham, and all but one of those who had their copies available were cottagers. The

[1] At some point in its history the Grange of Chicksands acquired the name of the "Brent" or "burnt" grange. Since the site was over a mile from the village, it can hardly have been burnt on this occasion, unless arson was the cause, but it is a curious coincidence.

[2] On the Cambridgeshire estates of the abbey of Crowland neglect in the repair of houses had started in 1350 and reached its peak in 1366–8.—F. M. Page, op. cit., p. 147. At Forncett, the greatest decay of holdings was certainly before 1422, and probably before 1376, when 250 acres of bond land was already in hand.—F. G. Davenport, op. cit., p. 52.

[3] See below, pp. 37–8.

[4] Similar signs of decay are found in the court rolls of Owston Abbey in the fifteenth century, and in Leicestershire also repair clauses were added to leases in this period. For the significance of the clauses, see R. H. Hilton, op. cit., pp. 127–8.

fire marked the end of leasehold tenancy in the village; presumably copyhold tenure had lost the disadvantage of service, and there was therefore no inducement, in the apathy and chaos which followed the fire, for tenants to suffer the disadvantage of short, non-hereditable farms. From now until 1544 the farmers of any sizable tenements in Chippenham were copyholders. Recovery was very slow, however; between 1457 and 1471 an average of under one transaction of any size came into the court yearly. Even in the 1470's, when there were general signs of economic recovery,[1] only one transaction a year was being dealt with, and the average rent had dropped to its lowest yet, 5d. an acre, or between 6s. and 7s. a holding. Between 1509 and 1523 things improved: an average of over two holdings were being taken a year, and rent had risen, although at 6½d. an acre, or 8s. a holding, it was still only back to the level of the 1420's.

## THE RISE OF THE YEOMAN

The importance of the factors illustrated by the rolls, low population, a slackening land-market, falling rents, and a superfluity of holdings, lies in the way in which they made the emergence of a new rural class possible, and made it possible in time for this class to take advantage of the renewed growth of population in the sixteenth century, and the rising prices of agricultural produce. The existence of two relatively complete surveys of land-holding in Chippenham, the Hundred Rolls at the end of the thirteenth century, and the survey carried out after the dissolution in the 1540's, pin-points the appearance of the big peasant farmer; the court rolls show his farm in the process of growth.

In the late fourteenth century the manor court at Chippenham was mainly concerned with the lease of single 15-acre holdings, readily identifiable as the villein holdings of a century before. Only something like a fifth of the tenements which passed through it were certainly of 30 acres or more; and this proportion remained constant between 1433 and 1446. This did not prevent the accumulation of holdings into one man's hands, even if only at farm for a term of years. John Lenote took two 15-acre holdings to farm in 1384 and another in 1392. In 1399 he took a messuage and fifteen acres by the rod; and in 1400 another. It is hardly surprising that he was at the same time being presented for not repairing a tenement. In 1419 a John Lenote, possibly son of the first, died seized of four yardlands.[2] In 1426 another tenant died holding three "terrae nativae." Holdings were being split, as well as consolidated; in the

[1] M. M. Postan, 'Revisions in Economic History; The Fifteenth Century', *Econ. Hist. Rev.*, IX, 1939, p. 162.

[2] Approximately 60 acres at this date.

1380's the tenements called Heylokkes, Plots, and Toymannesland were all split into 7½-acre divisions.[1] As early as 1385 messuages were being divided from their appurtenant land, and examples of tofts remaining in the hands of the lord are sprinkled throughout the fifteenth-century rolls. The physical effects of this activity were presumably being specified, when in 1428 all who held villein land were ordered "qd fac' divisionē inter eas ad cognoscend' particionē inter eas." The laying together of strips in the open fields was causing confusion.

Until 1446 customary 15-acre holdings were usually thought of as separate units, and conveyed as such, even though more than one might come into the same tenant's hands. Between 1471 and 1483 this was changing.[2] Over a third of the holdings passing through the court, instead of a fifth, were definitely of 30 acres or more, and holdings, once combined, showed a tendency to remain combined. In 1473 John Gerrard was admitted to an 18-acre tenement and a 13-acre tenement which had previously been acquired from two different tenants by a certain John Persyvale. At the same court, John Gerrard took another croft and half a yardland. When he died, two years later, his wife was admitted to the whole holding, and on her surrender in 1481, it passed as a block to John Branch. By the early sixteenth century the process of accumulation had speeded up considerably. Between 1509–26 nearly two-thirds of the transactions passing through the courts were of 30 acres or more, and in some cases there was little attempt to maintain the traditional integrity of the holdings. In 1516, for instance, Thomas Rawlings was admitted to one messuage "edificatam" and 40 acres of land, and one messuage "vacuam" with 38 acres of land.

## V. THE SURVEY OF 1544

### THE TENANTS

THE survey made of Chippenham in 1544 is a palimpsest, which both illustrates the early growth of the village, and anatomizes the effect of the fifteenth-century changes.

Chippenham was dominated by the figure of the demesne lessee, Thomas Bowles. His father had acquired the farm of the manor and its stock for forty-

---

[1] The comparative absence of fragmentation of complete "terrae nativae" into divisions smaller than seven acres perhaps argues that the preceptory was still keeping firm control of its tenants at this date. So do the seizures for alienating property without licence, and perhaps most of all, the ability of the lord to extract a "farm" of 6d. a year from various tenants for permission to use hand-querns and evade the demesne mills.

[2] The development of large tenancies at Chippenham follows the same dating as that at Forncett.— F. G. Davenport, *op. cit.*, pp. 85–6.

A CAMBRIDGESHIRE COMMUNITY

six years from 1529,[1] and was also farmer of Chicksands Grange.[2] Since he had acquired the property of Walden Abbey in Chippenham from the Audley family,[3] his son was at the time of the survey farming over one-fifth of the open fields. Thomas Bowles also held five farms acquired by seizure or forfeiture in the 1520's or 30's and not regranted.[4] The histories of at least two of these holdings throw some light on the disappearance of the freeholds in Chippenham, which was by now almost complete. A bondman could not, of course, hold free land, and in 1526, Richard Akes, a villein who had acquired a messuage and 30 acres of freehold, was dispossessed. About 35 acres "late Akes" was still in hand in 1544. The farmer of the demesne in 1461, Robert Morys or Mosse, had built up a considerable holding of copyhold, which came into the hands of the lord for lack of tenants, and his purchases of small freeholds can also be traced through the rolls. In 1522 his grandson surrendered these lands, which he had inherited, to Henry Lucas, gentleman, "against the custom of the manor" and they were seized. The tenement "late Moss's" which was also still in hand in late 1544 contained over 110 acres, and had with it eleven or more decayed 'mease grounds' and two standing houses. The surveyors were uncertain of the tenure of the whole holding, and it probably contained a considerable amount of free land.

Analysis of the 1544 survey shows that forty-five men, excluding the lord of Fordham, held or had recently held land in the village, and at least another fifteen householders were landless.[5] In all, half the tenants held a house only, or a house and a couple of acres. The proportion, although not the number, of those with inadequate land had risen since the thirteenth century, unless so many sub-tenants were concealed by the Hundred Rolls that a comparison between the two sources is invalid. On the other hand, while only two of the 143 tenants of 1279 had held thirty acres or more, no less than a third of those of 1544 had farms of this size. Indeed, a yardland had the look of a compara-

---

[1] P.R.O., S.C.6/Hen. VIII/7268 m.7.     [2] P.R.O., S.C.6/Hen. VIII/11 m. 13d.

[3] C.R.O., R.55.7.7.1–4 (notes made by an eighteenth-century antiquarian for the purchaser of the manor. See letter in C.R.O., R.55.7.11.1a*).

[4] C.R.O., R.55.7.5.1(15), fo. 79.

[5] It is impossible to estimate these exactly, since the consolidation of holdings had led to such an involved tenurial situation that only half the landholding tenants had one standing house attached to their land. Nearly a quarter of them had apparently no house built at all, but the remainder each had two or more houses, presumably indicating that those unoccupied were available for subletting. In all, there were six houses in the village in 1544 which seemed to be surplus and might have been sublet to swell the number of landless men; but there is of course no evidence that they were actually occupied. Unfortunately the taxation returns for Chippenham in 1524 and 1525, which would have offered a very useful check on the early sixteenth-century population, do not survive. No episcopal return for the diocese of Norwich, in which Chippenham lies, exists for 1563 either, so mid-sixteenth-century information is also lacking.

# A CAMBRIDGESHIRE COMMUNITY

## TABLE IV

### LAND TENURE IN 1544
(Customary measurements corrected to nearest acre)

| Range of size | Demesne and Chicksands | Unknown tenure | Free tenure | | Copyholds including seized | | Total | |
|---|---|---|---|---|---|---|---|---|
| | | | No. | Acreage | No. | Acreage | No. | Acreage |
| Town land Parsonage Vicarage | 480a. (arable & meadow) 300a. (heath) | 86a. (no occupant) | | 13a. 91a. 9a. | | | | 780a. 86a. 13a. 100a. |
| Over 100a. | | | | | 2 | 212a. | 2 | 212a. |
| 74–83a. | | | | | 3 | 232a. | 3 | 232a. |
| 51–63a. (2 yardlands) | | | | | 6 | 340a. | 6 | 340a. |
| 41–48a. (1½ yardlands) | | | | | 4 | 174a. | 4 | 174a. |
| 27–37a. (1 yardland) | | | | | 6 | 192a. | 6 | 192a. |
| 13–19a. (½ yardland) | | | | | 6 | 94a. | 6 | 94a. |
| 7–10a. (¼ yardland) | | | | | 2 | 16a. | 2 | 16a. |
| 3–4a. | | | 1 | 3a. | 1 | 4a. | 2 | 7a. |
| Under 2a. | | | 5 | 7a. | 11 | 12a. | 16 | 19a. |
| Total | 780a. | 86a. | 6 | 123a. | 41 | 1276a. | 47* | 2265a. |
| Messuage only ** | | 1 (+4) | 3 (+1) | | 11 (+1) | | 15 (+6) | |

\* One holder of both a copyhold and a freehold appears twice, hence there were in reality only forty-six landholders.

\*\* For figures in brackets, see p. 39 n.5.

tively small holding in 1544. A sixth of the tenants farmed over fifty acres, and the largest copyholder, Thomas Rawlings, had acquired 101 acres with three decayed and two standing messuages and two cottages. The later Middle Ages had greatly reduced the proportion of farmers with subsistence holdings, which had predominated in the thirteenth century, and enlarged the numbers both of the landless, and of men with a size of holding hitherto unknown.[1] The step from a grossly overpopulated community with enforcedly equal holdings providing a bare subsistence, to a community half the size, in which the larger landless section of society was probably worse off, but the much more considerable number of large farmers was vastly better off, is a long one, and judgement on the relative prosperity of the township in the late thirteenth century and the mid-sixteenth century depends to some extent on the doctrinaire preconceptions of the historian.

### THE OPEN FIELDS

Over 60 per cent of the lordship of Chippenham was arable in 1544, lying in the eight fields, which by now had firmly established boundaries. There was considerable variation from field to field in the size of the strip which preponderated, but in all, half-acre strips made up 31 per cent of the total, and rood strips only 22 per cent (Table V). Strips of a rood and a half were almost as common as rood strips, and therefore their multiple of three roods formed another considerable class. Acre strips, surprisingly for the sixteenth century,[2] formed as much as 11 per cent of the total number. Only 7 per cent of strips were over one acre, although these accounted for over a quarter of the whole open-field acreage. The overwhelming majority of the larger strips and blocks of arable were demesne or Chicksands land.[3] Only 30 acres of copyhold land, and no freehold, lay in strips of two or more acres; whereas all but eight out of a total of 379 acres of demesne and Chicksands land lay in such strips. The tenants' farms, with few exceptions, exhibited the typical proportions of strip sizes found in the open fields as a whole. There were variations: William Kirke's 56 acres lay in 89 strips, while his neighbours,

---

[1] This is very similar to the results obtained by R. H. Hilton in three Leicestershire villages (*op. cit.*, pp. 100–5) and F. G. Davenport in Forncett (*op. cit.*, pp. 81–3).

[2] W. G. Hoskins, *The Midland Peasant*, 1957, pp. 151–2, describes acre strips as a "text-book myth" on the basis of sixteenth-century evidence. The proportion of acre strips at Chippenham had fallen since the thirteenth century (see above, pp. 20–2), but if the interpretation of the evidence suggested above is correct, strip size had fallen sharply with the pressure on land and the division of holdings in the thirteenth century, and risen again considerably with the consolidation of holdings by 1544.

[3] There is not enough thirteenth-century evidence to be conclusive, but the incidental references to the demesne in the cartularies, like the one referring to the "culturam hospitalis iuxta Smythemere" in West Field (A fo. 38v), strongly suggest that it was then a block demesne. The land of Chicksands had lain together since the original grant.

John Kydd and James Clements, with similar acreages, had over 110 strips each. The most striking example of a consolidated farm was that of Richard Taylor, who held 27½ acres in only 16 strips, over half of which were of an

TABLE V

STRIP SIZE IN THE SIXTEENTH CENTURY (CUSTOMARY MEASUREMENT)

| Size a. r. | Demesne and Chicksands* | Sample tenants | | | | | | Total strips 1544 |
|---|---|---|---|---|---|---|---|---|
|  |  | *Thomas Rawlings* | *John Kydd* | *William Kirke* | *James Clements* | *Mr Myrphrim* | *Richard Taylor* |  |
| 2+ | 43 | 1 | — | 1 | — | — | 4 | 73 |
| 2    0 | 2 | 2 | — | — | — | — | 2 | 40 |
| 1    2 | — | 3 | 1 | 2 | 1 | — | — | 68 |
| 1    0 | 4 | 21 | 9 | 14 | 7 | 2 | 4 | 283 |
|     3 | — | 18 | 11 | 10 | 12 | 9 | 2 | 246 |
|     2½ | — | — | — | 1 | 1 | — | — | 13 |
|     2 | — | 61 | 43 | 36 | 39 | 26 | 4 | 805 |
|     1½ | 1 | 37 | 17 | 10 | 23 | 8 | — | 463 |
|     1 | — | 40 | 37 | 15 | 27 | 19 | — | 566 |
|     ½ | — | 1 | 1 | — | 1 | — | — | 10 |
| Other | 2 | 4 | 1 | — | — | 4 | — | 34 |
| Total strips | 52 | 188 | 120 | 89 | 111 | 68 | 16 | 2601 |
| Farm size | 480a. | 100a. 2r. | 56a. | 55a. 2½r. | 53a. ½r. | 29a. 2r. | 27a. 2r. | 1965a.[1] |

* Omitting 300a. heath.

acre or more. There were other men who held more, rather than less, than the usual number of strips in proportion to the number of acres they farmed.

The survey of 1544 shows that there had been a tendency for land on the poorer soils to go out of cultivation. The main example was of course the heath itself; where the arable of Chicksands and of Blatherwyck had lain in the twelfth century was now simply "a pece of heath ground being parcell of the demaynes called Blethewick" and a "parcell of chicksond londe ... heathe grounde."[1] Chippenham was by no means alone in this diminution of arable; the jurors who surveyed the neighbouring parish of Snailwell in 1560 observed when they came to the edge of the heath, "patet per le fforowes qd quondam fuer' arrat'."[2] North of the heath, in the area where we find thirteenth-century references to ley, there were ley strips scattered in 1544; but this was no indication of sixteenth-century improved farming. Lands called 'ley' were more likely to be abandoned than improved. Very often they were of unknown tenure.[3] Elsewhere there were three acres of ley "being wast ground" and right down by the heath "a parcell of grounde being ley over growen w$^{th}$ ffiris."

The heath and the fen together amounted to some eight hundred acres, but only five hundred acres of this was common to the tenants. All two hundred acres of the fen was common, and presumably was theoretically usable as pasture, since the two lakes within the parish on which the fen abutted had no acreage assigned to them. Apart from the fen, and half the heath area, the tenants had common rights at certain seasons over about eighteen acres of demesne pasture in various places south and east of the village, and on the Hallmore and Townmore and the heath by the rabbit warren.

The arable area may have retreated, but the farmers of the demesnes in the sixteenth century were attempting to increase the amount of stock kept, and particularly to enlarge the sheep flocks. There was trouble in 1518, when the homage presented that the farmer of Walden, who had not over 40 acres of fallow, was keeping at least 200 sheep. He was ordered to reduce the number to 120, or three for each acre of fallow. Similarly, the farmer of Chicksands, who had only 20 acres of fallow out of 100, was keeping at least 400 sheep. He was likewise ordered to reduce the number to 200, or two for every acre he held.

The presentments in 1544 show that the effort to control the growth of sheep flocks had been fruitless.[4] The jury stated, wrongly in view of the evidence of 1518, that the farmer of the parsonage had not previously kept sheep; there were now 300 or 400, although the jurors were not clear if they were kept by tenure of the parsonage or of Chicksands, not surprisingly since Thomas Bowles was farming both. There were also, or had been, 300 wethers on the land of Chicksands. The jury also presented that whereas the main

---

[1] C.R.O., R.55.7.5.1(15), ff. 77, 77v.    [2] C.R.O., R.55.7.43.2.
[3] One parcel of eight acres in Blackland Field was "common ley w$^{ch}$ hath not ben eared by the space of lx yeares or more."
[4] C.R.O., R.55.7.1(15), ff. 78v, 79.

demesne flock had never been over 1140, Thomas Bowles was now keeping between 1640 and 1740 beasts. Bowles was then, in 1544, running a minimum of 2,000 sheep at Chippenham, and, according to the tenants, he was also trying to deny their right to common their own sheep.[1] Bowles was also infringing the by-laws governing rights of pasture generally, by putting his sheep into the stubble before the cattle, putting his horse on to the common with the tenants' beasts against precedent, and possibly attempting to prevent the right, which is all that is known of the Chippenham crop rotation at this date, of sowing a furlong with peas "in every shifte . . . in the ffyld left for ffallowe" which the tenants "have ever had before." There was obviously great discontent.[2] The next lord of the manor, Sir Thomas Rivett, made an attempt in 1565, which seems to have been successful,[3] to enclose the fen. The village seems to have fallen into the hands of the profiteering landlord denounced by the pamphleteers of the sixteenth century.

## VI. THE ENGROSSING OF HOLDINGS AND THE END OF THE OPEN FIELDS

THE latter part of the sixteenth and the course of the seventeenth centuries saw the continuation of the changes which had so altered Chippenham by the end of the fifteenth. Crude comparison of incomparable materials suggests that the population of Cambridgeshire rose by something like 34 per cent between 1563 and the Hearth Tax return of 1664, after a negligible rise or even a slight fall in the earlier part of the sixteenth century.[4] The materials for this comparison do not exist for Chippenham. It is not even possible to compare directly the 63 or so houses standing in the village in 1544[5] with those taxed in 1664, since no separate Hearth Tax assessment was made of the hamlet of Badlingham. Seventy-six houses in all were taxed in Chippenham, probably including those in Badlingham. When Badlingham was mapped only five years earlier, there had been at least nine houses there.[6] It seems from this that the population of Chippenham did not rise during the period. Even if any houses in Badlingham

---

[1] The word "sheep" has been torn off the page but it is clear that it is correct.—*Ibid.*, fo. 79.

[2] Thomas Bowles's attempt to overstock the foldcourse whilst denying the tenants' right to contribute to it was very much in line with similar developments in Norfolk.—K. J. Allison, 'The Sheep-Corn Husbandry of Norfolk in the Sixteenth and Seventeenth Centuries', *Ag. Hist. Rev.*, v, 1957, pp. 12–20.

[3] C.R.O., R.55.7.5.1 (4).

[4] Margaret Spufford, *Rural Cambridgeshire, 1520–1680* (unpublished M.A. thesis, Leicester, 1963), p. 47.

[5] See above, p. 31 and p. 39, n. 5.    [6] Map in possession of Spalding Gentlemen's Society.

are disregarded, the increasing number of houses between 1544 and 1664 would suggest a rise of only just over 20 per cent in the number of families inhabiting them. While the occupants of the village increased by a maximum of a fifth, however, the available land continued to accumulate into fewer and fewer hands.

### LAND TENURE AND DISTRIBUTION

This accumulation was hastened by the successful conversion of copyhold to leasehold on a large part of the manor. A rental of 1560[1] exists showing that out of approximately 1200 acres accounted for[2] almost exactly a tenth was in the hands of the lord. The half-yardland of this "sometime holden by court roll" at 8s. a year and now "letten to farm" for 20s. a year, shows which way the wind was blowing. In 1636, when the rental was annotated, another 585 acres had joined this nucleus of leasehold.

|      | Leasehold   | Copy and Freehold | Total        |
|------|-------------|-------------------|--------------|
| 1560 | c. 126 a.   | c. 1099 a.        | c. 1225 a.   |
| 1636 | c. 711 a.   | c. 523 a.         | c. 1225 a.   |

Well over half the land which had previously been free and copyhold was leased. The notes in the rental suggest, though inconclusively, that there were ten leasehold farms in 1636 and that not all of them were large. Four were under forty acres, and three more the conventional two-yardland size of between fifty and sixty acres, although the others ran up from ninety to two hundred acres. The conversion to leasehold was not, however, the cause of the continuing disappearance of the smaller farms and concentration of the land into larger and larger units. This trend continued spontaneously amongst the copyholders and is best illustrated by the history of the Dillamore family. The seventeenth-century annotations on the rental of 1560 show that in 1636 Thomas Dillamore held mainly copyholds and one very small lease; a parallel set of annotations on the rental of 1544 show which of the copyholds then in separate hands were concentrated into his. No less than nine of the holdings of 1544 had come in whole or part into his tenure in 1636. Other evidence suggests that he may before his death, in 1638–9, have acquired one of the largest leasehold farms in the parish as well.[3] When he died, Thomas Dillamore left free and copyhold lands in three other villages besides Chippenham.[4] He was the outstanding example of the yeoman farmer in a position to

[1] C.R.O., R.55.7.5.1(1).
[2] Comparable with the total freehold and copyhold land shown in Table IV.
[3] C.R.O., R.55.7.7.88, pp. 4–6, 13–14.
[4] Bury St Edmunds and West Suffolk Record Office, Register Muriell, ff. 28–9.

profit from high agricultural prices in the village at this date, but he was not the only one; John Francis had in 1636 acquired all or part of five of the copyholds of 1544 as well.[1]

It is not surprising, in these circumstances, that the Hearth Tax return of 1664 should indicate that half of the houses in Chippenham had only one hearth, against just under a third with three or more hearths.[2] In Cambridgeshire at this date, the occupancy of a house with one hearth indicated a status and wealth not much higher than that of the average labourer, whereas a house with three or more hearths was usually occupied by a yeoman or prosperous craftsman.[3] The distribution of land in Chippenham in the seventeenth century abundantly accounted for the predominance of small houses there.

### EMPARKING

In 1696 Edward Russell, later Lord Orford, bought up most of the remaining copyhold in the village, which had amounted to just over 500 acres in 1636. The 'lands' he bought were then concentrated in the hands of five men;[4] and the three of them whose farms were described in detail in the court rolls held farms of from 120 to 155 acres apiece. The process of accumulation begun in the fifteenth century had then reached its logical conclusion, in the emergence of these yeomen's farms of over 100 acres.[5] It was perhaps ironic that the net result of their endeavours was to simplify Lord Orford's way to achieving his ambition, since the vast majority of the tenants with whom he had to deal were virtually landless.

"Your petitioner," ran Orford's letter to William III, "has A Seat called Chippenham Hall . . . about which he is desirous to make a Park."[6] His action probably did more to change the landscape of the parish than any other in its history, at least since the Hospitallers laid out their infirmary in the twelfth or thirteenth century. The park was to include part of the village south of the manor, taking in the bottom part of the High Street and the whole

---

[1] It is even possible that Thomas Dillamore had bought out John Francis by 1638, when his will mentions the copyhold of John Francis in Chippenham. He need not, of course, have been the same man.

[2] P.R.O., E.179/84/437.

[3] Margaret Spufford, 'The Significance of the Cambridgeshire Hearth Tax', *Proc. Cambs. Antiq. Soc.*, LV, 1961, pp. 53–64.

[4] C.R.O., R.55.7.4(d), 8, 9, and 10, list Orford's copyhold purchases and grants between 1696 and 1701.

[5] By the end of the seventeenth century the tenant of the small farm of under 50 acres had virtually disappeared from Chippenham. He seems already to have been a rare bird by 1660, the date which A. H. Johnson in *The Disappearance of the Small Landowner* adopted as the beginning of the crucial period marking the extinction of the small farmer.

[6] C.R.O., R.55.7.35.1.

of South Street. Licence to block these roads was obtained in 1702,[1] and when Heber Lands surveyed the remodelled estate for its owner in 1712, their positions, and those of the crofts along them, were only visible from the surviving pattern of trees which still outlined them. Two cottages still stood on what had been the north side of South Street, but they were the sole surviving relics to show where half a village once lay. Aerial photography shows less than the map; only the outlines of one or two closes survive into the twentieth century, together with the line of the High Street and its crossing with South Street.

Apart from the closes of the village houses, the park area was mainly made up of demesne land; the manor gardens themselves, the Hospitallers' South Croft, part of the block of demesne where one of their windmills stood in the thirteenth century, other blocks of demesne in the open fields, and the Hallmore. The main loss to the village, apart from the few acres of open-field land at the southern edge, was the right of half-yearly common it had enjoyed over the Hall Moor, and the threat to the adjoining Town Moor. This loss was justly dealt with. In 1702 the "Inhabitants and Owners" of Chippenham, then numbering only eleven, agreed to release the piece of fen called the Moor "lately enclosed" and their rights of common over it and the half-yearly common, together with all other emparked land. This they judged to be some 166 acres. In return, Orford granted them rights of common for cattle, not sheep, over all the Lammas land in Chippenham, and over the part of the fen in the occupation of the demesne lessee.[2] The village then regained some at least of the fen common which it had presumably lost in the 1560's, although the right to run sheep on the fen was never restored.

The bulk of Orford's purchases between 1696 and 1701 had consisted of at least 25 houses.[3] Some provision was made for their inhabitants. Nine of those who surrendered were admitted to other cottages or tenements, and of these, six at least were new. Four of them lay in Vicarage Lane, or "New Street." This had not at any time previously been built up, and the map shows at least fourteen cottages there. Some of them still survive today, to represent a piece of late seventeenth-century estate planning. It was not adequate, however; the map shows a maximum of only fifty houses in the village.[4] There must have been migration elsewhere, and the fact that one yeoman was enfeoffed of a messuage and two pieces of waste in the gravel pits at the end of New Street in 1712 on the understanding that extra relief should be paid if he built other

---

[1] C.R.O., R.55.7.35.2a.    [2] C.R.O., R.55.7.7.55.
[3] There were 40 houses and cottages still standing in 1544 in the area later to be emparked.
[4] It is not possible to be more precise, since the subdivision of closes often makes it uncertain whether one or two houses are shown on the map. New Farm, in the open fields, is omitted from this total.

houses there, suggests that it may have been unwilling.[1] If speculative building on such a site was profitable, there must have been a demand to satisfy, and also a shortage of land for it.

### THE TENANTS IN 1712

In 1712 only eighteen men held land in Chippenham. Of these five had a mere couple of acres. At least twenty-six householders were landless.[2] The

TABLE VI

FARM SIZE IN 1712

(Statutory measurements with customary equivalents)

| Range of Customary size | Range of stat. equiv. | Number of farms | Statutory acreage a. r. p. | | |
|---|---|---|---|---|---|
| Town Vicarage Non-parishioners | | | 37 | I | 02 |
| Over 290a. | Over 240a. | 3 | 1021 | 2 | 18 |
| 100–150a. | 85–125a. | 4 | 427 | I | 01 |
| 51–67a. (2 yardlands) | 43–56a. | 2 | 99 | 0 | 20 |
| 13–19a. (½ yardland) | 11–16a. | I | 12 | I | 14 |
| 3–5a. | 2a. 2r.–4a. | 3 | 10 | 0 | 13 |
| Under 2a. | Under 1a. 3r. | 5 | 5 | 3 | 37 |
| Total landholders | | 18 | 1613 | 2 | 25 |
| House or cottage only | | 26 (+5) | | | |

proportion of those with only a house, or a house and one or two acres, had again risen, from half in 1544 to nearly three-quarters. Farm size had risen equally sharply; three men now farmed over 290 acres apiece.[3] John Tetsal

[1] C.R.O., R.55.7.7.88, p. 89. He had already been admitted to a messuage and piece of waste in the gravel pits in 1699 and had also built two houses elsewhere.—C.R.O., R.55.7.4(d).9. There were two cottages in the gravel pits in 1712 besides John Chapman's own messuage, according to the map.

[2] Again, as in 1544, it is impossible to estimate the number of landless men more precisely since various houses were available for subletting. Furthermore, some of the new cottages appear on the map to be in two tenancies, whether they were originally built as semi-detached or had been divided by 1712. Others may also have been subdivided. There may thus have been up to five further landless householders.

[3] For the sake of convenience all the acreages given in this section are customary, not statutory, since they are thus comparable with the acreages given earlier in the text for 1279 and 1544. The map deals in statutory measurement, and the farm sizes in Table VI are statutory, with customary equivalents given, reckoned at the rate of 120 customary to 100 statutory acres.

and Thomas Elliot were demesne lessees, since they shared land in positions described as demesne in 1544. Thomas Elliot also farmed the parsonage. Ambrose Davy's "New Farm," later La Hogue, or Hog Hall, the first farmstead to appear outside the village, stood by the side of what had formerly been the rabbit warren in Blackland Field, and he occupied Chicksands and demesne land in the southern fields. These men were not merely farmers of the demesne and parsonage land. Together, they held over two-thirds of the arable with over 1000 acres in the open fields. Half of the landholders, instead of one-sixth as in 1544, farmed the equivalent of over 50 acres, and the typical 'large' farm of the sixteenth century, which had ranged between 30 and 70 customary acres, had now almost disappeared. The two exceptions were the farms of William Harwell and Robert Hawes who farmed just under 70 and just over 50 acres each. The yardland holding had vanished, and the sole half-yardland to survive was that of George Abbot, the village butcher. Below him eight cottagers farmed under six acres.

Consolidation of holdings on this scale was inevitably marked by the physical amalgamation of strips. The notes made in 1636 on the survey of 1544 show Thomas Dillamore holding groups of strips lying together, which had previously been in different hands. The map shows the same process carried further, although the largest and most striking blocks of arable illustrated by it were in fact demesne, and had probably existed since the thirteenth century. All the blocks of land of considerable size which appear on the map had been described in the 1544 survey, although inspection shows that in some cases this original core had been much enlarged by the addition of other holdings. In 1544 there had been 42½ acres of demesne and Chicksands land where New Farm stood in 1712. At that date it was surrounded by nearly 100 acres of Ambrose Davy's land.

Other changes, less striking to the casual eye but even more far-reaching, are betrayed by a detailed analysis of the strip sizes given by the map (Table VII). The survey of 1544 describes in detail some 2600 strips and parcels of land. The map of 1712 illustrates and gives the acreage of only some 820 strips covering the same area within the same boundaries. In just over 150 years the number of individual parcels in the fields had been reduced by over two-thirds. A comparison of the sizes of strips in the survey with those on the map show that where half those of the mid-sixteenth century had been of a rood, a rood and a half, or half an acre, in the early eighteenth century over half were the equivalent of more than one customary acre. The open fields were much altered by the changing pattern of landholding, as they had presumably already been altered by similar amalgamations before 1544.

The high number of large strips was not accounted for merely by the activi-

TABLE VII

STRIP SIZE IN THE EIGHTEENTH CENTURY

| Size in stat. acres a. r. p. | Equiv. in cust. acres a. r. | John Tetsal | Thomas Elliot | John Godfrey | Robert Seeker | William Harwell | Robert Hawes | George Abbot | Total strips 1712 |
|---|---|---|---|---|---|---|---|---|---|
| over 2 0 20 | over 2 2 | 68 | 28 | 22 | 13 | | | | 212 |
| 2 0 19 ⎫ 1 2 20 ⎭ | 2 0 | 16 | 1 | 7 | 7 | 3 | 2 | 1 | 61 |
| 1 2 19 ⎫ 1 0 20 ⎭ | 1 2 | 24 | — | 9 | 9 | 7 | 5 | 2 | 98 |
| 1 0 19 ⎫ 0 3 20 ⎭ | | 12 | 1 | 14 | 9 | 4 | 1 | 3 | 66 |
| 0 3 19 ⎫ 0 2 20 ⎭ | 1 0 | 12 | — | 5 | 7 | 9 | 6 | 2 | 62 |
| 0 2 19 ⎫ 0 2 10 ⎭ | 3 | 9 | — | — | 5 | 11 | 10 | 1 | 47 |
| 0 2 9 ⎫ 0 1 30 ⎭ | 2½ | 3 | — | 5 | 4 | 23 | 16 | 3 | 84 |
| 0 1 29 ⎫ 0 1 10 ⎭ | 2 | 6 | — | 7 | 7 | 19 | 26 | 3 | 99 |
| 0 1 9 ⎫ 0 0 30 ⎭ | 1 | 6 | — | 1 | 2 | 22 | 14 | 1 | 75 |
| under 0 0 29 | ½ | — | — | 2 | 1 | 2 | 1 | — | 12 |
| Total strips | | 30 | 156 | 72 | 64 | 100 | 81 | 16 | 816* |
| Farm size. Stat. | | 245a. | 393a. | 123a. | 98a. | 56a. | 43a. | 12a. | 1613a. 2r. 25p. |
| Cust. | | 293a. | 471a. | 147a. | 117a. | 67a. | 52a. | 15a. | c. 1935a. |

\* There were also 8 parcels of unknown size or occupant.

ties of the three largest farmers, and the reorganization of the land which came within their hands. Each of the other four farmers with over 100 customary acres had approximately two-thirds of his parcels of land in units of more than one acre, and illustrated the general change. No sign of the traditional predominance of the rood and half-acre survived. The only exceptions were, again, those whose farms were a recognizable survival of an earlier type.

A half and just under a half of the strips of William Harwell and Robert Hawes were between a rood and half an acre in size. In these circumstances, it becomes highly significant that their selions are the only ones which frequently ran across and divided the areas of land in Ambrose Davy's possession, which were otherwise so large that they appeared, from the acreage, if nothing else, to justify the term 'field'. The only holdings of 1712 which can definitely be shown to be copyholds from the court roll extracts are William Harwell's 67 acres and George Abbot's 15.[1] The Harwell holding had been built up between 1704 and 1711 from the surrenders of four other copyholders,[2] which included one full yardland. George Abbot was running into difficulties, and after his land had been mortgaged in 1714, it was added to William Harwell's holding. The tendency for the smaller holdings to disappear, which was independent of the change of tenure from copy to leasehold, was continuing. With the extinction of George Abbot's tenement as a separate entity, the last farm of recognizable medieval size in Chippenham vanished.

The continued existence of the Harwell and Hawes holdings at such obvious inconvenience to the bigger lessees shows that it had been possible for the more stubborn to resist the conversion to leasehold, which had been accomplished piecemeal, by purchase and economic pressure, during the sixteenth and seventeenth centuries. The Harwell holding was in fact the last copyhold of any considerable acreage to survive, and was not bought out by the lord of the manor until 1791.[3]

The effects of the changes in tenure on the organization of the open fields may have been considerable. The land of the three chief lessees of 1712 appears to have been divided with more care for geographical compactness than any rotation which may have existed, since Davy held no land at all in the northern fields, and the Tetsall and Elliot farms lay principally, although not entirely, in them. Furthermore, the map shows the New Farm surrounded by a group of closes, and at enclosure this was the only farm in the village, apart from the one which included the medieval demesne pastures round the fen, which had any appreciable area of "old inclosures."[4] Blackland Field, within which the New Farm lay, had largely disappeared into these closes by 1712, or been emparked, and the remaining fragments of it had become "Lodge Field." It seems possible that a considerable part of the old field was taken out of the common rotation completely when the New Farm was built. The surviving seventeenth- and eighteenth-century orders of the homage do not help gauge the effects of these changes.[5] The descriptions of two small

[1] C.R.O., R.55.7.2(b).     [2] C.R.O., R.55.7.4(b).     [3] C.R.O., R.55.7.7.89, pp. 6–7.
[4] C.R.O., R.55.7.8.4.
[5] C.R.O., R.55.7.4(d). 12 (1689) & 11 (1691), and R.55.7.4(a). 6 (1753).

copyholds surrendered immediately before enclosure makes it clear that there was then a three-course rotation based on West Field, Mill Field (the old North Field), and Sound Field.[1] Another copyhold was described as lying in these fields and also in Lodge Field and Littlebeck Field.[2] Other fields still existed, therefore, but can have had little importance if they had lost any separate function they may once have had as units in the rotation. Themhowe Field seems to have lost all identity by this time. It is perhaps for that reason that when the large leaseholds were surveyed in 1780, the land of all but "New Farm" was described as simply in West, Mill, and Sound Fields.[3]

The changes which could take place within the existing framework of the open fields were so far-reaching, at Chippenham at least, that possibly one reason for the lateness of enclosure in Cambridgeshire has been found. The county was overwhelmingly arable, and an exporter of grain. There was relatively little pressure for enclosure for improved arable in the sixteenth and seventeenth centuries, and indeed, until the advent of modern drainage it is difficult to see why there should have been. The chief disadvantage of open-field arable farming was the inconvenience of scattered holdings, and at Chippenham it appears that this disadvantage could partly be overcome without enclosure, by the amalgamation of holdings. There was scope for the ambitious within the open fields, which perhaps explains why they survived so long.[4]

The map of Chippenham in 1712 shows that the large leasehold farm was by then fully developed, and in many ways the eighteenth century merely provided a footnote to this development, with the gradual disappearance of the remaining small copyholds. These were negligible by enclosure.[5]

### ENCLOSURE

In 1780 the owners of the estate were anxious to sell; they had the leaseholds surveyed with this in mind,[6] and noted at the time "an act to be got to enclose

---

[1] C.R.O., R.55.7.4(d). 3 & 5.        [2] C.R.O., R.55.7.4(d).6.        [3] C.R.O., R.55.7.10.3.

[4] The main disadvantage of this theory is that the amalgamation of holdings obviously made enclosure easier, and might therefore advance it rather than the reverse. Chippenham was in fact one of the first half-dozen parishes in the county to be enclosed (C.R.O. unpublished hand-list, *Cambridge Inclosure Records*, 1963). Any judgement on how common or unusual the degree of consolidation found there was must await further investigations; two other parishes of which I have examined the sixteenth- and seventeenth-century history showed a medium amount of amalgamation, and an almost total lack of it (Margaret Spufford, *Rural Cambridgeshire 1520–1680*, unpublished M.A. thesis, Leicester 1963). But it did take place elsewhere, as Vancouver's comment on Madingley shows. There, in 1794, "the Whole of the lands in open fields, lie in large pieces; as such, no enclosure is meditated or desired."—Vancouver, *General View of the Agriculture in the County of Cambridge*, London, 1794, p. 105.

[5] C.R.O., R.55.7.4(d). 1, 3, 5, 6, 13 and R.55.7.7.89.        [6] C.R.O., R.55.7.10.3.

... this estate would be amazingly improved."[1] The Act was passed in 1791. The award does not survive, but the purchaser of the estate in 1792, John Tharp, was possessed of a meticulous turn of mind, and his notebook preserves much of the relevant information from it.[2] There were eight enclosed farms in Chippenham in the 1790's, all of which were leasehold. Four of them were over 350 acres, running up to nearly 650; three were between 95 and 155 acres, and the sole remaining small farm was the 44 acres farmed by the lessee of the New Goat Inn. Only two other allotments of under two acres were listed by John Tharp.[3] The distribution of size varies little from that in 1712. John Tharp noted that there were 11 acres of copyhold in Chippenham parish not accounted for in his calculations,[4] and apart from these, there were 13 freehold and copyhold houses and cottages in the village. The rest, possessing between them 45 rights of common, were bought with the estate by its new owner.

It was over common rights that enclosure caused trouble at Chippenham. Some time between 1756 and 1780 the heath had been divided between the three largest farms, and had come again, for the first time since the Middle Ages, under the plough. The notes on these farms made in 1770 make it plain that 'shackage' had been abolished over the area. The village had thus lost one of its chief resources, and the process of attrition of communal rights, perhaps begun by the de Mandevilles in the twelfth century, had at last been completed.

The other chief waste area, the fen, and its outliers, Latchmere common and the Marsh, had already been in dispute in the sixteenth and seventeenth centuries. In 1791 it was excluded from the enclosure award, because—it was believed in the nineteenth century—it was of little value, "being all inundated the greater part of the year." In 1796 the new, improving landlord set about amending this. The orders of the homage on May 14th that year, which present the lord of the manor for encroachment on the fen and the droveways leading to it, reflect his preparations, as they do the rights which were about to be lost. No cottager was to cut more than three loads of "Hassacks" or turves, and this was only to be done under the orders of the fen reeve; no commoner was to give away or sell turves, and no one from outside the parish was to dig them.[5] John Tharp exchanged the common rights of the thirteen cottages which still possessed them for an allotment of just over three acres each by

[1] C.R.O., R.55.7.10.1 & 2.   [2] C.R.O., R.55.7.8.4.
[3] These and other acreages quoted from now on are in statutory measurement.
[4] It is not clear if these were really the same acres as the 13 acres 1½ roods said elsewhere (C.R.O., R.55.7.117.16) to have been accepted by the cottagers in lieu of common rights, excluding those over the fen.
[5] C.R.O., R.55.7.4(b).

agreement.[1] In addition he acted generously and set aside thirty-six acres for the poor to cut turves for fuel, and put this area under the management of the Court Leet. This allotment was presumably to cater for the needs of the lease-holders, who had technically no rights.

The way was then clear for John Tharp to drain, enclose, and plant the remainder of the fen. His proceedings met with the strong approval of Arthur Young, who wrote that "This before Mr Tharp's improvement was constantly flooded; when fed it was with cows and young stock, but to little profit . . . the whole the residence of snipes, wild ducks, and herons: cows and horses mired and lost, and their skeletons found when the drains were cut."[2] The approval of the village was less strong, although the full effect of the encroachment on common rights was not felt by most of it until the agricultural depression of the 1820's and 30's. In 1830 "several of the lower orders of the poor in Chippenham" set up a claim to right of turbary for the poor over the whole area exempted from the enclosure Act, irrespective of their occupancy of houses with such rights.[3] The claim was no doubt unlawful,[4] but it reflected the desperation of the landless, who had been bought out, and sometimes generously bought out, of the rights they enjoyed under a different form of tenure. In 1831 there were disorders at Chippenham, and the new fen closes were broken into, "in a riotous and disorderly manner with Spades and other implements" by several of the "pauper" inhabitants of the village. When challenged, they said "the Land was theirs." So they voiced an old claim, bad in law, that may, or may not, have been true in the days of Cippa, long before the de Mande-villes asserted their lordship over the waste. The paupers' protest was the last overt sign of life given by the old open-field society of Chippenham.

In many ways the history of the village adds a fresh example to a picture already clear in outline; the build-up of population and fragmentation of holdings to the end of the thirteenth century, the conversion of customary tenure to terms more favourable to the peasant by the end of the fourteenth century, the stagnation of the fifteenth century, and through it the emergence of a new 'rural aristocracy' and its copyhold farms. What is perhaps newer is the illustration that conversion to leasehold in the sixteenth and seventeenth centuries and the continued process of amalgamation of holdings by a few families could, within the existing framework of the open fields, utterly disrupt the society which had once farmed them. Enclosure is sometimes thought of as

---

[1] The history of the fen enclosure is given in C.R.O., R.55.7.117.16. Some of the original agreements survive as C.R.O., R.55.7.4(b). 1-8 & C.R.O., R.55.7.7.28 & 231, and John Tharp's memorandum book, R.55.7.8.4, gives the full list of those who exchanged their rights with him. The effects of the fen enclosure and the ·'Pauper Riots" of the 1830's are described in C.R.O., R.55.7.16.20, 21 & 22.

[2] Arthur Young, *Annals of Agriculture*, XLIII, p. 51. I am indebted to Mr R. H. Hills for this reference.

[3] C.R.O., R.55.7.117.16.    [4] C.R.O., R.55.7.16.20.

the death-knell of the 'small peasant' farm. In Chippenham it was no creator of inequality; it set the seal on a process which had begun by the late fourteenth century.

## ACKNOWLEDGEMENTS

The publication of this work has been assisted by a grant from the Twenty-Seven Foundation, the trustees of which I thank for their help.

I am also indebted to Dr Claire Cross who, as County Archivist of Cambridgeshire, first drew my attention to the map of Chippenham, and to Mr J. M. Farrar, her successor, who has coped with my demands for material over a long period. Mrs Bacon of Chippenham Park has kindly allowed me to visit her grounds, her house, and even her cellars whenever my field-work required. My thanks are also due to Professor M. M. Postan, Dr Joan Thirsk, and Dr Esther de Waal for their trouble in reading my draft and for their comments and criticisms of it.

Lastly, my acknowledgements go to my supervisor, Professor H. P. R. Finberg, for his persistent encouragement and help, which has always been available but never obtrusive. Without it, this work would never have reached the press.

NAMED FURLONGS

MILL FIELD
1. King's Path
2. Broke
3. Middle
4. Middle next Broke
5. Gore Acre
6. next Latchmere
7. cross over Sequysse
8. Sequysse
9. Latchmere
10. Pyncheden
11. Broke (or Alditch)

PUDMANHILL FIELD
1. Church Croft
2. Middle
3. Broke
4. Thaxted Way

STONEHILL FIELD
1. Broke
2. Middle
3. Thyvissche Ditch
4. Another

BLACKLAND FIELD
1. Thyvissche Ditch
2. Moulton Way
3. Broke
4. Blackland
5. Ditchway
6. Albone

LITTLEBECK FIELD
1. Ashley Hill
2. By Moulton Way
3. Other by Moulton Way
4. Over Ashley Way
5. Littlebeck Valley
6. Wronglands

SOUND FIELD
1. Fordhowe Marsh
2. Ditchedway
3. Cross above Ditch Way
4. Ditchway
5. Middle above Ditch Way
6. Heath
7. The Butts

THREMHOWE FIELD
1. Portway
2. Middle
3. Middle next Sound
4. Soundhill?
5. Sound
6. The Butts

WEST FIELD
1. Marsh
2. Middleway
3. Middleway
4. Portway
5. The Butts

A. Mill
B. Parson's Meadow
C. Guildhall
D. Monks' Meadow
E. The Holmes
F. Great Garden
G. Manor
H. Chicksands Grange

| | |
|---|---|
| Roads and Tracks | |
| Streams | |
| Field Boundaries | |
| Furlong Boundaries | |
| *SOUND* Field names | |
| Demesne | |
| X Messuage | |
| M Mease Ground | |
| Area Emparked by 1712 | |
| Direction of Strips | |
| Chicksands | |

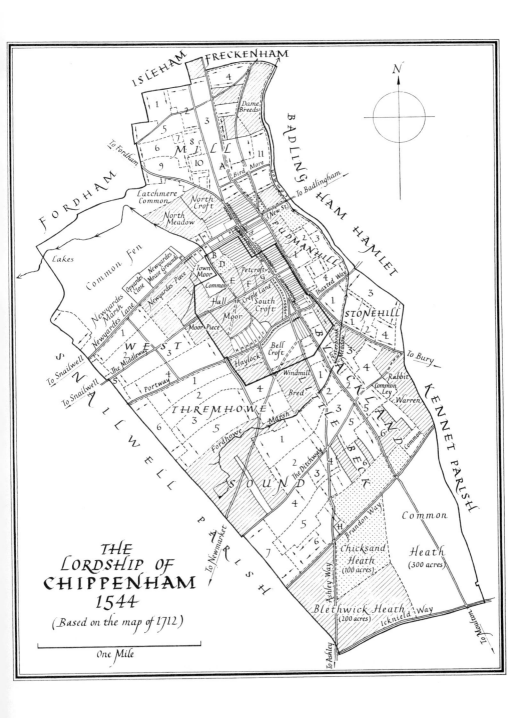

THE
LORDSHIP OF
CHIPPENHAM
1544
(Based on the map of 1712)

One Mile

# VI

# Isaac Archer's Chippenham, and Chippenham Hall: a Postscript

By the time *A Cambridgeshire Community* emerged from the press in 1965, I had already moved on in my thinking, and was working on the first drafts of *Contrasting Communities*, which included literacy and religion as well as village economies in its compass. It also included, very importantly, my first attempts at thumb-nail sketches of the inhabitants of the villages. *A Cambridgeshire Community* had been restricted to the history, in so far as I could do it, of land-distribution in Chippenham from before the Conquest until enclosure. Specifically because of my work on Chippenham, I inserted Professor Le Roy Ladurie's quotation 'J'avais commencé, tout au début, par additioner les hectares et les unités cadastrales; j'aboutissais, en fin de recherche, à regarder agir, lutter, penser les hommes vivants'[1] at the beginning of *Contrasting Communities*. I had indeed begun by counting up the 2,601 strips in the written survey of the manor and parish in 1544, as well as the 816 strips shown on the magnificent map of 1712, after engrossing and emparking. I had performed this very tedious chore in 1962 on the hand-wound adding-machine belonging to the Professor of Psychology at Leicester, which he kindly let me use. In my survey of landholding, I did pay due attention to the economic influence of the medieval hall of the Knights Hospitallers in Chippenham, which served as the infirmary for the whole of England, and indeed, to the major economic effect later of the actions of Lord Orford, lord of the manor in 1696, who wrote to William III 'Your petitioner has A Seat called Chippenham Hall ... about which he is desirous to make a Park'. However, when I moved onwards in my thinking in *Contrasting Communities* I did not make adequate acknowledgement of the influence of these resident gentry and nobility in Chippenham Park on the village which surrounded them.

I only realised the full extent of my omission when I read the newly-found *Diary* of Isaac Archer,[2] who was mainly resident in Chippenham from 1662–71, and was incumbent there until 1688. From 1662–67 Isaac Archer lived in the Hall itself, before removing to the Vicarage. His patron from 1664–69 was

---

[1]   *Contrasting Communities*, p.xix.
[2]   *Two East Anglian Diaries, 1641–1729: Isaac Archer and William Coe*, Matthew Storey (ed.), Suffolk Records Society XXXVI (1994), especially p.8, pp.87–137.

Sir John Russell, who was married to Frances Cromwell, fourth daughter of Oliver Cromwell. Archer's stay in the Hall was interrupted by removals from time to time to the household of Colonel Henry Cromwell, himself fourth son of the Protector, at Spinney Abbey, nearby, who in turn had married Sir John Russell's sister, Elizabeth Russell. Isaac Archer was a barely-conformist young man, with a very tender conscience. He was interrupted by the temptations of life at Chippenham Hall, and reproached himself greatly: the aim of his removal to Spinney Abbey, six miles away, in 1664,[3] a 'more private place was to serve God more closely, having such pious governours of the family, and prayers every evening, which were not regarded at Chippenham. I had contracted much guilt, and filth by living with those at Chippenham Hall, who did not so much mind the forme of religion as they should'.[4] He recorded this was 'to the grief of all, unless they dissembled with me, for I blesse God I gave some content to all sides'. But despite his resolve on that occasion, he was fencing with Sir John Russell in 1665[5] after being pressed back into his old place at Chippenham 'to the content of the towne, and all that were lovers of sobriety and the feare of God'. For all that, he was flirting with a widowed 'gentlewoman' resident at the Hall in 1665[6] as well as succumbing to playing cards at Christmas at the end of the year. He was still only twenty-four. Yet despite these misdemeanours, which loomed very large to him, and which he greatly repented, he made a very considerable impact by his preaching, by his gentle handling of nonconformist local meetings, the existence of which were previously unknown in Chippenham, and for which this Diary is the only source. Above all, his tactful approach to celebrating the first Communion to be held in Chippenham for 20 years in 1663 when he was twenty-two[7] was notable.

> I preached twice about it, laying downe such qualifications as the strictest divines make use of, and went to the houses of such as would receive, to speake with them concerning so weighty a busines. I found them generally honest in their way, but ignorant, wherfore I told them what I could of the grounds of religion, and particularly about the sacrament, and shewing the great dangers they incurred by unworthy receiving. I left it to their owne consciences what to doe.

---

[3]   Ibid, p.97.
[4]   Ibid, pp.97–8.
[5]   Ibid, p.104.
[6]   Ibid, pp.109–110.
[7]   Ibid, p.89.

153

*Postscript. Isaac Archer's Chippenham, and Chippenham Hall* 3

I thought they would take it ill, that so young a man as my selfe should examine them about such things, but I found them very thankfull, and willing to be instructed. The reason of this may be ... because I went mildly to worke, and included my selfe in those sinns I spoke against in them.[8]

Despite this, he reproached himself, the village, and the example set at the Hall for his failing to curb drinking in the alehouses. There were no 'godly' constables in Chippenham, and when he asked the constable to come with him in 1663 to reproach men drinking in the alehouse on the Lord's day in harvest-time, the constable replied 'he should gett the ill will of his neighbours' and would not go. In 1665, he recorded his expostulation with 'A chiefe man in the towne, who had made a profession of religion, [who] was become a common drunkard'.[9] Later in 1665 he wrote:[10]

Chippenham was growne worse now of late then when I came first. ... I expostulated with them, and asked when it would once be that they would reforme their alehouses...it so affected the officers ... that they consulted, of their own accord, together how to redresse thees things; and presently went with mee, and we looked that no children played, and I went to search the alehouses, and frighted them with threatening seveerly to execute the law against them etc. Thus after a promise from all of them that they would be strict hereafter in their offices I dismissed them; and hope that the whole towne will grow better, for they were come to a height of profaneness, by the ill examples of some of the Hall, and of those that came, sometimes, as strangers thither. I prayed for the cleansing of towne and house... I intend, when I have a fitt season, to tell Sir John of the abuses he hath suffered in his house to the scandall of his friends, and the ill example of others whom I cannot tell of their drunkennes, but they reflect upon him, and what is done, and suffered in his house.

The minister continued to be much concerned by the amount of drunkenness in the village, and laid the blame squarely on the influence of the Hall, and its many noble visitors, whose sojourns he dreaded. When he eventually left in 1671, he wrote 'the maine reason was a being wary of seing and hearing what I

---

[8]    p.89. Compare with the ministry of Ralph Josselin in a similar situation after a nine-year gap in the celebration of Communion, below, XIV, p.317.
[9]    Idem, p.110.
[10]    Idem, pp.111–112.

154

4          *Postscript. Isaac Archer's Chippenham, and Chippenham Hall*

mett with; and the rudenes of the towne, being overrun with grooms and racehorses, and too near the court sometimes'.[11]

Most of this I was necessarily unaware of, when I wrote *Contrasting Communities*. Some of the ungodliness he perceived may be discounted, for Isaac Archer was indeed a man of over-scrupulous conscience. His home as a child had been strict and rigid in the extreme, and the rapier-play, Christmas games of cards, and mild flirtation he found at the Hall were probably not serious. In so far as I considered the Hall, and its resident nobility, I thought a house governed by one of Cromwell's daughters was likely to be an influence for good, and for piety. However, I should have considered the proximity of Newmarket, and the probability of guests for the racing, in such a household. I should also have thought more of the power of the influence that such a great house must have had, when its visitors included Charles I himself, who played a game of bowls at Chippenham Hall, during his enforced stay in Newmarket in 1647, and Oliver Cromwell, who must have visited his daughter, married to a son-in-law who had distinguished himself in the battle of Marston Moor.[12] It was myopic not to look at the ties of Chippenham with the central figures of the century. However, it comes as a very interesting surprise, from this new evidence, that the influence of these Cromwellians was thought of by their minister as almost entirely bad, and that the prosperous yeomen of Chippenham, who had enlarged their farms to such effect during the seventeenth century, had not supplied a godly group of the more prosperous, or 'chiefer sort', to exercise 'social control' there at all, in the eyes of this hardworking and hardpreaching cleric. On the contrary, nobility, gentry and the parish officials were, to Isaac Archer, mainly a bad influence. His evidence comes as a very useful corrective to an historian concentrating exclusively on Archer's parishioners, and ignoring their lords of the manor.

I was led to this emphasis by my attempts to escape the whole tradition of 'local history' rooted in the seventeenth-century antiquarian writers, and still prevalent in the *Victorian County Histories* when I began to write. This tradition was based on the history of the descent of the manor. I allowed the pendulum to swing too far against this approach, and my lack of emphasis on the great importance of Chippenham Hall was the result. Isaac Archer's *Diary* puts the Hall firmly in its dominant position in the village.

---

[11]   Ibid, p.137.
[12]   M.J. Ross, *Chippenham: an East Anglian Estate Village* (Whitby, 1995) pp.15–18.

# VII

# Who made a will in village society?[1]

Who, in village society, made a will? Were the will-makers exceptional men, whose behaviour followed patterns which were not typical of their societies in general?

It is generally assumed that only the more prosperous in village society made wills.[2] This seems an important assumption to test. There are opposing generalisations in print, one to the effect that only the richer in village society made wills, and the other contradicting this. There are no figures demonstrating either view conclusively.

I examined the forty-nine wills which survive from Willingham from the last quarter of the sixteenth century. These are the years immediately following the survey of Willingham land made in 1575.[3] Some testators who died before the end of the century can easily be identified with tenants holding land in

---

[1]    This piece first appeared in 1976. I have not updated it. To do so would demand another article since it provoked so much debate. This, and the large bibliography which resulted, has recently been very ably summarised by Professor Eric Josef Carlson in his 'Historical Value of the Ely Consistory Probate Records', *Index of the Probate Records of the Consistory Court of Ely, 1449–1858*, I, British Record Society (London, 1994), pp.xvii–lix.

[2]    Most recently (1976) tentatively suggested by R.S. Schofield, 'Some Discussions of Illiteracy in England, 1600–1800', not yet in print, when he suggests that wills are 'socially selective, with a bias towards the upper social classes ... Wills, for example, may have been made more frequently by the richer men in each occupational group'.

[3]    About 45 per cent of the tenants who held land, or a commonable house, in Willingham in 1575, made a will, or were represented by a will, in the next 28 years. I do not know how many non-commonable houses, or subtenanted divided houses there were in Willingham in 1575, so that this figure of will-makers is a maximum. Mr Motoyasu Takahashi has continued, to make an exhaustive study of will-makers in Willingham, which has just (1999) appeared in Japanese, under the title *Village Inheritance*. He has compared the surviving Willingham wills from 1515–1732 with the family reconstitution forms prepared for the Cambridge Group for the History of Population and Social Structure by Miss Glynis Reynolds. Of the 470 surviving wills, 174, or 37 per cent, were made by testators with under-age, or unborn, children. 84, or 18 per cent were made by testators with no obvious heir. Only 212, or 45 per cent were made by testators without either of these reasons for making a will, but these included those who had two or more adult sons to provide for, let alone those with unmarried daughters. (Carlson, ibid. pp.xxlv–v). Professor Carlson also finds that in the diocese of Ely, the third largest group of testators were labourers. So in this diocese at least, it was true that the less prosperous did appear in quite sizeable numbers amongst testators in the early modern period (Carlson, ibid. p.xxx).

156

1575. Others, who cannot yet be connected to a particular tenant of 1575, still made such specific bequests of, for instance, stock, that they must have had common rights. Others left such specific acreages to their several sons, that their minimum acreage is calculable. Others left only their tools, and are readily identifiable as landless craftsmen. Others again left stock and small acreages, very carefully described. They are often men who had appeared in the survey of 1575 as landless, and must therefore have acquired this small acreage between the survey and their deaths. The approximate wealth, disposable goods, and economic standing of the men making wills in Willingham at the end of the sixteenth century can, therefore, be compared with the economic standing of the whole village community in 1575.[4] It is possible to see whether the will-makers were evenly distributed through society in this particular village, or whether, as the general assumption suggests, only the comparatively wealthy made wills.

### Table 1  Wills and status in Willingham

| | Tenants in Survey of 1575 | Makers of Wills, 1575–1603 | Percentage of landholding group |
|---|---|---|---|
| Half-yardland and over | 33 | 7 | (21%) |
| 2 acres to half-yardland | 21 | 8 | (38%) |
| With under 2 acres of arable including landless | At least 53 | 34 | (64%) |
| Totals | At least 107 | 49 | (46%) |

The results of this comparison are startling. The forty-nine will-makers in Table 1 were indeed distributed through the whole of village society in Willingham. But they were not evenly distributed. All the groups holding land were represented by wills, but landless men, or men who held a cottage with

---

[4]    This sounds an artlessly impressionistic method of comparison. In fact, all the court roll entries for Willingham land have been checked as well, and all entries relating to testators added to the information in these wills. I am satisfied that I have fairly accurate figures for their acreages at death.

rights in common, or up to two acres of land, were most heavily represented. Sixty-four per cent of this group of tenants (nearly two-thirds) made wills. Thirty-eight per cent of the men with between 2 and 16 acres, or up to half a yardland (over one-third) made wills. Only a fifth of the most prosperous group in Willingham society, the half-yardlanders and yardlanders, left wills.

This is a very curious picture which does not coincide at all with the generalisations usually made. A family reconstitution of Willingham is now in progress, and when it is completed, it will be possible to associate most of the wills made by 1700 with specific tenants, and so correct the impressionistic element in the figures and provide a much bigger sample of will-makers. Meanwhile, it is possible to say that, although all groups in the village produced wills, at the end of the sixteenth century it was the poorer groups that produced most wills.

But it is also possible to look at the will-makers in another way, by identifying their family responsibilities.

### Table 2  Makers of Wills at Willingham 1575–1603

| | |
|---|---|
| 16 | had two or more adult sons to provide for |
| 17 | had unmarried daughters, children under age or unborn children to provide for |
| 5 | were childless and had no obvious heir |
| 11 | had no obvious domestic reason for will-making |
| 49 | |

If the family circumstances described in the wills are taken into account it turns out that of the forty-nine making wills, a third had two or more sons to provide for, and seem to have been making a will for this reason. The second and subsequent sons were being set up with subsidiary holdings which their fathers had managed to acquire, or with cash sums, or stock, or tools. Another third of the will-makers had unmarried daughters to provide for, or children under age, right down to those with only unborn children. The most pathetic example of the latter was Henry Greaves, who in 1585 left to his wife his copyhold half-cottage on the Green 'and after her death to my child, be it man or woman, if it please God she be with any'. A small number, five of the forty-nine testators, were either unmarried or childless, and made a will because they had no obvious heir.

Under a quarter of the testators had no obvious family reason, in the form of a child under age to provide for, to make a will. So, in all, over three-quarters of the testators made a will, not because they were rich or poor, but because they had to provide for children who were not yet independent. This reason lay alike behind the wills of George Crispe, the man who held over ninety acres of free and copyhold land in Willingham in 1575, and died leaving sons aged three-and-a-half and one-and-a-half, between whom he divided his land; and Mathew Ewesden, who appeared as a landless cottager in 1575, and acquired a piece of leasehold land by the time he died in 1595. He left half the profits of the lease to his wife, and half to his two eldest sons, as well as leaving to his two sons his eight sheep with which to renew the lease. His boat and fishing nets went to his second son, the residue to his first.

If over three-quarters of the makers of wills in Willingham had to provide for children, I suggest that this need to provide for a young family must have been the dominant reason behind the making of a will. Again, the family reconstitution now in progress will check the exact demographic status of the testators. Willingham had remarkably high death rates until after the fen drainage.

There are obviously other reasons as well. I have shown that more wills were made in Willingham by the landless and near-landless than by the more prosperous tenants. Over two-thirds of the surviving wills were made by this group. If it is true both that the poor made more wills, and that the main reason for making a will was for a man to provide for children under age, then it looks as if poor men may have died younger, or married later, leaving more young children. This is an important question for the historical demographer to resolve.

All sort of other motives also probably operated. The half-yardlanders who left comparatively fewer wills had holdings which were to some extent regulated by the custom of the manor.[5] Many of the comparatively numerous men who had up to a couple of acres and left wills had held only a landless cottage with rights of common in the 1575 survey. By the time they died, they had often acquired a lease of a couple of acres, or a bit of fen, or the subtenancy of a second cottage. Like Mathew Ewesden, they were concerned with dividing up this bit of leasehold or the extra subtenancy, which was not controlled by manorial custom, in order to establish their under-age children as well as

---

[5]    Most of the half-yardlanders who did make wills were concerned with the disposal of exactly the same sort of fragments of leasehold and freehold land, and of subtenancies, as their less prosperous brethren.

possible. They must have been making wills partly because they were dealing in fragments of land outside the customary framework. One of the motives of their will-making must have been care for their relatively precarious holdings.

We are therefore left with two dominant reasons for will-making. The need to provide for an under-age child, or children, was the most important. Yet after that came the need to dispose of tiny holdings, not provided for by the custom of the manor, which was most keenly felt by the relatively poor men who were predominant amongst the testators in this fen-edge parish.

# VIII

# Families, Will Witnesses, and Economic Structure in the Fens and on the Chalk: Sixteenth- and Seventeenth-Century Willingham and Chippenham*

*Margaret Spufford* and *Motoyasu Takahashi*

The debate on whether or not seventeenth-century village society was increasingly polarized between parish notables and prosperous households, who tended both to appropriate Protestant virtues of "order and godliness" to themselves and impose them on the indifferent or even hostile laboring poor, is not yet over. On one side is Tessa Watt, who has summarized the arguments against polarization that do not fit with the distribution of her "godly" woodcuts, broadsides, and chapbooks,[1] and Martin Ingram, who says "the evidence from Wiltshire and elsewhere suggest it is a mistake to overemphasize either the presence of `godly' groups, or the existence of people largely indifferent to religion." In the village of Keevil, he found the relatively few pious villagers "quite widely scattered in the social scale, and as a group, not particularly literate....They did not form a close-knit nexus in village society, and...did not dominate the structure of local office-holding." He concludes that "both ecclesiastical and religious issues were of sufficient significance in parish life to serve as a focus for parish rivalries and in so far as religious and moral issues were socially divisive, the splits were as much vertical as horizontal."[2] On another side are Anthony Fletcher and John Stevenson accepting the increased polarization of a "Protestantized culture" of the gentry and some of the middling ranks, and the "tra-

*Professor Spufford would like to point out that although she has written this paper, the work on the kinship networks, the will-witnessing and the credit for it, are all Dr. Takahashi's. The work is entirely his own, and only the introduction is hers. She is responsible for any errors of interpretation, expression, and deductions in the summary, and he is responsible for the figures, tables, and maps. The introduction to the paper is drawn together from the work of a group of former research students, Dr. Christopher Marsh, Dr. Derek Plumb, and Dr. Bill Stevenson who, with Mrs. Nesta Evans, cooperated as a team with Professor Spufford in doing the research for her *The World of Rural Dissenters, 1520–1725* (Cambridge, 1995), where interpretations of relative economic status will be found more fully set out. References to this group are subsumed under "the team" and "they," whereas for Dr. Takahashi's work and her own, she has used the pronoun "we." Professor Spufford is grateful to her husband, Dr. Peter Spufford, to Dr. Eric Carlson and Dr. Helen Robinshaw for reading and commenting on this paper in draft.

[1] Tessa Watt, *Cheap Print and Popular Piety, 1550–1640* (Cambridge, 1991), pp. 71–73 and 326–28.

[2] Martin Ingram, *Church Courts, Sex and Marriage in England, 1570–1640* (Cambridge, 1990), pp. 80–81, 93–94, 116, 118.

ditional culture of the laborers and the poor."[3] In doing so, they leaned heavily on Keith Wrightson and David Levine's picture of Mildmay's Terling in Essex as a village community that was divided by religion as a form of cultural differentiation, and which increasingly detached yeomen, substantial tradesmen, and even husbandmen from their poorer neighbors.[4]

In the last ten years, our knowledge of testamentary records, particularly wills made at the village level, has changed and deepened significantly. Our understanding of the meaning of being a witness to a will has therefore changed also. Christopher Marsh has investigated forty disputed will-cases from all over the country and found that normally the dying testators sent out wives, servants, or children to carefully-selected "friends" and "neighbors." The role of a group of witnesses was an intimate one, bringing harmony, smoothing out discord, and promoting fellowship. Witnesses were therefore important, or relatively important, people in a testator's life: "testators generally selected their witnesses quite deliberately, basing their choices upon personal friendship and social respect," Marsh concludes.[5]

Investigations of the social and economic status in rural society of the later Lollards in the upper Thames valley, including the Buckinghamshire Chilterns,[6] and the Family of Love on the Cambridgeshire border with Essex and Suffolk, found the witnesses to wills of these named, persecuted, and "known" heterodox groups a vital key to so far unknown co-religionists, who often came from considerable distances and often had business links. Matthew Storey has also found that Quakers in Mildenhall witnessed, or wrote, one another's wills when possible,[7] while Derek Plumb and Christopher Marsh have advanced our knowl-

---

[3]A. J. Fletcher and J. Stevenson, "A polarized society?" in Fletcher and Stevenson, eds., *Order and Disorder in Early Modern England* (Cambridge, 1985), p. 3.

[4]Keith Wrightson and David Levine, *Poverty and Piety in an English Village, Terling, 1525–1700* (New York and London, 1979), pp. 17–18, 176.

[5]Christopher Marsh, "In the name of God? Will-making and faith in early modern England," in G. H. Martin and Peter Spufford, eds., *The Records of the Nation* (Woodbridge, 1990), pp. 232, 233.

[6]Derek Plumb, "John Foxe and the later Lollards of the mid-Thames valley" (Ph.D. thesis, University of Cambridge, 1987), pp. 341–428. Christopher Marsh, "The Family of Love in English society, 1550–1630" (Ph.D. thesis, University of Cambridge, 1993), and The *Family of Love, 1550–1630* (Cambridge, 1994), pp. 190–96. Again, the appendix (pp. 267–87) lists witnesses, along with other important evidence of involvement with the Family. It demonstrates the importance of will-witnessing among co-religionists. See also Christopher Marsh, "The gravestone of Thomas Lawrence revisited," in Spufford, *The World of Rural Dissenters*, p. 216. Keith Wrightson, without discussing witnessing as such, incidentally provides a similar picture of the group of people round death-beds, and their function in *Whickham: The Making of an Industrial Society* (Oxford, 1991), pp. 288–94.

[7]Matthew Storey, "The Diary of Isaac Archer," chapter on "Nonconformity" (Ph.D. thesis, University of Cambridge, 1994). As he points out, Bill Stevenson, "The Economic and Social Status of Protestant sectaries in Huntingdonshire, Cambridgeshire and Bedfordshire, 1650–1725" (Ph.D.

edge of the spread and linkages of these radical nonconformists, by investigating these witnesses to wills. Marsh concludes: "The witness lists can...yield invaluable information, enabling the historian to establish local religious networks, albeit imperfectly. Witnesses were, as we have seen, generally chosen deliberately." We are therefore entitled to say that the act of witnessing a will generally indicated the family, social, religious, business, or "neighborly" significance of that witness to the testator, even though we must not forget that, very occasionally, an odd witness was merely a passer-by pressed into helping, and missing the opening of a game of ball.[8]

This team of historians (see note * supra) had established the significance of witnessing among religious groups. The team also needed to know, however, whether those affiliated to these same groups crossed the whole of society.

Derek Plumb and Bill Stevenson, investigating the economic levels of religious radical belief in the 1520s and the 1670s respectively, demonstrated conclusively, by tying adequately large groups of "known" late Lollards to their tax-levels in the 1524/5 subsidy returns, and persecuted Protestant dissenters to their entries in the appropriate Hearth Tax returns respectively,[9] that these radical groups crossed the whole taxable social and economic spectrum at both dates,[10] including the wage-laborers and the "exempt" at one end of the taxable spectrum, and those taxed on £10 and over, or 5 hearths and over at the other.[11] The

thesis, University of Cambridge, 1990) pp. 280 ff, especially case cited on p. 320, found that those divided on religious grounds could also act as witnesses, or even scribes, for their opponents. A witness list can therefore be taken as a possible pointer for religious affiliation, fit for further investigation, no more. But it is because adherents of the same sect so often acted as witnesses for each other, that the converse, their acceptance as desirable witnesses by non-sectarians, can also be used as evidence of community tolerance of these sects.

[8]Christopher Marsh, "In the name of God," *Roger Hopper missed his game*, p. 253.

[9]W. Stevenson, "The economic status," and chs. 8 and 9 in Spufford, The *World of Rural Dissenters*.

[10]Spufford, *The World of Rural Dissenters*, esp. Nesta Evans, ch. 7 and appendices.

[11]This is not a suitable place to discuss the validity of using the tax-bands of the 1524–25 Great Subsidy, and the numbers of hearths on which householders were taxed in the Hearth Taxes 150 years later in a comparative way, as Wrightson and Levine did throughout *Poverty and Piety*. Such a discussion forms an article in itself. I first attempted to justify, the procedure in my M.A. thesis, "Rural Cambridgeshire, 1520–1680" (M.A. with Distinction, University of Leicester, 1962), pp. 63–67, in which I connected individual taxation bands in 1524–25 with standard landholdings of a yardland or half a yardland, and also connected 100 probate inventories of the relevant Hearth Tax entries. This discussion mainly appeared in my *Contrasting Communities: English Villagers in the Sixteenth and Seventeenth Centuries* (Cambridge, 1974), pp. 34–45. Parts of the latter work also appear in "The significance of the Cambridgeshire Hearth Tax," *Proceedings of the Cambridgeshire Antiquarian Society* 55 (1962): 53–64. W. Stevenson, "The economic status," has greatly expanded our knowledge of the accuracy of the Hearth Taxes and has an article in preparation. But there is now a whole literature accumulating on the subject. The best guide to it is in Kevin Schürer and Tom Arkell, eds., *Surveying the People: The Interpretation and Use of Document Sources for the Study of Population in the Late Seventeenth Century* (Oxford, 1993). The work of

numbers of Plumb's Lollards in each taxation band were roughly proportionate to those of the taxable population at large. Thirty-eight per cent of Stevenson's post-Restoration dissenters were either exempt from tax on the grounds of poverty, or lived in cottages with only one hearth. The median value of the goods of five exempt householders in Huntingdonshire in 1674–79 was £5, the median value of the goods of thirty-eight paying on one hearth was £24, whereas the forty-three people paying on two hearths was £37. It may turn out that this is a lesser proportion of the very poor than in society at large.[12] On the other hand, it is far too sizeable a proportion to dismiss as in any way insignificant. This social spread of dissenters involved their meeting together and the cooperation of richer and poorer in sectarian groups: a significant number of licensed meeting places in the 1670s were in cottages with only one or two hearths.[13] Furthermore, radical dissent was frequently a family affair.[14]

Since various members of our team have shown that families had religious links that spread across the social and economic spectrum at widely separate dates, and that will-witnessing was a significant and important activity frequently demonstrating kinship, friendship, or business or religious links, we were therefore interested to know whether these kinship links were maintained in the vitally important matter of will-making in other families when they became economically polarized, even when they were not necessarily united by religious beliefs. We were also interested not only in kin continuing to cooperate across the economic spectrum, but also rich and poor members of the same community generally doing so. If witnesses were called to a death-bed from the different eco-

Arkell and Christopher Husbands is especially relevant. Keith Wrightson has recently used the Hearth Tax as a guide to the comparative wealth and poverty of communities in his superb *Whickham*, p. 157. However, possibly the best check on such a system is that Gregory King, in his work as a herald, used these contemporary records as a fast rule-of-thumb guide to possible gentility. Anyone with five hearths or more was a possible candidate. See Margaret Spufford. *Poverty Portrayed: Gregory King and the Parish of Eccleshall, Staffordshire* (Staffordshire Studies, 1995), and Philip Styles, "The heralds' visitation of Warwickshire, 1682–3," *Transactions of the Birmingham Archaeological Society* 71 (1953): 98–103. No one has done the further work connecting and refining the amounts assessed and acreage farmed in 1524–25, which my initial work in my M.A. thesis demanded. I hope that Dr. Richard Hoyle of the University of Central Lancashire has it under way.

[12]The proportion of Stevenson's dissenters compared with the distribution of hearths in society at large awaits a full analysis of the Hearth Tax. This is a major enterprise, currently being explored by the Department of History at The Roehampton Institute. For the purposes of this argument, the "very" poor have been taken to be those either exempt from the tax or paying on only one hearth. Stevenson, "Economic and Social Status," pp. 5–13. See, however, Tom Arkell, "The incidence of poverty in England in the later seventeenth century," *Social History* 12 (1987).

[13]See "Introduction" to Spufford, *The World of Rural Dissenters*, p. 21. See also chs. 1, 2, 5, 8, and 9 by their respective authors.

[14]Ibid., esp. Mrs. Nesta Evans, ch. 7 and appendices.

165

*Families, Will Witnesses, and Economic Structure* 383

nomic sections of village *strata*, and particularly if the poorer were called to witness the last testaments of the richer, the gulf in village societies caused by the economic polarization of land must have been at least partially bridged, since Marsh has demonstrated that witnesses were normally carefully chosen. It seemed to us that if these bridges existed at the village level, this would be relevant to the debate about social polarization in the seventeenth century and to the possible "cultural divide" opening up between the "chiefer sort" of inhabitant[15] and the landless laborer, especially in the great "champagne" corn areas of England.[16] We were encouraged to look at this by the individual examples of two families.

Samuel Pepys is well known as an omnivorous collector whose library demonstrates an interest in both "high" and "low" culture. He collected first folios of Shakespeare, but also collected almanacs, chapbooks, and ballads at the other end of the print spectrum. His omnivorous habits probably related in part to the way his family and kin spread across the whole social spectrum, from country gentleman to his father, who was a London tailor, and from holders of government office, to much humbler country cousins, with whom he kept up. Pepys had been educated at a grammar school in Huntingdonshire and had brothers at school at St. Paul's in London, but he was in touch with his less elevated relations. In 1661, he sent a fiddle to his "cousin," Perkin, the miller, whose windmill had blown down, and was now earning a living by fiddling at country feasts.[17] There is no reason to suppose he was behaving differently from other gentlemen in keeping up with his poor relations.

Neville Butler of Orwell in Cambridgeshire, who was born in 1609 and educated at the Perse School and Christ's College, sensibly married an heiress, and was able to buy the manor of Barnwell and move away from his own village. He served on the County Committee for Cambridgeshire, and was undoubtedly accepted as the county gentleman he was. His grandfather had been a yeoman who had managed to send his eldest son up to Gray's Inn to study law. However, although Neville Butler moved away, both socially and physically, from the place of his birth, he did not sever his links with his second cousins, who remained malsters, husbandmen, and even smallholders, any more than his father, educated at Gray's Inn, had done with his first cousins. On the contrary, in the middle generation the humbler cousins were used as rent-collectors by their more fortunate relations. Neville himself acted as co-witness to villagers'

[15]Henry French (Ph.D. Thesis, University of Cambridge, 1993) did not find the terminology "the middling sort" used in contemporary society in Essex and Suffolk.

[16]For one example, take Chippenham, where the engrosser had done his village worst by 1700, and society was split into "coqs de village" and landless village laborers (Spufford, *Contrasting Communities*, pp. 64–76 and 90–92)

[17]Margaret Spufford, *Small Books and Pleasant Histories* (London, 1981), pp. 50, 177.

384

wills with his second cousin. Even after he moved away to his new manor he travelled back across the county to witness his dying second cousin's will.[18] It is unlikely that Neville Butler was unaware of what his second cousins read, and what cheap print circulated in his own village where he had been brought up, or that he was ignorant either of all the oral stories and news that must also have been current there. He cooperated too often with his relations for such ignorance to be possible.

When such family ties spread right across the social and economic spectrum at both village and county level, and still meant something in realistic terms of human cooperation and contact, it is unreasonable to suppose a wide, or total, cultural divide. Samuel Pepys was not alone among the gentry in having an interest equally in first folios and chapbooks. In the same way the gentlewoman, Frances Wolfreston, who was a Staffordshire lady, began acquiring books after her marriage in 1631 and went on doing so until the 1660s. She died in 1677. She is known among bibliophiles for her Shakespearean folios and collection of drama, poetry, and criticism, but Tessa Watt has found that she had also made the earliest known collection of "small godly" and "small merry" books, probably purchased from chapmen at the same dates.[19] Her eclectic interests are a powerful argument for the generally well-informed cultural situation among the gentry, particularly since she was a gentlewoman living in the West Midlands at a considerable distance from London.

One of our team, Motoyasu Takahashi, therefore, took up the task of investigating both kin linkage and witnessing by members of different economic strata in village society, following Keith Wrightson's and David Levine's model for Terling, in two villages where we already knew society developed extremely differently: the "egalitarian" fen village of Willingham, where the traditional holdings of half a yardland or fifteen acres tended to break down over the period 1575–1720 and the number of smallholders rose by twenty-five per cent, and Chippenham, on the great barley-growing chalklands of Cambridgeshire, where engrossers had already done their worst by 1700 and village society was split into "coqs de village" and landless laborers.

It was obvious early in the study that we could only obtain partial results. In two isolated villages, where we already knew about the very different social structure and changes in land-distribution, we were bound to lose a high proportion of linkages through immigration and emigration. Moreover, although the parish register at Willingham was in a good state, and even had a family reconstitution based on it, the register at Chippenham was in appalling condition,

[18]Spufford, *Contrasting Communities*, appendix I, "The Butlers of Orwell," pp. 354–55, and 179–80, 197, 323–24, and illustration of Neville Butler witnessing his villager second-cousin's will, p. 198.

[19]Tessa Watt, *Cheap Print*, pp. 315–17.

having been deliberately mutilated. Very little can be done with it to support the wills. Dr. Takahashi had 470 surviving wills from Willingham, dated from 1515 to 1730, with a family reconstitution to back them, against 109 wills from Chippenham, for the period between 1520 and 1730. However, Willingham had 150 households taxed in 1674, and Chippenham only seventy-two, so using the crude measurement of the number of wills surviving over the period compared with the number of households, we have three survivors per household in Willingham against only two in Chippenham. If the difference is significant, it is probably accounted for by the high and ea1ly death rates in the fens. In Chippenham only fifteen testators mentioned their under-age children, while in Willingham over thirty per cent of wills referred to minor children. It appears that in Chippenham fewer wills were made, due to the lesser need to provide for the maintenance of young families.[20] The age at death may have been higher, although without a family reconstitution, which is impossible, we cannot be certain. We know that fen-ague was responsible for a very high early death rate among adult males in Willingham. We knew because of the mutilated register and the lower number of wills for each household that we would find only a very low proportion of families with the same surname in Chippenham. On the other hand, since we now knew that will-witnessing was most frequently a significant function, we were anxious to know if it continued when families spread across the social spectrum. It would be significant if even a small number of families and neighbors continued to cooperate with each other across the great economic and social gulf in landholding that opened up in Chippenham between the 1590s and 1712. If kin, and rich and poor, continued to cooperate, it would cast considerable doubt on the theories of a similar gulf developing between "elite" and "popular" culture, and the polarization of village society. We already felt the "gulf" in the spread of religious ideas between "rich" and "poor" had been bridged by the proven work by different members of our team. Therefore, despite the damaged parish registers, the lack of a family reconstitution, and the impossibility of establishing relationships accurately in consequence, the wills of Chippenham, where we were fully aware of dramatic changes in economy and land-distribution, and where, if anywhere, social polarization should have developed, presented us with a particularly important challenge.

Our team had produced evidence of co-religionists of different status witnessing each others' wills at various dates, and David Cressy has provided striking evidence of the way

> awareness of kinship by affinity and blood stretched much further than the immediate family of siblings and surviving parents to embrace a range of relations, un-

---

[20]Margaret Spufford, "Peasant inheritance customs and land distribution in Cambridgeshire from the sixteenth to the eighteenth centuries," in *Family and Inheritance: Rural Society in Western Europe, 1200–1800*, eds. Jack Goody, Joan Thirsk, and E. P. Thompson (Cambridge, 1976), pp. 169–72, esp. table 3.

386

cles and aunts, in-laws and cousins at various degrees of removal....We find distant relations, virtual strangers who lived on opposite sides of the Atlantic, seeking assistance and offering mutual support on the sole ground of acknowledgement of kin.[21]

Thus, a wine cooper who emigrated with his sisters to New England, but came
back to run a London tavern, kept up with news of his sisters and his new
nephews and nieces by contact through a Massachusetts yeoman who regularly
visited him on return trips. A young man from Connecticut confided business
trustingly to a "cousin," a yeoman of Warwickshire who was brother-in-law to
his father's wife's first husband. A Lancashire draper wrote to as important a
figure as Increase Mather about emigration in 1686, not as a co-religionist, but
on the apparently more important grounds of relationship between them, which
he considered close:

> These lines are to acquaint you how nearly my wife is related to you viz; her
> grandmother on the mother's side was Abigail Holt, and sister unto your mother,
> and by marriage changed her name to Isherwood, and by that husband had two
> daughters, whereof Ann the elder married John Holme of Bolton, and had by him
> three sons and one daughter, which daughter, through providence, is my wife.

Even more interestingly, he also claimed relationship on the grounds that his
wife's first husband shared a surname with Mather, and also came from the
same parish, so presumably he was some sort of kin. He did get an answer from
his newly-claimed "cousin." These "distant" kin relations were normally called
on in situations of extreme economic stress. Since no evidence of other cooperation between kin had been investigated, Dr. Takahashi took up the search.

Cressy claims that awareness of kin was much wider than is suggested by the
narrow awareness of the nuclear family usually found in wills. He even produced
some cases where, for lack of an obvious heir, or other reasons, a testator makes
us aware of his much wider kin-universe.[22] Although Cressy's findings and those
of Wrightson appear in conflict, they are not necessarily so at all. Wrightson
draws attention to the range of kin recognised beyond a nuclear family in Whickham in the seventeenth century and concludes:

> All in all, kinship recognition in wills seems to have been genealogically narrow
> and shallow; nevertheless it is clear that within that circumscribed range, testators
> could attach considerable significance to relationships with other households
> closely related by blood or marriage.[23]

These were what they called their "friends." Wrightson cites an extraordinary
will left by a childless widower in 1750, naming forty-seven nephews or great-

[21]David Cressy, *Coming Over: Migration and Communication between England and New England
in the Seventeenth Century* (Cambridge, 1987), pp. 287, 267–68, 270, 273.

[22]David Cressy, "Kinship and kin interaction in early modern England," *Past and Present* 113
(1986): pp. 41, 42–43, 46–47, 50, 61, 63–65.

[23]Wrightson, *Whickham*, pp. 329–39.

nephews and nieces, and fourteen cousins and/or their children; but he concludes that "it was utterly untypical."[24] So it was atypical for a will; Cressy would almost certainly argue that it probably provides a much more realistic glimpse into the realities of the kin-universe in which many people moved, than does the normal will, which performs the specific function of transmitting property within the nuclear family. Only if there were no obvious heirs does the more distant web of relationship become apparent in a will.

In view of this debate on social polarization and its importance not only for social history, but also for the spread of religious belief, Dr. Takahashi embarked on his exploration of the kinship network and network of "friends" and possibly co-religionists, revealed in the wills for the fen village of Willingham from 1515–1730, which can be matched with family reconstitution forms in 253 cases.[25] The matching exercise showed that wills regularly, as one might expect, lead the reader to underestimate the number of young children a family had had, since the testator naturally omits children who did not survive until his or her death (Figure 1). We thought it possible that Willingham might provide a better opportunity than normal to study kinship networks, since no less than thirty-three per cent of the testators had one or more children under age, and eighteen per cent more were people without obvious heirs, bachelors, spinsters, or widows. This was partly because the parish was badly affected by fen-ague, and life expectancy for adult men was abnormally low. There was, therefore, more chance of atypical wills being left by people without obvious heirs. Indeed, a substantial number of them were left by young men who had pregnant wives at the time of their deaths. The wills of Willingham are also a good subject for study, because they provide an excellent social cross-section. Examination of the occupational status of will-makers in the whole diocese of Ely in the six-teenth and seventeenth centuries shows that the habit of will-making spread among "ordinary people" there from the second half of Elizabeth's reign.[26] By the 1620s and 1630s as many as twenty-two per cent of all wills proved in the Ely Consistory Court were those of self-styled laborers. Willingham followed this general fashion.

[24]Ibid., p. 330 and n. 122.

[25]The reconstitution was carried out by Miss Glynis Reynolds.

[26]For this spread, see Motoyasu Takahashi, "The number of wills proved in the sixteenth and seventeenth centuries. Graphs, with tables and commentary," in G. H. Martin and Peter Spufford, eds., *The Records of the Nation* (Woodbridge, 1990), pp. 209–11. The diocese of Ely was possibly unusual in having such a high proportion of wills made by the lower social groups, but this was to our advantage. Chippenham, unfortunately, lies in the Diocese of Norwich. The low proportion of wills made there may reflect either different diocesan habits or community tradition. It is most likely to reflect a lesser need to provide for underage heirs, however, since life expectancy there was more normal for the seventeenth century among adult males than in the Fens.

388

Dr. Takahashi continued to examine relationships and will-witnessing in a similar way in the gentry-dominated engrossing village of Chippenham, on the chalk near Newmarket. Here relationships could not be established with anything like the same precision. However, it was important to continue the study onwards to make a comparison, because the economic history of the place and its social structure were completely contrasted.[27] Since a dramatic economic divide opened up in Chippenham between the 1590s and the early eighteenth century, it seemed particularly relevant to see if the same divide appeared in social relationships.

The wills of Willingham are likely to have had some co-religionists as witnesses, since Willingham parsonage was the meeting-place of a conventicle at the end of Mary's reign, and also probably had members of the Family of Love.[28] Its non-conforming minister in 1662, Nathanial Bradshaw, nursed a flourishing congregation that competed with Quakers. We were particularly interested to discover whether Willingham families and "neighbors" spread across the social and economic structure of the village, and whether poorer, and richer, kin continued to cooperate with each other.

Before this paper was conceived Wrightson had examined kinship networks and cooperation between kin in Terling in Essex. He has completed a similar study in Whickham, County Durham.[29] We owe a great deal to his work. Wrightson, like Professor Spufford in her earlier work, divided the hearth tax payers into four groups in rural Terling, although he divided them into five groups in industrial Whickham.[30] The direct comparisons from rural Willingham and Chippenham must be made with rural Terling. The 122 households of Terling seemed to divide up into groups near to the norm for the 21,000 households in Essex analyzed by Tom Arkell, and cited by Wrightson.[31] Essex does, however, seem to differ quite markedly from the parts of five other counties also analyzed by Arkell. If the households of Willingham are divided into the same four groups as at Terling, it is clear that there were fewer big houses than at Terling, because of the lack of resident gentry or very substantial yeomen. At the other end of the spectrum, Willingham also had fewer houses whose occupants either paid

[27]See below, pp. 395-99.

[28]Spufford, *Contrasting Communities*, pp. 245–48, 293, 302–04. Marsh, *The Family of Love*.

[29]Keith Wrightson, "Kinship in an English village: Terling, Essex, 1500–1700," in Richard M. Smith, ed., *Land, Kinship and Life-cycle* (Cambridge, 1984), pp. 313–32, and Wrightson, *Whickham*, pp 153–65.

[30]See n. 12 above for a brief discussion of the methodology here.

[31]Wrightson, *Whickham*, p. 157.

on one hearth or were exempted from payment on account of their "smallness of estate."

The economic and social difference between fen Willingham and the chalk parish of Chippenham, which comes up clearly from its estate surveys and maps as a paradise for engrossers, is clearly demonstrated also in the Hearth Tax of 1674 (Table 1). The seventy-two households of Chippenham included seven per cent of houses with six hearths and over, the occupiers of which, according to Gregory King's criteria, might have laid claim to gentle status. They were led by Chippenham Hall itself with its thirty-four hearths. More to our purpose, it had twenty-six per cent of householders living in houses with three to five hearths, as against fourteen per cent in Willingham.[32] The most striking difference is that there were only eighteen per cent of the moderately comfortable with only two hearths, in Chippenham, against forty-six per cent in Willingham, where such people prospered exceedingly. There were also, of course, more landless laborers, and no less than a quarter of Chippenham householders in 1674 were exempt from the tax on the grounds of poverty, against one seventh (fifteen per cent) in Willingham. Chippenham seems to have had a social structure much more like that of Terling, where we do not know a great deal about the economic distribution of land and the changes in land distribution.

Willingham had both a lower proportion of large houses and a lower proportion of small and exempt houses than any of the sections of six counties analyzed by Arkell. Willingham, therefore, had a much narrower range of house size, and correspondingly its householders were heavily concentrated in the ranks of small yeoman and husbandmen. This result obtained from the Hearth Tax is exactly what the historian would expect from its very thorough set of land surveys.[33] Industrial Whickham, by contrast, had a vastly higher proportion of exempt householders and occupants of one hearth houses than either Terling or Willingham, or indeed any rural areas, towns, or other industrial areas analyzed by Arkell.[34]

Dr. Takahashi has established kin linkage at Willingham from family reconstitution of the parish registers, and from wills and a wide variety of other sources. Both minima of "certain" kin and maxima of "probable" kin have been

[32]The number of taxpayers in houses with three to five hearths argues there were householders who had lost land in the engrossing process living on in houses that had once reflected yeoman status. In the same way, the number of "husbandmen" with two hearths reflects the earlier number of half yardlanders and yardlanders with 15–40 acres who had been forced off the land between 1598 and 1636. They had obviously been able to build before the poor harvests and engrossing boom hit them (Spufford, *Contrasting Communities*, pp. 82–84, 90–92).

[33]Ibid., pp. 134–51, where these surveys are fully described and analyzed.

[34]The only rural community with a higher proportion of exempt householders than any other on Wrightson's table so far known is Eccleshall in Staffordshire, which had 53% (Spufford, *Poverty Portrayed: Gregory King and the Parish of Eccleshall, Staffordshire* (1995), Table 1).

established, as at Terling (Table 2). "Certain" kin were those whose relationship could be proved from the family reconstitution forms. The relationship of "probable" kin was based on groups of identical surnames, and on contextual evidence, where relationship to a named person was stated in a will, but there were two or more persons of that name in the family reconstitution forms. Although the proportion of "certain" kin at Willingham was slightly lower than at Terling, the proportion of "probable" kin was considerably higher, suggesting a society substantially less mobile than at Terling. However, the proportion of householders at Whickham "certainly" related to other householders in the parish was under fourteen per cent, suggesting a society greatly more mobile even than at Terling. We know that there was a great deal of immigration into the fen villages, which could support families on much less land, because of the rich resources of the fen commons during the population rise of the sixteenth and seventeenth centuries.[35]

At Terling, Wrightson specifically looked at first order kinship links between households; that is, those in which one member of the married couple who headed the household (or the single head of a household) was son, daughter, father, mother, brother, or sister to one member of the married couple or single head of another household in the parish. Dr. Takahashi carried out a similar exercise at Willingham (Table 3).

The proportion of "close" kin at Willingham, like that of "certain" kin, was considerably lower than at Terling (Table 4). These "close kin" were presumably the old established families, not the incomers. However, those who did have "close" kin within the village had more of them. When the same exercise was carried out for all "certain" kin and all "probable" kin, it became apparent that the density of "probable" kin at Willingham was much greater than at Terling, which again suggests a lower overall mobility of population at Willingham than Terling, despite the known influx of newcomers to Willingham.

For Terling this exercise was only carried out at one instant in time, that of the hearth taxes, but for Willingham Dr. Takahashi was able to carry out the same operation at four other points of time, not only from the Great Subsidy of 1524/5, but also in 1575, 1603, and the 1720s, because an abnormally good series of field books and a map survive from these years as bases to work from (Table 5). For these purposes, householders with more than six hearths were taken as equivalent to "gentlemen" or to farmers of over fifty acres of arable, or those assessed on £10 or over in the Great Subsidy.[36] Householders with three to five hearths were taken as equivalent to farmers of half yardlands of arable, or assessed at between £5 and £10 in the Great Subsidy. In this village they were the prosperous backbone of society, the yeomanry, although on the

[35]Spufford, *Contrasting Communities*, pp. 16–22 and map 5, p. 17.

[36]For the rationale of this passage, see n. 12 above.

chalk uplands of Cambridgeshire, like the inhabitants of Chippenham, a half yardland holder was a negligible man, likely to be in trouble in the price rise and the bad harvests of the 1590s. Households with two hearths were taken as equivalent to farmers of smaller holdings, while householders either paying on one hearth or exempt from payment were taken as equivalent to the landless in the field books, or those assessed on wages in the Great Subsidy. Nominal linkage provided the base for these near equivalences.

The number of householders at different times in each of these categories in the field books and on the map were compared with the hearth tax returns. These field books and the map omit sub-tenants, perhaps as many as thirty of them in the case of the field books of the 1718/20s. It is, nevertheless, apparent that as the population grew the number of farmers of complete arable half-yard-lands diminished, and the number of farmers of smaller arable holdings increased dramatically.

We already knew that the community of Willingham formed, not a special case, but the sort of different social and economic picture to be found in fen (and forest) landscapes, with their additional resources of common and by-employments. The population rise at the edge of the Ouse was one of the steepest in the old county of Cambridgeshire between 1524 and the Hearth Taxes: immigration heavily exceeded emigration there.

We have some indication of the possible origins, and certainly the current social universe, of these incomers from the mentions of other places in the wills right through from 1518 to the 1720s (Figure 2). Willingham looked south to the "uplands," from the references to kin and property mentioned in the wills all through the period. The barrier formed by the river Ouse was emphasized by the few scattered references to the north of it. South of Willingham, the market town of Cambridge itself, less than ten miles away, formed the boundary. There was a dense group of references to parishes on the clays, as far as eight miles away to the west, in which population density in general tended to drop during the period. This cluster provides a possible clue to the origins of incomers. All movement took place within a ten-mile radius of Willingham, with the exception of three atypical people from the fen village of Isleham, from Royston, the next market town south of Cambridge, and from Bassingbourn on the chalk, one parish outside Royston. There were also the usual infrequent references to London.

Basic agricultural holdings broke down, under the pressure of this influx of people, and the original twenty-eight half-yardlands of 1575 in Willingham were, by the 1720s, divided up among no less than seventy-six tenants. In other Cambridgeshire villages, the rising numbers of landless was an obvious phenomenon: in Willingham, the most striking change was the huge rise in the seventeenth century in both the numbers and proportion of those who were more than cottagers, but still held less than a half-yardland, or between two and sixteen acres.

This change in the numbers of those with smallholdings, which would have been under subsistence level in the uplands, from thirty-seven per cent of the community in 1603 to fifty-seven per cent in the 1720s, was reflected in the Hearth Taxes. The whole group of parishes along the Ouse had a uniformly lower proportion of houses taxed on one hearth (or exempt) than in the uplands, and an "abnormally" high proportion of the middlingly prosperous, in village terms, paying tax on two hearths. This is not to say economic polarization did not exist in Willingham. It did, as our tables show. What they do not show, and cannot show, is the probably abnormally large group of the really poor sub-tenants who had no common rights and were therefore without visible means of subsistence. We have no information about them outside the hearth taxes, except that from scattered wills that demonstrate real poverty in their lack of material goods to bequeath.[37]

The effect of these changes over time on kin linkage is indicated in Table 6. It appears that a slightly higher proportion of tenants were related to each other in 1603 than in 1575, which suggests a relatively static population over the intervening generation. By contrast, in the course of the seventeenth century when the population rose substantially in this parish, the number of interrelated tenants dropped considerably. The hearth tax evidence fits with this pattern and suggests that the growing population of Willingham, even if less mobile than in Essex or Whickham, had still become more mobile through its increase, so that the tenants of Willingham had become more likely to have kin outside the village and less likely to have them within.

When the analysis is limited to first order kin and the number of kin-links between tenants is counted and the kinship density calculated, this pattern of kinship decline within the village in the course of the seventeenth century is further emphasized (Table 7).

Once again the hearth tax evidence fits into the pattern. All this is, of course, only the background to the investigation of whether those whose relations did live within the village had kin there whose landholding and house size were at all different from their own, and, if so, how much they cooperated.

Despite the immigration, all though our period, at least a quarter of the heads of household were recognizably related. The proportion of these related heads of household with kinship links crossing the economic spectrum was always at least half throughout the whole period from 1575 to the 1720s. The household heads who were recognizably related to members of different social groups therefore always equalled, if they did not substantially exceed, those who were only related to heads of household in similar economic circumstances (Table 8).

[37]Spufford, *Contrasting Communities*, pp. 143–44.

175

Because the physical layout of the village in itself reflected the economic divisions that existed in Willingham society it has also been possible for Dr. Takahashi to present some of the information on which Table 8 is based in the form of maps (Figures 3, 4 and 5). They are all based on the 1603 estate map and indicate the amount of land associated with each messuage. This is the first time that kinship and social relationships have been mapped together with economic information on the landholding of the parties. The village formed an inverted "U" shape, with the church at the closed end of the "U," and the fen beyond it, to the north. The new school, to which even some landless villagers contributed in 1593, was in a room over the church porch. The Green and its pond lay to the east. The houses of the most prosperous, the yardlanders and half-yardlanders lay round the "U." The cottages of the landless, however, including that of the schoolmaster and his three-acre smallholding, were built either infilling on the Green, on the two roads out towards the fen, or in a "poor" area at the east end of the "U."

The significant point is that members of these families continued to cooperate across any economic categories we impose on them. For example, they witnessed each other's wills, and acted as executors, or supervised the execution of wills of family members from different social groups. This cooperation did not only consist in the most prosperous members witnessing the wills, and acting for, their poorer relatives. The reverse procedure also happened, although it happened much less often. Yet lesser kin were also called to the deathbeds of their more prosperous relations.

This family co-operation was only part of a general pattern of poorer and richer villagers acting for each other under such circumstances. Most wills were not usable for these purposes, since only for heads of households can a firm economic category be determined. Therefore, in only seventy-five of the wills surviving from Willingham between 1575 and 1640 can a related head of household be identified as a witness. Of these thirty-nine per cent were of the same economic status as the testator, but sixty-one per cent were of a different economic status. Table 9 shows the way in which poorer and richer heads of household acted for each other as will witnesses. Mapping patterns of witnessing from the material on which Table 9 is based, where it has been possible to identify the houses of both testator and witness, shows visually how visits to act as a witness were made (Figures 6 and 7). The poverty of the houses at the southeast end of the "U" did not prevent the visits of wealthier neighbors. We should remember that, even in a relatively unpolarized village, there was an enormous economic distinction between a half-yardland holder (Group II) and a landless man (Group IV) in Willingham.[38] It was not only kin but neighbors who joined

[38]Spelled out in detail in ibid., ch. 5.

together across very substantial economic divides in the intimate circumstances of death and inheritance.

We can illustrate family cooperation to some extent by a brief history of the Biddall family.[39] William Biddall, senior, who died in 1586, leaving a will, was typical of the prosperous half-yardland holders. His widow, Cecily, did not die until 1595, and then left an enormously useful will, as widows tended to, showing her interest in her many grandchildren. William and Cecily had four sons and a daughter; the latter very suitably married another half-yardland holder. The eldest son may already have been established when his father died: some of his children were named in his father's will, as well as his mother's. Another son inherited the half-yardland. The other sons were set up with fragments of land, two-and-a-half acres or cash, and so joined the ranks of those with more than a cottage, who depended, however, on fen common. The most interesting bequest was one of the very few examples from the early modern period that illustrates care for someone in some way handicapped. William Biddall, junior, was established by his father with cash, food for life, and space in the haybarn to make a shop.[40] He was a shoemaker, and he did well. When he died unmarried, also leaving a will in 1593, he left numerous small cash bequests to all his nephews, nieces, and small cousins. He and two of his brothers cooperated, because they ran a common sheep-flock. Most significantly, perhaps, he had become a small-scale money lender and remitted debts owed to him by an older brother and by another William Biddall "the weaver." The relationship of the two Williams, one a handicapped shoemaker living at home, the other another small-scale artisan, cannot be established. The latter may have been a cousin of old William Biddall or his wife Cecily. He had apprenticed his own son to Robert Ward, another weaver and a landless man, who died in 1589 leaving not only the tools of his trade back to William Biddall the weaver, but also listing debts owed to him by eight men, including a half-yardland holder.

William Biddall the weaver was not the only "poor relation" of this family that was "very prosperous" in fenland terms. Our crippled shoemaker left 10/- to be shared by the children of John Biddall "the soldier," and 6/8 to his "kin" Christopher Biddall. And on the outer edge of this family group, lay the really poor, like Roger Biddall, the landless man with three sons who died in 1589, leaving one of his sons one sheet and 3/-. The whole Biddall family, which was so helpfully prolix in its will-making despite the poverty of some of its members,

[39]Ibid., pp. 140–43.

[40]No other son, in all the thousands of wills I have read, was left food for life from his inheriting brother, rather than a sum to establish himself independently. It seems reasonable to assume that independence was impossible for him. The only other case I know from this social level is of a girl with cerebral palsy in the 1690s, who was left the income from £20 as provision, in a complex set of arrangements (Spufford, *Poverty Portrayed,* pp. 66–67).

provides a concrete example of connection among kin that stretched across the economic spectrum, and therefore helpfully illustrates the spectrum for social groups II to IV in Table 8. On the basis of this evidence we concluded that seventeenth-century village society in the fens was not socially polarized, even when it was economically divided.

Few families in Willingham in 1674 were spread as far across the economic spectrum as the Butler family of Orwell. Yet it was not at all uncommon for Willingham families to include both prosperous yeomen holding a half-yardland and the landless, although as broad a spread as that of the Butlers from gentlemen to landless laborers was unknown. This very wide economic gulf was bridged by kinship. It is not, in this social environment, surprising to find non-kin heads of household of very different economic circumstances also witnessing each others' wills. The Willingham community was a surprisingly homogenous social, if not economic, whole, because the very diverse members of it acted in cooperation. It therefore looks as if translating the economic gulf into a rigid social cleavage is purely a historians' construct. If, as historians we have been imposing our own interpretations on the past, in ignorance of social communications of this kind, we have falsified the past rather than interpreted it.

For comparison Dr. Takahashi made a similar examination of circumstances in the contrasting village of Chippenham, which, like Terling, was becoming much more economically polarized than Willingham in the course of the seventeenth century. The distribution of Chippenham houses with different numbers of hearths clearly points at the gap that had opened between rich and poor villagers, unlike the continuum from rich to poor found in the fens.[41]

Chippenham also had its numerous nonconformists, although we would not suppose so from the Compton Census, which only records two of them.[42] This is because the incumbent who made the return, Isaac Archer, whose *Diary* we now have, was so sympathetically disposed to nonconformity that he found it difficult to subscribe in 1662 himself.[43] He also himself attended nonconformist meetings within the parish and baptized a Quaker baby. None of this could be deduced from the Compton Census. Unfortunately for the historian, even within his own *Diary*, Archer scrupulously omitted the names of his parishioners. Only the name of John Tetsal, a yeoman who on principle failed to pay his tithes, is deducible from the evidence. Archer was perennially hard up and needed his tithes, despite the seven hearths in the draughty vicarage in which his children

---

[41]See Table 1. For details of economic polarization at Chippenham, see Spufford, *Contrasting Communities*, ch. 3, pp. 65 ff.

[42]Anne Whiteman, ed., *The Compton Census of 1676: A Critical Edition* (Records of Social and Economic History, ns 10 [Oxford, 1986], p. 231).

[43]Matthew Storey, ed., *The Diaries of Isaac Archer and William Coe* (Suffolk Record Society, 36 [1994]), and idem, "The Diary," chapter on Nonconformity.

died so often, so he presented John Tetsal and his wife as dissenters. We have no idea how many more there were: we do know there were both Quakers and Congregationalists there, so it is reasonable to suppose both rich and poor assembled at meetings and witnessed each other's wills, just as they did elsewhere, although compared to Willingham, the number of surviving wills is many fewer.

As we were aware from the beginning, the shortage of information in the mutilated parish registers makes it difficult to identify definite kin relationships.[44] The results in Table 10 must necessarily be crude. There are still some intriguing findings. Firstly, almost one-half of the householders appearing in the 1544 survey and the 1560 rental were probably related to each other. In the 1674 Hearth Tax return, despite the polarization of landholding that had largely taken place, thirty-five out of seventy-two household heads, still nearly half, were probably related. Furthermore, well over half of these thirty-five were plurally related. The data from the 1712 map suggest that the kin relationship links were only slightly looser.

The same economic categories of landholding cannot be transposed wholesale from Willingham in the fens to Chippenham on the chalk. A half-yardlander in Willingham, with his resources of fen common, was a prosperous man, as was William Biddall.[45] He was the cream of the village community. However, a tenant of fifteen acres in Chippenham with no such resources was in such a precarious position that his holding was likely to have been mortgaged and squeezed out by the disastrous harvests of the 1590s.[46] Such holdings mainly disappeared between 1598 and 1636, and only one tenant of a single one of these holdings was left, a reminder of a pre-engrossing past on the map of 1712. We therefore have to adjust our categories accordingly. Group I laid claim to gentry status with freehold or copyhold of fifty acres or more in Willingham and 290 acres or more in Chippenham. Group II "yeomen" were tenants of sixteen acres or more of arable, plus marsh and fen grazing in Willingham and forty acres or more in Chippenham. Group III "husbandmen" were tenants of only three to fourteen acres in Willingham, thirteen to thirty-seven acres in Chippenham. The laborers made up Group IV whether they were absolutely landless or tenants of tiny holdings. Those exempt from the Hearth Tax almost certainly were landless anywhere, except that they had far more chance of mak-

[44]See above, p. 385.

[45]See above, p 394. Spufford, *Contrasting Communities*, pp. 43–44, 139–42, 144.

[46]Ibid., pp. 66–70.

[47]We have actual surveyors' acreages for 1575 and the 1720s in Willingham, 1544 and 1712 in Chippenham. We have chosen to use customary acreages of the earlier/later dates, because error is always possible adjusting from customary to statutory acres on a large scale. Furthermore, I have used the acreages for Chippenham in my earlier publication, *A Cambridgeshire Community, Chippenham from Settlement to Enclosure*, Dept. of English Local History, Occasional Papers, First

ing a living in the fens, where they might have fen fishing, fowling, and common rights at their disposal (Table 11).[47]

The apparent increase in numbers between the 1560 rental and the 1674 Hearth Tax return does not represent an increase in the size of the Chippenham community, since the 1544 survey and the 1560 rental naturally ignores sub-tenants and those without land. However, the village did genuinely become smaller between the 1674 Hearth Tax return and 1712, when the very full and beautiful estate map was made, because emparking had taken place meanwhile, and more than half the village had been physically moved.[48]

We can only consider proven and highly probable individual kinship links in different economic categories in the 1674 Hearth Tax return (Table 12), since the 1544 survey and the 1560 rental did not include the landless. Although the numbers are small it is interesting to note that much more prosperous family members commonly existed in the same parish as their poorer relations. The economic polarization that had largely taken place was as much *within* families as between families. Case-studies demonstrate this.

In 1636, the remarkable detailed survey of Chippenham made for its new lay lords in 1544 had been annotated. From these incomplete annotations, it is possible to work out that engrossing, by substantial tenants as well as the lord of the manor, was then in full swing, and had been going on for some considerable time. Most notably, one Thomas Dillamore had acquired the holdings of fifteen other tenants, as well as his own. From his will, made in 1638, it was apparent that he was a substantial man indeed, able to set up no less than seven sons with land or mortgages due to fall in, in several parishes,[49] not all of which were immediately adjacent.

It is not surprising that we read in the 1674 hearth tax return for Chippenham of a "Mr." Dillamore with four hearths (see Tables 11 and 12). We also read of a "Thomas Dillamore" also with four hearths, in the same social group, but without the term of respect, and a "John Dillamore" with three hearths. The descendants of Thomas Dillamore had done well. As another up-and-coming yeoman, Robert Furze of Devonshire, who had been a contemporary of the sixteenth-century Thomas Dillamore's, wrote with pride of his ancestors that "from little acorns great oaks do grow." But in some ways the most interesting point about this family from our present point of view is that on the list of those "discharged by legall Certificates" from paying the tax on a single hearth

---

Series, no. 20 (Leicester, 1965), Tables IV and VI, pp. 40 and 48, because they are more clearly set out in terms of acreages rather than yardlands. Dr. Takahashi unfortunately analysed the kinship links of the householders appearing in the 1712 map as if the same landed categories could be applied in Chippenham as in Willingham.

[48]Spufford, *A Cambridgeshire Community*, pp. 46–48.

[49]Ibid., ch. 3, pp. 76, 81, 84 (Thomas Dillamore), and pp. 81–87.

398

was Robert Dillamore (Class IV). We cannot, in the state of the register, know how he was related to the three prospering descendants who also bore the same name; but he will have been another descendant of the successful yeoman, Thomas, and he will have been kin. We are entitled to think here of another possible example such as that of Neville Butler and his cousins.[50]

The case of the Kents and the Tebbutts is an absolutely certain one. Both Tebbutts and Kents had prospered in pre-Civil War Chippenham: Robert Tebbutt held ninety-six acres of leasehold in 1636, and had acquired part of the farm of the glebe, as well as substantial copyhold land, by his death in 1668.[51] His widow, the extremely able Phillippa, paid tax on five hearths in 1674, and his son, another Robert, lived in very fine style, with a closet with books, a tankard, and wine cups off his bedroom. This comfort he owed, as he stated in his own will, to the efficiency of his mother, who had paid off his father's debts without selling land, as she had been instructed in her husband's will. The capable Phillippa Tebbutt had been born a Kent. Her son Robert, when he had finished enjoying his wine, left £15 in 1682 between John and Joseph Kent, sons of "my uncle," Christopher Kent.[52] A John Kent had held over eighty-three acres of copyhold long ago, in 1636, and had then been only a little less prosperous than Robert Tebbutt.[53] But the Kents did not continue to rise economically after that. There were six of them in the 1674 Hearth Tax, four paying on one hearth apiece, including two Christopher Kents and one Widow Kent. But two more were exempt from paying tax on their single hearths on the grounds of poverty. One of the widows left only £9 worth of meager moveables. Christopher Kent may by now have been a poor relation, but he still had witnessed his brother-in-law's will in 1668,[54] despite the economic gulf that had developed between Tebbutts and Kents in the later seventeenth century. It is also interesting that the same Christopher Kent was called to witness the will of prosperous John Dillamore of the three hearth-house in 1679,[55] and that when he himself died, properly styled only as "husbandman" in the 1680s,[56] the equally prosperous

---

[50]See above, pp. 383–84.

[51]Spufford, *Contrasting Communities*, pp. 72, 74–75, 80, 89–90, for the Tebbutts, including the powerful Phillippa, née Kent.

[52]Bury St. Edmunds R.O., IC500/1/136/82.

[53]Spufford, *Contrasting Communities*, pp. 69, 84 (Table 3) for John Kent. Inventory of Mary Kent, widow, 1680, p. 65.

[54]Bury St. Edmunds R.O., IC500/1/120/54.

[55]Bury St. Edmunds R.O., IC500/1/133/29.

[56]Bury St. Edmunds R.O., IC500/1/139/78.

John Cheesewright, whose family also had a long yeoman history, came to witness his will. The dramatic economic polarization of Chippenham, where six of the heads of households were related to as many as four others (Table 10) does not seem to have divided it socially in the same way, at all, even though the number of kin we could identify were tiny, because of the state of the register.

When we looked for cases of household heads witnessing wills, we found only twenty-three wills in which a witness could be found who was a head of household whose economic status could be identified (Table 13).

In both the periods from the 1540s to the 1590s, and after the Commonwealth, poorer relations witnessed the wills of their richer relations. It is particularly significant that this continued to happen after the great economic gulf had developed between yeomen and their agricultural laborer relations at Chippenham where land distribution was typical of the chalk uplands. It is also significant that poorer kin and villagers from the laboring section of village society were summoned to the deathbeds of their more prosperous relations and neighbors, as well as the other way round. Relationship continued to matter. Significant friendships and "neighborliness" could, and did, survive and transcend economic polarization.

We think the width of family-spread across the economic spectrum of the seventeenth century should be reconsidered, as one of the major factors in the debate for, and against, polarization within village society, and indeed for and against the total divorce of the minor gentry, which had sprung from yeomen origins in village society. But such a consideration will only be useful if it takes into account the size of landholdings. Too often recently, the economic base of prosperity in landholding, and therefore of the basis of social dominance, has been lost sight of by social historians. Back in the 1970s, historians needed to expand the social history of rural society from its economic base. Now it is time to redress the balance, and root our social history back in its economic foundations. But, as Dr. Takahashi's work shows, social and family relationships could transcend deep economic divisions.[57]

---

[57]In 1967 my husband wrote a powerful plea for the importance of lateral genealogy (Peter Spufford, "Genealogy and the historian," *Genealogists' Magazine* 15 [1967]: 431–47.) It is unfortunate that the family reconstitution forms used in parish reconstitutions by the Cambridge Group for the History of Population and Social Structure do not allow for any lateral relationships, and therefore do not encourage awareness of them.

Table 1. Taxpayers divided into economic groups

| | Industrial Whickham 1666 | Rural Essex 1669/70 | Rural Terling 1671 | Rural Chippenham 1674 | Rural Willingham 1666 | Rural Willingham 1674 |
|---|---|---|---|---|---|---|
| I 6 hearths & over | 10(3%) | 8% | 10(8%) | 5(7%) | 1(1%) | 2(1%) |
| II 3-5 hearths | 24(7%) | 25% | 29(24%) | 19(26%) | 21(14%) | 28(19%) |
| III 2 hearths (inc. exempt) | 42(11%) | 19% | 21(17%) | 13(18%) | 68(46%) | 61(41%) |
| IV 1 hearth (inc. exempt) | 291(79%) | 48% | 62(51%) | 35(49%) | 59(40%) | 59(39%) |
| Total taxpayers | 367 | 20,897 | 122 | 72 | 149 | 150 |
| Of which exempt | 79% | 34% | 33% | 17(23%) | — | 23(15%) |

Table 2. Certain and probable kin

| | Terling 1671 | | Chippenham 1674 | Willingham 1666 | | Willingham 1674 | |
|---|---|---|---|---|---|---|---|
| | Min. (certain kin) | Max. (probable kin) | (probable kin) | Min. (certain kin) | Max. (probable kin) | Min. (certain kin) | Max. (probable kin) |
| Recognizably related to other house-holders | 48(39%) | 64(52%) | 35(49%) | 53(36%) | 101(68%) | 36(24%) | 104(69%) |
| Total house-holders | 122 | | 72 | 149 | | 150 | |

Table 3. Recognizable first-order kinship links

| | Terling 1671 (%) | Willingham 1666 (%) | Willingham 1674 (%) |
|---|---|---|---|
| Related to "head" of one other household | 26 | 10 | 11 |
| Of two other households | 7 | 6 | 5 |
| Of three or more other households | | 8 | 3 |
| Total closely related to other households | 33 | 25 | 19 |
| Total households | 122 | 149 | 150 |

Table 4. Kinship links: all recognizable links

| | Terling 1671 | | Willingham 1666 | | Willingham 1674 | |
|---|---|---|---|---|---|---|
| | Min. (certain kin) | Max. (probable kin) | Min. (certain kin) | Max. (probable kin) | Min. (certain kin) | Max. (probable kin) |
| Related to 1 other | 32(26%) | 39(32%) | 22(15%) | 34(23%) | 18(12%) | 34(23%) |
| Related to 2 others | 10(8%) | 16(13%) | 12(8%) | 17(11%) | 7(5%) | 24(16%) |
| Related to 3 others | 4(3%) | 6(5%) | 5(3%) | 16(11%) | 6(4%) | 15(10%) |
| Related to 4 others | 2(2%) | 3(3%) | 14(9%) | 15(10%) | 5(3%) | 6(4%) |
| Related to 5 or more others | | | | 19(13%) | | 25(16%) |
| Total related | 48(39%) | 64(53%) | 53(36%) | 101(68%) | 36(24%) | 104(69%) |
| | 122 | | 149 | | 150 | |

Table 5. Householders at Willingham

| | | 1575 Field Book | 1603 Map | 1718/20s Field Books | 1666 Hearth Tax | |
|---|---|---|---|---|---|---|
| I | Over 50 acres | 1(1%) | 1(1%) | 2(2%) | 1(1%) | 6 hearths and over |
| II | Half yardland | 31(43%) | 29(34%) | 23(19%) | 21(14%) | 3-5 hearths |
| III | Smallholders | 23(32%) | 31(37%) | 69(57%) | 68(46%) | 2 hearths |
| IV | Landless | 18(25%) | 23(28%) | 27(22%) | 59(40%) | 1 hearth |
| | total tenants or taxpayers | 73 | 84 | 121 | 149 | |

Table 6. Recognizable kin linkage in Willingham

| | 1575 Field Books | | 1603 Map | | 1718/20s Field Books | | Equivalents in 1666 Hearth Tax | |
|---|---|---|---|---|---|---|---|---|
| | Min. (certain kin) | Max. (probable kin) | Min. (certain kin) | Max. (probable kin) | Min. (certain kin) | Max. (probable kin) | Min. (certain kin) | Max. (probable kin) |
| Related to other tenants | 32(44%) | 49(67%) | 51(61%) | 72(86%) | 42(35%) | 71(59%) | 53(36%) | 101(68%) |
| Total tenants | 73 | | 84 | | 121 | | 149 | |

Table 7. Recognizable first order kinship links at Willingham

|  | 1575 Field Books | 1603 Map | 1718/20s Field Books | 1666 Hearth Tax |
|---|---|---|---|---|
| Closely related to 1 other tenant | 23% | 21% | 18% | 10% |
| Closely related to 2 other tenants | 11% | 11% | 4% | 6% |
| Closely related to 3 or more other tenants | 5% | 10% | 4% | 8% |
| Total % closely related to other tenants | 40% | 42% | 26% | 25% |
| Total no. of tenants | 73 | 84 | 121 | 149 |
| Absolute kinship density | 0.62 | 0.71 | 0.39 | 0.48 |

404

Table 8.  Proven and highly probable kinship links in different social categories, Willingham, 1575–1720s

| Years | Total tenants/taxpayers in each category | | | | | Proven, and highly probable, individual kinship links in different social categories — status difference (by economic groups) | | | | | | | | | Grand Total |
|---|---|---|---|---|---|---|---|---|---|---|---|---|---|---|---|
| | | | | | | 3 degrees apart (I-IV) | 2 degrees | | | 1 degree | | | | |
| | I | II | III | IV | Total | | I-III | II-IV | Subtotal | I-II | II-III | III-IV | Subtotal | |
| 1575 | 1 | 31 | 23 | 18 | 73 | 1 | | 4 | 4 | | 10 | 3 | 13 | 18 |
| 1603 | 1 | 29 | 31 | 23 | 84 | | | 7 | 7 | 2 | 9 | 9 | 21 | 27 |
| 1666 | 1 | 21 | 68 | 59 | 149 | | | 4 | 4 | | 8 | 18 | 26 | 30 |
| 1674 | 2 | 28 | 61 | 59 | 150 | 2 | 1 | 5 | 6 | 1 | 3 | 13 | 17 | 25 |
| 1718/20s | 2 | 23 | 69 | 27 | 121 | | | 3 | 3 | | 12 | 10 | 22 | 25 |

| Years | Proven and highly probable individual kinship links in the same social categories | | | | Total highly probably related individual heads of households | % of these with kinship links crossing the spectrum |
|---|---|---|---|---|---|---|
| | II | III | IV | Total | | |
| 1575 | 8 | 3 | 2 | 13 | 31 | 58 |
| 1603 | 7 | 10 | 4 | 21 | 48 | 60 |
| 1666 | | 10 | 7 | 17 | 47 | 64 |
| 1674 | 1 | 7 | 6 | 14 | 39 | 64 |
| 1718/20s | 5 | 19 | 1 | 25 | 50 | 50 |

Table 9. 17 Will-Witnesses etc. who were heads of household in Willingham, whose status can be indentified, compared with status of testators (details in footnote)

| Years | Poorer Witness Richer Testator | Richer Witness Poorer Testator | Witness and Testator of same status |
|---|---|---|---|
| 1575-1603 | 5 | 14 | 15 |
| 1603-1640 | 10 | 17 | 14 |
| Total | 15 | 31 | 29 |

Note to Table 9. Heads of Household witnessing wills in Willingham

Witnessing for different economic groups. Difference by economic groups

| Years | 3 degrees apart downwards (I→IV)* | 2 degrees apart downwards I→III | II→IV | upwards III→I | IV→II | 1 degree apart downwards II→III | III→IV | upwards III→II | IV→III | Subtotal |
|---|---|---|---|---|---|---|---|---|---|---|
| 1575-1603 | 1 | | 10 | 1 | 2 | 3 | 1 | 2 | | 19 |
| 1603-1640 | | 1 | 8 | | 1 | 4 | 3 | 6 | 3 | 27 |

| Years | Witnessing in the same economic categories II | III | IV | Subtotal | Total witnessing individual heads of households |
|---|---|---|---|---|---|
| 1575-1603 | 14 | | 1 | 15 | 34 |
| 1603-1640 | 7 | 3 | 4 | 14 | 41 |

* Arrow demonstrates which member of social group is witness, executor, overseer or supervisor. The member on the left is always acting for the testator on the right.

406

Table 10. Probable kinship links in Chippenham

|  | 1544<br>Survey | 1560<br>Rental | 1674<br>Hearth Tax | 1712<br>Map |
|---|---|---|---|---|
| Total number of householders | 36<br>excluding landless | 29<br>excluding<br>landless | 72<br>(including<br>exempt) | 35<br>(after emparking) |
| Related to 1 other | 9 | 4 | 15 | 4 |
| Related to 2 others | 3 | 9 | 8 | 6 |
| Related to 3 others | 4 |  | 6 | 4 |
| Related to 4 others | 2 |  | 6 |  |
| Total probably related to other householders | 18 | 13 | 35 | 14 |

Table 11. Households at Chippenham

|  |  | 1544<br>Survey | 1674<br>Hearth Tax | 1712<br>Map |
|---|---|---|---|---|
| I | "gentle" | 2 | 5 (6+ hearths) | 5 (over 290a) |
| II | "yeomen" | 15(41-112a)<br>1 ½ yardlands & up | 19(3-5) hearths)* | 6(51-150a) |
| III | "husbandmen" | 12 (½ yardland and<br>yardland 13a-37a) | 13 (2 hearths) | 1 (½ yardland) |
| IV | "labourers and smallholders" | 35(+6?)<br>(landless and up<br>to 10a) | 35 (1 hearth<br>including exempt) | 34(+5?)<br>(landless and up<br>to 5a) |
|  |  | 64(+6?) | 72 | 46(+5?) |

* The number of taxpayers in houses with 3-5 hearths argues there were householders who had lost land in the engrossing process living on in houses that had once reflected yeomen status, and the land that went with it.

Table 12. Probable individual kinship links between Chippenham householders

| | Probable individual kinship links in different economic categories | | | Probable individual kinship links in the same economic categories | |
|---|---|---|---|---|---|
| | across two divisions | across one division | | | |
| | II-IV | II-III | III-IV | II | IV |
| 1674 | 6 | 8 | 6 | 1 | 5 |

Table 13. Witnesses and Testators at Chippenham

Twenty-three witnesses who were heads of household, whose economic status can be identified, compared with status of testators

| | Poorer Witness Richer Testator | Richer Witness Poorer Testator | Witness and Testator of same status |
|---|---|---|---|
| 1544-91 | 6 | 3 | 7 |
| 1674 | 3 | 2 | 2 |
| TOTAL | 9 | 5 | 9 |

**Figure 1**

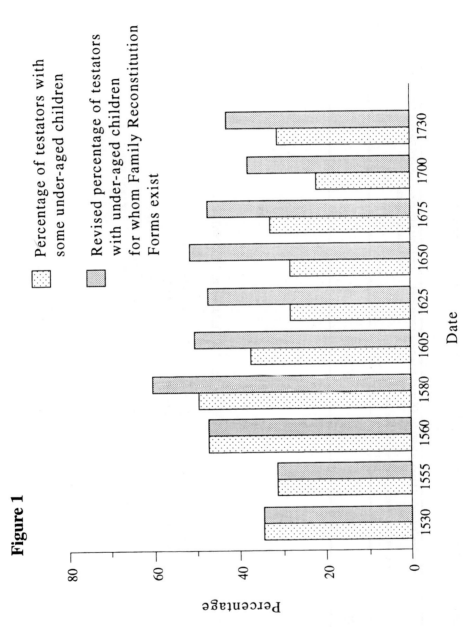

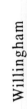

Willingham

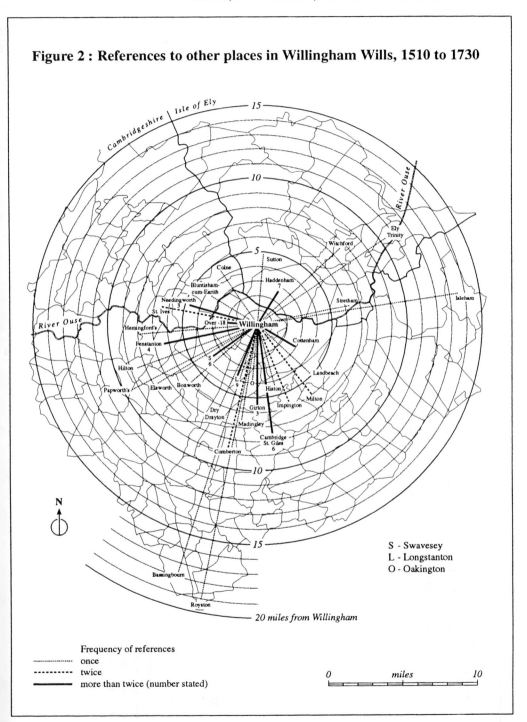

**Figure 2 : References to other places in Willingham Wills, 1510 to 1730**

S - Swavesey
L - Longstanton
O - Oakington

20 miles from Willingham

Frequency of references
once
twice
more than twice (number stated)

0        miles        10

410

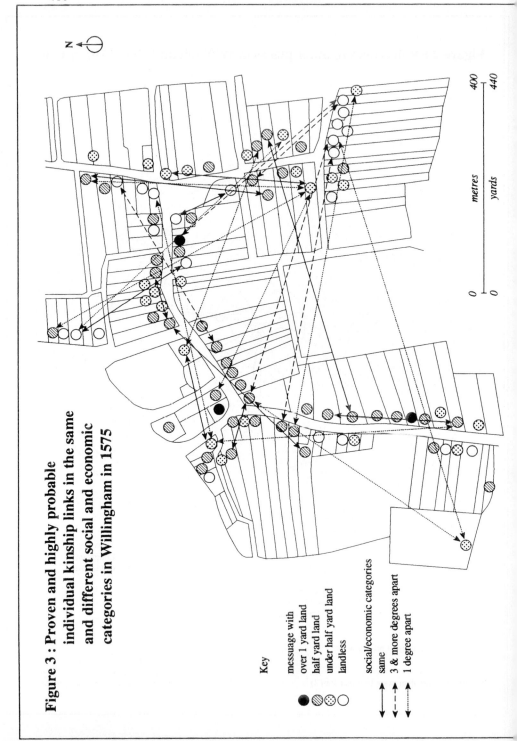

**Figure 3 : Proven and highly probable individual kinship links in the same and different social and economic categories in Willingham in 1575**

Key

messuage with

● over 1 yard land
◍ half yard land
◌ under half yard land
○ landless

social/economic categories

↔ same
⇠⇢ 3 & more degrees apart
⋯ 1 degree apart

N

metres
yards

0    400
0    440

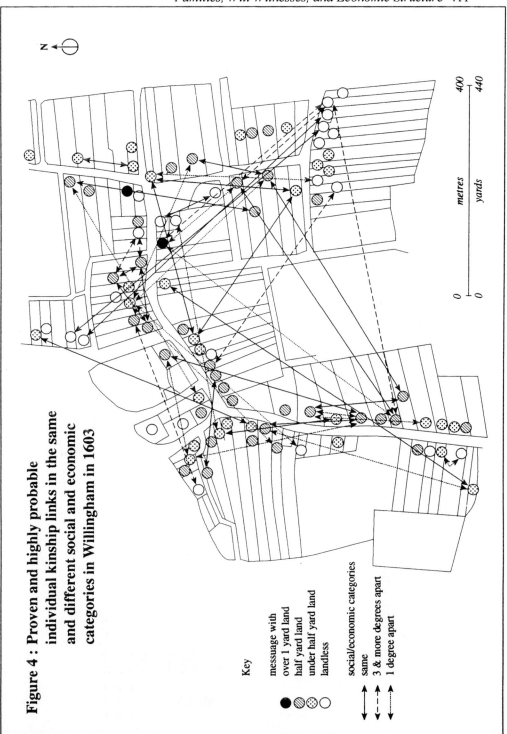

**Figure 4 : Proven and highly probable individual kinship links in the same and different social and economic categories in Willingham in 1603**

Key

messuage with

- ● over 1 yard land
- ◪ half yard land
- ◌ under half yard land
- ○ landless

social/economic categories

- ⟷ same
- ⤑ 3 & more degrees apart
- ⇢ 1 degree apart

412

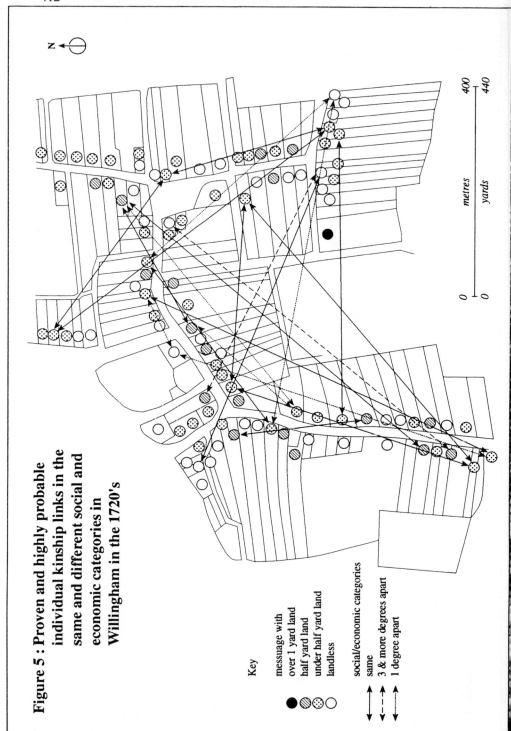

Figure 5 : Proven and highly probable individual kinship links in the same and different social and economic categories in Willingham in the 1720's

Key

messuage with
● over 1 yard land
◑ half yard land
◒ under half yard land
○ landless

social/economic categories
same
3 & more degrees apart
1 degree apart

N

metres
yards

0        400
0        440

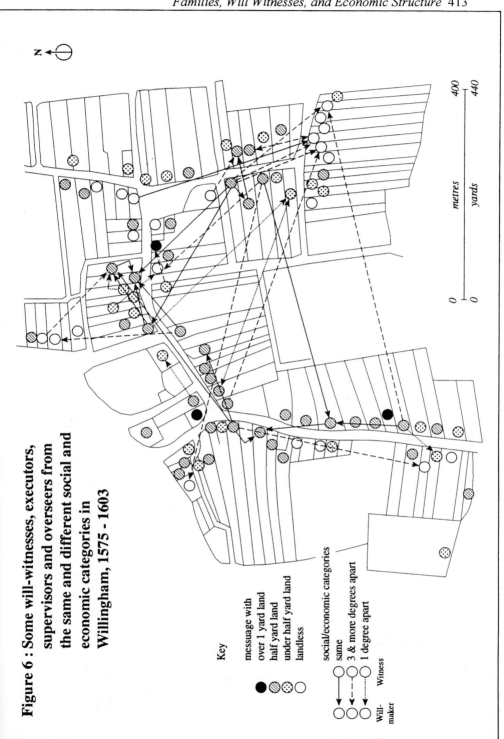

Figure 6 : Some will-witnesses, executors, supervisors and overseers from the same and different social and economic categories in Willingham, 1575 - 1603

Key

messuage with
over 1 yard land
half yard land
under half yard land
landless

social/economic categories
same
3 & more degrees apart
1 degree apart

Will-maker

Witness

0                    400
0                    440

metres
yards

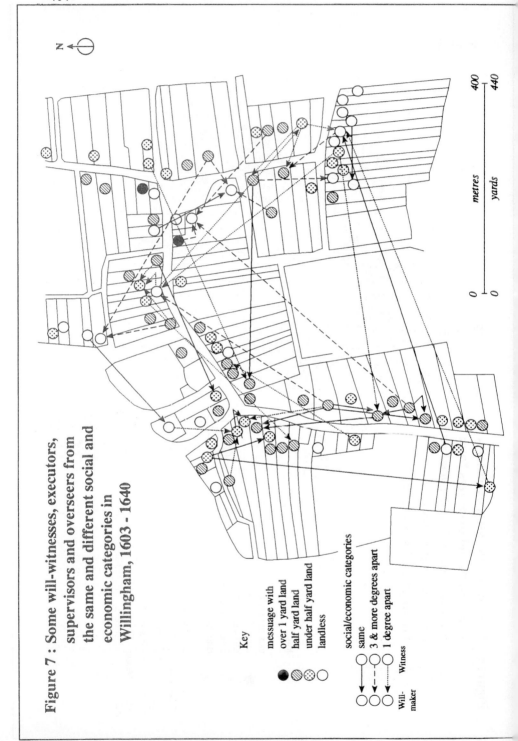

414

Figure 7 : Some will-witnesses, executors,
supervisors and overseers from
the same and different social and
economic categories in
Willingham, 1603 - 1640

Key

messuage with

over 1 yard land
half yard land
under half yard land
landless

social/economic categories

same
3 & more degrees apart
1 degree apart

Will-        Witness
maker

# IX

# The Pedlar and the Historian:
# Seventeenth-Century Communications

*Introduction*

For some time now, folklorists, especially those interested in traditional drama and contemporary legend, have been aware of the relevance of the content and availability of cheap print.[1] However, it must not be overlooked that interactions between, on the one hand the written word and mass communications, and on the other hand the oral tradition, are no less significant for other forms of folklore and at times other than our own. At the popular level, there has been too much interchange between written and spoken stories, rhymes, songs, plays and words for the interrelationships to be ignored. Therefore the aim of this paper is to bring to the attention of folklorists the range of writing and research now available on both the content of cheap print and its distribution in the sixteenth and seventeenth centuries.

Only when I began to prepare this paper did I realise what a revolution had taken place in the last decade, and is still taking place now, in our knowledge of cheap print and its accessibility even to the very poor in these centuries. As recently as 1979, Patrick Collinson in his Ford Lectures spoke about the dissemination of the religious messages of the Reformation as follows:

> Many shepherds, carters, and milkmaids ... were initiated through the catechism into the lower reaches of a literate, print-based culture to *which...their natural inclinations made them strangers ... [and which they] had little use for.* [my emphasis][2]

---

[1]    Ronald L. Baker, 'The Influence of Mass Culture on Modern Legends', *Southern Folklore Quarterly* 40 (1976), pp.367–376; Bengt af. Klintberg, 'Modern Migratory Legends in Oral Tradition and Daily Papers', *Arv* 37 (1981), pp.153–160; Georgina Smith, 'Chapbooks and Traditional Plays: Communication and Performance', *Folklore* 92 (1981), pp.208–218; Paul Smith, 'Tradition – A Perspective: Part II – Transmission', *Lore and Language* 2.3 (1975), pp.8–13; Paul Smith, 'Contemporary Legend: A Legendary Genre?', *The Questing Beast: Perspectives on Contemporary Legend IV*, Gillian Bennett and Paul Smith (eds) (Sheffield, 1989), pp.91–101. I am very grateful to Gillian Bennett for bringing these references to my attention.

[2]    Patrick Collinson, *The Religion of Protestants* (Oxford, 1981), pp.233–234.

At the time, this was a perfectly reasonable conclusion to draw, even though Bernard Capp's splendid and scholarly study of almanacs, demonstrating their huge print-runs and popularity, came out in the same year[3] and Peter Burke's scintillating display of intellectual fireworks *Popular Culture in Early Modern Europe* had come out the year before that.[4] At the same time as the Ford Lectures were in press so was my *Small Books and Pleasant Histories*, which drew attention to the output, cheapness, very diverse contents and varied readership of the chapbooks collected by Samuel Pepys, especially in the 1680s.[5] I followed this up with a study of the pedlars who were the chief distributors of both ballads and chapbooks.[6] By 1986, Collinson had considerably modified his opinions and referred to the 'fertile imagery' of the Bible being 'as accessible to the obscure and ordinary bible scholar and sermon-goer as it was to the erudite...the imaginative world of the Bible became the mentality of the literate or scarcely literate lay person'.[7]

However by the mid-1980s, there was still no scholarly study of the contents and main themes of the ballads and woodcuts, which were the cheapest form of cheap print and which came pouring off the presses in the sixteenth and seventeenth centuries. In 1985, Barry Reay's admirable volume of essays appeared and pulled together what was then known on the influence of cheap print: but the chapters on the seventeenth century – 'London', 'Bristol', 'Sex and Marriage', and 'Popular Literature' – could still only use ballads in a limited and impressionistic way.[8] Similarly, in his 1988 article, 'The Common Voice: History, Folklore and Oral Tradition in Early Modern England', D.R. Woolf was able to draw attention to the way the early topographers and antiquarians (and, he could have added, lawyers) drew on oral traditions and memories, but was still forced to concede that:

> An exhaustive treatment of the topic of oral tradition would include a more thorough discussion of such aspects of oral culture as the ballad,

---

[3]     Bernard Capp, *Astrology and the Popular Press* (London, 1979).

[4]     Peter Burke, *Popular Culture in Early Modern Europe* (London, 1978).

[5]     Margaret Spufford, *Small Books and Pleasant Histories: Popular Fiction and its Readership in Seventeenth-Century England* (London, 1981; reprint Cambridge, 1985).

[6]     Margaret Spufford, *The Great Reclothing of Rural England: Petty Chapmen and their Wares in the Seventeenth-Century* (London, 1984).

[7]     Patrick Collinson, *The Birth Pangs of Protestant England: Religion and Cultural Change in the Sixteenth and Seventeenth Centuries* (Basingstoke, 1988), p.124. (First delivered as the Anstey Memorial Lectures at the University of Kent in 1986.)

[8]     Barry Reay (ed.), *Popular Culture in Seventeenth Century England* (London, 1985; reprint London, 1988), pp.49–50, 69–70 and 150–156.

as well as the sort of tales and songs purveyed by strolling players and mummers, than can be made here.[9]

Now, at last, there is a lot of new information to offer. Scholars' knowledge of the contents of the surviving ballads from before 1640, and the origins of the 'small godly' chapbooks, has been transformed by the publication of Tessa Watt's *Cheap Print and Popular Piety, 1550–1640*.[10] Thanks to Watt, we also have a much more complete idea of the visual surroundings and influences on the 'common sort' than ever before – for what she also remarkably did was to establish the nature of the visual material in the early modern domestic house, ale-house and church – from woodcut pictures to paste on the walls, images on painted cloth, and paintings on the walls themselves. In addition, the facsimile volumes of *The Pepys Ballads*[11] are at last emerging from the press. These will make available a very important subject-index of the contents of the collection. Already it is plain, for instance, that the four issues which the publishers concentrated on, and which the reading public therefore presumably bought, were: religion; politics; issues regarding identity within the family, the region and the nation; and above all, marriage, courtship and sexuality. A subject index of the woodcuts which decorated the ballads is available in the Pepys Library, so the folklorist or historian interested in subjects as diverse as religion, superstition, domestic furniture, dress, sexuality and working tools will have a new 'visual dictionary' at his or her disposal. Work is also going on on the antecedents of the 'small merry books' which, like the 'small godly books', may have emerged as a distinct genre in the same period, the 1620s.[12] Last of all, work is being completed on road communications and the emergence and distribution of newsbooks in the 1620s:[13] in this work the author suggests that up to five million copies of newsbooks may have been produced and distributed between 1620 and 1641. In short, it is not too much to call the increase in information about the period a 'quantum leap' in historical knowledge.

---

[9]     D.R. Woolf,. 'The Common Voice: History, Folklore and Oral Tradition in Early Modern England,' *Past and Present* 120 (1988), p.27, n.3.

[10]    Tessa Watt, *Cheap Print and Popular Piety, 1550–1640* (Cambridge, 1991).

[11]    W.G. Day and Helen Weinstein (eds), *The Pepys Ballads*, 5 vols (Woodbridge, 1987). A set of cassettes, organised by subjects, of these early modern ballads has been available from Dr C. Marsh, The History Department, Queen's University, Belfast. Dr Marsh is now (1998) working on a book on music and the relationship between the oral and the aural, in the early modern period. It will be accompanied by cassettes.

[12]    David Harrison, 'Ancestral Subject Catalogue of Chapbook Themes', unpublished Ph.D. thesis (Roehampton Institute, London, 1996).

[13]    Michael Frearson, *The English Corantos of the 1620s*, unpublished Ph.D. thesis (Cambridge, 1994).

In this paper I want to focus on the vendors of this cheap print, the pedlars, on the way they got about, and some of the contents of the print they distributed. They are of as much interest to the folklorist as to the historian, because the printed materials they sold fed into, and helped to shape, oral traditions and folk stories from a very early date indeed.

I came to be interested in pedlars by a logical progression. I began my work on village communities unaware of whether, or how much, the 'common sort' were actively involved in the Reformation. When I had established that they were, literacy became very important. How much were they open to influences other than oral ones, from the manor house or the pulpit? What was there cheap enough for them to read anyway?[14] As I discovered, there was a great deal – far too much for one scholar's lifetime.

I also met my first pedlar, who appeared by accident in an ecclesiastical court case, selling 'lytle books' from a bag in a village off the main road in 1578. Now that I had focused on the availability of reading matter, the contents of that bag of little books suddenly became enormously important. The little books I found to work on were those collected by Samuel Pepys in the 1680s,[15] which their specialist publishers described in their trade-lists as 'small godlies, small merries, and pleasant histories'. These were the linear descendants of the 'lytle' books of the 1570s ('chapbook' is merely a nineteenth-century term for them). These books were not printed for, or aimed at, the educated. They were aimed at the urban artisan or the country labourer who could perhaps read, but not write. Any discussion of the possible readership of the books had, in part, to consider the size and efficiency of the distribution network which handled them: and so I arrived at the ubiquitous figure of the pedlar.

*Pedlars and their ware*

The pedlar is a very elusive figure indeed, not only because he or she is peripatetic, literally always walking off over whatever administrative boundary represents the edge of the historian's working area, but also because many of them lived near the edge of society, the vagrant fringe.

Vagrants and print have not usually been thought to go together, but they were not necessarily unfamiliar with each other at all. It is worth recording that printed goods were often the first recourse of the destitute, those who were in

---

[14]    Margaret Spufford, *Contrasting Communities* (Cambridge, 1972), pp.208–211.
[15]    Spufford, *Small Books*.

very real danger of being whipped as vagrants.[16] A shipwrecked sailor with no possessions, in the far-from-metropolitan north, for example, might acquire 'some pictures and ballads and other paper wares' on credit; or an ex-servant whose husband beat her might get hold of some 'books and ballads' and go 'about the country from place to place' bartering paper-ware for food or a night's lodging in a barn.[17] The very poorest of the pedlars appeared to have sold only cheap print. Extraordinarily enough, there still remains the record of a vagrant from as early as 1653. The Fenstanton Baptist church, of which she was an active member, agreed to take the financial responsibility for her if she was allowed to settle in the village of Melbourn. She seems to have been a chapwoman, or pedlar, since the members of the church 'upon diligent search found the best way for the satisfying of her necessities was to provide her a stock to trade withall, as formerly she was accustomed' and to that end supplied her with one pound to buy goods.[18]

What very few historians have recognised is that these people, peddling their goods on the vagrant fringe of society, walked all over England[19] – and even further: some Scots lowland pedlars got as far as Poland; it is impossible to believe that they did not walk all over France too (see below p.205). Peddling was very frequently an occupation worked from Alpine regions, which took up part of the year.[20] Research has shown that there were over 2,500 pedlars licensed to sell goods in 1697–98, in various places all over England.[21] They constituted a group in society who went everywhere, who were the humblest people, and who were responsible for the diffusion of ideas, stories, news, ballads, cheap 'godly' and 'merry' books, jokes and almanacs.

The sixteenth century had been a time of diversification in English industry and the seventeenth century saw the spread of new rural occupations demanding little capital and much labour, from pin-making to copperas-boiling, from

---

[16]    Paul Slack (ed.), 'Poverty in Early Stuart Salisbury', *Wiltshire Record Society* 31 (Devizes, 1975).

[17]    Margaret Spufford, *The Great Reclothing*, pp.25 and 43.

[18]    E.B. Underhill (ed.), *Records of the Churches of Christ Gathered at Fenstanton, Warboys and Hexham, 1644–1720*, The Hanserd Knollys Society (1854), pp.82–83 and 86. Bill Stevenson brought this woman to my attention. She is discussed in W. Stevenson, *The Economic and Social Status of Protestant Sectaries in Huntingdonshire, Cambridge and Bedfordshire, 1650–1725*, unpublished Ph.D. thesis (Cambridge, 1990), p.355 n.17.

[19]    See Spufford, *The Great Reclothing*, p.43 (Mary Rice); pp.23–25 (Mary Prosser, Ann How and Jane, Sarah and Thomas Broderick *alias* Young); and pp.26–30 (for a group of men).

[20]    Laurence Fontaine, *History of Pedlars in Europe* (Cambridge, 1994).

[21]    Spufford, *The Great Reclothing*, p. 18. We know this number from taxation figures. Unlike most taxation, which leads to avoidance, there was every incentive for these people to pay for a licence, for it gave them immunity from being whipped as beggars, a fate which often befell them.

starch-making and lace-making to tobacco- and flower-growing and stocking-knitting. Such products could be produced in the countryside in different qualities and finenesses; laces and ribbons, buttons and thread, cheap and gay consumer goods thus came within reach of working men and women in the period from 1650 to 1750.[22]

The high prices of the late sixteenth century had benefited the yeoman and the largest tenant farmers, but the wage labourers, their employees, had suffered enormously. The real purchasing power of wages was lower at the end of the sixteenth century than it had been for the whole of the previous three centuries, or, indeed, the following three centuries. It was lower even than it had been from 1264 to 1854 – even than it was in the dreadful years at the beginning of the fourteenth century or during the Napoleonic crisis.[23] But in the 1650s population pressures at last slackened off,[24] and the purchasing power of wages rose too; at last the poverty-stricken rural poor felt some relief. At the same time the cheap new goods from America and Asia - tobacco, sugar and the Indian textiles – were starting to trickle, then to flood, in. In the second half of the seventeenth century these goods were reaching a quite new consumer market in England and becoming available to all social classes.[25] But did they reach the humblest people, and was there indeed a 'humble consumer society' in the late seventeenth century?

The pedlars provided the answer – and, interestingly, it is because the pedlars fulfilled an economic role that they became cultural mediators. Indeed, where the economic factor has been overlooked, as it has been by the *Annales* school, it has led scholars to think that cheap print arrived in rural villages at a later date than it actually did. Roger Chartier, for example, has suggested that:

> In the first century of its existence, the Bibliothèque bleue [that is, the little blue covered-books printed in large numbers in Troyes from the early seventeenth century onwards] seems to have reached a public that was essentially urban ... it was perhaps only in the eighteenth century

---

[22]     Joan Thirsk, *Economic Policy and Projects* (Oxford, 1978), from the Ford Lectures, delivered in 1975.

[23]     H. Phelps-Brown and Sheila Hopkins, 'Seven Centuries of the Prices of Consumables, Compared with Builders' Wage Rates', *Essays in Economic History*, vol. 2, E.M. Wilson (ed.) (London, 1962), pp.168–189.

[24]     R.M. Smith, 'Population and its Geography in England, 1500–1730', *An Historical Geography of England and Wales*, R.A. Dodgshon and R.A. Butlin (eds) (London, 1978), pp. 199–237.

[25]     Ralph Davis, 'English Foreign Trade, 1660–1700', *Economic History Review* 7, 2nd series (1954), pp.151–153.

203

Figure 1: 'Map' handkerchief, 1688. Victoria and Albert Museum. Courtesy of the V&A.

Figure 2: News Sellers outside a Cobbler's Shop, Norwich.
From MS book of illustrations by Thomas Starling,
painter-stainer of Norwich, late 17th/early 18th century.
Courtesy of the Library of Congress.

Figure 3: Cobbler's Shop, Norwich.
Caption reads: 'Three or foure common people at a Coblars Shop one reading the
News paper, þe others arguing þe Case.' From MS book of illustrations by Thomas
Starling, painter-stainer of Norwich, late 17th/early 18th century.
Courtesy of the Library of Congress.

that peddling escaped the confines of the cities to carry the little blue booklets ... into the small towns and villages that had no book stores.[26]

This judgement is based on the fact that the seventeenth-century sources on book peddling in France derive from royal ordinances attempting to control subversive literature and in response to complaints of competition from keepers of bookshops. Naturally, the complaints from the bookshops came from urban sources; villages did not, and still do not, have bookshops.

But Chartier's statement is mistaken for two other reasons. The very successful Oudot family who inaugurated and profited from the *bibliothèque bleue* sold their books to pedlars on a sale-or-return basis,[27] so the pedlars must have worked out of, and back to, Troyes itself. Furthermore, Troyes was one of the old Champagne fair towns which had an economic revival in the sixteenth and seventeenth centuries based on the making of cotton caps and the knitting of stockings.[28] It was also a centre for the creation of ribbons, laces and small wares. Men may live without print, perhaps, but definitely not without stockings. Stockings were ideal pedlar's goods and it is inconceivable that the main distribution network out of Troyes was not based on *bonneterie* carried by pedlars.[29]

In my view it was precisely because of the true economic function of the pedlars as distributors of the 'new' seventeenth-century luxuries as well as necessities – above all the linens – available to the poor, that they were also such important distributors of their *marginal* goods – the woodcut picture, the reading primer, the ballad, the chapbook, the 'newsbook' – and indeed the 'news' – and the idea.

Let us take a concrete case. In 1683, Roland Johnson died in Penrith, in England.[30] Cumberland was one of the poorest areas of the British Isles, yet, from Johnson, the local purchaser could buy hollands and cambric from the Low Countries; Bengals, calicoes and muslins from India; silks, linens, which were probably dyed in England; Scotch cloth as a cheap alternative to calico for the new-fangled window curtains; and gloves, muffs, bone-lace, ribbons, combs and band-strings for adornment. Men like Johnson were to be found all

---

[26]    Roger Chartier, *The Cultural Use of Print in Early Modern France*, trans. Lydia G. Cochrane (Princeton, 1987), pp.176–177.

[27]    Robert Mandrou, *De la Culture Populaire aux 17ᵉ et 18ᵉ Siècles* (Paris, 1964; reprint 1975), p.102 n.9; and Spufford, *The Great Reclothing*, p. 80.

[28]    Spufford, *Small Books*, p.129.

[29]    Why has no French historian done a detailed study of pedlars in the region of Troyes?

[30]    Cumbria, R.O., Roland Johnson, ADMON. 1683.

over England. So the consumer could buy bone-lace, and other small luxuries, as well as pins and needles, a wide variety of fabrics of very diverse origins and all the requirements for clothing a family, which have been too lightly dismissed by male historians who simply assume the domestic framework of living. They have therefore been more interested in the growth of heavy industry than its concomitant niceties, like the proliferation of the pin.

The social skills necessary to people like Roland Johnson, who were essentially *salesmen* working in and out of markets, were the oral story, the gossip, the latest bawdy joke and, very important, the latest song. The ability to tell a joke or sing a song, or the musical skill to play a simple instrument to a catchy tune, were vital devices to the salesman, who frequently had to pay for his night's food and lodging by entertaining. It is precisely because these people were so important in the distribution of goods like shirts and underclothes that were, or became, essential that the news, jokes, songs, ideas and few books they carried had so much chance of spreading so widely. It was because they were primarily salesmen of linen and haberdashery, that their 'cultural' goods had such a good chance of reaching the widest possible audience: they became cultural intermediaries because they had a vital economic function.

*Communications: roads and maps*

A pedlar on foot, or even on horseback, was only the humblest of the distributors of goods, news and cheap print; and all of them were dependent on communications in a literal geographical sense. There is evidence of improvement of communications in seventeenth-century England, and with it the growth of awareness of routes, of roads and of space. Not only were there enormous advances in map-making, but in the spread of the map even at the humblest social levels.

There had been regular services of carriers' carts and pack horses out of London to distant parts of the country at least as early as Elizabeth's reign and probably long before.[31] By 1637 John Taylor, the low-life 'water poet', who was always eager to make a quick penny in print, wrote his *Carriers' Cosmographie*. This was a description of all the weekly services run by carriers out of London, the days of the week on which they left and the inns that were their regular points of departure. If you wanted to go to Bristol in 1637, for instance, you went either to 'The Three Cups' in Bread Street or to 'The Swan'

---

[31]      David Hey, *Packman, Carriers, and Packhorse Roads: Trade and Communications in North Derbyshire and South Yorkshire* (Leicester, 1980), pp.211–216.

near Holborn Bridge on Thursday.[32] The importance of these services was, in part, their regularity. Parcels, packages, foodstuffs, bonds for debts, letters and news all travelled by these means. In the 1650s, a young gentlewoman, Dorothy Osborne, living in Bedfordshire, was able to grumble to her fiancé because his letters were not coming on the carrier's cart (which arrived every Thursday) as they should have been and as she had a right to expect. In the 1680s, a Quaker prisoner in a Somerset jail in the west of England revealed accidentally that 'parcels of Quaker books' were sent to him regularly on the carrier's cart from London and were left at the inn for him to pick up.[33] Communications between London, and therefore the printing trade of which it was the centre, and the rest of the kingdom were much more regular than has been supposed: with good communications went both increase in trade and awareness of political events, and news.

One of the reasons, or consequences perhaps, of this desire was to improve communications was the awareness of spatial relationships and the ability to express this new, closer articulation of the kingdom in cartographic form. There was an explosion of cartographical expertise in the sixteenth and seventeenth centuries in England,[34] and an increased ability to understand the concept of space and distance expressed in these new forms, which spread downwards through society, until, by 1700, as we shall see, cartographical images were probably familiar to almost everyone. The spread of government, and the increase of government interference in business both central and local, was one of the triggers for this cartographical explosion: another was the need to record the new accessions of the gentry in an easily-assimilable form in the post-Reformation land-market. The same need recurred a century later after the Restoration. Initially, the county maps – which were the fruit of the queen's Council's acquisitiveness, the need to record the sphere of their influence and perhaps the dominance of the country gentry – were not aides to travel at all. Christopher Saxton's first county maps of the 1570s which were made at the behest of the Council recorded, not roads, but rivers and the seats of the gentry. The gentlemen, noblemen or administrators who wanted to get about used a different method. Elizabeth's Secretary of State, William Cecil, had a set of routes between places and the distances between them, verbally described,

---

[32]    J.A. Chartres, 'The Capital's Provincial Eyes: London's Inns in the Early Eighteenth Century', *London Journal* 3.1 (1977), pp.31–32.

[33]    Spufford, *Small Books*, p.46.

[34]    Sarah Tyacke (ed.), *English Map-Making, 1500–1620: Historical Essays* (London, 1983), and Sarah A. Bendall, *Maps, Land and Society: A History with a Carto-Bibliography of Cambridgeshire Estate Maps, c.1600–1636* (Cambridge, 1993).

amongst his papers.[35] Exactly the same method was used by the pedlars. We know this because a pedlar, John Hewitson, a chapman typically accused of theft in Cambridge, described his route from the north of England to Stourbridge Fair, in terms of his overnight stops in a list of places:

> The night before he reached Cambridge, he spent in St Neots. The night before 'he knoweth not': the night before that, he was at Wansford. The night before that again he was at a place 'he knoweth not'.[36]

By 1685, the number of chapmen had increased to such an extent in England that it was worth publishing an almanac especially for them, with information that would especially appeal and which they especially needed,[37] such as the market days in the towns throughout England and the routes of the main roads throughout England. These were described in lists exactly like William Cecil's a century before.

But things were changing, and changing fast. In 1685, John Ogilby issued the first road atlas of England, showing these routes in pictorial form. This was an immense advance. The two types of map, the route map for the traveller in strip form, and the county map for the gentleman and the administrator, had already been fused by Morden ten years before, when he issued a pack of playing cards with all the counties of England and Wales on them, showing the roads newly mapped by Ogilby superimposed on the bases of the old county maps. Now, for the first time, it must be supposed, the visual image of the cartographer became familiar in a multiplicity of social environments and levels, for other pictorial playing cards were everywhere used and provided a very important leisure activity. The innumerable prosecutions in ecclesiastical courts of parishioners, and the poorer parishioners at that, for playing cards in service time on Sundays is sufficient demonstration of that: and there was no objection to anyone playing cards outside service time. Playing cards were themselves goods sold by chapmen: the rare itemised lists of a chapman's goods which survive in their probate inventories frequently list 'cards', which sold cheaply.[38] So after 1676, the cards sold by chapmen may have carried the images of maps.

---

[35]     I am very grateful to Dr Victor Morgan for this information. Burghley's 'working atlas' with notes in his own hand is B.L. Royal Ms. 181.0.3 ff. 4v–12v.

[36]     Spufford, *The Great Reclothing*, p.24.

[37]     There is an example in the Pepys collection of almanacs, Magdalene College, Cambridge.

[38]     But note that there is confusion between 'cards' for carding wool, and 'cards' for playing games, which I have been unable to resolve safely since the retail prices for both types of objects are unknown. Robert Carr of Newcastle, chapman, had three and a half dozen 'cards'

Indeed the form of the map may have become familiar before that, amongst the humblest sort. (It had already become so amongst the gentry, of course.) The content of the woodcut pictures which were among the cheapest of the chapman's cultural goods, and the simplest of all the cultural messages sent out by the printers, is one of the most mysterious puzzles of all. Woodcut pictures to stick on the cottage wall were the most ephemeral of all the ephemera, and until the appearance of Tessa Watt's book, the least known. Amongst these really cheap woodcut pictures from 1550 to 1640, both the 'godly' pictures to incite the sinner to repentance, and the portrait of notable royal and political figures had a place – and so did the map.[39] In 1656, a list of eighty-eight woodcuts were registered with the Stationer's Company: unhappily, none of them survives. Nearly three-quarters of them were religious and moral and a quarter were portraits. Amongst the portraits were three maps. John Bunyan refers to a map in his *Pilgrim's Progress*: so he had seen one. And we know not only that Bunyan was a poor man, but also that he ministered to an outstandingly poor congregation.[40] He would not refer to utterly unfamiliar objects. Work on consumption from 1660 onwards traces the spread of a group of 'luxury goods' distributed by social group, region and decade. Amongst these 'indexed' goods are pictures which were rare in 1675 and much more commonly owned by the early eighteenth century, and amongst the pictures were maps.[41] For instance James Bradstreet, who kept a shop in Manchester, when he died in 1669 had in his parlour, fourteen pictures, fourteen cushions and a 'Mapp', together worth one pound, one and two-pence.[42] Luxury indeed.

But you didn't have to invest in luxuries to become familiar with maps. Not only were there playing cards, but I suspect that the commonest way that maps became familiar was printed on silk handkerchiefs. (The Victoria and Albert Museum has a splendid collection of silk handkerchiefs.[43]) But until I put the two together, historians did not know what was printed on them, and the

---

at 2/6d the lot. I have presumed that wool cards would be too heavy and too awkward, and the profit margins too low, to make them convenient objects for a chapman to carry. Playing cards were used as propaganda devices also: cards conveying political messages appeared at least from the pack satirising the Rump Parliament in 1659 onwards. One pack advertised in 1689, represented in 'lively cuts' the 'history of the late times', and sold at 12d, or a day's wages; Lois G. Schwoerer, 'Propaganda in the Revolution of 1688–89', *American Historical Review* 82 (1977), pp.866–868, and J.R.S. Whiting, *A Handful of History* (Totowa NJ, 1978), p.2.

[39]   Watt, *Cheap Print*, p.162.

[40]   Stevenson, *The Economic and Social Status*, thesis cit.

[41]   Lorna Weatherill, *Consumer Behaviour and Material in Britain, 1660–1760* (London, 1988), p.26 table 2.1, pp.28, 49 table 3.3, and p.88 table 4.4.

[42]   Will 25 October, 1699. Inventory 10 December, 1699.

[43]   Victoria and Albert Museum, Textile Department.

museum curators did not know that they were peddled, or what their selling price was. Pedlars commonly sold silk handkerchiefs, and they were quite cheap.[44] What is exciting is that among the handkerchiefs in the Victoria and Albert's collection, the earliest survivor, from 1688, is a map with the roads of England and the market days of the various towns on it. It is big, the size of a modern head-square (see figure 1, p. 203). It is inconceivable that the gentry would have wished to wear the market days of England round their necks or would have flaunted them in their top pockets. So it looks as if it was the pedlars' customers who bought them, and that the form of the map was becoming more familiar to the 'common sort' and particularly to the trading community throughout the seventeenth century by this means.

*Communications: social groups*

Did pedlars also act as 'cultural intermediaries' in the sense of communicating between social levels, as well as literally trudging the roads of England and Wales alongside and on top of the carrier's cart, establishing communications over physical distance and space? It is very difficult to prove. But there is one outstanding example from the mid-sixteenth century of the way in which such a man and his wife did act as cultural intermediaries between social levels. Richard Sheale was a 'minstrel' to the Earl of Derby. Minstrels were a group very much frowned upon by 'proper musicians'. Thomas Whythorne, who was himself a music teacher in great houses and a madrigalist, wrote in his autobiography of 1576 of:

> those who do use to go with their instruments about the countries to cities, towns and villages, where also they do go to private houses, to such as will have them, either publicly or privately: or else to markets, fairs, marriages, assemblies, taverns, alehouses and such like places...these in ancient times were named minstrels ... they (have) been of late in this realm restrained somewhat from their vagabond life.

He also described minstrels as the 'rascals and offscum' of that profession who did or do 'make it common, by offering of it to every Jack'.[45] Richard Sheale would certainly have fallen into this category.

---

44    Inventory of George Pool, a poor packman in Cumbria, Cumbria Record office (probate 1695, George Pool).

45    James M. Osborn (ed.), *Autobiography of Thomas Whythorne* (Oxford, 1961), pp.193–194.

The Earl of Derby kept his household in Lancashire, in the northwest of England, and Richard Sheale was a maker of verses who sometimes lived within it, judging from the ballads he wrote to his patron listing the delicacies to be eaten from his table, the 'ale and wine and beer', the 'fresh salmon and conger' in Lent, and the beef at other seasons:

> Both mutton and veile
> Is good for Richard Sheill
> (he rhymed)
> Ser, for the good chear
> That I have hade heare
> I gyve youe hartté thankes,
> With bowing of my shankes.

Another of his verses was a lament for the death of the Countess of Derby, his patron's wife, which included a note of genuine personal sorrow, as well as a description of her lavish funeral ceremony at Ormskirk in Lancashire, which was so detailed that he was obviously there. There was a manuscript collection of songs, made between 1557 and 1565, mostly copied from broadside printed ballads, including some of Sheale's own originals. Sheale's own songs were so bad that it is thought that only he himself, or another member of the Earl of Derby's household, can have had any interest in noting them down.[46] However it came about, we do have a collection of the ballads and songs sung in a noble household, and a little knowledge of one of the minstrels.

The chief interest is that one of Sheale's own songs, made after he had been robbed, describes his wife and her trade. And here his plodding literal style is a great ally, for we get given a full shopping-list, or rather selling-list of her goods:

> My wyff is in dede is ys a sylke woman by her occupation
> And linen cloth most chiefly was her greatest trade
> And at fairs and markets she sold sale-ware she made
> As shirts, smocks, partyttes, headcloths and other things

---

[46]    *Commonplace Book of Songs and Ballads, 1557–1565*, B.L. MS Ashmole 48; reprinted Thomas Wright (ed.), *Songs and Ballads, with Other Short Poems, Chiefly of the Reign of Philip and Mary* (London, 1860); Watt, *Cheap Print*, pp.16–21. A.P. Fox, *Aspects of Oral Culture in Early Modern England*, unpublished Ph.D. thesis (Cambridge, 1993), is a most important work showing the way ballad forms were picked up by the lower orders of society and used in excruciating rhymes libelling their social superiors. These are even worse than Richard Sheale's work.

> As silk thred and edgings, shirt bands and strings
> At Lichfield market and at Atherstone good customers she found
> And also in Tamworth, where I dwell, she took many a pound.

It seems likely that Richard Sheale, like his wife, also worked the markets, for he explained his prosperity as a minstrel by saying that he had friends in London who were always willing to lend him twenty pounds of ware ('ware' is the word used for a chapman's stock-in-trade, or selling goods). So here we have a minstrel familiar with, and sometimes resident in, a household of the high nobility, who may also have worked the markets as a pedlar, selling cheap goods. Whether he did himself or not, his wife did. It is inconceivable that they didn't sing, in the Staffordshire markets, the songs recorded in the collection mostly made in the 1550s and 1560s, some of which were Richard Sheale's own verses which never made it to print and others of which were the printed broadside ballads which were obviously sung in the Earl's own household. So here we have a pedlar couple, man and wife, singing songs and selling linen and clothing in a noble household and in the markets of northwestern England in the mid-sixteenth century. Cultural mediators indeed! But we only know about them from a chance and very fortunate survival.

There is a theory among English social historians at present that the seventeenth century saw a polarisation, a drawing apart among social levels, and between 'high' and 'low' culture. I suspect this theory a little for many reasons, among others on the grounds that we can easily show that the pedlars supplied both the 'common sort' and the gentry. Of course they supplied the common people. One chapbook was specifically dedicated to 'Bakers, Millers and Smiths as a means to "increase ... Trade and call Customers to you".' The latter were all rural craftsmen at whose bakehouse, mill or smithy the customer had to wait and therefore had to be entertained. But schoolboys in London, and as far away as Wales, formed one of the markets at which the publishers of chapbooks aimed their sales, and we know that the chapbooks were indeed read by these boys, who were, by definition, at grammar school.[47] And it is inconceivable that the jokes, stories, news, songs and patter of the pedlar failed to ease him through the back door and make him a welcome guest, whose news was willingly heard by the lady of the house.

---

[47]    Francis Kirkman, son of a London merchant at St Paul's was so carried away by them that he fancied himself the son of a great person: but no lesser people than Samuel Johnson and Edmund Burke later confessed to their addiction. They were also used as school-readers, Spufford, *Small Books*, pp.72–75).

Sir Nicholas Le Strange, son of the High Sheriff of Norfolk (1603–55) and therefore prominent amongst the county gentry of Norfolk, kept a book in which he recorded jokes in the first half of the seventeenth century.[48] Amongst these, he wrote of the gentlewoman who loved to bubble away her money in 'Bone-Laces, pinnes and such like toyes, often used the short Ejaculation; God love me as I love a Pedlar'. Sir Nicholas was not merely using a literary convention. Again, the surviving household account books of the Rydal family of Cumbria in the northwest of England in the 1680s and 1690s show the lady of the house regularly purchasing calico, linen and muslin from pedlars.[49] The most concrete evidence that the chapman did indeed make his way into gentle drawing-rooms is provided by Mrs Frances Wolfreston. She was a Staffordshire lady who began acquiring books after her marriage in 1631 and went on until the 1660s. She died in 1677. She was known amongst bibliophiles for her Shakespearean folios, and other works of drama, poetry and criticism, but no-one noticed until recently that she also made the earliest known collection of 'small godly' and 'small merry' books, which she probably purchased from chapmen between 1631 and the 1660s.[50] Her eclectic interests are a powerful argument for the generally well-informed cultural situation amongst the gentry, particularly since she was a gentlewoman living in the West Midlands at a considerable distance from London.

Another reason for suspecting the theory that social groups drew apart at this time can be seen by looking at the family background of another omnivorous collector, Samuel Pepys, who also collected almanacs, chapbooks and ballads at the other end of the spectrum of print and went on doing so until 1702. His omnivorous habits probably related in part to the way his family and kin spread across the whole social spectrum, from country gentleman to his father, who was a London tailor, and from holders of government office, to much humbler country cousins, with whom he kept up. He himself was educated at a grammar school in Huntingdonshire and had brothers at school at St Paul's in London, but he was in touch with his less elevated relations. In 1661, he sent a fiddle to his 'cousin', Perkin, the miller, whose windmill had blown down, and who was now earning a living by fiddling at country feasts.[51] There is no reason to suppose he was behaving differently from other gentlemen in keeping up with his poor relations.

---

48  Spufford, *Small Books*, p.67.
49  Spufford, *The Great Reclothing*, p.89.
50  Watt, *Cheap Print*, pp.315–317.
51  Spufford, *Small Books*, pp.50 and 177.

Neville Butler of Orwell in Cambridgeshire, who was born in 1609 and was educated at the Perse School and Christ's College, sensibly married an heiress, and was able to buy the manor of Barnwell and move away from his own village. He served on the County Committee for Cambridgeshire and was undoubtedly accepted as the country gentleman he was. His grandfather had been a yeoman who had managed to send his eldest son up to Gray's Inn to study law. However, although Neville Butler moved away, both socially and physically, from the place of his birth, he did not sever the links with his cousins, who remained malsters, husbandmen and even smallholders, any more than his father, educated at Gray's Inn, had done. On the contrary, in the middle generation the humbler cousins were used as rent collectors by their more fortunate relations, and Neville himself acted as co-witness to villagers' wills with his second cousin. Even after he moved away to his new manor he travelled back across the county to witness this dying second cousin's will.[52]

Such behaviour was not at all uncommon. Motoyasu Takahashi has examined the will-witnessing behaviour of families both in the more egalitarian fen village of Willingham, and the arable chalk village of Chippenham, where society was almost completely economically polarised between the 1590s and the early eighteenth century. Very interestingly, in both places in these completely different economic circumstances, some kin continued to cooperate with each other in the important and intimate business of witnessing each others' wills at death.[53] When such family ties spread right across the social and economic spectrum at both village and county level, and still meant something in realistic terms of human co-operation and contact, it is unreasonable to suppose a wide, or total, cultural divide. Frances Wolfreston and Samuel Pepys between them illustrate the interest the gentry could have equally in first folios, and chapbooks. It is highly unlikely that Neville Butler was unaware of what his second cousins read, and what cheap print circulated in his old home-village, or that he was ignorant either of all the oral stories and news which must also have been current there. He co-operated too often with his relations for such ignorance to be possible.

---

[52]     Spufford, *Contrasting Communities*, pp.179–180, 323, 24, 354–355 and illustration p.198.

[53]     Margaret Spufford and Motoyasu Takahashi, 'Families, Will-Witnesses and Economic Structure in the Fens and on the Chalk: Sixteenth and Seventeenth Century Willingham and Chippenham', *Albion* 28 (1996), pp.382–384, 397–399 and tables 8, 9, 12 and 13. See chapter VIII below, pp. 164–166, 179–181 and tables 8, 9, 12 and 13.

*Print and oral tradition*

Having now looked at communications within England in the seventeenth century, and at the pedlars like the Sheales of Tamworth and Ormskirk who were supplied from London in the sixteenth and the seventeenth century – and established their ubiquity – we can begin to think of the way the cheap print they carried fed into the oral tradition and, perhaps, out again.

One of the ways in which the sensibility of English rural society has been permanently modified by the influence of one of the types of cheap print was demonstrated with great force by Robert Thomson in his study of English folksong survivals.[54] Thomson gives convincing statistical evidence of the general importance of literacy, not only to exceptional men like Clare and Bunyan but to the wider population. He has shown that at least eighty percent of the folksongs gathered in the major collections made early in the twentieth century were derived from printed broadsides. A suggestive series of maps shows the regions in which folksong collectors worked, overlaid on the routes taken by the chapmen working for the ballad and chapbook printers in the eighteenth and nineteenth centuries. There is a high degree of coincidence. This is conclusive evidence of the effects of eighteenth- and nineteenth-century literacy and its indelible impact on the popular imagination. The efforts of the ballad partners of the seventeenth century also left a permanent mark, even if this is naturally normally overlaid by later printing. Thomson has also identified just over ninety songs gathered by folksong collectors which can only derive from broadsides printed before 1700. His work has proved that it is impossible to study English folk songs without also studying the development of the broadside ballad trade.

A similar exercise may be undertaken with Katharine Briggs's *Dictionary of British Folk Tales (1970–71)*. It can be shown that forty-nine chapbooks and eighty-five ballads (6 per cent) have titles which either possibly, or definitely, overlap with titles in the index.[55] Six percent is not a large proportion but nevertheless it is enough to show that there is, and was, a considerable mutual influence between print and oral communication. It is interesting, too, to compare the Index to Briggs's *Dictionary* and the equally large ballad and chapbook indices, for the focus of each is rather different. Briggs has a much

---

[54]    R.S. Thomson, *The Development of the Broadside Ballad Trade and its Influence on the Transmission of English Folk-songs*, unpublished Ph.D. thesis (Cambridge, 1974).

[55]    I am deeply grateful to my former research students, Helen Weinstein and David Harrison, who between them took Briggs's 'Index of Story-Titles' in both volumes and checked the titles against Hyder Rollin's *Analytical Index to the Ballad Entries, 1557–1709*, and their own indices to the Pepys and Roxburghe collections of ballads, the Pepys Chapbook collection and the earlier *Short Title Catalogue Entries to Chapbooks*. I am much indebted to them both.

greater emphasis on animals, fairies, devils, ghosts, haunted places, giants and witches – the supernatural, in brief. The ballad and chapbooks, on the other hand, have a much greater emphasis on the occupations, religion, marriage, courtship and cuckolding: Christ, God and Judgement appear as real figures and real possibilities in the religious ballads, and people like the 'jolly coachman', the 'country blacksmith', a 'Tailor and his Maid', and the 'Maulster's Daughter of Marlborough' figure largely in the rest. The reason for this difference of emphasis would be a major research subject in itself. I suspect that it would be useful to undertake a detailed consideration of the way in which Briggs put her *Dictionary* together. Meanwhile we know that six percent of her folk-stories, and of the stories and legends she collected, were available in cheap print already before 1700.

*Conclusion*

Before 1550 provincial England was a late medieval peasant society, in which people were well aware of the value of the written instrument but in which reading and writing were still special skills exercised by experts on behalf of the community. Between 1500 and 1700 however, it was transformed into a society in which writing, and particularly reading, were widely used in many areas of human activity, including pleasure and self-education, by more members of the community including some of the labouring poor (see figures 2 and 3 above). This transition can, and does, involve far-reaching changes, which are usually left to the literary specialist and the anthropologist. But historians and folklorists, too, must take it on board. We have to be aware of the content of printed cheap popular literature feeding into the oral tradition in bulk, at least from the 1620s onwards when the cheap print trade seems to have sharply expanded. The form of the 'small godly' book, the 'small merry' book and the 'new book' all seem to have evolved and been mass marketed in this decade, but there is evidence that printed and literary work fed into oral culture long before 1620. I would like to end up by evoking the image of an alehouse, constructed by Tessa Watt:

> Perhaps we might bring back the visual dimension by following the example of the 'art of memory' practitioners, projecting the collective early seventeenth-century mind out onto the external representation of a building. Not a grand hall or cathedral, since we are in post-Reformation England, but an ordinary village alehouse.

This is ... an 'honest alehouse' where established householders, whether poor or relatively prosperous, could respectably be seen. Above the entrance is a very protestant painted cloth which reads 'Feare God', almost illegible from the ravages of smoke. On the same wall has been nailed a rather Catholic-looking woodcut of the nativity scene, surrounded by the arms of the passion. The long back wall is crudely painted with the story of the prodigal son in four scenes, with a black-letter text below. The third wall is hung with a plain cloth upon which is pinned a row of ballads decorated with woodcuts (including various figures kneeling in prayer, and a small faded scene which might be the resurrection). The final wall is dominated by the hearth, above which hangs a wooden plaque with rows of wise sayings: "Save us O Lord from heathens sword', 'An evil woman is like a scorpion', and so on. Of course, we are exaggerating the piety of this metaphorical alehouse: perhaps there are only one or two religious images in a room full of knights on woodcut horses, portraits of royalty [she could have added a map or two], scatological political satires and placards of strange fish or deformed pigs. Nevertheless, this is precisely the point. The profane and the pious, the verbal and the visual – all were accommodated within the same room, the same mind, the same experience. It is only the historian who, like an iconoclast, wants to rip down all the images on the walls which do not seem to fit. We need to recognise how the culture could absorb new beliefs while retaining old ones, could modify doctrines, could accommodate words and icons, ambiguities and contradictions. There may have been Reformation and Civil War, riot and rebellion, but the basic mental decor did not change as suddenly or completely as historians would sometimes lead us to believe.[56]

This image of the sixteenth and seventeenth-century alehouse world – in which orality and print ran side by side, and print enriched  but did not replace, the oral culture – sums up the theme of this paper. The pedlar was, in large part, the agent of that change. Take note of the print: it matters to us.

---

[56]    Watt, *Cheap Print*, pp. 331–332.

# X

# First steps in literacy: the reading and writing experiences of the humblest seventeenth-century spiritual autobiographers

The spiritual autobiographies of the seventeenth century include the first subjective accounts, written by men from the countryside from yeoman parentage or below, of childhood, education, the importance of literacy and the importance that their religious convictions had for them. They therefore contain first-hand accounts, or rather fragments of accounts, of the amount of education available, and its effects, by the relatively humble. They thus provide insight into the effects of literacy which is not provided by any other source.

There are very, very few of these accounts, and those which do exist suffer from the disadvantage of the *genre*. The spiritual autobiographers were Puritans and dissenters,[1] and therefore were socially slanted in whatever way Puritans and dissenters were socially slanted. They must also be considered even more a-typical than Puritans and dissenters in general, because the urge to write autobiography in itself defines an exceptional man.[2]

[1] I should like to thank Dr Roger Schofield for reading and commenting on this piece. I am also very grateful to Miss Sandy Harrison for collecting details from those autobiographies I could not myself see. The autobiographies have been extensively discussed in Owen C. Watkins, *The Puritan Experience* (1972) and Paul Delaney, *British Autobiography in the Seventeenth Century* (1969). Neither man is particularly interested in literacy, or the social origins of the humble autobiographer; indeed, the latter work includes the quite mistaken statement: 'Before 1700, no autobiographies by agricultural labourers or yeomen are known' (142, n. 25). Thirty-one of the 141 autobiographers whose works I have been able to examine describe the social status of the autobiographer's parents, and give some fragmentary details of the autobiographer's education. (Watkins, *op. cit.*, 241–59, lists autobiographies, and I have used this list as my base.) In addition, five more of the autobiographers give some information on their education

alone, and another dozen on their background alone. I have used this information to help build up a picture of the age at which reading and writing were taught. I have also used the diaries of men born in the seventeenth century of non-gentle rural origin, and, for good measure, the educational experience of the early eighteenth-century day-labourer poet, Stephen Duck.

[2] It is possible that the Quaker autobiographers were less exceptional, for the Quakers seem to have had an entirely deliberate policy of using print for evangelism and polemic. Quaker autobiographies are therefore much the most common. For the whole subject of humble autobiographers, see David Vincent's forthcoming study of the autobiographies of working men in the first half of the nineteenth century, *Bread. Knowledge, and Freedom* (Europa, 1980). I am very much indebted to Dr Vincent for drawing my attention to the relevance of the seventeenth-century autobiographer to my work. His

408

Lastly, even within the whole group of autobiographers, those who bothered to set the stage for their spiritual experiences within any framework of place, parentage and education were exceptional again. Most of them simply launched into the account of the work of God in their souls which was the purpose of their writing, without even the slightest account of their age, the region of England or the social group from which they came. There is no means of knowing whether those who do give some detail of parentage or education were drawn to do so by temperament, and were equally representative of the whole group of autobiographers whatever its social composition.

However, it is interesting, despite all these *caveats*, that those among the autobiographers who do bother to describe their social backgrounds were drawn mainly from just those groups in rural society which were most literate,[3] had more educational opportunity and also provided most converts to Quakerism than any other in some areas.[4] They were largely yeomen's sons, together with some wholesalers. They did not come exclusively from this sort of background, however. I have concentrated more here on the few who were either born in less prosperous circumstances, or who lost their fathers before their education was completed, and so abruptly descended the social scale, and, as they describe their surroundings, give us some account of the less literate world below the level of the yeoman. It is, therefore, the least typical of the autobiographers who are discussed most fully here.

·Despite the problem of typicality the autobiographers present, it seems entirely fair to assume that this group gives the reader some insight into the range of opportunities and experience in seventeenth-century England which was open to other, non-Puritan boys from similar social backgrounds. This account is therefore based on their experiences. Some of this group of autobiographers were only able to attend school for a very short time, and their accounts of the stage of proficiency in reading or writing they had reached by six, seven or eight years old give a very useful guide to the time it took to learn to read and write in the seventeenth century, and the ages at which it was customary to acquire the different skills. The incidental description of these autobiographers of their different social worlds and range of contacts also gives an impression of the diffusion of literate skills at different levels of seventeenth-century society.

The ability to sign one's name[5] has been conclusively shown to be tied to one's social

second chapter discusses both the seventeenth-century autobiographers and the eighteenth-century 'uneducated poets' as forerunners of the nineteenth-century working-class autobiographers, and was my point of departure.

[3] See below, p. 409.

[4] R. T. Vann, *The Social Development of English Quakerism, 1655–1755* (1969), ch. 2.

[5] The whole question of the use of signatures to provide a measure of the diffusion of literary skills over time, and of the crucial relationship of writing ability

to reading ability, is discussed in R. S. Schofield, 'The measurement of literacy in pre-industrial England', in J. R. Goody (ed.), *Literacy in Traditional Societies* (1968), 318–25 and 'Some discussion of illiteracy in England, 1600–1800' (unpublished). A part of the latter has appeared as 'Dimensions of illiteracy, 1750–1850', *Explorations in Economic History*, x, 4 (1973), 437–54. I am very grateful for Dr Schofield's permission to use the unpublished, definitive discussion of the relationship between signing and reading ability.

status in Tudor and Stuart East Anglia,[6] for the simple reason that some degree of prosperity was necessary to spare a child from the labour force for education as soon as it was capable of work. So literacy was economically determined. Between 1580 and 1700, 11 per cent of women, 15 per cent of labourers and 21 per cent of husbandmen could sign their names, against 56 per cent of tradesmen and craftsmen and 65 per cent of yeomen. Grammar school and even more university education was heavily socially restricted and only sons of yeomen from amongst the peasantry had much chance of appearing in grammar school or college registers.[7] This somewhat gloomy picture fails to stress the small but significant groups of signatories in even the most illiterate social groups who were able to write their names. It dwells on grammar and university education to the exclusion of the patchy, sporadic, but very real elementary education available in Tudor and Stuart England.[8] At the same time, Cressy admits, 'we do not know whether the acquisition of literacy was exclusively the product of formal elementary schooling, or at what stage in a person's life he learned, or failed to learn, to write the letters of his name'. The experiences of the spiritual autobiographers throw a great deal of light on just these problems.

Because the acquisition of reading and writing skills was socially stratified, I have organized this account in ascending order, starting with the poorest. Viewed from this angle, those yeomen's sons whose fathers could support them through a university education appear highly privileged, and I have in fact ignored them in favour of those autobiographers whose experiences represent those of that part of society which is outside the cognizance of historians working from college admission registers. The evidence is of course impressionistic. It is the qualitative evidence which puts at least some flesh on the quantitative skeleton of literacy provided by the signatures. It illuminates a murky and ill-defined world in which grammar schooling was practically irrelevant and yet reading and writing skills were sought after.

Useful though it is, such a discussion of basic 'literacy' which attempts particularly to gain an impression of the diffusion of the ability to read, and the period of schooling necessary to acquire the ability, necessarily comprehends very different degrees of the

[6] David Cressy, 'Educational opportunity in Tudor and Stuart England', *History of Education Quarterly* (Fall 1976), 314, and 'Literacy in seventeenth-century England: more evidence', *Journal of Interdisciplinary History*, VIII, 1 (Summer 1977), 146–8. Also *Historical Journal*, XX (1977), 4–8.

[7] Cressy, 'Educational opportunity', 309–13.

[8] Ironically, in view of his recent care to stress restricted access to education in 'Educational opportunity', the best survey of elementary educational facilities and their effects is in David Cressy, 'Education and literacy in London and East Anglia 1580–1700' (Cambridge Ph.D. thesis, 1972) which lists all schoolmasters appearing in the Dioceses of London and Norwich and show them relatively well provided with masters in rural areas in the 1590s and early seven-

teenth century. Alan Smith 'A study of educational development in the dioceses of Lichfield and Coventry in the seventeenth century' (Leicester Ph.D. thesis, 1972) and 'Private schools and schoolmasters in the Dioceses of Lichfield and Coventry', *History of Education*, V, 2 (1976) shows that in these dioceses there were more unendowed schoolmasters teaching in more places between 1660 and 1700 than in 1600–40. This might, of course, indicate merely an improvement in the records. On the other hand, it may indicate that the periods when most elementary education was available differed in different parts of the country. In this case, Cressy's periodization of improvement and stagnation in literacy rates does not necessarily apply to the whole country.

410

skill under one heading. Is one inquiring, Schofield asks, about the ability to read a simple handbill, a local newspaper or the works of John Locke?[9] Here, inevitably, I find myself discussing under the heading 'reading ability' a Wiltshire labourer who could read *Paradise Lost* with the aid of a dictionary, the Gloucestershire shepherds who could sound out words to teach an eager boy to read, and a blind thresher in Yorkshire who made a name for himself as a 'famous schoolteacher' whose pupils probably learnt to 'read' by rote learning only. It is obvious that completely different levels of fluency and skills are involved, but there is no way of distinguishing them. The problem can only be stated. I have deliberately let the autobiographers speak for themselves wherever possible. Since the point is to demonstrate that very limited educational opportunity did not debar at least a few people, who may of course have been highly exceptional, from the development of interests involving literary skills, the way in which men who left school at six, seven or nine later expressed themselves on paper is in itself meaningful.

Before working through the experiences of the autobiographers from the poorest upwards, it is useful to consider the specific information the autobiographies give us about the length of time it took some of them to acquire the skills of reading and of writing. This provides a background which makes it easier to assess the probable effects of the limited educational experiences of the poorer children. The seventeenth-century educationalists suggested that in the country schools, children normally began at seven or eight. Six was early. This fits well, on the whole, with the experience of the autobiographers, who learnt to read with a variety of people, mostly women, before starting writing with the 'formal' part of their education at seven, if they got that far.[10]

A bright child was able to learn to read in a few months in the seventeenth century, although so much must have depended on intelligence, the sort of teacher available, and the size of group he was in, that it is difficult to generalize. Oliver Sansom, born in 1636 in Beedon in Berkshire, wrote: 'When I was about six years of age, I was put to school to a woman, to learn to read, who finding me not unapt to learn, forwarded me so well, that in about four months' time, I could read a chapter in the Bible pretty readily.' Latin and writing began at seven.[11] John Evelyn, the diarist, began his schooling earlier, at four, when he joined the village group to begin the 'rudiments' in the local church porch. But he was not 'put to learn my Latin rudiments, and to write' until he was eight.[12] James Fretwell, eldest son of a Yorkshire timber-merchant, born in 1699, began lessons earlier still.

> As soon as I was capable of learning [my mother] sent me to an old school-dame, who lived at the very next door.... But I suppose I did but continue here but a few days, for growing weary of my book, and my dame not correcting me as my mother desired, she took me under her pedagogy untill I could read in my Bible, and thus she did afterwards by all my brothers and sisters.... And as my capacity

[9] Schofield, 'The measurement of literacy in pre-Industrial England', 313–14, and 'Some discussion of Illiteracy in England, 1600–1800'.

[10] See Cressy, *Education in Tudor and Stuart*

*England*, 70–2.

[11] Oliver Sansom, *An Account of the Many Remarkable Passages of the Life of Oliver Sansom...* (1710).

[12] John Evelyn, *Diary* for 1624 and 1628.

was able, she caused me to observe what I read, so I soon began to take some notice of several historical passages in the Old Testament.

He was admitted to the small grammar school of Kirk Sandall,

> my dear mother being desirous that I should have a little more learning than she was capable of giving me . . . where [the master] placed me amongst some little ones, such as myself . . . when he called me up to hear what I could say for myself, he finding me better than he expected, removed me higher, asking my mother if she had brought me an Accidence, which I think she had; so she had the pleasure of seeing me removed out of the horn-book class, which my master at first sight thought most suitable for me.

The master's assumption was not surprising. James was then aged four years and seven months.[13] He was obviously precocious. Other precocious children's achievements were also recorded because they were unusual. Oliver Heyward married the daughter of a Puritan minister who had learnt both to read and to write fluently before the normal age in the 1640s. 'She could read the hardest chapter in the Bible when she was but four years of age' and was taught to write by the local schoolmaster 'in learning whereof she was more than ordinarily capable, being able at six yeares of age to write down passages of the sermon in the chappel'.[14] Anne Gwin of Falmouth, daugher of a fisherman and fishmerchant, born in 1692, likewise 'took to learning very Young, and soon became a good Reader, viz. when she was but about Three yeares and a Half old, she wrote tolerably well before five'.[15] The biographers of these girls recognized their unusual forwardness; it seems safer to use Oliver Sansom as a specific example of the time it took normal children to learn to read.

The autobiographers give the impression that, unless their schooling had already been broken off, they were reading fluently by seven at the latest, even if, like young Thomas Boston, who 'had delight in reading' the Bible by that age, and took it to bed at night with him, 'nothing inclined me to it but . . . curiosity, as about the history of Balaam's ass'.[16]

Writing began with Latin, if a grammar school education was in prospect, whether the boy began this stage of his education at seven like Oliver Sansom, at eight like John Evelyn, or at four like the forward little James Fretwell. It is even more difficult to find evidence on the time it took to master the second skill than the first. Yet one piece of very precise evidence does survive. Alderman Samuel Newton of Cambridge kept a diary from 1664 to 1717.[17] It contains very little personal information, amongst the accounts

---

[13] James Fretwell, 'Yorkshire diaries', *Surtees Society* (1877), 183–4.

[14] The Rev. Oliver Heyward, B.A., 1630–1702 (ed. J. Horsfall-Turner), *His Autobiography, Diaries, Anecdotes and Event Books* (1882), I, 58.

[15] Thomas Gwin, *A Memorial of Anne Gwin* (1715) and the *Journal of Thomas Gwin of Falmouth* (1837).

[16] Thomas Boston (ed. George D. Low), *A General Account of my Life by Thomas Boston, A.M. Minister at Simprin, 1699–1707 and at Ettrick, 1707–1732* (Edinburgh, 1908), 3.

[17] J. E. Foster (ed.), 'The diary of Samuel Newton, Alderman of Cambridge (1662–1717)', *Cambridge Antiquarian Society*, Octavo Publications

412

of corporation junketings and funerals of prominent persons. But on 12 February 1667, Alderman Newton wrote: 'On Tewsday was the first time John Newton my sonne went to the Grammar Free Schoole in Cambridge'. In October the same year, between a note on the assembly of parliament and a family baptism, appears an entry in a child's hand:

I John Newton being in Coates this nineteenth day of October Anno Domini 1667 and not then full eight yeares old, wrote this by me
John Newton.

There is no paternal comment on this entry, but Alderman Newton must have shared his son's satisfaction in the new achievement to allow the entry to be made. Obviously, to the seven-year-old John, the new skill of writing, which had taken six months to acquire, was a matter of as much pride as his emergence into manhood in his newly acquired breeches.

It seems likely, as a rule-of-thumb guide, that children who had the opportunity to go to school until they were seven were likely to be able to read. Those who remained at school until eight were likely to be able to write.

If it took the autobiographers, who may have been exceptionally gifted, four to six months to learn to read, and they began to acquire the skill at various ages from four to six, it seems reasonable to double this learning period to allow a margin of safety for less intelligent or forward children.[18] A working hypothesis would then be that children who had the opportunity of going to school would have learnt to read by seven. Similarly, since the autobiographers normally began the writing part of their curriculum at seven, and it took John Newton six months to write a good hand, it seems reasonable to double this period also, and suggest that the ability to write was normally acquired by eight.

If these hypotheses are accepted, it follows from the evidence collected by Cressy on occupational differences in ability to sign, showing that only 15 per cent of labourers and 21 per cent of husbandmen, as against 65 per cent of yeomen could sign,[19] that these percentages roughly represent the proportion of those social groups which had the opportunity for schooling between seven and eight. Nothing could show more clearly that the economic status of the parents was the determinant of schooling,[20] along, of

XXIII, 17 and 23. The original is in Downing College Library, and the entry by John Newton appears on fo. 74 of the MS.
[18] This coincides well with the expectations of the early nineteenth-century monitorial schools, in which a child was expected to learn to read in eleven months. Schofield, 'Measurement of literacy in pre-Industrial England', 316.
[19] See above, p. 409.
[20] Pace Peter Clark, who suggests that my argument that 'the husbandman who depended entirely on familial labour was probably...unable to afford the loss of labour which his child's school attendance

entailed...is stronger in the context of higher education than in the case of primary instruction. It does not take into account those many longeurs in the agricultural year...when parents were probably quite happy to send a noisy son out to school for a month or so.' Peter Clark, English Provincial Society from the Reformation to the Revolution: Religion, Politics and Society in Kent, 1500–1640 (1977), 191. The acquisition of the ability to sign was certainly normally acquired young, probably between seven and eight, and Cressy's evidence shows quite conclusively that economic status determined education to this level.

course, with the existence of some local teaching. The children of labourers and, to a lesser extent, of husbandmen,[21] were needed to join the labour force as soon as they were strong enough to contribute meaningfully to the family economy.[22]

It is difficult to conceive that they could have made a real contribution before six. The case of Thomas Tryon, whose father urgently needed his son's earnings, but still sent him to school from five until he was nearly six,[23] bears this out. So does the literary evidence of Thomas Deloney, who was himself a weaver, who wrote in one of his extravagant novels glorifying the clothing trade in 1599 of a golden age in the past when:

> poor people whom God lightly blessed with most children did by meanes of this occupation so order them that by the time they were come to be six or seven years of age, they were able to get their own bread.[24]

Further evidence for a starting age of six or seven comes from workhouse regulations of the sixteenth and seventeenth centuries governing the ages at which children could be set to work. These seem particularly likely to be reliable, since a municipal workhouse was very unlikely not to try to profit from children's labour if it were possible to do so. Westminster workhouse, in 1560, sent its children over six, but not yet twelve, 'to wind Quills for weavers'.[25]

The Aldersgate workhouse, in 1677, admitted children of from three to ten, and its founder wrote 'as to young children, there is nothing they can more easily learn than to spin linen, their fingers, though never so little, being big enough to pull the flax and make a fine thread'. At the time, in 1678 and 1681 when he wrote, he had 'some children not above seven or eight years old, who are able to earn two pence a day'.[26] In 1699, the Bishopgate workhouse was established for all poor parish children over the age of seven. They were to be employed from seven in the morning until six at night, with an hour off for dinner and play, and two hours' instruction in reading and writing.[27] This

[21] See below, Thomas Carleton, pp. 417–18, for the sporadic opportunities of a husbandman's son had for learning, and John Bunyan, p. 418, who knew perfectly well that his ability to write was unusual in the economic circumstances of his home, and had to be accounted for.

[22] Christopher Wase in his *New Discovery of the Old Art of Teaching School* (1660) wrote 'many parents will not spare their children to learn if they can but find them any employment about their domestic or rural affairs whereby they may save a penny', although he also implied that such families spared their children to learn to read and write. Quoted by Cressy, *Education in Tudor and Stuart England*, 45.

[23] See below, p. 415.

[24] Thomas Deloney, *The Pleasant History of Thomas of Reading, or, the Six Worthy Yeomen of the West* (1599?) ch. 1. One of the claims to fame of another of Deloney's heroes, Jack of Newbery, was that he set ninety-six poor children on work wool-picking; *The Pleasant History of John Winchcomb, in his younger year called Jack of Newbery* (1597), ch. III; *The Works of Thomas Deloney* (ed. F. O. Mann) (1912), 213–37.

[25] Alice Clark, *Working Life of Women in the Seventeenth Century* (1919), 131. In the 1640s unskilled agricultural labourers were earning 12d. a day (Joan Thirsk (ed.), *Agrarian History of England and Wales*, IV, *1560–1640*, 864). This rate was the same as that for building labourers, which remained constant at 12d. a day until just after 1690. (E. H. Phelps Brown and Sheila V. Hopkins, 'Seven centuries of building wages', in E. M. Carus-Wilson (ed.), *Essays in Economic History*, II (1962), 172–3 and 177.) These children were earning a sixth of a man's wage. Exceptionally skilled children, like Thomas Tryon, could earn a third of a man's wage at eight.

[26] I. Pinchbeck and M. Hewitt, *Children in English Society* (1969), i, 161.

[27] *Ibid.*, 154–6.

414

workhouse, which was, incidentally, a humane one by contemporary standards, was obviously run on the assumption that its children could all work these hours. It is highly significant, therefore, that it did not admit children under seven. It looks very much as if seven was thought to be the age at which a child could cope with a full working day and start to earn a wage which began to be significant.[28] It was also the age at which Tudor parents had a statutory duty to see that their sons practised regularly at the butts, that is, were strong enough to begin to be thought significant in the adult world of the militia. Obviously, rural children could only be regularly employed in areas where textile industries provided the kind of outwork performed by these city orphans. In many areas, their opportunities for work were likely to be more seasonal, and more along the lines described by Henry Best. His 'spreaders of muck and molehills' were for the most part women, boys and girls, and they were paid 3d. a day for the 'bigger and abler sort' and 2d. a day for the 'lesser sort'.[29] Obviously a child was started at work before seven if there was a great need, as the cases of Thomas Tryon and the Westminster workhouse children show.[30]

If seven were indeed the age at which a child could earn significant wages, and was regarded as an embryonic member of the militia as well as the workforce, it also seems to have been the age at which reading had probably been mastered, but writing not yet embarked on. If this conclusion is true, it is an important one. It indicates that reading skills, which unfortunately by their nature are not capable of measurement, were likely to have been very much more socially widespread in sixteenth- and seventeenth-century England than writing skills, simply because the age at which children learnt to read was one at which children of the relatively poor were not yet capable of much paying labour, and were therefore available for some schooling. The restriction of writing ability to a small percentage of labourers' and husbandmen's sons, and its much wider spread amongst the sons of the yeomanry is at once explained. Reading skills are likely to have been very much more diffused. It was, of course, the ability to read (and not the ability to write) that laid the way open to cultural change.

The argument can, of course, be started the other way round. We know that 15 per cent of labourers' sons could sign their names and presumably could read; we know that a much higher proportion of yeomen's sons could do so. We therefore know that economic necessity is likely to have been the factor that limited the opportunity to learn. It seems that a boy was physically strong and co-ordinated enough to contribute to the family budget in a significant way at some age between six and eight. The crucial question is

[28] Ibid., 10.

[29] Henry Best, Rural Economy in Yorkshire in 1641; being the farming and account books of Henry Best, of Elmswell, in the East Riding of the county of York (ed. C. B. Robinson) (Surtees Soc., no. 33, 1857).

[30] Defoe, writing in the 1720s, is unusual by seventeenth-century standards in implying that children commonly started work before six. He says Yorkshire children could earn their living at four, round Taunton at five, and in east and mid-Norfolk 'the very children after four or five years of Age could earn their own Bread'. Quoted by Pinchbeck and Hewitt, op. cit., 310–11. Either he exaggerated, or there had been a social change, and work started earlier, perhaps because the numbers of agricultural labourers were swelling so much as the pace of engrossing increased.

First steps in literacy                                           415

whether this point was nearer six, or nearer seven. On the answer to this, as well as the local availability of schooling, depended the number of boys, from different occupational backgrounds, who could read.

No identifiable autobiographer was fathered by an agricultural labourer, although at least one autobiographer became an agricultural labourer. Thomas Tryon, of the autobiographers who identified their backgrounds, came from the poorest home, and he certainly had the most prolonged struggle to get himself an education. He was born in 1634 at Bibury in Oxfordshire, and was the son of a village tiler and plasterer 'an honest sober Man of good Reputation; but having many Children, was forced to bring them all to work betimes'.[31] Tilers and plasterers were building craftsmen, and as such were more prosperous than agricultural labourers, but the purchasing power of their wages was very low in the early seventeenth century.[32]

The size of the family did much to dictate educational opportunity, for obvious reasons.[33] Again and again, only children or those from small families amongst the autobiographers appear at an advantage. Despite his numerous siblings, young Thomas was briefly sent to school. 'About Five Year old, I was put to School, but being addicted to play, after the Example of my young School-fellows, I scarcely learnt to distinguish my Letters, before I was taken away to Work for my Living.' This seems to have been before he was six, although his account is ambiguous. At six young Thomas Tryon was either not strongly motivated, as he obviously thought himself from his mention of the importance of play, or he was not well taught. Yet it is worth remembering that he was removed from school to work at about the age Oliver Sansom began to learn. His failure to learn to read was going to take great determination to repair.

His contribution to the family economy began immediately and he obviously took tremendous pride in his ability to contribute: 'The first Work my Father put me to, was Spinning and Carding, wherein I was so Industrious and grew so expert that at Eight Years of Age I could Spin Four Pound a day which came to Two Shillings a Week.'[34] He continued to spin until he was twelve or thirteen but by the time he was ten 'began to be weary of the Wheel' and started to help the local shepherds with their flocks on Sundays, to earn a penny or twopence on his own account. When his father wished to

[31] *Some Memoirs of the Life of Mr Tho: Tryon, late of London, merchant: written by himself . . .* (1705), 7–9.
[32] J. Thirsk (ed.), *Agrarian History of England and Wales*, IV, *1500–1640*, 865. In 1586 in London their day-wages without food had been fixed at 13*d.* a day, along with masons, coopers and glaziers under the Statute of Artificers. This compared with 9*d.* a day for 'common labourers'. R. H. Tawney and Eileen Power (eds.), *Tudor Econ. Documents*, I (1924), 369–70.
[33] The brutal reality was most simply stated later by John Clare in his autobiography. He was born the son of a Northamptonshire day-labourer in 1793: 'As my parents had the good fate to have but a small family, I being the eldest of 4, two of whom dyed in their Infancy, my mother's hopeful ambition ran high

of being able to make me a good scholar . . . but God help her, her hopeful and tender kindness was often cross'd with difficulty, for there was often enough to do to keep cart upon wheels, as the saying is, without incuring an extra expence of pulling me to school . . . I believe I was not older than 10 when my father took me to seek the rewards of industry . . . [but] As to my schooling, I think never a year pass'd me till I was 11 or 12, but 3 months or more at the worst of times was luckily spend for my improvement,' Edmund Blunden (ed.), *Sketches in the Life of John Clare* (1931).
[34] Tryon, *op. cit.*, 10–11. This is approximately double the earnings of eight-year-olds quoted as an example of industrious good management. See above, p. 413.

416

apprentice him to his own trade he obeyed very reluctantly, for by this time he was determined to become a shepherd. 'My Father was unwilling to gratifie me herein . . . but by continually importuning him, at last I prevailed, and he bought a small number of Sheep; to the keeping and management whereof, I betook myself with much satisfaction and delight, as well as care.' But now, at last, at the age when his most fortunate contemporaries were about to go to University,[35] the desire for literacy gripped Thomas. It is worth quoting his account of the way he managed to satisfy it in full.

> All this while, tho' now about Thirteen Years Old, I could not Read; then thinking of the vast usefulness of Reading, I bought me a Primer, and got now one, then another, to teach me to Spell, and so learn'd to Read imperfectly, my Teachers themselves not being ready Readers: But in a little time having learn't to Read competently well, I was desirous to learn to Write, but was at a great loss for a Master, none of my Fellow-Shepherds being able to teach me. At last, I bethought myself of a lame young Man who taught some poor People's Children to Read and Write; and having by this time got two Sheep of my own, I applied myself to him, and agreed with him to give him one of my Sheep to teach me to make the Letters, and Joyn them together.[36]

The difficulty Thomas found in learning to write, as opposed to learning to read, seems very important. Although his fellow shepherds, as a group, were not 'ready' readers, they did, again as a group, possess the capacity to help him to learn to spell out words. He was not dependent on only one of them to help him. But although these Gloucestershire shepherds could read, they could not write at all. A semi-qualified teacher was called for, and it took some effort to find him.

Thomas Tryon eventually went to London as an apprentice. His addiction to print continued. He made time to read by sitting up at night for two or three hours after his day's work was finished. His wages went on education. 'Therewith I furnished myself with Books, paid my Tutors and served all my occasions.' He was particularly interested in the art of medicine which he defined as the 'whole study of Nature' and within that, astrology, which he defined as the 'Method of God's government in Nature . . . [which] ought no more to be condemned because of the common abuse of it, than Religion ought, because its so commonly perverted to Superstition, or made a Cloak to Hypocrisie and Knavery'. Even after his marriage at thirty-five, he remained an incurable self-improver and then took music lessons:

> About Five and Thirty Years, I attempted to learn Musick and having a natural propensity thereto, made a pretty good progress on the Base-viol, tho' during the time of my learning, I . . . stuck as close to my working Trade, as ever before; so that I could only apply an Hour or Two to Musick, taking my opportunities at Night,

[35] The autobiographers whose parents were prosperous enough to enable them to go to university quite frequently went as early as fourteen. This conflicts with Cressy's findings that the mean age for entry to university was sixteen (*thesis cit.*) and bears out the suggestion that the autobiographers were probably an exceptionally gifted group.
[36] Tryon, *op. cit.*, 13–15.

or in a Morning as best I could; and the time others spent in a Coffee-house or Tavern, I spent in Reading, Writing, Musick or some useful Imployment; by which means I supplyed what I could the defect of Education.[37]

His written works which reflected his own range of interests included *The Country Man's Companion, The Good Housewife made a Doctor, Dreams and Visions, Book of Trade, Friendly Advice to the People of the West Indies, A New Method of Education* and, most surprisingly of all, *Averroes Letter to Pythagoras*. It is a remarkable publication list for a boy who left school at six before he could read.

When Thomas Tryon came to write down his 'Principles' for the religious group he founded, his own experiences, including his battle for literacy, were directly reflected in them. In his 'Laws and Orders proper for Women to observe', he wrote, amongst various rules for the upbringing of children which were, on the whole, remarkably sane and tolerant:

At a Year and a Half or Two Years Old, shew them their Letters, not troubling them in the vulgar way with asking them what is this Letter, or that Word; but instead thereof, make frequent Repetitions in their hearing, putting the Letters in their Sight. And thus in a little time, they will easily and familiarly learn to distinguish the Twenty Four Letters, all one as they do the Utensils, Goods, and Furniture of the House, by hearing the Family name them. *At the same time*, teach your Children to hold the Pen, and guide their Hand; and by this method, your Children, un-accountably to themselves, will attain to Read and Write at Three, Four, or Five years old... When your Children are of dull Capacities and hard to Learn, Reproach them not nor expose them, but taking them alone... shew them the Advantages of Learning, and how much it will tend to their advancement.[38]

His advocacy of flash-cards has a strangely modern ring about it, as does his suggestion of teaching writing at the same time as reading. His assumption that the teaching of reading is the natural function of the mother, is an interesting one, particularly since several of the autobiographers were in fact taught to read by their mothers. The few literate women in seventeenth-century society may well have had a disproportionately large influence.[39]

A boy from a husbandman's background, rather than a skilled labourer's, was more likely to be lucky enough to be spared from work for long enough to gain a rudimentary education, although his education was likely to be constantly interrupted by more pressing agricultural business. Thomas Carleton described the situation of such a boy very well.

I sprang of mean (though honest) Parents according to the flesh, my Father being a Husbandman, in the County of Cumberland, I (according to his pleasure) was educated sometimes at School, sometimes with Herding, and tending of Sheep, or

[37] *Ibid.*, 42–4.    [39] See note at end.
[38] My italics; *ibid.*, 117–18, 122–3.

418

Cattel, sometime with the Plow, Cart, or threshing-Instrument, or other lawfull labour.[40]

This background of sporadic schooling enabled him, when the spiritual need took him, to 'give myself to reading and Searching of the Scriptures'. Intermittent educational experience like this was probably typical of the fifth of the husbandmen[41] who were lucky enough to get as far as learning to write their names.

John Bunyan, the best known of all the seventeenth-century dissenters, came of poor parentage, although his parents were more prosperous or their family less numerous than Thomas Tryon's. He never had to struggle for a basic education as Tryon did. His father held a cottage and nine acres in Bedfordshire.[42] This was barely adequate for subsistence. He eked out a living by tinkering rather than by wage-labour, and so is classifiable either as a husbandman on his acreage, or as a poor craftsman on his trade. Despite their relative poverty, Bunyan wrote 'notwithstanding the meanness of...my Parents, it pleased God to put it into their Hearts to put me to School, to learn both to read and write'. He was fully conscious of having had educational advantages which exceeded his parents' social position.

Amongst the autobiographers who described their parentage[43] only Baxter and Bunyan also confessed to the reading of cheap print as a childhood sin. The yeoman's son, Richard Baxter, listed amongst his early sins committed about the age of ten, 'I was extremely bewitched with a love of romances, fables and old tales, which corrupted my affections and lost my time'.[44] He also gives a very rare glimpse of a chapman at work in the 1630s: 'About that time it pleased God that a poor pedlar came to the door that had ballads and some good books: and my father bought of him Dr Sibb's *Bruised Reed.*'

Bunyan is also likely to have got his reading matter from the chapmen, either at the door or at market. Elstow, where he was brought up, is two miles from the county-town of Bedford, which was not a large enough provincial town to have a bookshop in the seventeenth century. Moreover, the reading matter he describes is chapmen's ware. He was much more specific than Baxter about his tastes in his youth. He wrote:

[40] Thomas Carleton, *The Captives Complaint or the Prisoners Plea* (1688).

[41] The term 'husbandman' can be misleadingly used in a literary sense. Otherwise, it normally describes the group of farmers with medium-sized farms between fifteen and fifty acres who were becoming increasingly rare in arable areas in the seventeenth century. The plotting of values of the goods of men described as 'husbandmen' by their neighbours who drew up their inventories shows this quite clearly, although the range of values of husbandmen's goods is wide, and will overlap considerably with the bottom of the range of values of the more prosperous 'yeomen's' goods. Margaret Spufford, 'The significance of the Cambridgeshire Hearth Tax', *Cambridge Antiquarian Society*, LV (1962), 54, n. 3.

[42] Roger Sharrock, *John Bunyan* (1968; 1st edn 1954), 9, 11–12.

[43] Others, who did not describe their backgrounds, confessed to unscriptural reading. Vavasour Powell, from the Welsh border, also had 'no esteem for the holy scripture, nor cared not at all to look into them, but either Hystorical or Poetical Books, Romances and the like were all my delight'. V. Powell, *The Life and Death of Mr Vavasour Powell, that faithful minister and confessor of Jesus Christ...* (1671). Richard Kilby was so distressed by his besetting sin of lust that he recommended 'Whatsoever lewd ballet, book or picture cometh to your hands, teare it all to pieces or burne it to ashes'. R. Kilby, *The burthen of a loaded conscience: or the miserie of sinne...etc.* (1608).

[44] N. H. Keeble (ed.), *Autobiography of Richard Baxter* (1974), 5, 7. I am very grateful to Cedric Parry for drawing this particular passage to my attention.

First steps in literacy                                        419

give me a Ballard, a News-book, *George* on Horseback or *Bevis of Southampton*, give me some book that teaches curious Arts, that tells of old Fables; but for the Holy Scriptures, I cared not. And as it was with me then, so it is with my brethren now.[45]

The implication is plain that either Bunyan's relations or his peer group were, at the time Bunyan was writing in the 1660s, commonly readers of the ballads and chapbooks which Bunyan himself avoided after his conversion.[46]

Bunyan's reading seems to have left some mark on him.[47] *Bevis of Southampton* was a typical, breathless, sub-chilvalric romance in which adventure follows adventure in quick succession.[48] The hero's mother betrays his father to death and marries his murderer. Her son first escapes and keeps his uncle's sheep on a hill near his father's castle, then is sold into slavery to the 'paynims'. There he refuses to serve 'Apoline' their god, kills a gigantic wild boar, is made a general over twenty thousand men, and wins the love of the princess. Alas, he is betrayed, and thrown into a dungeon with two dragons who quickly get the worst of it. He is still able to kill his jailer, after seven years on bread and water, and runs off with the princess and a great store of money and jewels. He is next attacked by two lions in a cave, meets 'an ugly Gyant thirty foot in length and a foot between his eyebrows', defeats him and makes him his page, and kills a dragon forty foot long. He then has the heathen princess baptised, and after numerous further adventures invades England, avenges his father's death, marries his paynim lady, and

---

[45] John Bunyan, *Sighs from Hell* (2nd edn, 1666?), 147–8. The italics are his own. In 1631, Richard Brathwait in *Whimzies: or, a New Cast of Characters* had not been complimentary about the 'Corranto-Coiner' who was presumably the source of the news-books Bunyan enjoyed. 'His mint goes weekly, and he coins monie by it . . .', Brathwait wrote. 'The vulgar doe admire him, holding his novels oracular; and these are usually sent for tokens . . . betwixt city and countrey . . . You shall many times find in his corrants miserable distructions; here a city taken by force before it bee besieged; there a countrey laid waste before even the enemy entered . . . He is the very landskip of our age . . . Yet our best comfort is that his chymeras live not long; a weeke is the longest in the citie, and after their arrival, a little longer in the countrey; which past, they melt like *Butter*, or match a pipe, and so Burne.' Quoted by Joseph Frank, *The Beginnings of the English Newspaper 1620–60* (1961), 276.

[46] It is an interesting one, since his education was abnormally good for his economic and social background, and he had learnt to write as well as to read. It might imply that his 'brethren' who had not learnt both skills, did read the chap literature.

[47] When Mrs Leavis wrote of the literary inade-quacy and emotional poverty of twentieth-century mass fiction in 1939, she was unaware of the existence of the voluminous chap-literature of the seventeenth and eighteenth centuries, the content of which would have provided her with an apt comparison with modern bestsellers. She wrote of Bunyan's prose, as if only the *Authorised Version* was available to form his style, and of the cultural contacts of working-class men up to the 1850s as if only the *Bible*, the *Pilgrim's Progress*, *Paradise Lost* and *Robinson Crusoe*, works by Addison, Swift and Goldsmith and so on, were on the market. 'No energy was wasted, the edge of their taste was not blunted on bad writing and cheap thinking', Q. D. Leavis, *Fiction and the Reading Public* (1939), 97–102, 106–15.

[48] A copy survives in Samuel Pepys's collection of *Vulgaria, III*, item 10, Pepys Library, Magdalene College, Cambridge. '*George* on Horseback' is probably the chapbook *St George*. There is a copy in Pepys's *Penny Merriments*, II, 105–28, of the edition printed in the 1680s. The title page bears a really impressive woodcut of a knight on horseback, and Bunyan, working from memory, might well have arrived at his title from this visual recollection, combined perhaps with a disinclination to give the hero his saintly title.

420

is made Lord Marshall. There is no attempt at characterization and the whole piece of blood-and-thunder writing seems aimed at pre-adolescent or adolescent males; very successfully, if Bunyan's testimony is to be believed. Although his own writing was very far removed from this, some of his imagery does seem to have come from his early reading. The lions Christian met by the way, the description of the monster Apollyon and the cave where the giants Pope and Pagan dwelt all owe something to it, as perhaps, does Giant Despair himself. It is worth remembering also that Bunyan's own voluminous output was surely aimed at the rural readership he knew in the villages around Bedford amongst which he had his ministry. He knew his readership was familiar with the giants, lions, dragons and battles of the chapbooks, just as it was with the cadences of the Authorized Version.

Arise Evans, who came from the Welsh border, was born in 1606 or 1607.[49] His father was a good deal better off than either Bunyan's or Tryon's, and sounds indeed like a prosperous yeoman, or even a minor gentleman, from his son's description:

> My father being a sufficient man of the Parish did entertain the Curate always at his Table, and gave him a little Tenement of Land to live upon; and by reason of this kindness to the Minister, which had but small allowance from the Parson of the Parish, that had all the Tithes. The Minister was diligent to do my father's family what good he was able: and as soon as I began to speak plain, I was put to school to him.

But when Arise was only six, his father died.

A surprisingly large number of autobiographers who give any factual details of themselves at all dwell on the deaths of one, or both of their parents.[50] It seems that as many as one eighth of children may have lost their fathers by the time they were seven, the age at which I suggest they might have learnt to read, but not to write.[51] The death of the father leaving a young family always meant that the family economy collapsed. A son still at school usually left, either to earn his living, or to help his mother. Frequently he seems to have slithered down the social scale permanently; it is for this reason that some account of the life of a farm labourer survives. It was written by a boy who was at grammar school until his father's death, but who became an in-servant in

[49] A. Evans, *An eccho to the voice from heaven. Or a narration of the life, and manner of the special calling, and visions of Arise Evans...* (1652).

[50] Nine of the thirty-one who describe both their parentage and their education. The extreme example is John Whiting of Somerset who was born in 1656, son of a 'reputable yeoman', who died when John was two 'while I was very young, so that I cannot remember him'. His mother remarried in 1661, but died in 1666 'when I was about ten years old, which was a great trouble to me, she being a tender mother'. The orphaned ten-year-old let his step-father remain in possession of his lands to bring up his three younger half-brothers, but he, in turn, died in 1672,

so the young John chose a guardian until 1675, when he 'went to his own house', and presumably assumed headship of his family. John Whiting, *Persecution Expos'd...* (1715).

[51] In eighteenth-century France, about one eighth of children had lost their fathers by this age, and by fourteen, the age at which apprenticeship normally seems to have started, a quarter of children had lost their fathers. Calculated from Harvé Le Bras, 'Parents, grands-parents, bisaieux', *Population* (1973), 34. I am told by the Cambridge Group for the History of Population and Social Structure that these figures should apply to seventeenth-century England.

233

husbandry after his mother's remarriage. The death of the mother involved less economic hardship, but often considerable psychological distress for the child. Historical demographers have so far emphasized infant mortality rates a good deal more than parental mortality rates. It seems that the social and personal consequences of as many as one child in eight losing its father when it was seven or less, were considerable, and deserve more attention.

The death of Arise Evans's father involved both economic and psychological hardship for him; indeed, it seems from his autobiography that the trauma involved could well have been one of the causes of his later emotional unbalance and rather dubious visions. He had thought that he was his father's favourite child. Certainly his father had shown great pride in his ability to read aloud and had shown him off to visitors.

> It was not long before I attained to reade English perfectly, to the admiration of all that heard me: and because I was so young and so active in learning, all concluded that God had designed me for some great work....But...death takes away my father before I was seven years old, and now he forgets me at his death, that was his delight a little before; and making his last Will, he leaves a Portion to all his children by name, and to many of his kindred,...but I was not so much as mentioned in his Will, nor any thing left for me, so that I came soon to know the folly of vain confidence in man....After this I was taken from school, when I had learned the *Accidence* out of Book, but never came to *Grammar*, or to write.[52]

Arise never tells us how or when he did learn to write. Certainly, he had no opportunity at the normal age. At eight when he should have learnt to write, he was apprenticed to a tailor, far younger than usual. He retained from his brief period of education until some time in his seventh year a passion for the written word which he was hardly ever able to satisfy. One of the stories he tells dramatically illuminates this thirst for information and for books which he would satisfy at the cost of enormous personal discomfort, if only it were possible. At twenty-two he set off, like so many others, to work his way to London.

> And at Coventre I wrought and stayed a quarter of a year, by reason of an old Chronicle that was in my Master's house that showed all the passage in Brittain and Ireland from Noahs Floud to William the Conquerour, it was of a great volume, and by day I bestowed what time I could spare to read, and bought Candles for the night, *so that I got by heart the most material part* of it.[53]

This desire for information, together with the problems of even finding time to absorb it during the working day, or a source of light to read it by at night, seems to have been common to all largely self-educated working men at all periods. The physical difficulties the autobiographers encountered in the seventeenth century were fundamentally the same as those of their nineteenth-century heirs.[54]

[52] Evans, *op. cit.*, 6.
[53] *Ibid.*, 13.
[54] Vincent, *op. cit.*, Ch. 5. See below, p. 433, for Thomas Boston.

422

Thomas Chubb,[55] like Arise Evans and Thomas Tryon, was a boy from a rural background who moved to town, although in his case the town was Salisbury, not London. Also, like Arise Evans, the death of his father affected his prospects, though not so seriously. He was the son of a maltster[56] of East Harnham, born in 1679. His father died when he was nine, leaving a widow and five children, of which he was the youngest. He wrote of himself in the introduction to a lengthy work on the Scriptures.

> The Author was taught to read English, to write an ordinary hand, and was further instructed in the common rules of arithmetick; this education being suitable to the circumstances of his family and to the time he had to be instructed in. For as the Author's mother laboured hard, in order to get a maintenance for herself and family, so she obliged her children to perform their parts towards it. Accordingly, the Author was very early required to perform such work and service as was suitable for his age and capacity; so that he had neither time nor means for further instruction than the above mentioned.[57]

When he was fifteen, in 1694, he was apprenticed to a glover in Salisbury. It is not certain from his account that he left school at nine, on his father's death, but it seems probable, since he would then have had two years in which to learn writing and elementary arithmetic. He had obviously attended one of the schoolmasters who was so frequently licensed in visitation records to teach 'to read, write and caste an accompte'.[58] He was never intended, or never had the chance, to embark on a grammar school curriculum. After he had served his apprenticeship he became a journeyman, but was handicapped as a glover by his weak sight. So, after 1705 he lived with, and worked for, a tallow-chandler. He served in the chandler's shop, and made gloves part-time only.

---

[55] T. Chubb, *The Posthumus Works of Mr Thomas Chubb... To the whole is prefixed, some account of the author written by himself...* (1748).

[56] Maltsters are wholesale tradesmen, who are usually, but not always, more prosperous than husbandmen, but less prosperous than the more substantial yeomen. The two maltsters whose inventories survive from the 1660s in the Lichfield area, for instance, left goods worth £48 and £132 respectively. The nine men whose contemporaries described them as husbandmen all left under £100, but the fifteen men described as yeomen left goods ranging in value widely from under £50 to just under £300. D. G. Vaisey (ed.), *Probate Inventories of Lichfield and District, 1568–1680*, Collections for a History of Staffs, 4th series Vol. v (Staffordshire Record Society) (1969). Thomas Boston (see below, p. 433), the other son of a maltster discussed here, was born in the same decade as Thomas Chubb, but in the Scottish Lowlands.

[57] Chubb, *op. cit.*, ii–iii.

[58] Although it seems that there was no hard and fast distinctive line drawn between a schoolmaster licensed to teach 'reading, writing and arithmetic' and one licensed to teach 'grammar'. At one visitation a man might well be licensed to teach grammar, who had previously been licensed to teach reading and writing, and vice versa. It does not seem as if there was a clear distinction, in the small 'private' schools which were both so numerous and so impermanent in the seventeenth century, between 'English', or 'petty' schools, and grammar schools. The masters probably taught according to the aptitudes of the different children, the desires of their parents, and the length of time the children could be spared for education from the labour force, as well as their own ability and training. The flexibility frequently found in seventeenth-century education is indicated by the licenses to Thomas Orpe, *literatus* 'to teach boys in English as well as in Latin as long as they were able' at Norton, Salop, in 1695. Alan Smith, 'Private schools and schoolmasters in the Dioceses of Lichfield and Coventry in the seventeenth century', *History of Education*, vol. 5, no. 2, (1976) 125; Margaret Spufford, *Contrasting Communities* (1974), 187.

First steps in literacy

He never married and it sounds as if his experience of poverty after his father's death had influenced him heavily in this:

> The Author . . . [judged] it greatly improper to introduce a family into the world, without a prospect of maintaining them, which was his case; such adventures being usually attended with great poverty. . . . And tho', according to the proverb, God does not send mouths without sending meat to fill them; yet our Author saw, by daily experience, that meat to some was not to be obtained but with great difficulty. And as to trusting to providence, in such cases, the Author . . . did [not] find, that providence interposed to extricate it's . . . dependents out of their difficulties.[59]

Thomas Chubb gives an account of the way his first tract came to be published. The fascination of this lies not in the account of the tract itself, but the way it reveals his own habits of written composition since his boyhood, and the literary activities of a whole group of young men like himself in Salisbury.

> When the reverend Mr. Whiston published his historical preface to those books he entitled *Primitive – christianity revived* . . . about 1711, that preface happened to fall into the hands of the Author and some of his acquaintance, who were *persons of reading* in Salisbury; and as some of his friends took part with Mr. Whiston in the main point controverted, viz. the single supremacy of the one God and the father of all; so some were against him, *which introduced a paper – controversy betwixt them.* And as the Author's friends were shy of expressing themselves plainly and fully upon the question, but chose rather to oppose each other by interrogations; so this appeared to the Author a way altogether unlikely to clear up the case, and bring the point debated to an issue . . . he was naturally led to draw up his thoughts upon the subject in the way that he did, as it appeared to him a more probable means of bringing the controversy to a conclusion. And this the Author did without . . . even a thought of it's being offered to publick consideration, but only for his own satisfaction, and for the information and satisfaction of his friends in Salisbury, to whom then his acquaintance was confined; *he having accustomed himself from his youth to put his thoughts into writing*, upon such subjects to which his attention had been called in; . . . thereby to arouse and satisfy himself, and then commit them to the flames, *which had been the case in many instances.*[60] The Author . . . arranged his sentiments on the aforementioned subject . . . it was exposed to the view and perusal of his acquaintance . . . some of whom approved the performance, . . . but others thought the contrary, and this induced a controversy in writing betwixt the Author and some of those who thought differently . . . and several letters and papers passed betwixt them.

Eventually one of Chubb's friends took the manuscript he had composed on this latest occasion to Whiston himself to ask for his opinion. Whiston had the manuscript published, and so the work of the Salisbury journeyman first reached the printed page.

[59] Chubb, *op. cit.*, iv.          [60] The italics in this passage are mine; *ibid.*, v–vii.

424

He had a cool, rational, exploratory cast of mind. He was a theist, who denied the divinity of Christ, and looked with a critical eye on the Scriptures.

> This collection of writings has been the parent of doctrines most dishonourable to God, and most injurous to men; such as the doctrine of absolute unconditional election and reprobation, of religious persecution and the like...
> Besides, this book, called the holy Bible, contains many things that are greatly below, and unworthy of, the Supreme Deity...That [God] should...approve of, or countenance, such malevolent desires as these, 'Let his children be fatherless and his wife a widow; let his children be continually vagabonds, and beg...let his posterity be cut off, and in the generation following let their name be blotted out'.
> I say that such trifling observations, and such malevolent desires as these, should be considered as the offspring of God, is playing at hazard indeed.[61]

His collected works, which included a treatise on 'Divine Revelation in General, and of the Divine Original of the Jewish, Mohometon and Christian Revelation in Particular' ended with a typical statement 'in what I have offered to the world, I have appealed to the understandings, and not to the passions of men'.[62] His achievement is not as startling as Thomas Tryon's, but the vivid image of this urban artisan, too poor to marry and support a family, a part-time journeyman-glover with bad sight, a part-time assistant to a chandler, weighing out candles in the shop and at the same time ordering his thoughts to commit them to paper for his own pleasure, or that of his friends, in their next 'paper-controversy' is a fascinating one. This lively literate atmosphere of serious debate on theological subjects amongst the journeymen who were 'persons of reading' in early eighteenth-century Salisbury was, of course, urban, but Thomas Chubb participated in it, and apparently led it, from an education in a rural hamlet which taught him to read, write and count, probably all before his tenth year, in the 1680s.

Shortly before Chubb began to write for publication in the second decade of the eighteenth century, Stephen Duck, the first of the eighteenth-century poets of the countryside to come from a humble rural background himself, was born at Chorlton St Peter, at the northern edge of the Salisbury Plain.[63] His education was exactly similar to that of Thomas Chubb; he learnt to read and to write English and the 'Arithmetic [which] is generally join'd with this Degree of Learning'. His first biographer, Joseph Spence, wrote that he was not taken from school until he was fourteen, which sounds improbably late. His father was able to set him up on a small-holding after he left school, but after its failure he made his living as a day-labourer. His great opportunity for self-improvement came when he made friends with a man who had acquired two or three

---

[61] Chubb, op. cit., I, 6–7.
[62] Ibid., II, 355.
[63] Michael Paffard, 'Stephen Duck, The Thresher Poet', History (1977), 467–72, on which I have drawn heavily here. See also Rayner Unwin, The Rural Muse (1954). These critics have assumed that Duck must have acquired his education at a charity school, although there was not one near Chorlton St Peter. There is, of course, no reason why he should have been at a charity school. The rudiments he had been taught were the normal basic ones for which most of the sixteenth and seventeenth-century schoolmasters were licensed. See above, p. 422, n. 58.

dozen books while in service in London. Amongst these were seven of Shakespeare's plays, Dryden, Virgil, Seneca, Ovid, the *Spectator* and Milton's *Paradise Lost*, which Duck read twice with the aid of a dictionary before he could understand it. He relied extensively on his memory, just as Arise Evans had done. When he first read Pope's *Essay on Criticism* he memorized almost the whole of it overnight. The verses in the *Spectator* first triggered him into composing his own poetry. His own personal experience of day-labour and his absorption with these literary models and their vocabulary lay behind his most original poem, *The Thresher's Labour.*

Even though we are now considering a period in the 1720s, Stephen Duck's ability to read Milton, Dryden and Shakespeare and his ability to compose his own verses is invaluable evidence of the degree of literacy a basic seventeenth-century education could bestow. Of course, this day-labourer, like his older contemporary in Salisbury, the chandler's assistant, was a highly exceptional man. Nevertheless, he demonstrates the literate skills a boy from a poor rural background could develop, given an education until eight or nine in the seventeenth-century basic subjects, reading, writing and simple arithmetic.

Josiah Langdale was the first of the autobiographers considered here whose background was prosperous enough for long enough to bring him within reach of a grammar school education.[64] He was born in 1673 in the village of Nafferton in the East Riding, and went to school 'after I grew up', as he wrote. His labour was not required until the death of his father, before he was nine. Then his mother found his labour essential to the family economy. Like Tryon, he took great pride and pleasure in his skills, which in his case were specifically rural, not industrial.

> I then was taken from School, and being a strong Boy, of my Years, was put to lead Harrows and learn to Plow, Also, in the Summer Time, I kept Cattel (we having in our Country both Horses and Oxen in Tethers) and moved them when there was Occasion with much Care, for I loved to see them in good Liking. In those Days, both when I followed the Plow and kept Cattel in the Field, I was religiously inclined...I had not time for much Schooling, being closely kept to what I could do in our way of Husbandry, yet I made a little Progress in Latin, but soon forgot it; I endeavoured however, to keep my English, and could read the Bible, and delighted therein....
>
> I now being about Thirteen Years of Age, and growing strong, did my Mother good service; having attain'd to the knowledge of ordering my Plow, and being expert in this Employment could go with Four horses, and plow alone, which we always did except in Seed time; I very much delighted in holding the Plow, It being an Employment suitable to my Mind, and no Company to disturb my Contemplation, therefore I loved it the more, and found by experience that to have my mind inward

[64] Josiah Langdale, 'Some Account of the Birth, Education and Religious Exercises and Visitations of God to that faithful Servant and Minister of Jesus Christ, Josiah Langdale' (died 1723) Friends' House Library, MS Box 10/10. All the passages quoted here are taken from pp. 1, 2, 3, 5, 7, 8.

and to contemplate the Ways and Works of God was a great Benefit and Comfort to me.

Josiah's inclinations were not all devotional, however, and he was much drawn towards dancing, which was an important adolescent pastime in Nafferton. He gives the only account I have seen of the way this important leisure activity was learnt in the countryside. At this point his account becomes confused, for he seems to have learnt dancing after school at night, before he was fourteen, even though he had left regular school, and lost his Latin before he was nine. It sounds as if he attended sporadically when agricultural routine allowed it, after his ninth year. Just possibly the schooling that included Latin, before this, had been outside Nafferton, unless country masters able to teach grammar also frequently taught dancing at night.

> Dancing took much with the young People of our Town... Much Evil was
> committed at this School... The Dancing Master was a Fidler and Jugler, and after
> we broke up School every Night he went to play his Tricks. I did not learn many
> Dances before it became an exceeding Trouble to my Soul and Spirit... After some
> time my Playfellows would entice me to Feasts, where young men and women meet
> to be merry... and such Like was I invited to, under a Pretence to improve our
> Dancing.

Josiah's fortunes changed again when his mother remarried after seven years of widowhood, and no longer needed him. At that point the fifteen-year-old became an in-servant in husbandry. His spiritual search continued, and was fed by an influential close friend in his second year as a servant. His account of his friend shows just how limited seventeenth-century literacy could be.

> After I was come to my new Master, he had a young strong Man that was his
> Thresher, but he was blind, and had been so for about Twenty Years, who had
> lost his Sight when about Ten Years of Age; He was never Taught further than
> the Psalter as I have heard him often say; yet this Man taught our Master's Children,
> and afterwards became a famous Schoolmaster.... He was a Man of great Memory,
> and of good Understanding.

If reading could be taught by the blind, the role of memorization and rote-learning must have been very great indeed.

Josiah's description of his conversations and recreations with this friend gives some insight into the world of this literate pair of labourers in the 1680s, and the astonishingly cool and appraising round of sectarian sermon-tasting they indulged in, and their worries about the necessity of the sacraments, which held them back from Quakerism for some time. Their opinions were based on Bible reading.

> We would walk out together on First-Day mornings in the Summertime several Miles
> a-foot, to hear such Priests as were the most famed for Preaching; and as we walked
> together we should have such Talk as was profitable. One Time as we were coming

home from hearing one of the most famous and learned of these Priests in our Country, Well, said he, Josiah, I am weary with hearing these Priests, they are an idle Generation, they cannot be Ministers of Jesus Christ; This Sermon that we heard to Day I heard this man preach some years ago; as soon as he took his Text I thought how he would manage it, and accordingly as I thought he would go on so he did – I do not know, said he, what People to join in Society with – I have looked in my Mind over the Church of England, Presbyterians, Baptists and the Quakers, and do say the Quakers excel all people in Conversation. . . but, said he they do not use Baptism and the Lords Supper. . . So, as I followed my Business, which was mostly Plowing, serious thoughts began again to flow afresh in upon me. . . We Two would often go on First Day Mornings into the Field, taking a Bible with us, and there we would sit down together, and after I have read a while, we have sat silent, waiting with Desires in our Hearts after the Lord.

The blind thresher and the literate ploughman had possibly become in-servants for the same reasons that their education had been disrupted, in one case the accident or disease that had caused blindness, in the other the demographic accident of parental loss. But there must have been a constant trickle of semi-literate people into agricultural labour for just these reasons, and although this literate pair in Yorkshire were probably unusual, they were certainly not unique. Richard Baxter's first 'stirrings of conscience' in about 1630 in rural Shropshire were prompted by 'a poor day-labourer' in the town who normally did 'the reading of the psalms and chapters' in church, and who lent Baxter's father 'an old, torn book. . . called *Bunny's Resolution*' which influenced young Richard.[65] These examples of literate labourers may be taken to represent the 15 per cent of labourers between 1580 and 1700 who could sign their names.[66] We may firmly deduce from the evidence of the order in which reading and writing was taught, and the experience of the autobiographers given above, that those who could sign their names could all read. The existence of this literate group amongst agricultural labourers is one of the reasons which leads me to stress the magnitude of the change in English society between 1500 and 1700. It proves my contention that illiteracy was everywhere face to face with literacy, and the oral with the printed word. Schofield suggested some time ago that 'there were probably groups in the population, such as agricultural labourers in certain parts of the country, which were entirely cut off from any contact with the literate culture'.[67] Cressy recently concurred. Although he concedes that the presence of even one reader amongst a group of rural labourers could act as a significant bridge to the literate world, he feels that 'normally these ordinary people were indifferent to the political and religious controversies which exercised their betters'.[68] Langdale's account of lively debate scarcely bears him out. I think the combination of the existence of a measurable proportion of labourers able to sign over a period of time, combined

[65] Keeble, *Autobiography of Richard Baxter*, 7.
[66] Cressy, 'Educational opportunity in Tudor and Stuart England', 314.
[67] Schofield, 'The measurement of literacy in pre-Industrial England', 313.
[68] David Cressy, 'Illiteracy in England, 1530–1730', *Historical Journal*, xx, 1 (March 1977), 8–9.

428

with the amount of cheap print in circulation, combined again with the brief impressions I am able to gather from Langdale, Baxter, and Thomas Tryon's group of reading shepherds, justifies the disagreement. It seems, from the life expectancy for adult males in the seventeenth century, and the proportion of children who lost their fathers early, that there was a constant slithering down the social ladder.[69] The steady trickle of semi-educated orphaned boys into apprenticeship and into service was one of the ways largely illiterate groups came to contain 'literate' members in the sixteenth and seventeenth centuries.

All the autobiographers quoted so far either come from too poor a background, or suffered too much from their father's early death to go to grammar school. The next group of men come from yeomen or trading backgrounds, and their education was interrupted by their fathers at an appropriate point in time when they had absorbed as much as would be of use. They were never intended for the universities. A third of the autobiographers who identified their social backgrounds and their educational experiences fully became apprentices at fourteen.[70] Here is a very important correction to a view of seventeenth-century education based on university entrants alone. Such a view necessarily completely neglects the flow of boys from the schools into the various trades. The evidence of the autobiographers suggests this flow was very considerable. The boys involved came from a tremendous social and economic range.

George Trosse of Exeter was the son of a prominent lawyer who had married the daughter of a merchant who had twice been Mayor. George shone at grammar school and his master objected when he was removed at fifteen 'having a mind to be a Merchant'. Alderman Newton of Cambridge certainly took great pride in his son's intellectual achievement, or he would not have allowed him to celebrate his new skill of writing at seven by making an entry in his own diary; but proud as he was of this grammar school product, he apprenticed him to a dry-salter at fourteen.[71] The boys concerned were not merely sons of townsmen, however. The autobiographies contain ample evidence of the degree of magnetism exerted by the towns. London was, of course, pre-eminent. The autobiographies provide a mass of evidence on the formative effects of their apprenticeships then, and the Puritan meetings and occasions they then attended. Their backgrounds were as diverse as the distances they travelled to get there. Arise Evans had walked across country from Wales, Thomas Tryon from Gloucestershire. William Crouch was the son of a substantial yeoman of Hampshire, and his father's early death and the Civil War combined deprived him of both his inheritance on the land which he expected from his father's will, and also the grammar education he regarded, with some justification, as his right as a yeoman's son. He also ended up, after much wandering, as a London apprentice.[72] Benjamin Bangs, son of a prosperous Norfolk yeoman who died when he was a small child, has a similar history, except that he was more humbly apprenticed to a local shoemaker, and ended in London more by accident than design.[73]

[69] See above, p. 420, n. 50.
[70] Eleven of the thirty-one, including six of the nine orphans.
[71] See above, p. 412.

[72] William Crouch, *Posthuma Christiana*. . . (1712). See below, p. 432, n. 83.
[73] Benjamin Bangs, *Memoirs of the Life and Convincement of that Worthy Friend*. . . (1757).

The provincial towns also drew in boys from rural backgrounds. Thomas Chubb was only one of the boys who went to Salisbury. The fanatic William Dewsbury was apprenticed to a clock-maker in Leeds at thirteen, specifically because he wanted to explore Quakerism and knew he could do so there.[74] William Edmundson, yet another orphan, the youngest of six children, of a Westmorland family whose mother died when he was four, his father when he was eight, also lost his portion under his father's will. He was apprenticed to a carpenter and joiner in York. George Bewley was a second generation Quaker, born in Cumberland in 1684. He attended a school about a mile from home until he was twelve, when he was sent to board with an uncle to attend a school twenty miles away. This sounds like a grammar education. At fourteen, he was sent as apprentice to a Quaker linen-draper in Dublin. His parents kept in touch with him by letter, and more interesting, his sister, the eldest child, frequently wrote him long letters also.[75] Apart from these boys from the country apprenticed to masters in provincial towns, many others were simply apprenticed to local craftsmen in their own area. The outstanding example is, of course, George Fox, the Leicestershire weaver's son apprenticed to a shoemaker.[76] The main utility of a seventeenth-century education, judging from the autobiographies, was to prepare boys for an apprenticeship. A university education beginning for some of the autobiographers at about fourteen was a highly specialized and rare type of apprenticeship preparing boys for the Church.

Boys who came from slightly more prosperous backgrounds than those just described or who had not been precipitated down the social ladder by their father's death, sons of wholesale traders and yeomen, were given a grammar education to an appropriate level of usefulness, before being claimed from school by their fathers. Some of them were simply sons of yeomen, being prepared for the activities and lives of the more prosperous farmers who acted as local officials in their areas, with no thought of a university training. Grammar education often seems to have been assumed by such people, university education was not. The next group of autobiographers gives some insight into the social world of the yeomen, and its expectations.

James Fretwell, who was born right at the end of the seventeenth century, came from a family of yeomen and traders, timber merchants, horse-breeders and dealers, carpenters and brasiers. James's father, who was born in the 1670s, went to grammar school, but his father removed him to 'put him to his own business' after 'he had learn'd so far as my grandfather thought was needful'. He was a substantial timber-merchant. The family pattern was repeated. James went to grammar school before he was five.[77] Because this school was five miles away it was too far for such a small child to walk, although he began by trying it, so he was boarded out during the week with a widow who lived near the school. The autobiographers were commonly boarded out like this, to get over the problems of accessibility caused by scattered schools. Between five and fourteen, James and his younger brother went to three separate schools and were

---

[74] William Dewsbury, 'The first birth', in *The Discovery of the Great Enmity of the Serpent against the Seed of the Woman...* (1655).

[75] George Bewley, *A Narrative of the Christian Experience...* (1750).

[76] George Fox, *A Journal, or the Historical Account of the Life, Travels, Sufferings* (1694).

[77] See above, p. 411.

430

boarded with three different families. It is just possible from his account that the availability of relatives or ex-servants with whom to board the children dictated the change of school. By the time he left the second, at thirteen, he 'had made an entrance into Greek'. When he was fourteen, his father 'thinking I had got as much of the learned languages[78] as would be of service to a tradesman. . . thought it time to learn something which was more immediately related to the qualifying of me for business: therefore he sent me to Pontefract, to learn to write and to accompt'. He was taught by a Quaker linen-draper, who kept a school which was partly run by his apprentice who 'was a good penman'. James who was fluent in Latin and had had two years Greek seems to have been astonishingly uncertain of his writing. Again, the separation between the two skills is emphasized: 'I had learn't some little to write before, but nothing of accounts that I remember. Here it was that I got what learning I have of that kind. I went through most of the rules of vulgar arithmetick and decimal fractions, with some little of practical geometry.' Then James, like his father before him, left school. There was never any thought of university for him.[79]

Oliver Sansom had been born over sixty years earlier, at Beedon in Berkshire, and was also the son of a timber-merchant, who had married a yeoman's daughter. His educational experiences closely paralleled James Fretwell's. He began later. At seven, he was sent to board with an aunt to learn 'latin, and writing'. He had another change of schools at ten, but 'stayed not long there, my father having occasion to take me home to keep his book, and look after what I was capable of in his business, which was dealing in timber and wood'. Oliver Sansom's autobiography, together with that of the Quaker John Whiting of Somerset gives most insight into the literate yeoman world of the seventeenth century. It was a world in which the ability to read was assumed, without question. The very unself-consciousness of the incidental remarks that give away the

---

[78] James never learnt a modern language. The normal way to learn a modern language seems to have been by exchange, usually at about fourteen, before commencing a trade. Prosperous merchants exchanged their sons: George Trosse, son of a lawyer, was sent off at fifteen in 1646 to a French minister who took in a group of English youths for two years (*Life of the Rev. Mr George Trosse, late Minister of the Gospel at Exon* [1715]). This followed his grammar schooling and preceded his apprenticeship to a Portuguese merchant. The extraordinary Henry Lamp who eventually settled down at Ulverston in the Lake District as a respected Quaker, after running an apothecary's shop in Lynn and spending some years searching abortively for the philosopher's stone, was the son of a Prussian merchant. He trained as a physician at Leyden. He first came to England to visit his brother who was living with a merchant at King's Lynn, whose son had been taken in as a member of the family at Conisburg to learn German. Henry Lamp, *Curriculum Vitae or the Birth, Travels and Education of Henry Lamp*, M.D., written by himself (1710, ed. J. J. Green, 1895). Thomas Gwin of Falmouth went to grammar school until fourteen, and then was removed to enter the family business of fishing and fish-merchandising. The first step was to send him to France. Thomas Gwin, *The Journal of Thomas Gwin of Falmouth* (1837). Exchanges to learn foreign languages were not only arranged between prosperous merchant families, however. Edward Coxere, who became a merchant seaman, lost his father shortly after his birth. His mother then remarried a cordwainer. She sent him to a French family at fourteen, in 1647, taking a French boy into her house in exchange. He had no preparation for this visit at all, and 'was like one dumb' for two months, although he was fluent after eleven months. E. H. W. Meyerstein (ed.), *Adventures by Sea of Edward Coxere* (1945).

[79] James Fretwell, 'Yorkshire diaries', *Selden Soc.* (1877), 172, 174, 183-7.

First steps in literacy

manner in which literate skills were used in everyday living, amongst wives and daughters as well as friends, are revealing of the way in which literacy was an accepted skill. Oliver Sansom 'took great delight, even in my tenders years, in reading the Holy Scriptures, and other godly books which I met with'. When he married, his wife was 'of a good yeomanry family and had been brought up in a sober and suitable way of education...I walked as before, in great seriousness of mind, and spent much time in reading good books, the holy Scriptures more especially; with which my wife and her relations, as well as my own, were greatly affected.' Oliver's autobiography includes a whole series of letters written to his wife during his lengthy series of imprisonments. More important, when he had smallpox he adjured his wife, 'I desire thee not to venture to come to me, until thou hear further from me, but let me hear from thee as often as thou canst'. His wife's sister also wrote to him in prison. In 1670 he wrote, 'I would have thee remember me dearly to thy sister, and let her know that I received her letter and was sweetly refreshed in the sense of the love of God which is manifested in and through her'.

Oliver Sansom's father had bought him a 'copyhold estate' at Boxford, near Newbury, after his marriage, and he settled down to lead the life of a yeoman farmer. He had one serving man to help him, so his acreage cannot have been very large. But he was a person of consequence in the neighbourhood, well liked by his neighbours despite his Quaker beliefs. On one of his releases from prison after a two-year spell, 'many of my neighbours came running to welcome me home'. Indeed, in 1665, a situation reminiscent of pure farce arose when the priest spent an evening searching for the tithingman and the village constable to break up a Quaker meeting at Sansom's house. He failed to find them, because they were at it. This same priest was responsible for an event which reveals more of Sansom's assumptions about literacy than any other. In 1668, he embarked on a public tirade against Sansom, at the Court Leet of Boxford and Westbrook, when he accused him of denying the Trinity and the Sacraments, and

> made a long clamourous speech against me, using many bitter, reviling words. And not satisfied with that, he in his fury with his own hands plucked my hat from my head two several times, in the presence of all the people...thus he spent much of the time until he went to dinner, endeavouring...to make me a gazing-stock to the whole assembly.

Oliver Sansom was very upset, obviously partly because the Leet contained 'the chief men of three or four parishes'. He objected to being made a spectacle in front of such a group. His immediate redress to re-establish his credit and defend himself was to write a paper of rebuttal. 'This little Paper, I fastened to a post in the middle of the great hall where the court was kept, *that it might be seen and read of all those present.*' He took it down after 'it had stuck there some time and was pretty well viewed'. His implicit assumption was that 'the chief men of three or four parishes' could, and did, read, so that his paper of defence was as good a means of answering the charges against himself

432

and re-establishing himself in their eyes as the speech he apparently lacked the opportunity to make.[80]

John Whiting of Naylsey in Somerset[81] was born in 1656, the son of a convinced Quaker yeoman 'having a competent estate in the same parish, where my ancestors lived for several generations'. Despite the early deaths of his father, his mother, and then his stepfather, this estate was evidently considerable enough to keep John at school.[82] He does not tell us at what age he left. He was certainly still there at twelve and may have been there until fourteen. He went to grammar school, along with the sons of the local minister, but there was never from his writing any suggestion of his going on to university. At nineteen he left his guardian and took up active farming, which was frequently disrupted by imprisonment for his beliefs.

Whiting's autobiography is in itself the most compelling piece of evidence that he shared the assumption of that other yeoman, Oliver Sansom. Unlike all but a very few of the autobiographies, it is a piece of work of which parts can still be read for their intrinsic interest. Whiting was a sober, shrewd and perceptive observer. He noted his own reactions as a child when his conscience impelled him to put Quaker beliefs into practice and 'the plain language also cost me very dear, it was so hard to take it up, that I could have gone miles about rather than to have met some of my relations to speak to them'. He noted the shocked reactions of the prisoners who watched Jeffries's retribution for Monmouth's rebellion, and recorded 'they forced poor men to hale about mens quarters like horse-flesh or carrion, to boil and hang them up as monuments of their cruelty'. He inserted potted biographies of the other Friends he talked about, and they frequently come off. His gossip is interesting too, as when he wrote of a proclamation from Elizabeth Bathhurst's pen in 1679: 'This treatise was so extraordinary, both for depth of matter and expression that some would not believe it was written by her, being but a weakly maid, though it was known to be her own writing.' His considering, unhysterical cast of mind comes through very clearly,[83] and it is no surprise that he

---

[80] Oliver Sansom, *An Account of the Many Remarkable Passages in the Life of Oliver Sansom* (1710), 1–10, 18, 41, 47, 75, 132. A similar situation of course already existed a century earlier amongst at least a group of the yeomanry. C. J. Harrison, 'The Social and Economic History of Cannock and Rugeley, 1546–1597' (unpublished Ph.D. thesis, University of Keele, 1974), 118–23, demonstrates the social importance of the court Leet meeting and also the legal capacities and attitudes, and network of correspondents, of a sixteenth-century yeoman farmer. He himself, although technically untrained, acted as both under-steward and steward of the manor, advising his lord on legal affairs in Staffordshire. A small group of such men regularly acted as legal advisors and representatives of the other peasantry in the manor court.

[81] John Whiting, *Persecution Exposed* (1715).

[82] Although in 1676 the acreage of winter and spring corn together only amounted to ten acres, which is of course extremely meagre by yeoman standards at this date, *ibid.*, 21.

[83] The only other Quaker autobiography which I have read which compares with it comes from the previous generation of Quakers, and from the pen of a boy who shared the same yeoman background, but lost both estate and education because of the Civil War. William Crouch was born in 1628, son of a substantial yeoman in a small Hampshire village. Like so many others, he lost his father. 'My father was taken from us in the Prime of his Years, leaving his Children Young. And by reason of the Wars which happened in England, with the Unsettledness of our Family by frequent Removings, I was deprived of a great part of what fell to my Share, by the Will of my Father, and by Sundry Interruptions was prevented

First steps in literacy

continued to hold local office in his parish, where he was overseer of the poor in 1679, despite his Quakerism, which had first cut him off from his peer group when he reluctantly gave up playing with the other boys after school at night when he was twelve.

Although the quality of his autobiography is the best testimonial for John Whiting's education, there is plenty of other evidence in it for the importance that reading held for him. Of course, he read 'the scriptures of truth, which I diligently read as well as fireside books' as a boy. He also produces evidence on the remarkable degree of organization reached by the Quaker book trade. In one of his imprisonments he remarked incidentally, 'I had a parcel of friends books, etc., come down from London, as I used to have. . .and the carrier left them, as he used to do for me, at Newberryinn.' His reading spread wider than the Bible and sectarian propaganda though; he refers to Eusebius, and to Bishop Burnet.

All the autobiographers touched on so far were without benefit of university education. Another third of those who identified both their social backgrounds and their educational experiences did go on to university. Most, though not all, of them came from more prosperous yeomen, small gentry, merchant and ministry backgrounds. I have not considered them here, because their experiences are more familiar[84] than the struggle to acquire basic literary skills displayed by the poorest autobiographers. These boys appear from the worm's eye view of the humbler autobiographers as an educational élite. But to summarize their circumstances as 'prosperous' or 'privileged' is of course relative. To the Chubbs and Tryons of seventeenth-century society, they were indeed privileged; but the plight of Henry Jessey, who in 1623 at Cambridge had 3d. a day for his 'provision of diet' and spent some of this on hiring the books he could not afford to buy, demonstrates just how relative this 'privilege' was.[85] The most succinct description of the physical difficulties of finding privacy and quiet in which to work which were suffered by boys from a humble background acquiring an education is provided by Thomas Boston. His father, who was a maltster, could put him through grammar school; but at the end of it Thomas spent two years trying to find notarial work, or raise the fees for university somehow. In that time he battled to keep up his Latin, and re-read his Justinian 'the malt-loft being my closet'.[86]

The general impression given by the autobiographers is that boys from non-yeoman backgrounds quite frequently had a year or two's sporadic education, but it was often broken off before seven either by family needs or demographic mishap. Those boys who

---

of that Education in Grammar Learning, which otherwise I might have enjoyed.' His lack of grammar schooling did not prevent his pen travelling; he became an apprentice in London, and his careful, first-hand observations of Quaker meetings and events in London from 1656, published as *Posthuma Christiana. . .or, A Collection of some Papers* in 1712, have the same kind of sober and intelligent approach as John Whiting's.

[84] Cressy, 'Educational opportunity in Tudor and Stuart England', *passim*. To him, of course, yeomen's sons at university appear a minority, sober and straitened group. This, as an overall view, is undoubtedly correct.

[85] Henry Jessey, *The Life and Death of Mr Henry Jessey. . .* (1671).

[86] Thomas Boston, *A General Account of my Life by Thomas Boston, A.M., Minister at Simprin, 1699–1707 and at Ettrick, 1707–32* (ed. G. D. Low) (Edinburgh, 1908), 13. For the prosperity of maltsters, see above, p. 422, n. 56.

434

were fortunate enough to be supported at school until fourteen divided into two groups. Some went into apprenticeships; some to the universities as an apprenticeship to the Church, or to teaching. The latter almost all came from yeomen, or more prosperous families.

Oxford and Cambridge had nothing to do with the 'literate' worlds of the Yorkshire labourers Langdale and his friend Hewson, and the Wiltshire labourer Stephen Duck, the Gloucestershire shepherds who taught Tryon to read, the Bedfordshire small craftsman, John Bunyan, whose tastes in reading changed, the urban artisans with rural educations, Tryon, Chubb and Crouch, and the more assured and confident Berkshire and Wiltshire yeomen, Sansom and Whiting. Much more important, only Langdale, Sansom and Whiting amongst them owed anything to the grammar schools. The picture they jointly convey is one of a society in which a boy even from a relatively poor family might have a year or two's education up to six or seven. If he was at school until seven he could read, if he was at school until eight or at the latest nine, he could write. Either way he would be able to make sense of whatever cheap print the pedlars brought within his reach. Either way, his mental environment had undergone an enormous and very important change.

There is, of course, no real conflict between recent work stressing the social restrictiveness of grammar and university education in Tudor and Stuart England and the glimpses the autobiographers give us of the spread of elementary skills, particularly reading, amongst the very humble. Yet emphasis on the first, however well justified, gives an incomplete picture unless it is tempered by the second. It is particularly incomplete in view of the likelihood that boys below the level of yeomen were quite likely to learn to read, since reading was taught at an age when they could earn little, whereas writing was commonly taught at an age after the meaningful earning lives of such boys had begun. An account of 'literacy' based on the only measurable skill, the ability to sign, necessarily omits this possibility that reading was a much more socially diffused skill than writing. Since the psychological and social changes brought about by the spread of reading skills were very great, the evidence of the humbler autobiographers of their acquisition of reading skills ought to be taken into account, if a balanced picture of the effects of the combined spread of cheap print and elementary education in the sixteenth and seventeenth centuries is to be obtained.

**Additional note on the influence of 'literate' women**

'Literate' by definition implies the ability to write. It seems quite likely, however, that many schooldames taught reading who could not themselves write, and who also escaped the episcopal licensing procedure. Bishop Lloyd compiled a very detailed shorthand survey of the small market town and parish of Eccleshall in Staffordshire in which he himself had a seat, between 1693–8. It contained the names of no less than one man and five women from whom he described as 'schoolteachers,' as well as a visiting 'writing master' who came twice a year for six weeks. (Transcripts of the Survey of the Township of

First steps in literacy                                    435

Eccleshall, 1697, and the Parish of Eccleshall, 1693–8, compiled by N. W. Tildesley (1969) in the William Salt Library, Stafford.) Not a single one of these people appears in the diocesan records at all, although Eccleshall is, admittedly, a peculiar. (I am much indebted to Dr Alan Smith for this information.) Four of the five women were wives of day-labourers and of small craftsmen. This is a social group of women who have completely escaped observation. They may have played a very important part in preliminary education, as the frequency with which authors, from Dr Johnson down to Oliver Sansom and James Fretwell, refer to their schooldames who taught the first steps, shows. This runs counter to David Cressy's suggestion that 'since women were rarely educated themselves, it is unlikely that they played a great part in expanding the literate public' (*thesis cit.*, 179–81). The autobiographies do contain a number of examples of mothers teaching reading, however. They included mothers like Benjamin Bangs' mother, daughter of a Hertfordshire clergyman married to a Norfolk yeoman, who was left widowed with nine children in the mid 1650s. She was obliged to sell the farm as soon as the oldest children were old enough to be put to service, but the youngest three she kept at home 'under her Care and Instruction... We were all indeed indifferently well brought up both in reading and writing; and although we of the younger sort were most behind, yet we were able to signify our Minds to one another by our Pens'. Benjamin Bangs, *Memoirs of the Life and Convincement* (1757). Of more interest socially than this example of a woman spreading literate skills downwards socially through demographic accident are those of women who could not themselves write, who deliberately fostered reading skills. Oliver Heywood's mother, wife of a Lancashire fustian-weaver, seems only to have been able to read. As a young girl after her conversion in 1614 she 'took her bible with her and spent the whole day in reading and praying'. Later her son went with her to Puritan exercises and sermons. Afterwards he wrote, 'was in some measure helpful to her memory by the notes of sermons I took'. He regularly sent her notes of sermons when he went up to Cambridge, and as an old woman she meditated on these: 'it was her constant course in the night when she lay waking to roll them in her mind, and rivet them there'. She took great pains over her children's education: 'She was continually putting us upon the scriptures and good bookes and instructing us how to pray...' and this work extended outside her own family. 'It was her usual practice to help many poore children to learning by buying them bookes, setting them to schoole, and paying their master for teaching, whereby many a poore parent blessed god for help *by their childrens reading*' [my italics]. *The Rev. Oliver Heywood, B.A., 1630–1702: His Autobiographies, Diaries, Anecdote and Event Books* (ed. J. Horsfall-Turner) (1882), I, pp. 42, 48, 51 and

# WOMEN TEACHING READING
# TO POOR CHILDREN IN THE
# SIXTEENTH AND
# SEVENTEENTH CENTURIES

The historians of education sometimes seem still to be partially befogged by the last remaining tatters of an old myth that education for the poor really began with the Charity School movement. Although I hope to focus this chapter on the subject of women teaching both their own, and also other people's children to read, I wish first to blow away these remaining wisps of fog for good, if I can.

Brian Simon wrote a splendid article on 'Leicestershire Schools, 1625–40' as long ago as 1954.[1] When I wrote *Contrasting Communities*, which appeared in 1974, I mapped the references to masters teaching between 1570 and 1620,[2] when the episcopal licensing system was working well. These masters were licensed to a variety of functions, but very frequently to teach 'to write, read and caste an accompte'.[3] Girls, on the other hand, were normally taught 'only' to read, and those gainful occupations, knitting and spinning. One of the very rare school curricula we have for such a school, for Orwell in Cambridgeshire, specified boys were taught to read, write, and cast accounts, girls to read, sew, knit and spin.[4] I was astonished by what I found (see Figure 3.1). Schooling was available within walking distance all over much of the county of Cambridgeshire, although, since most of these schools were unendowed, it was an ephemeral business: the teachers were young men trying to stay alive, just down from university, and seeking their first benefice, here today and gone tomorrow. Oddly, though, the old market towns which today have village colleges also had permanent schooling: the Sawstons and the Lintons and the Swaveseys were not newly equipped when Henry Morris came along in the 1930s with his great new idea of schools that acted also as rural community centres.[5]

I thought Cambridgeshire might be abnormal; its proximity to Cambridge University made it obviously accessible to these young men. However, Peter Clark carried out a similar exercise for Kent in 1977[6] (see Figure 3.2). Cambridgeshire was not abnormal at all. Kent also had this pattern of sporadic, but commonly found, schooling, with some centres when it was always to be found. And we already had the Leicestershire evidence. So I would like at the start of this chapter to correct the persistent and erroneous notion that 'schooling for the poor' was a new phenomenon in the eighteenth century.[7] Indeed, it is beginning to seem likely that the S.P.C.K. Charity School movement adopted and set on firmer foundations village schools already in being in the seventeenth century.

The fog has, I hope, vanished. Yet there remain major difficulties with my subject of women teaching reading before 1700. I need to approach it via the schooldames who probably taught reading only, and who are not only elusive, here today and gone tomorrow, like the schoolmasters, but nearly, if not quite, impossible to find. This is because the Bishops, who ought to have licensed them, very rarely, if at all, did so. Mrs Karen Smith-Adams, during her period as a research-student in Cambridge, was working on midwives. They, like schoolmistresses, were supposed to have episcopal licences. She very kindly carried out a parallel search for schooldames for me. They are not, with highly unusual exceptions which she diligently collected, to be found in the ecclesiastical registers.[8] But we know they were there, working alongside mothers, teaching reading. The fullest example comes from outside my period. James Raine, who was indeed a very poor boy, son of a village blacksmith and a dressmaker, founder of the Surtees Society, wrote an autobiography which describes his early schooling, by schooldames and both his grandmothers between his birth in 1791, and 1797.[9] By the time he was six he was in the hands of a 'superior master', by which time he wrote, 'for two or three preceding years I had been able to read almost anything that fell my way'.[10] He could already write too – and that was abnormal for a six-year-old. He had been taught that skill by a master, which was normal for England.[11] But what really interests us is how he had been introduced to print. In the mental worlds of his grandmothers, print and oral tales fused. The picture is necessarily confused, however, because his maternal grandmother, who was poor enough to live in an almshouse, was blind. She took 'a particular pleasure in teaching me Watts's Hymns, which I was not slow in committing to memory'. She had these by heart. But also 'many a tale would she tell me with a moral at its end'.[12] Despite her earlier extreme poverty as a wife, she had managed to send her daughter, James's mother, to school for a long period.

James's mother was a highly unusual girl, because she had learnt not only to read, as was normal for girls in England, but was also, in her son's words, 'the writer of a very beautiful hand, and an excellent arithmetician'. This was rare indeed.[13] James Raine describes her as the 'great scholar of the village, writing letters for fathers and mothers to their

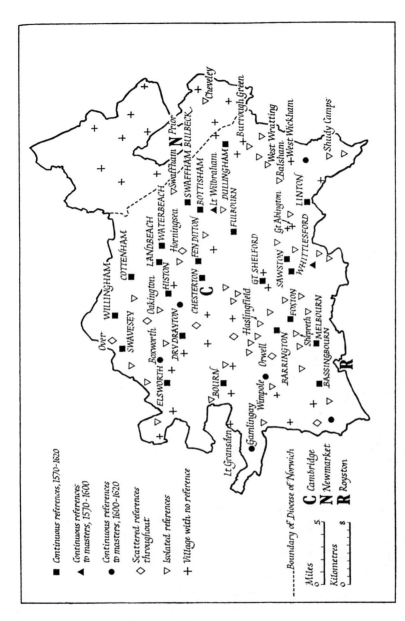

*Figure 3.1* Schools in Cambridgeshire, 1570–1620 (reproduced with the permission of the author)

252

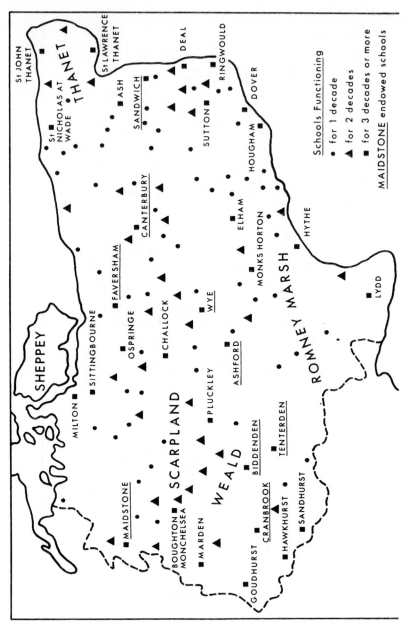

*Figure 3.2* Schools in Canterbury diocese, 1601–40 (from Peter Clark, *English Provincial Society from the Reformation to the Revolution*, Harvester, reproduced with the permission of the author)

absent children and their relations'.[14] To our great loss, he simply assumes her effect on him and does not describe either the school she had gone to, or the help she undoubtedly must have given him. But he waxes lyrical about his paternal grandmother, by whose spinning-wheel he spent all the time he could as a very small child. She had few books, but two in particular caught his fancy: she had a 'life of Christ ornamented at the head of each chapter with a rude [i.e. crude] woodcut ... It belonged to the earlier part of the seventeenth century. She also had a copy of Aesop's Fables, tattered and torn and imperfect, equally ornamented with woodcuts, over which I used to pore with infinite delight. This book ... was of an earlier date.' But she also had an 'immense bundle of penny histories and ballads [so I] made myself intimately acquainted with giants, witches, fairies and their doings, and had the Seven Champions of Christendom and the ballads of Robin Hood at my fingers' ends.' But his grandmother had a 'very considerable' stock of tales, as well.[15] We are vividly reminded of the mental world of John Clare.[16]

James was formally taught his letters from a 'battledore', which had just taken over from the hornbook as the basic piece of first-reading equipment, by a schooldame in the village, with whom he remained for a year. He probably started at three and a half. Two other schooldames taught him next, both of whom were the wives of day-labourers. The second had been a maidservant before her marriage. Yet he makes it plain they did actually *teach*.[17] There is no ambiguity.

He went on to describe his teaching by two schoolmasters, beginning when he was still only five. The first, an ex-manual labourer,[18] worked in a tumbledown shack, covered with thatch and open to the roof. There he taught 20–25 boys and girls. By the time he was six, James had been taught to write, which was highly unusual.[19] The Dutch genre painter, Egbert van Heemskerk, whose paintings suddenly became so very popular in the 1680s and 1690s, painted such men at work (see Figure 3.3). So did his followers. They sold: they were of familiar, identifiable subjects. Again from the 1690s comes a piece of quantifiable evidence. The Brewers' Company of London ran a school at Aldenham, in Hertfordshire. Three times, in 1689, 1695 and 1708 a survey of the *reading*, not the writing, abilities of the incoming boys was carried out. It showed that together, out of the 127 boys covered, 10 per cent of the incoming 3 and 4-year-olds could read, but almost one-third of the 5-year-olds and just over half of the 6-year-olds could.[20]

Now, if children as young as 3, 4 and 5 years old were reading, the argument that some of them had been taught by their mothers is a very likely one. Of course, it is just possible that they had come in to the Aldenham school via a schooldame. Dr Samuel Johnson, no less, was taught to read by a woman before going to the Free Grammar School at Lichfield. He bitterly repented, as many others did, that as a boy 'he was

51

*Figure 3.3* Egbert van Heemskerk: *Schoolroom*, present location unknown (reproduced with the permission of the Courtauld Institute, the University of London)

inordinately fond of reading romances of chivalry'. They sold well on his bookseller-father's stall at Uttoxeter market.

In the 1690s, too, the then Bishop of Lichfield had a highly eccentric survey made of his own manor of Eccleshall, in Staffordshire, which lay surrounding its own little market town. The insight this survey gives us of the women who taught reading in it is unusual: the pity of it is that we cannot tell, for lack of other evidence, whether the women were unusual, or only the insight. For they were not women from the higher social orders at all: they were labourers' wives, who had this skill to sell to help them eke out the family budget. One of them 'Stephen Dimock's wife' was the wife of a day-labourer living on the common. Thomas Alsop's wife, 'the best knitter in my parish', a valuable gainful skill she would have taught girls, was also the wife of a day-labourer. 'Barnet's wife' was married to a shoemaker, and 'Curly Wollam's wife' was married to a labourer who thrashed and thatched part-time, was a weaver the rest of the time, and earned the Bishop's approval as a 'very honest man, laborious and religious, sings Psalms in Church'. It is highly improbable that all these schooldames merely acted as childminders, which is one aspersion commonly thrown at them.[21] We have already seen that the day-labourers' wives who taught James Raine were not. Without any extrapolation through time, the shop of the Eccleshall mercer, Jeffrey Snelson, which would have supplied these women at the time, carried a large number of hornbooks (see Figure 3.4) and primers.[22]

No one who runs a business keeps useless stock. Also, inspection of the wills of Eccleshall people shows that a larger proportion than normal of poorer men went on to learn the ancillary skill of writing there. There is also a thesis in progress which, very excitingly, shows the enormous volume of hornbooks and ABCs being produced by the monopolists, the Stationers' Company, after the Restoration.[23] From these numbers, England was saturated with the basic equipment for learning to read: and once again, the Stationers' Company was a hard-nosed company, in business to make profits, not losses. We saw the fruits in Aldenham School, in those 3-, 4- and 5-year-olds who could read. And lastly, there are just too many odd anecdotes, casual, incidental comments, demonstrating, by accident, that yet one more child had learnt to read from a woman, before going to a formal school. Oliver Sansom, a yeoman of Berkshire, was one of these. He was born in 1636, and wrote:

> when I was about six years of age, I was put to school to a woman, who finding me not unapt to learn, forwarded me so well that in about four months time, I could read a chapter in the Bible pretty readily.[24]

It may be that this Berkshire woman was more able than her counterpart in Yorkshire who taught James Fretwell, the son of a timber merchant born right at the end of the seventeenth century: or it may just be that James Fretwell's mother was a more ambitious parent. For, James later wrote:

> As soon as I was capable of learning [my mother] sent me to an

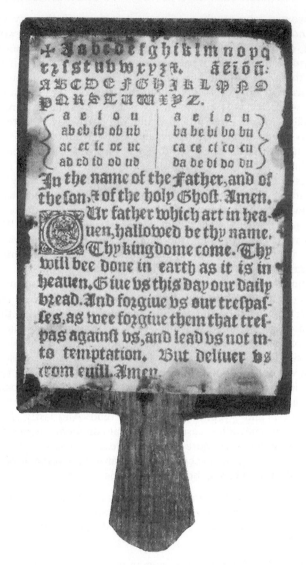

*Figure 3.4* Seventeenth-century hornbook

old schooldame, who lived at the very next door. But I suppose I did not continue here but a few days, for growing weary of my book, and my dame not correcting me as my mother desired, she took me under her as pedagogy until I could read the Bible, *and thus she did afterwards by all my brothers and sisters* [emphasis added].[25]

So we reach the heart of the matter. Jane Johnson, gentlewoman, was not alone in the 1730s and she did not, by any means, set a precedent. Mrs Fretwell of Yorkshire was a highly successful teacher. When James was only four and a half he was admitted to the small local grammar school

my dear mother being desirous that I should have a little more learning than she was capable of giving me ... when the master placed me among some little ones, such as myself ... when he called me up to hear what I had to say for myself, he ... removed me higher, asking my mother whether she had brought me an Accidence, which I think she had; so she had the pleasure of seeing me removed out of the horn-book class

It is hard to find other examples like Mrs Fretwell, teaching all her children. But Thomas Tryon, born in 1641, who is in so many ways the best example we have of seventeenth-century literacy, was not only the poorest boy, son of a Gloucestershire tiler and plasterer, to write his *Autobiography* (*and* wrote the most detailed and vivid account of how he learnt to read *from his own workmates*),[26] but also tantalizes us further, for he went on to write a series of treatises which are fascinating, set in the context of this poor background. One of them gives us the most mouth-watering glimpse of a whole possible group of mothers teaching reading.

Tryon founded a religious sect. He wrote not only a treatise called *A New Method of Education*, but probably was also the 'TT' who, together with 'GF' and 'GC' also produced *The Compleat School Master or Child's Instructor* of 1700. In the 'Principles' for his religious group, he wrote a section called 'Laws and Orders proper for Women to observe', giving them detailed directions on how they should teach their young children to read, pleasurably. 'Pleasure' in education was extremely important to him.

At a Year and a Half or Two Years Old, shew them their Letters, not troubling them in the vulgar way with asking them what is this Letter, or that Word; but instead thereof, make frequent Repetitions in their hearing, putting the Letters in their Sight. And thus, in a little time, they will easily and familiarly learn to distinguish the Twenty Four Letters, all one as they do the Utensils, Goods, and

Furniture of the House, by hearing the Family name them. At the same time, teach your Children to hold the Pen, and guide their Hand; [this is, of course, extraordinary for the seventeenth century, when writing began at seven] and by this method, your Children, un-accountably to themselves, will attain to Read and Write at Three, Four, or Five years old . . .[27]

So, if these women actually carried their instructions out, there were women in the 1680s and 1690s who were building up their own little collections of seventeenth-century 'flash cards' and materials to teach their children to read, forty years at least before Jane Johnson. Maybe, some day, someone will find another shoebox, complete with the contents from a slightly different social background and an earlier period. It is by no means impossible. James Raine's grandmother had had a collection spanning two centuries.

*

So, if schooldames and mothers taught reading, what was there available to read, after the ubiquitous hornbook and primer, which always taught the child the basic tenets of religion, as well as reading?

Evidence mounts up to show that the 1620s marked a revolution in the cheap print trade. The ballad had existed for well over a century in affordable form. Now the chapbooks made their appearance as a genre, both those called 'small merries' and those called 'small godlies'.[28] So also did the serial newsbook.[29] Not only did the Ballad Partnership form, to market these things: even the Worshipful Company of Playing Card Makers made its first appearance. This is more serious a matter than it sounds: playing-cards were ubiquitous, and used by all social groups. They made alphabetical symbols familiar, they spread political news and satire as the 'Armada' pack and the Rump Parliament pack did, and pilloried famous persons and types, as the 'South Sea Bubble' pack did. They also educated: they made familiar the form of the map, both in John Ogilby's pack of 1676, and the 'New England' pack.

However horrified she might have been by playing-cards, even out of service time, we know the basic books Hannah Gifford taught from in the school newly established by the reforming Dorchester Corporation in the town Hospital. They set up Hannah there to teach in 1651, with the very considerable salary of £10 a year for less than thirty children, £12 if there were more. She was still there in 1668, and for most, if not all, of that time, she had been paid £12 a year. The most exciting thing is that we know something of her teaching material. In 1658, she was sent bibles, testaments, primers 'and other small books' to the value of £3.5s.7d by the local bookseller.[30] In May 1666, she was supplied with twelve hornbooks at 1d each, thirteen Primers at 3d each, eleven single

Psalters at 1/- each and eight Testaments at 1/6d each. The total was £1.7s.3d. At the end of April 1668, the local bookseller was paid for six hornbooks at 1d each, twelve Primers at 3d each, nine single Psalters at a total of 10/6 and nine Testaments at a total of 15/-.[31] It was, as I have said elsewhere, impossible to learn to read without being also taught the basics of religious belief: this was true quite separately from the Puritan nature of this school, the woman who ran it, and the Corporation which set it up. What we long to know is what were those 'other small books' of 1658? Did Goody Gifford permit her most virtuous pupils a glimpse of a 'small godly book' as a reward? Dr Michael Frearson's important evidence of the book-list of a 'godly' shoemaker in the 1620s is relevant here: *The Rich Cabinet* and *A Godly Garden of Comfortable Hearbes* and *Smug the Smith*[32] do not all sound forbidding. There was an ingenious plea in the 'Preface' to the chapbook *The Wise Mistresses*,[33] that

> History ought to be praised, not condemned; for it doth encourage Youth through the pleasantness of the Story, whereby he doth sooner attain to his English Tongue, and is still more desirous to read further. For many thousands at School, in their innocency, are more naturally given to learn first Historical Fables, by which they sooner come to read perfect, then to begin first in hard Books appertaining to Divine knowledge; which made that rare and learned Scholar Æsop, to put forth his Fables in the Schools, which being composed with such incomparable and acute Wit, Jeast and Merriment, that each Scholar daily strove who should outvie the other in the Dispute and Rehearsal of them.[34]

This may not have appealed to Goody Gifford, but is it perhaps possible that Aesop's *Fables* might have passed her guardianship? We have already seen[35] what an effect a seventeenth-century copy of Aesop had on little James Raine: one large enough, indeed to justify this selling hyperbole.

We have scattered references all through the century to the reading matter beloved of the poor. It was picked from the whole medley of what was available. Young Richard Baxter repented of the love of 'romances, fables and old tales' which had 'corrupted his affections' in the 1630s. We know James Raine's grandmothers had collected a seventeenth-century book illustrated with woodcuts, as well as the hymns of Isaac Watts, which he was circulating in the late seventeenth century,[36] as well as a heap of ballads. The Old Testament was more popular than the New amongst seventeenth-century children, just as it is amongst twentieth-century children: young Thomas Boston was ashamed to recollect that nothing had moved him to read the Bible when he was seven but 'curiosity, as about the history of Balaam's ass'.[37] He hid underneath the bedclothes with it, and a candle-end. London schoolboys swapped the whole corpus of romances later collected by Samuel Pepys. Older, print-starved poor men were held captive by tougher meat. One pitiable unhinged journeyman, Arise Evans, stopped his walk from the Black Mountains to London at Coventry for six months, simply because the master he found there had a copy of a *History of the World*, which he wished to get by heart. The passion for print could consume these readers.

Women were affected as well as men. I have used my favourite character, Sister Sneesby, the Cambridgeshire Quaker who earned her living by day-labour in her widowhood, too often.[38] But she was such a shining example because she was deaf, and was converted from her General Baptist beliefs to Quakerism, in the 1650s, by what I myself found a peculiarly indigestible Quaker tract. Let me hastily set up against her Widow Robinson, who caused deep offence to her Open Baptist brethren by singing 'carnal' songs and dancing on the table, at the shoemakers' feast fifty years or so later.[39] I don't know whether it was the contents of her ballads, which were almost certainly taken from print at that date, or dancing on a table when high-flown with ale that gave offence – but she should be noted, in case women are only thought to be readers of pious material.[40]

Let me finish with John Bunyan. For John Bunyan also repented his early reading, and gives us the best list, probably from the 1640s, of any of those who did so. He had, he wrote, thought

> give me a Ballad, a News-book, *George on Horseback* [a quarto chivalric romance – see Figure 3.5] or *Bevis of Southampton*, give me some book that touches curious Arts, that tells of old Fables: but for the Holy Scriptures, I cared not. And as it is with me then, so it is with my brethren now.[41]

Apart from covering the whole spectrum of cheap print that I outlined for you earlier, and thereby demonstrating it did percolate to the lowest social levels, the most telling thing about this quotation is the simple, easily overlooked statement '*so it is with my brethren now*' (my italics). My 'brethren' were presumably not Bunyan's own flock of Bedfordshire Open Baptists – who were, incidentally, the poorest group of post-Restoration dissenters we know about[42] – but his fellow-villagers and relations round about Bedford in the 1660s when he wrote the autobiography from which this quotation comes. Such stuff was common in men's – and women's – reading.[43]

In the circumstances, it becomes highly significant that John Bunyan wrote one of the first books deliberately aimed at children. His emblem book, *A Book for Boys and Girls or Country Rhimes for Children*, came out in 1686. My ignorance of the field is too great for me to say it was the first deliberate attempt to write suitable substitution literature for children, instead of all the fanciful histories John Bunyan and others had

*Figure 3.5 St George on Horseback* (reproduced with the permission of Dr Richard Luckett, The Pepys Library, Magdalene College, Cambridge)

reported reading with such monotonous regularity. But it must have been one of the first.

However, the very concept of 'children's books' becomes suspect, and possibly meaningless, when the first version of *Tom Thumb* had been printed in 1621, and all the chivalrics that entranced young Bunyan, as well as the extraordinary *Old Women of Ratcliffe Highway*, which uniquely competed with Lewis Carroll for sheer nonsense, were in print.

So I will leave you with a picture of schooling relatively readily available, schooldames and mothers actively teaching the rudiments, a semi-literate society able to read, if not write, gulping up new trash from the presses. And perhaps amongst these people were the forebears of Jane Johnson, like Mrs Fretwell, diligently teaching their own offspring, and perhaps indeed collecting suitable material for teaching reading, just as Thomas Tryon advocated. There is 'very little new beneath the visiting moon'.

## NOTES

1 Brian Simon, 'Leicestershire Schools, 1625–40', *British Jo. of Ed. Studies* III (1954), pp. 42–58.
2 Margaret Spufford, *Contrasting Communities* (1974), Map II, p. 185.
3 Margaret Spufford, 'The Schooling of the Peasantry in Cambridgeshire, 1575–1700', *Land, Church and People: Essays Presented to H.P.R. Finberg*, ed. Joan Thirsk (Reading: British Agricultural History Society 1970) p. 127. 'Casting an accompte' was the skill of arithmetic, taught by using counters on a cloth, board, or table marked in squares. It was also known as 'reckoning'. There is a rare survival of a very grand reckoning table in the city of Basle. 'Ciphering' was the much greater skill of using written arabic numerals. Continental teachers charged more to teach the latter. See Margaret Spufford, 'Literacy, Trade and Religion in the Commercial Centres of Europe', *A Miracle Mirrored: The Dutch Republic in European Perspective*, eds Karel Davids and Jan Lucassen (Cambridge, 1996), pp. 254–5, 265, 266–7 and n. 91, p. 277. For the importance of the earning capacity given by knitting and spinning, which might indeed keep a labouring family afloat and off the poor-rates, see Margaret Spufford and James Went, *Poverty Portrayed: Gregory King and the Parish of Eccleshall*, ed. Robin Studd (Keele, 1996), Table III, p. 63, and discussion on labouring women's work, pp. 64–6.
4 Spufford, *Contrasting Communities*, p. 203, n. 32.
5 Nikolaus Pevsner, *Cambridgeshire*, 2nd edn (Harmondsworth, 1970), pp. 413, 454.
6 Peter Clark, *English Provincial Society from the Reformation to the Revolution: Religion, Politics and Society in Kent, 1500–1640* (Hassocks, 1977), Maps 4 and 5, pp. 202, 203.
7 For the medieval period, see J.A.H. Moran, *The Growth of English Schooling, 1340–1598* (1985); and Nicholas Orme, *Education in the West of England, 1066–1548* (Exeter, 1976) and *English Schools in the Middle Ages* (London, 1973).
8 Margaret Spufford, ed., *The World of Rural Dissenters, 1520–1725* (Cambridge, 1995), pp. 67–8, n. 230. David Cressy in his vast thesis 'Education and Literacy

in London and East Anglia, 1580–1700' (Cambridge Ph.D., 1973) which lies behind his *Literacy and the Social Order: Reading and Writing in Tudor and Stuart England* (Cambridge, 1980) also found very few licensed schooldames in his exhaustive initial study. Professor Cressy's opinion that schooldames were often merely childminders probably lies behind much received wisdom. However, English schooldames were undoubtedly called on to do much less than those in the Low Countries (see n. 13).

9 James Raine was born in 1791 and had a 'village' education until he went to weekly boarding grammar school in 1804. 'A Raine Miscellany', ed. Angela Marsden, *Surtees Society*, CC (1989).

10 Ibid., p. 45.

11 Ibid., p. 43.

12 Ibid., p. 17.

13 Poor English girls were not officially taught, nor did schooldames teach, arithmetic. This is a very strong contrast with, for instance, the Low Countries. In Antwerp, after the decline set in, from 1595–1645, 122 men and 120 women teaching were examined on their skills. Thirty-three per cent of the men and 45 per cent of the women taught 'only' Dutch reading *and writing*: I have yet to find a single seventeenth-century woman teaching writing in England. But, much more remarkably, 38 per cent of the men, and as many as 25 per cent of the women, taught *arithmetic*. This was utterly unheard of in England: see Spufford, 'Literacy, Trade and Religion', pp. 253–4, 258, 259–61 and Plate 8.2. Note that in a Utrecht orphanage, the girls were apparently taught writing from 1600, as well as reading. Girls in Amersfoort Sunday School may very well have been taught arithmetic, as well as reading and writing.

14 Ibid., pp. 31–2.

15 Ibid., pp. 14–15.

16 Margaret Spufford, *Small Books and Pleasant Histories: Popular Fiction and its Readership in Seventeenth-century England* (London, 1981), pp. 3–6.

17 'A Raine Miscellany', pp. 36–41.

18 In 1606 in the Isle of Ely, Edward Browne 'labourer' faced the Ecclesiastic Court for 'teaching of Children without any licence.' His wife was accused with him. The pair were dismissed, Ely DR, B/2/66, fol. 121v. I owe this reference to the kindness of Dr Christopher Marsh.

19 'A Raine Miscellany', pp. 41–6.

20 I am greatly indebted to Dr Roger Schofield, who worked out the figures for me (personal communication) from an unpublished paper of Newman Brown's, held at the Cambridge Group for the History of Population and Social Structure. It is possible that the distribution of reading skills was much greater in wood-pasture areas: see Spufford, *The World of Rural Dissenters, 1520–1725*, pp. 44–7, elaborated on in Spufford and Went, *Poverty Portrayed*, pp. 50–2.

21 See, for instance, David Underdown, *Fire from Heaven* (London, 1992), p. 225. Professor Underdown is merely repeating a received wisdom, see above, n. 8.

22 Spufford and Went, *Poverty Portrayed*.

23 Helen Weinstein, 'Rudimentary Religion and National Identity in Late Seventeenth Century England' (Cambridge Ph.D in progress, 1996).

24 Quoted in Spufford, *Small Books*, p. 24.

25 Ibid., p. 24.

26 His account of learning to read and write and the prices of primers and hornbooks may be found in full in Spufford, *The World*, pp. 68–70.

27 *Some Memoirs of the Life of Mr Tho: Tryon, late of London, merchant: written by himself...* (1705), pp. 117–18, 122–3.
28 Tessa Watt, *Cheap Print and Popular Piety, 1550–1640* (Cambridge, 1991). David Harrison, Roehampton Institute London, has completed a Ph.D. (1996) on the antecedents of the chapbooks.
29 Michael Frearson, 'The English Corantos of the 1620s' (Cambridge Ph.D., 1994, to appear in the Cambridge *History of the Book* series, ed. David McKitterick).
30 Underdown, *Fire from Heaven*, pp. 225–6.
31 I am particularly grateful to Professor Underdown, who took the trouble to look these lists of books and prices out for me from his collection of materials.
32 Spufford, *The World*, p. 53. I am much indebted to Dr Frearson for allowing me to use this important find of his.
33 Thomas Howard, *The Wise Mistresses*, Penny Merriments, III(6), p. 634, (Pepys Library, Magdalene College, Cambridge).
34 Preface to Thomas Howard, *The Wise Mistresses*, Penny Merriments, III(6), p. 634.
35 See p. 51.
36 Spufford, *The World*, p. 95.
37 Spufford, *Small Books*, pp. 25, 73.
38 Spufford, *Contrasting Communities*, pp. 216–17 and n. 39, and *The World*, p. 64.
39 Spufford, *The World*, p. 86, n. 297.
40 Ibid.
41 Spufford, *Small Books*, p. 7.
42 Bill Stevenson, 'The Social and Economic Status of Post-Restoration Dissenters, 1660–1725', in Margaret Spufford, *The World*, pp. 334–6 and Table 9.
43 See also David Harrison, *An Ancestral Subject Catalogue of Chapbook Themes* (Scolar Press, 1996), an invaluable finding-aid to scholars interested in the topics available to those who could read.

# XII

## THE DISSENTING CHURCHES IN
## CAMBRIDGESHIRE FROM 1660 TO 1700

THE Commonwealth saw the rapid growth of 'gathered' churches, which drew in their members from a wide area. For instance, the Baptists of Fenstanton in Hunting-donshire and Caxton in Cambridgeshire, united between 1644 and 1666, baptized members from no less than thirty villages and towns in Cambridgeshire, Huntingdon-shire and Bedfordshire.[1] As John Cook wrote, 'A Union of hearts rather than a vicinity of Houses, is to make up a Congregation according to the New Testament'.[2] The Restoration marked the end of the toleration which all but the Quakers had enjoyed for most of the preceding twenty years. It also marked the beginning of official inquiries by the re-established Anglican church, into the number of these gathered churches, and the number of parishioners who had switched their allegiance from the parish church to the nearest Congregational, Baptist or Quaker meeting. These Anglican inquiries were naturally made on a parochial basis, whereas the whole aim of the sectarian churches they were attempting to examine was to bring together believers in a conscious act of choice, wherever they lived. The Church Book of Gamlingay Old Meeting defined a true church of Christ as 'visible saints, and...a congregation of visible Believers in Christ who are separated from the wicked world, and give themselves up unto God, and unto one another'. The returns made by the ministers on the numbers of dissenters in their parishes therefore only give dis-membered fragments of the nonconformist churches in the area. It is usually im-possible to reconstruct the whole body from these fragments. However, the Anglican reports of the late 1660s and 1670s do give statistical information on the extent of nonconformist growth in the preceding period. They are therefore valuable, particularly since they come at a time when the records of the dissenters themselves become extremely thin.[3]

The printed sources available for the diocese of Ely which show the extent to which nonconformity had spread under the Commonwealth are the returns made

---

[1] *Records of the Churches of Christ gathered at Fenstanton, Warboys and Hexham, 1644–1720*, ed. E. B. Underhill for the Hanserd Knollys Society, 1854, pp. 251–4. (Henceforth, *Fenstanton Records*.)

[2] Quoted G. F. Nuttall, *Visible Saints* (1957), p. 108, n. 2.

[3] The Quaker records are the only ones for Cambridgeshire which continue through the 1670s, and they in any case record the doings of a hard core of converts which had been under persistent pressure since the sect was founded in the 1650s. They may be regarded as untypical. The continuous records of the Fen-stanton Baptists end in 1658/9 (*Fenstanton Records*, p. 250) and the records of the Open Baptists of Bedford become too scrappy in the 1670s for a reconstruction of their history (*Church Book of Bunyan Meeting 1650–1821*, ed. G. B. Harrison). Even the earliest history of the Cambridgeshire Congregationalists is extraordinarily thin, never mind their history in this time of persecution.

68

by the bishop, Benjamin Laney, in 1669, the licences issued for dissenting meeting places and preachers after the Declaration of Indulgence of 1672,[1] and the Compton Census of 1676,[2] listing the numbers of papists, conformists and nonconformists in each village. Two unpublished visitations of the diocese, carried out in 1679 and 1682,[3] form extra evidence to support or disprove this general information gathered by central authority, as do the detailed memoranda made for the visitation of the archdeaconry of Ely in 1685.[4] Of these sources, the licences issued in 1672 and the visitations of the diocese carried out at the end of the decade are the most trustworthy, in so far as they are issued to, or they present, specific named individuals, whose existence can be safely assumed. Neither, of course, is any guide to the extent of nonconformity in a particular parish. Licences were usually, but not always, issued only to the larger congregations. The fact that a licence was issued in 1672 is therefore only proof that nonconformity did exist in a specific place, and the absence of such a licence is no evidence. Similarly, the presentation by the churchwardens of parishioners as conventiclers is proof that the nonconformists they named inhabited their parish. There remains the problem of what proportion were so presented, and of how far this proportion varied from parish to parish depending on the tolerant, or unsympathetic attitude, and on the laziness, or devotion to duty, of the individual churchwardens concerned. The necessity for caution is underlined by the example of the Warwickshire churchwarden who was presented for holding conventicles at his house.[5] His previous reports, made by virtue of his office, on nonconformists in his parish, seem unlikely to have been very thorough. However, the existence of a licence, or of presentations, for a particular parish is useful confirmatory evidence to collate with the episcopal returns of 1669, and with the Compton Census.

The returns of 1669 give details of the places within the diocese where the bishop knew, or suspected, that a conventicle was held, together with an estimate of its probable size, and the names of its teachers, and the social background of those who attended, where possible. The Compton Census listed the numbers of papists, nonconformists and conformists in each village. Both these surveys are useful bases for forming general impressions of the extent of nonconformity in the late 1660s and 1670s, but both are, of course, liable to be inaccurate in specific cases.[6] The Quarter Sessions records for Cambridgeshire, as opposed to the Isle of Ely, are unfortunately seriously defective. The volume of presentations for dissent at Quarter Sessions would provide a useful check on the numbers of dissenters recorded in various parishes in 1669 and 1676, but the session rolls only survive from 1730. Only the order books,

[1] Both printed in G. Lyon Turner, *Original Records of Early Nonconformity under Persecution and Indulgence* (1911), I, pp. 34–42 and II, pp. 862–75.
[2] William Salt Library, Stafford. Soon to be printed in the Staffs. Historical Collections, ed. A. Whiteman.
[3] Cambridge University Library, Ely Episcopal Records, B2/66 ff. 13–28v and 39–53r.
[4] Henry Bradshaw, 'Notes of the Episcopal Visitation of the Archdeaconry of Ely in 1685', *Proc. C.A.S.* III (1875), pp. 323–61.
[5] *Warwick County Records*, VII (1946), p. lxxvii.
[6] See note on the Compton Census at the end (p. 94).

and a book of recognizances survive from the 1660s.[1] The former do give registrations of meeting houses after the Toleration Act of 1689, but these, at least until 1715, are so sporadic, and omit so many major congregations known to be in existence, that they are very little help.[2]

The census showed that the villages of Cambridgeshire[3] contained between 4 and 5 per cent of nonconformists in 1676. This proportion was almost exactly typical of the country as a whole.[4] An average figure is, however, deceptive because a detailed survey of the distribution of nonconformity shows that it had obtained a really strong grasp in some areas, and was almost completely non-existent in others.

The census recorded the existence of dissenters in over thirty more parishes than the bishop had done in 1669, perhaps because dissent had spread up to 1675, after the Declaration of Indulgence in 1672. Even so, parishes with congregations which were entirely conformist made up the largest single group amongst the parishes of the diocese of Ely. Nearly half the parishes in the diocese had only two dissenters at most. The parishes which stood out in the census as centres of nonconformity were those with a group of ten or more dissenters. There were twenty-five of these in southern Cambridgeshire,[5] and, on the whole, all the available evidence agreed, with remarkable unanimity, on the part they played as strongholds of dissent. Bishop Laney had recorded a conventicle in, or a licence had been issued for, seventeen of them. Moreover twelve of them also had significantly large numbers of presentations for dissent in the visitations of 1679, 1682, and 1685. Only six other parishes appeared from the visitations to have large numbers of nonconformists at the end of the 1670s which would not have been selected as significant nonconformist strongholds on the basis of the Compton figures alone.[6]

The episcopal returns for the country as a whole showed that in 1669 the Presbyterians, with well over 40,000 adherents, were by far the strongest sect. The Baptists, with 7,000 or thereabouts, were equally noticeably the weakest. The Congregationalists competed with the Quakers for second place.[7]

This order was almost completely reversed in Cambridgeshire,[8] where the pitifully small group of thirty-odd Presbyterians put the county lowest amongst those which had Presbyterians at all.[9] The Congregationalists were, by Bishop Laney's reckoning, the strongest sect in the shire,[10] in 1669. There were just over 700 of them. Only London, Kent and Norfolk in eastern England, and Monmouthshire in the

---

[1] Cambridgeshire Record Office, Q.S. 2 I a, etc. and Q.S. 4 (i).
[2] Mapped on Map B. Registrations began in 1699, Q.S. 2.2. See also 'Nonconformist Places of Worship Licensed under the Toleration Act, 1688', *Tr. Cong. Hist. Soc.* VI (1913–15), pp. 200–1, 206.
[3] Including the Isle of Ely.
[4] I.e. 4·4 per cent in Cambridgeshire compared with 4·5 per cent (or 1:22) over the whole country.
[5] Excluding Cambridge itself and the parishes of the deanery of Fordham in the diocese of Norwich.
[6] These were in any case missing for two of them, Swaffham Bulbeck and Willingham.
[7] Lyon Turner, *op. cit.* III, p. 119.
[8] Numbers of conventiclers tabulated by denomination in Lyon Turner, *op. cit.* III, p. 110.
[9] Lyon Turner, *op. cit.* III, pp. 127–9.
[10] All these figures include the Isle.

268

70

west, had more,[1] and apart from the last they all, of course, had much larger popula-
tions on which to draw.

The evidence for the early growth of the Congregational church in Cambridgeshire is very scanty. The work of Francis Holcroft,[2] fellow of Clare, seems to have
been fundamental. He accepted the living of Bassingbourn in 1655, and, according to
tradition, founded a Congregational church there almost at once. Only the wording

Map A.

[1] Lyon Turner, *op. cit.* III, pp. 130–2.
[2] For Holcroft, Bradshaw, and Holcroft's assistants Oddy and Lock, see A. G. Matthews, *Calamy
Revised* (1934), pp. 271–2, 69–70, 325–6, 371.

of the covenant which bound the members of this first church survives.[1] There is little evidence which shows how extensive the growth of the Bassingbourn church was before the Restoration, apart from the account of Richard Conder, junior, who became pastor of a branch of Holcroft's church at Croydon-cum-Clopton after his death in 1692. At about that time, when he was in his early forties, Richard Conder wrote a note on the work of 'God's servant' Francis Holcroft, at the beginning of his Church Book, which afterwards became the Church Book of Great Gransden.[2] In his account, he described how, after Holcroft had begun to preach at Bassingbourn:

the lord oned him much in converchon of soolls and their began to be a talk of him, and my father being a ancient profeser then being feri son in this contri heard of his meting on one of the holi days as they calle them at Eastr or Whisantid.  he maid his servant and chilldren to goo with him to the meeting thou it much displeased us and he preached then from them woords 'the ston that was regectid by yow builders is becom the head ston of the corner'.

and i being yong did not understand what he preached but thought he was a strang man to talk so much about stoons.  and when wee cam away he followed us out and tallcked with my father about several things, and my father being feri plain with him he askid him what he thought in him, and his ansour was that he toock him to bee on of the reformed prests of that day, and hee claped him on the shoollder and said 'thow dost not know my mind, but thow maist know it hearaftor'.

and soo hee partid with him and soon after the woorck of God went forward and soolls was convertid and the lord was much with him and soonn seet his hart to buildd him an hows.  and the lord's hand was seen in that day in calling seaverall of the yong schollers in the unifarciti which did preach about in the cuntri towns, as mister Oddi at Melldrid and mister Ecins at Chisell and mister Ponder at Whadon.

[1] Quoted by Robert Robinson, 'Historical Account' in his *Posthumous Works*, ed. B. Flower (Harlow, 1812), pp. 257–9. Most of Robinson's material is drawn from the near-contemporary account of Francis Holcroft's work preserved at the beginning of the Great Gransden Church Book (see below), which appears to be the only seventeenth-century documentary evidence on the spread of Congregationalism in Cambridgeshire, apart from the list of members of the church made in 1675. The wording of the covenant taken at Bassingbourn was recorded in the Gransden Church Book when the members of the Croydon church renewed their covenant in the 1690s. The 'Statistical Survey of Dissent' in the *Congregational Magazine or London Christian Instructor*, II (1819), p. 437, also records the Bassingbourn tradition, as, in a modified form, does the first surviving Church Book of Cottenham Old Meeting (in the keeping of the secretary and deacons, to whose kindness I am much indebted). The latter only begins in 1780, and includes two passages of meditation on the earlier history of the church inserted amongst the minutes of meetings in 1823 and 1829 (pp. 107–8 and 163). The writer of the second seems to have had an earlier church book in front of him. W. T. Whitley, 'Willingham Church', *Congregational Historical Society Transactions*, XII (1933–6), pp. 120–30, prints 'An Authentick Account of the Church of Christ at Willingham from the year 1662 to 1781' probably written in 1811.

The only other possible reference to early Congregationalism in the county is the reference made by the Quaker, Margaret Killam, in 1654 to a church she attended in Cambridge 'where most of those meet which are comers from the other priests, and have one, as they say, that speaks freely without hire' (*Early Quaker Letters from the Swarthmore MSS. to 1660* (1952), no. 83 calendared G. F. Nuttall). Dr Nuttall suggests that this separatist congregation might well have paved the way for the work of Holcroft and Oddy after 1662. A. G. Mathews, 'The Seventeenth Century' in *Congregationalism through the Centuries* (Cambridge, 1937), pp. 45–7, was baffled because he had not been able to find any trace of a Congregational church nearer to Cambridge than Wisbech at this time.

[2] H. G. Tibbutt, 'Pattern of Change', *Cong. Hist. Soc. Trans.* XX, pp. 170–3, and 'Memoir of the Late Rev. John Conder, D. D.', *Evangelical Magazine*, III (1795), pp. 393–5. I am deeply indebted to Mr Tibbutt for his generosity in lending me his transcript of the Great Gransden Church Book.

and God's servant, being ficxed for the rulls of God's hous, was soonne set apart pastor by mister Staloms and soom others which I hafe forgat, then being feri yong, but this I remember they cept the day and all the night after with great joy and singin. and I remember that my father and mother cam hom in the morning and as soonne as my mother had doon milleking shee cam in and toolld my father that shee must goo to Basingbon again, and they toock their hors and weent away.

their was shuch a mighti preasenc of God amongst them that they ware redi to forsack all to follow Crist.

Holcroft was obviously drawing large audiences to Bassingbourn before his ejection, although it sounds as if the formation of his church did not take place very long before 1662. Richard Conder added that his father 'stood out a priti whil' before he joined the covenant 'but the Lord brought him...to see into it afterwards and in the time of builldin this church it was a tim of trobell, for now king Charls cam in and God's servant...was turned out of the publick placises'.

The lack of references to tension between the Open Baptists of Fenstanton and Caxton, and the Congregationalists, in the later 1650s seems to argue that, although Holcroft's church was formed, and had considerable drawing-power, there was no overlap in the areas from which the two dissenting congregations were drawn, and therefore little opportunity for friction before the recorder of the Fenstanton church completed his volume in 1658/9. Holcroft's work before that date must therefore have been carried on to the south of Great Shelford and Harston, the most southerly villages within the orbit of the Fenstanton Baptists. Negative arguments are admittedly dangerous, but the struggles between the Quakers and the Baptists are so fully noted by the Baptists after the arrival of the Quakers in 1653 that it is difficult to believe that debate between the Calvinist Congregationalists and the Armenian General Baptists would find no place in the record.

After Holcroft refused to subscribe in 1662, he became a peripatetic minister in south Cambridgeshire, aided by a team of ex-fellows of Trinity, including Joseph Oddy. In Richard Conder's words, 'the woork of God went forward and their was daly adid to the church'. By 1663, he had meetings of several hundred people in southern Cambridgeshire and the neighbouring counties.[1] Most of his time between 1663 and 1672 was spent in prison, but according to tradition he was allowed out to preach. Conder testified that with Holcroft's imprisonment 'the churchis aflicton began upon her but the moar she was aflicted the moar she gru'. At the same time, Nathanial Bradshaw, the non-subscribing rector of Willingham, continued to preach in his own house there as well as the neighbouring villages,[2] until he made the place too hot to hold him in about 1667. He then retreated to London for a space. Joseph Oddy took over his work and became the itinerent Congregationalist minister of north-west Cambridgeshire.

The Baptists, who were generally so weak, were extremely well established in Cambridgeshire in 1669. Their congregation in the county numbered over six

[1] Lyon Turner, *op. cit.* III, pp. 294–6.
[2] *Cottenham Old Meeting first Church Book* (unprinted), p. 163.

hundred, and was probably more considerable than that of any other area except London and Buckinghamshire.[1] Kent and Sussex, in the south-east, also had a strong Baptist element. The only other counties where Baptists were found in considerable numbers were Wiltshire and Warwickshire.

The Baptist church in western Cambridgeshire owed its genesis to Henry Denne,[2] the famous preacher, who was presented to the living of Eltisley by the Disborough family under the Commonwealth. The first members of the church all lived within easy physical reach of Eltisley, which was once described as 'an asylum for the most extravagant fanaticism...psalm singing was as heineous a sin at Eltisley as bending a knee to Baal, and it was then as much noted for the devout exercises practised there, as any other canting place within the kingdom'. Denne's son, John, became elder and recorder of the General Baptist church which was established round the joint centres of Fenstanton in Huntingdonshire and Caxton in Cambridgeshire in the early 1650s. John Denne lived at Caxton Pastures, a farm in Caxton parish a mile or so from Eltisley, which therefore became one of the principal meeting places of the church. The fullness and vivid reporting of the first Fenstanton Church Book, which covered the period up to 1659 and includes comment on the relations between the Baptists and other religious groups, makes it not only the most complete source for the history of the dissenting churches of Cambridgeshire but also the principal source for Baptist history under the Protectorate. Even so, little is known of the origins of the other Baptist churches in Cambridgeshire, like those at Melbourn and Burwell, which were not affiliated to Caxton. These were conveniently listed by the Fenstanton Baptists in 1654, when they had occasion to send out a fund-raising letter, but nothing more is known of their early history.

There were probably over 600 Quakers in Cambridgeshire, but the county did not stand out as a predominant centre of Quakerism in the way that it did as a centre for

[1] Lyon Turner, *op. cit.* pp. 133–6, discusses the Baptist figures. The order in which he lists the size of Baptist, or, indeed, any, congregations in the counties, depends on the theoretical size given to conventicles for which the bishops gave no number of attenders. Lyon Turner adopts the nominal figures of 90 and 50 for these meetings of unknown size, and gives two alternative tables for each sect, based on them. In these tables, Cambridgeshire, which certainly had 610 Baptists, plus three meetings of unknown size, comes out sixth and seventh respectively, well behind such counties as Kent, which had 236 Baptists, plus the members of 13 meetings of unknown size.

I feel myself that figures of 90 and 50 are much too large. The whole baptized membership of the church of Fenstanton and Caxton, which had been one of the strongest in the kingdom, was only 84 in 1676. This included many local meetings, which would have been listed separately by the bishops (*Fenstanton Records*, pp. 255–6). Quaker meetings were undoubtedly smaller than this, judging from the records of the prosecution of attenders under the second Conventicle Act in 1670. The largest Cambridgeshire meeting recorded was one of just over twenty. If this figure of twenty is adopted for the Baptists, whose numbers were certainly diminishing under persecution, Cambridgeshire had more Baptists than anywhere except Buckinghamshire and London.

[2] The career of Henry Denne is described in most works on the General Baptists. It is given in the introduction to the *Records of the Churches of Christ gathered at Fenstanton, Warboys and Hexham, 1644–1720*, ed. E. B. Underhill for the Hanserd Knollys Society (1854), pp. v–xxiii. Adam Taylor, in his *History of the English General Baptists* (London, 1818), I, described both Denne's career and the history of the Fenstanton church, pp. 99–100, 101–7, 137–57, 218–24. W. H. Whitley listed Denne's printed works in *A Baptist Bibliography*, I (1916). B. Nutter, *The Story of the Cambridge Baptists* (1912), mainly concentrated on the central figures in the Baptist church rather than its local developments.

74

Baptists. Yorkshire, in the north, and Wiltshire and Somerset in the south-west, all had over 1,000 Quakers. Almost all the eastern and south-eastern counties had over 600 apiece,[1] even though they were also mostly larger counties.

Organized Quakerism had first reached Cambridgeshire with the visit of Mary Fisher and Elizabeth Williams to the county town in 1653. In the following year, Richard Hubberthorne was jailed for visiting a woman imprisoned for 'testifying against a false prophet' in Cambridge. There they were joined by James Parnell, who was to be the principal Quaker apostle of Cambridgeshire. He had heard, some-where in the north, of two of his friends, who were presumably the two women visitors of 1653, being whipped for declaring the truth in Cambridge. Although he was frightened, and was only seventeen or eighteen, he was moved to come to the town and there 'found those that were worthy that received me' before himself being jailed. Sometime after his release from prison in the autumn of 1654, Parnell returned to Cambridge, and spent six months evangelizing and 'declaring the Truth in the Countries about', whence he found many 'that received the Truth gladly, but more Enemies'. By mid 1655 he was in Essex, where he was finally martyred, still only aged eighteen.[2]

It was no wonder that Parnell found some willing converts, for the records of the Baptist church show that, even before Elizabeth Williams and Mary Fisher reached Cambridge in 1653, spiritual seeking and unrest were extremely widespread at the lowest parochial level. Many villagers had already reached the Quaker position, like the maid Isobel at Kingston, who in 1653 'tried the Scriptures by the Spirit, and not the Spirit by the Scriptures'.[3] The ground was well prepared to receive Quaker teachings. Converts were also made at a higher social level. In 1655, the year of Parnell's evangelism, James Docwra, a gentleman of Fulbourn, who was married to Ann, daughter of Sir William Waldegrave of Wormingford in Essex, settled a close of pasture and about sixty acres of arable in Fulbourn on his wife for 500 years. The

[1] Lyon Turner, *op. cit.* III, pp. 127–9. I have again used 20 as a theoretical number for meetings of unknown size.

[2] Information on the persecution of individual Quakers is taken from the *Volume of Sufferings* preserved in the Friends' Meeting House, London, 1, pp. 101–35 covering Cambridgeshire and the Isle of Ely. The original book of sufferings of the Cambridgeshire meetings, from which the transcripts preserved in Friends' House were presumably made, did not survive. The first sufferings book in the Cambridgeshire Record Office covering Cambridgeshire as well as Huntingdonshire only begins in 1756. Most of the information from the *Volume of Sufferings* is printed in J. Besse, *Collections of the Sufferings of the People called Quakers* (1753), pp. 84–99, but he sometimes leaves out entries, or vital information, like the name of the village from which the particular sufferer comes. The humbler the Quaker, the more risk of omission. The rest of the history of early Quaker evangelism in the shire can be pieced together from G. F. Nuttall (ed.), *Early Quaker Letters from the Swarthmore MSS to 1660* (1952), particularly numbers 57, 76, 83 (Richard Hubberthorne from prison in Cambridge), 84 (Margaret Killam to George Fox), 367 (George Whitehead at Cottenham and Ely), 440, 476, and 486. James Parnell, referred to in letter 83, gives his own account of his Cambridge-shire ministry in the 'Fruits of a Fast' printed in *A Collection of the Several Writings Given Forth from the Spirit of the Lord, through that Meek, Patient and Suffering Servant of God, James Parnell* (1675). The minutes of the Quarterly Meeting of Friends in Cambridgeshire and the Isle of Ely survive from 1673, Cambridgeshire Record Office R. 59.25.1.5. The register of Quaker births, marriages and deaths is in the Public Record Office, R.G./6/1219.

[3] *Fenstanton Records*, p. 78.

income was to support various Quaker causes, including £3 a year towards the charges of 'Travelling Preachers and Horses at Cambridge'.[1] This argues a high degree of organization by the end of Parnell's ministry. With both this, and popular support, it is not surprising that Quakerism flourished, and that despite the intense persecution suffered by Quakers, both under the Commonwealth and later, a considerable hard core of adherents still remained in the late 1660s.

The arid figures and estimates given in the bishop's returns of 1669 in fact partially reflect the successful evangelism of Henry Denne, James Parnell, and Holcroft and his associates in the 1650s.

All the official sources of the 1660s and 1670s, taken together, show that dissent had gained a really strong footing in three well-defined areas of the country.[2] These were a cluster of nearly a dozen villages in south-west Cambridgeshire in the upper valley of the Rhee, with a couple on the western clay uplands nearby, another cluster on the edge of the fens north-westwards from Cambridge, and yet a third group of villages sited just above the edge of the fens running north-eastward from Cambridge. Just as there were areas where nonconformist influences were strongly felt, there were also areas where nonconformity had very little, if any, footing. The villagers in the south-east of the county on the chalk ridge had almost no organized centres of dissent, and another group of villages west of Cambridge on the north of the clay plateau had none at all.

## CONGREGATIONALISTS

Congregationalism was represented in all three areas. By the time the series of official returns on dissent began in 1669, the position once held by Bassingbourn as the centre from which Holcroft formed his first church was only a memory. Yet the work he had done there had had a lasting effect, as the amount of nonconformity in the villages of the upper Rhee valley showed. Amongst them were Meldreth, Shepreth, Fowlmere, and Thriplow, together with Orwell and Barrington, which lay a little further away at the foot of the western clay uplands. Orwell, which had fifty-eight nonconformists in the Compton Census, had more than any other parish in the county, and Thriplow with forty-eight, Barrington with forty, and Shepreth with thirty-nine ran it close. The only contemporary Congregational document is a church list of 1675.[3] It shows that there were two groups of adherents here, one of which was mainly derived from Bassingbourn and Meldreth, and the other from Barrington, Thriplow, Croydon, and Orwell. These two congregations with ninety and a hundred and twenty-four members apiece were the strongest in the county, apart from the one in Cambridge town itself, which had a hundred and ten adherents.

---

[1] W. Geoffrey Stevens, *Old Time Links between Cambridgeshire and the Lake District*, II, 'The Knights Hospitallers and the Docwra Family' (typescript 1966), pp. 27–31 (copy available in C.R.O.). Ann Docwra gave the 'Meeting House Yard' estate to the Friends in her will of 1700. The codicil of 1710 confirmed the annual payment of £3 for preachers, and added £20 towards a new burial ground. The present Meeting House was built in 1772.

[2] See Map A (p. 70) and Map B (p. 76) throughout this discussion.

[3] Bodleian Library, MS Rawl. D. 1480, ff. 123–6.

76

This strength of membership reflected Holcroft's early work, as did the significant inclusion of three women from Bassingbourn and Meldreth, along with Holcroft himself and Joseph Oddy, amongst the 'ten stones of the foundation' listed in the register.[1]

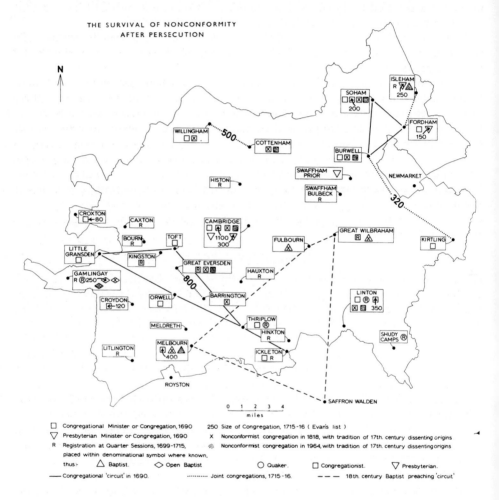

Map B.

[1] Only eight names were in fact given; the other two identifiable ones were brethren from Cambridge itself. This list is a very corrupt copy. It is arranged by groups of members under the headings of the villages from which they came. These headings are certainly not complete, and other villages must have contributed as well as those named, which presumably sent the largest contingents. The Bassingbourn and Meldreth church, for instance, included ninety names, whereas the Compton Census recorded only forty-two

Amongst this cluster of villages, Meldreth and Orwell had both Congregational conventicles in 1669 and Congregational licences issued in 1672.[1] They must therefore have been the respective meeting places for each of the groups of members in the area. In these centres Oddy, Corbin and Lock, who had all been ejected from Trinity College, nursed Holcroft's converts.

Congregationalists were also found in the second nonconformist area amongst the villages north of Cambridge on the edge of the fens, Histon, Oakington, Willingham, and Over. This was the region in which the influence of Nathaniel Bradshaw, rector of Willingham, who was a non-subscriber in 1662, had been felt. He had, he said, 'left four score and ten praying families in Willingham at...ejectment'.[2] Joseph Oddy moved from Meldreth to minister to this congregation after Bradshaw temporarily retired from the vicinity in 1667. Most of these villages had large numbers of dissenters in 1676[3] and Willingham and Oakington had both had conventiclers meeting in the parish in 1669 and licences issued in 1672. There were again two Congregational groups hereabouts listed in the church list of 1675. The stronger one, with seventy members, included Over, Willingham, and Oakington, and was led by Oddy himself. He was assisted by Samuel Corbin at Willingham and by James Day at Oakington.[4] The church of Willingham and Cottenham, which is now known as Cottenham Old Meeting, preserves a continuous tradition of worship ever since Bradshaw's ejection in 1662. It had 500 hearers in 1715–16, and was the largest in the county after the Barrington and Eversden church, and the Congregational church in Cambridge itself. Later in the eighteenth century it fell on evil days, but was refounded in 1780, with eleven members, under the guidance of a supply from Isleham. It adopted Baptist principles in 1813.

The weaker group, with only thirty members in 1675, covered Histon, Cottenham, Landbeach, and Waterbeach. Histon had had an independent conventicle in 1669,

dissenters in these two villages. But the census also recorded twenty-four dissenters at Litlington, the next parish to Bassingbourn, where Holcroft had preached. These must surely have been Congregationalists included under the Bassingbourn and Meldreth heading in the Congregational church list. The list also contains mis-spellings and duplication. As well as the Bassingbourn and 'Meldred' list, there is a separate one for 'Mildred' which appears to bear no relation to the first. It is very likely that the Bassingbourn and Meldreth list is itself seriously defective, for the latter part of it includes Brother John Day as deacon. Brother John Day had been licensed at Eversden in 1672, and appears to have been living there in 1682, when a certain John Day was presented for absence from church. It is likely therefore that part of the list of members of the Barrington and Orwell church, which included members from Eversden, was wrongly copied under the heading of Bassingbourn and Meldreth.

[1] Lyon Turner, 'Classified Summary' of the 1669 returns and licences of 1672 (*op. cit.* II), makes several wrong attributions. Thus he enters meetings and licences at Eversden, Orwell and Barrington as Presbyterian (p. 863) although the people involved in them appear in the Congregational church list of 1675. He entered Moses Crab of Little Wilbraham, who also appeared in the Congregational list, as a Baptist (p. 872).

[2] A. G. Matthews, *Calamy Revised* (1934), pp. 69–70. *Congregational Magazine or London Christian Instructor*, II (1819), p. 439, and III, pp. 168–9.

[3] Led by Over, with forty-two, and Oakington, with thirty-seven dissenters. The figures were missing for Willingham in the Compton Census. Quakerism was also strong here however, and the conventicle at Oakington in 1669 was entered by the bishop as Independent and Quaker.

[4] The entry for 'Haginton', printed by Lyon Turner as for a separate place, II, p. 869, should be under Oakington, p. 865, which was frequently spelt thus.

78

as had Milton, which was nowhere mentioned in the church list, but no licences permitted the group to function independently in 1672. Possibly the list was mistaken in ascribing a separate identity to the group, which was obviously absorbed into the joint Willingham and Cottenham church soon afterwards.

Congregationalism was not nearly so strong a force in the last area in which it was found, east of Cambridge in a group of parishes stretched along the edge of the fens from Stow-cum-Quy and Little Wilbraham to Burwell, and out to Snailwell. A further group included Soham and members in the Isle of Ely and Needingworth. Stow-cum-Quy had had a flourishing Congregational conventicle in 1669. It was attended by fifty to a hundred people, many of whom came from other places, according to Bishop Laney. The conventicle was licensed in 1672, but there were only eleven dissenters in the parish in 1676 according to the census.[1] Burwell, the only other village in the group for which a licence was taken out in 1672,[2] had a much larger number of thirty-three dissenters in 1676, but these may well have been Baptists rather than Congregationalists. There had been a Baptist church in Burwell in 1654,[3] and the Congregational list of 1675 only included between twenty and thirty members in the whole area. Amongst these were the Crabb family of Little Wilbraham, who were to prove indefatigable dissenters for several generations.[4] The discrepancy between the numbers of nonconformists recorded by the census and those recorded in the church list is confusing, unless a Baptist group did indeed survive at Burwell. No other churches were strongly represented in the area, although there was a small Quaker meeting at Soham[5] and single staunch Quaker families at Little Wilbraham and at Quy. The later history of the Burwell district is almost entirely Congregational, and there may well have been some continuity between the members of Holcroft's church who lived in the area in 1675, and the membership of the Congregational church thereabouts fifteen years later. The survey of the Congregational and Presbyterian churches made in 1690 recorded that a Scottish minister had been working in Burwell, Soham and Fordham for some considerable time, although he was discouraged and about to leave.[6] George Doughty, a 'Mechanick', had already been introduced as a replacement, although the Congregational church of Burwell and Soham was not formally founded by him until 1692.[7] It included members from Isleham, Burwell, Reach, Bottisham and Soham, and was soon joined by others from the old Holcroft area of Wilbraham, Swaffham Prior and Snailwell. Baptist ideas did not reassert themselves, unless the present Baptist church of Isleham, which

[1] See below, p. 96.
[2] Not identified by Lyon Turner. See 'Classified Summary', II, p. 870, no. 25, for 'Barrell Hightown'. The later Congregational chapel in Burwell was in Burwell High Town.
[3] See below, p. 85.                    [4] See below, p. 82.
[5] No Soham entries appear in the Quaker register for Cambridgeshire, although the elders were occasionally listed amongst the witnesses at weddings. This makes the size of the meeting difficult to gauge.
[6] 'Review of the State of the Severall Counties in England and Wales', 1690-2, ed. Alexander Gordon, *Freedom after Ejection* (1917), p. 14.
[7] The Church Book of George Doughty's church is printed in the *Transactions of the Congregational Historical Society*, VI (1913-15), pp. 415-28, and VII (1916-18), pp. 3-15.

claims seventeenth-century origins,[1] has an early Baptist tradition. It is recorded that the minister who was working round Burwell in 1690 was discouraged because 'the people are many of such od opinions'.[2] Perhaps these represented a last memory of Baptist teaching in Burwell.

Congregationalism remained strong in the Meldreth and Orwell area, despite the renewed wave of persecution in the 1680s, and the eighteenth-century apathy which generally seems to have followed it. In 1679 and 1682, the relatively high number of eight Orwell parishioners had been presented for absence from church and for attending conventicles; an additional note in the visitation of 1682[3] listed no less than twenty-eight names presented by the churchwardens of Orwell at the visitation.[4] No other village in Cambridge had a similar indictment for nonconformity. This estimate was confirmed by the note in the visitation of 1685 that, of the sixty families in Orwell, there were many dissenters and about thirty disciples of Holcroft and Oddy, most of whom were excommunicated already.[5] No conventicle met in the village at that date however. Nevertheless, the survey of Presbyterian and Congregational churches made in 1690 recorded the existence of a Congregational preaching circuit in which a new generation of Holcroft's assistants preached every third Sunday, in Orwell, Thriplow, Ickleton, Toft and Gransden.[6] The circuit had extended its area a little, and Holcroft's old church groupings had been altered since 1675, but, although individual villages had changed from one group of the Congregational church to another, or been added to it, the Congregational church of west Cambridgeshire had visibly survived persecution and emerged as recognizable as ever in its old stronghold. There is, however, a certain amount of evidence that, although Congregationalism survived wherever Holcroft and his helpers had worked, his church met with considerable setbacks before the local branches were settled as separate churches. Holcroft had been imprisoned again in the later 1670s and 1680s, and tradition has it that his ill-health was combined with depression towards the end of the 1680s, and the end of his life. Oddy died in 1687, and Holcroft himself in 1692. Holcroft's successor, Joseph Hussey, did not openly adopt Congregational principles until 1694. The vacuum left was to some extent filled by the activities of Richard Davis of the Rothwell Congregational church, as his Church Book shows. Although Davis merely preached at the formation of the Burwell church in 1692,[7]

[1] I have not yet managed to investigate the records of this church, which dates its formation to 1693. So far, I have found no reference to a dissenting congregation there in general sources earlier than 1715–16, when there was a joint Presbyterian congregation there and at Fordham.

[2] There was some connection between the church of Burwell and Richard Davis's Congregational church of Rothwell in Northamptonshire, for Mr Davis preached at the formation of the Burwell church in 1692. This connection, as well as residual Baptist notions, may have accounted for the 'od opinions', for, in the same year, Richard Davis was accused of High Calvinism bordering on Antinomianism at Kettering. G. F. Nuttall, 'Northamptonshire and the Modern Question', *Journ. Theol. Stud.* n.s. XVI (1965), pp. 104, 106–8.

[3] Cambridge University Library, Ely Episcopal Records B 2/66, ff. 51–52 v.

[4] Almost all of these were additional to the eight already presented.

[5] See Map B throughout this discussion.

[6] 'Review of the State of the Severall Counties in England and Wales', 1690–2, ed. Alexander Gordon in *Freedom after Ejection* (1917), p. 13.

[7] See above, n. 2.

some of the members of Holcroft's church in Soham, Needingworth and the Isle of Ely were received into the Rothwell church itself in 1691, after messengers had been sent from Rothwell to inquire 'into a handfull of late converts in the Fens',[1] and the church had been 'exceedingly affected to observe how the Lord gloriously taught those poor people in those dark corners'. The churches of Needingworth and Guyhirn in the Isle eventually obtained their collective dismissions from Rothwell church in 1693.[2] Davis's activities went further. Oddy's death had obviously left the church of Cottenham and Willingham lacking a pastor, and in 1692 the Rothwell church agreed to send a preacher to them and 'assist and support' the meeting at Cottenham.[3] It is more surprising that amongst the many admissions to the Rothwell church from Needingworth and from the Isle in 1691 and 1692 were included half a dozen apiece from Willingham, and Swavesey, three or four from Cambridge itself, and, most startling of all, a man and his wife from Eversden and a man from Orwell.[4] It is no wonder that Davis's activities aroused resentment.[5] Some indication of the rudderless state of the church after Holcroft's death is given by Richard Conder, who wrote of the Croydon church

The Lord tacking our dear pastor away the lord sturid up som of us seing mani disorders amongst us to renew our cofenant and to purg the hous of God but meet with mani hinderances and coolld in no wise git forward but contention aroas about mani things to the greef of som of our sools and coolld by no means atain to a onnes to follo the lord fully but after much greef and trobell of solle the lord seet it upon our harts with desier to follow the lord as he shoold help us.

Only seventeen members of the church renewed their covenant at Clopton in 1694, led by the deacon John Day from Eversden[6] and the propriety of their renewal remained a cause of debate and dissension as late as 1702, when 'Brother Nicolls', pastor of the Melbourn and Chishill church, was amongst those who did not support the Croydon church in their desire to appoint a pastor. Richard Conder wrote:

the meshingors ansured us that if they shoolld stand by us in this woorck that they shoolld bring the churchis under blam and our answor was this that they brought them seellvs under blam... namly the church at Needingworth and Gyhorn and Chisill which had tacken our members without dismish or recomendation.

The survey of the main dissenting congregations in Cambridgeshire made by Joseph Hussey in 1715 or 1716 shows that the period of confusion after Holcroft's death had not permanently affected his church. There was one change; Orwell lost predominance as a meeting place and Great Eversden acquired it. The Eversden

[1] Rothwell Church Book transcript, pp. 14, 24, 25, 26, 29–30. I am again indebted to Mr Tibbutt for lending me this.
[2] *Ibid.* pp. 38, 42 and 46.
[3] *Ibid.* pp. 34, 36.          [4] *Ibid.* p. 36.
[5] G. F. Nuttall, 'Northamptonshire and the Modern Question', *Journ. Theol. Stud.* n.s. XVI (1965), pp. 107–8, 112.
[6] See above, p. 75, n. 1, and this page.

church later preserved a strong tradition of Holcroft's work of foundation and conversion there.[1] This is verified by Richard Conder's account of Holcroft's work. He wrote that after his ejection

God's servant was for gooing on in church order and for choosing ellders, and at a meting at Eavesden was chosen foor...and God's servant, after he was turnd out at Basingbon, preached in the publick at Croydon and then was turnd out their and then hee preached at Great Eavesdon publickly and their they toock him and woolld leet him preach no longer.

Despite this, the Compton Census had recorded only conformists in the parish in 1676. The census was certainly in error here, for John Day, Deacon of Holcroft's church, had had his house in Eversden licensed in 1672. Congregationalism was not numerically strong there, however, for, in 1682, John Day was the sole parishioner presented for absence from church. Presumably the Eversden church only acquired a strong resident membership after 1690, but by 1715 or 1716 the Barrington and Eversden church had eight hundred hearers, more than any other except Hussey himself in Cambridge. These hearers were of course drawn from the whole area round about, the self-same area in which Holcroft's largest church was rooted in 1675. The present Eversden congregational church is the heir of a long tradition in western Cambridgeshire.

The mother branch of Holcroft's church, lying in Bassingbourn and Meldreth, also survived the varying vicissitudes of both persecution and the eighteenth century, also in a somewhat changed form. Three years after the Compton Census, the visitation of 1679 recorded the persistence of nonconformity in Bassingbourn in the persons of five absentees from church, although the visitation memorandum in 1685 reported 'noe Dissenters, Many Sluggards'. In Meldreth, which had been the traditional meeting place of this group of Congregationalists since 1669, the existence of 'Many unbaptized dissenters, Holcroft's disciples' amongst the parishioners was noted. Twelve of the seventy families in Melbourn, the next village to the south of Meldreth, were Holcroft's disciples. This was new.[2] Melbourn had had a Baptist tradition since 1654 at least. However, Congregationalism now gained so strong a footing in Melbourn that, at some point in the next thirty years, the old Meldreth and Bassingbourn church moved its meeting place there.[3] Between 1716 and 1717 the charming house of brick which is still used by the Congregationalists today[4] was built in Melbourn, and by 1715–16 the meeting house, with four hundred hearers, was the fourth best

[1] R. Robinson, 'Historical Account', p. 260. By the time the recorder of Cottenham Old Meeting set down what was known of the origins of the Congregational church in Cambridgeshire in the nineteenth century, all memory of the work of Holcroft in Bassingbourn and Orwell was lost, and the church was supposed to have originated in Great Eversden.

[2] As far as the evidence so far goes. It is very likely, however, that some of the members of the Bassingbourne and Meldreth church in 1675 came from Melbourn, if they could be identified.

[3] Local tradition dates the move from 1694 when John Nicolls was chosen pastor of the church of Melbourn and Chishill, but there seems to be no direct evidence for this. J. Porter Chapple, *Congregationalism at Melbourn 1694–1894*, printed with an essay on *The Puritan in Melbourn 1640–88*, by W. M. Palmer as *A Nonconformist Bi-Centenary Memorial* (London, 1895).

[4] After a vicissitude during which it was used as a Sunday school in the nineteenth century.

82

attended in the county. Appropriately enough, a Bassingbourn man, John Jermans, a tailor, was one of the first feoffees of the new meeting house.[1]

The Congregational church in Cambridge also prospered greatly, far more than its Presbyterian rival. The Presbyterians in Cambridge were, according to the first historian of dissent in Cambridgeshire, 'not many, but they were rich'.[2] All the thirty-odd Presbyterians noticed by the bishop in 1669 were in the county town itself, and in 1672 they acquired two licences. After toleration, their numbers had increased to seventy-six by 1691, when the Presbyterian Joseph Hussey became their pastor. The lack of doctrinal dispute between Independents and Presbyterians, who disagreed only on church government, made it easy to drift from one denomination to the other. In 1694, Hussey's Presbyterian church was split, and Hussey himself with over half his communicants adopted Congregationalism. The Presbyterian remnant joined the church at Green Street in Cambridge which had hitherto been Congregational and now, in turn, became Presbyterian.[3]

Joseph Hussey, as head of the portion of the Congregational church in the centre of the county, inherited something of Holcroft's position. Despite the fact that after Holcroft's death in 1692 his Cambridgeshire church split up and settled itself on a local basis, Hussey's list of baptisms in his church book[4] shows him baptizing all over the county in most of the main Congregational centres like Barrington, Eversden and Linton, even though, after his adoption of Congregational views in 1694, his theological opinions gradually hardened until by 1707 he was an exponent of the extreme Calvinist view that the offer of God's grace should only be proclaimed to the converted.[5] Those baptized by Hussey are often stated to be sons and daughters of parents 'late of Mr Holcroft's church in the county of Cambridge'. The family continuity which existed in some cases between the early dissenters and their eighteenth-century brethren is vividly illustrated by an entry for 1716. In this year Hussey baptized Sarah Crabb of Little Wilbraham aged twenty, the daughter of the Widow Crabb, 'after her experience of the work of God laid upon her soul in the law of the church', together with her eighteen-year-old sister. These were presumably the great-grandchildren of Moses Crabb, water-miller, who had held a very small conventicle at his house in 1669, according to the bishop. The Crabb family were the only members of the meeting to come from the village itself.[6] In 1676, four nonconformists were entered for Little Wilbraham in the Compton Census; and in the visitation of 1679 four Crabbs and a Crabb son-in-law

[1] Title deeds of the Melbourn Congregational chapel, copied by W. M. Palmer, A. 27, in his collection of papers in the University Library, Cambridge.

[2] R. Robinson, 'Historical Account', p. 266.

[3] R. Robinson, *op. cit.* pp. 268–9. It attracted very small audiences compared with Hussey's new Congregational church, if Hussey himself is to be believed, for in 1715–16 it had just over two hundred 'hearers' compared with Hussey's eleven hundred. See also C. S. Kenny, 'The Earlier History of Emmanuel Church, Cambridge', *Trans. Cong. Hist. Soc.* IV (1909–10), pp. 183–90.

[4] Partially copied by W. M. Palmer in his 'Notes on the Non-Parochial Registers of Cambridge', B4/3, W. M. Palmer Collection, Cambridge University Library.

[5] G. F. Nuttall, 'Northamptonshire and the Modern Question', *Journ. Theol. Stud.* n.s. XVI (1965), pp. 111–13.

[6] See above, p. 78.

were being presented by the churchwardens of Little Wilbraham for joining conventicles. The validity of Sarah Crabb's marriage, which had presumably been
performed in a Congregational meeting, was also doubted by her co-villagers. The
Sarah Crabb baptized by Hussey was presumably her grandchild, and one of the
fourth generation to experience spiritual convictions deep enough to lead her to
separate herself off from her natural village community.

Hussey's pastoral work also took him to baptisms at meetings in many other
villages, some of which were traditionally held, as was that of the daughter of John
Giffard of Dry Drayton in 1700 'at a meeting there held in his barn'. As well as
inheriting some of Holcroft's peripatetic position in the county, Hussey also records
that he received some of the members of Holcroft's old church in Cambridge directly
into his Hog Hill church, after it had become Congregational. In 1698, he noted
in his diary 'On this great day, we joyfully received a dozen of Mr Holcroft's former
members'.[1]

Congregationalism was spreading. Just as Congregationalism moved into Melbourn, to challenge the Baptists, it now moved into Linton to challenge the Quakers.
There is no surviving evidence that there was any early Congregationalism at Linton,
apart from the tradition of the church there that during persecution the oldest
members had been to hear preaching in the woods a few miles away.[2] Apart from
this the early dissenting history of the place was all Quaker. However, only ten years
after Toleration, in 1698, the Linton Congregationalists were planning to build a
chapel.[3] In the eighteenth century this building was described, and the description
gives a vivid impression of the simplicity of the reformed worship, and the predominance in it of the preaching of the Word from the dominating pulpit. It also
shows that Congregationalism had acquired great social respectability by the end of
the eighteenth century at Linton, where the squire had his own pew, despite the fact
that the meeting house stood next to a tan yard, since the ground had been given by
a tanner, 'which rendered it most unpleasant'.

The pastor of Linton in the late eighteenth century wrote of his chapel:

In appearance it was rather rough, the shape was like unto a barn divided into three bays, to be
converted into a barn again if persecution revived...the doors opened outside, the windows
were all provided with shutters to prevent their being broken into by persecuting men, the shutters
being drawn up with pulleys. As you enter, opposite the doors, stands the pulpit, with a large
Cumbrous sounding board over it. In front of the pulpit is a long table pew across the building
capable of holding thirty persons or more, with a large brass chandelier hanging over it. There
is a square pew for the Squire, lined with green baize surrounded with silk curtains, with a devotional table in the centre; other large square pews lined with green baize capable of seating
fourteen or fifteen persons, other pews in variety, some long, some square, some three-cornered,

[1] Quoted by A. G. Matthews in 'The Seventeenth Century', one of the lectures in *Congregationalism
through the Centuries* (Cambridge, 1937).
[2] Typescript précis of the Rev. Thomas Hopkins and others, *History of Linton Congregational Church*,
W. M. Palmer Collection, B3/8, University Library, Cambridge.
[3] Copy of first trust deed in 'Notes on Linton Congregational Church', W. M. Palmer Collection B4/1,
University Library, Cambridge.

it appeared that each one built his pew as he pleased. On either side of the pulpit galleries were erected in 1704, and in front of the pulpit was a circular gallery where the singers like the sons of Asaph had their place. On the walls were many monumental tablets in memory of worthy men, the Malns, Jacksons, Fords and Taylors, whose voices once filled the house with praise.[1]

The later history of the Congregational church in Cambridgeshire shows that, wherever Francis Holcroft and his assistant planted Congregationalism in the county, it took lasting root. The descent is not direct, but, in each of the three areas where the list of members of the Congregational church in 1675 shows that Holcroft gained support, a Congregational church survives today. The present churches of Eversden and Melbourn represent Holcroft's cluster of believers round Orwell and Bassing-bourn and Meldreth. In the north-west of the county the present Baptist Cottenham Old Meeting descends from the adherents of 1675 in Cottenham and Willingham. In the north-east, the churches now to be found in Burwell and Soham probably derive from Holcroft's members in Stow, Wilbraham and Burwell in 1675.

BAPTISTS

The Baptist cause in Cambridgeshire had taken root in John Denne's farmhouse at Caxton Pastures and spread outwards from it in the early 1650s,[2] just as Congrega-tionalism had done from Francis Holcroft's vicarage in Bassingbourn. By the 1660s and 1670s, though, no trace was left of the early pre-eminence of the Caxton area. The list of members of what had once been the General Baptist church of Fenstanton and Caxton made in 1676 shows that there had been a radical change in the member-ship, and that the church now barely touched Cambridgeshire.[3] The strength of the Fenstanton church now lay in Huntingdonshire, in Fenstanton itself, Godmanchester, the Hemingfords, and St Ives, where John Denne was living by 1672. Fenstanton still provided more members than anywhere else, but not a single member in 1676 came from Caxton, which had once stood second only to Fenstanton, or from Eltisley, which had once figured so prominently among the 'canting places' of the kingdom. The Compton Census itself recorded five nonconformists in Caxton and three in Eltisley; but they were not General Baptists.[4]

Some disaster seems to have hit the Cambridgeshire part of the Fenstanton church. As it happens, the Quaker records of their trial at Assizes for refusing to swear the Oath of Allegiance in 1661 give some idea of what this had been. The Quaker spokes-

---

[1] Taken from the typescript précis of the *History of Linton Congregational Church* by the Rev. Thomas Hopkins and others, W. M. Palmer Collection, B 3/8, University Library, Cambridge. This building was pulled down in 1818, according to Hopkins, and the materials were used in the present meeting house which stands at right-angles to the original building in Horn Lane, Linton.

[2] This farm still stands today, but, according to the Royal Commission on Historical Monuments for Cambridgeshire, it is almost entirely a remodelled eighteenth-century building.

[3] *Fenstanton Records*, pp. 255–6, compared with pp. 251–4.

[4] Two at least of those at Eltisley were Quakers. Elias and Elizabeth Woodward of Eltisley were presented for absence from church in the visitations of 1682, and in 1674 Elias Woodward had been fined for holding a Quaker meeting in his house. *Volumes of Sufferings*, i, p. 126.

man recorded that 'Severall of Bunion's People and also Baptists' were tried along with the Quakers, and that among them was

> one John Denne, a teacher amongst you, to whom the Judge was very harsh, more than to any other of the prisoners...and did much upbraid him for getting up to ye Pulpitt for he and some others had crepen into a Steeplehouse to shelter themselves from the King's late proclamation against meetings in private, And it became a greater Snare to him, for he was taken in the Pulpitt not haveing orders as the Judg said.[1]

It sounds as if the Caxton meeting had taken refuge in Eltisley parish church, a mile or so away across the fields, when John Denne's father Henry probably still held the living.[2] The collapse of the Cambridgeshire section of the Fenstanton church seems very likely to have been related to whatever penalties it suffered in 1661. However, John Denne was not discredited amongst his fellow Baptists. He remained their acknowledged leader, for in 1672 he was responsible for applying for the licences for all the meetings in Cambridgeshire and Huntingdonshire.[3] These showed that one at least of the former local meetings of the Fenstanton church in Cambridgeshire had survived. The Baptists of Harston who had given Henry Denne hospitality on his evangelizing tour in 1653, were still meeting in 1669, and also acquired a licence in 1672.[4] At Melbourn, the church taught by the redoubtable farmer Benjamin Metcalfe, which had existed by 1654, was also still meeting in 1669, and was licensed in 1672.

The Baptists had had early meetings amongst the villages on the edge of the fen to the east of Cambridge, just as had the Congregationalists. Great Wilbraham[5] and Burwell had had meetings in 1654, but apparently only the one at Wilbraham survived to be reported in 1669.[6] According to the bishop, it was then a small conventicle of twenty to thirty people 'all of meane sought most from other places' taught in a barn by John Denne who came from Huntingdonshire. The Wilbraham influence had spread to Fulbourn All Saints, where there was another small Anabaptist conventicle 'neere White hall in a house fitted for it...their especiall Encouragement'.[7] The teacher was John Dennis, who really seems to have been a different individual from John Denne, for he was presented as a parishioner of Great Wilbraham for being an Anabaptist and attending conventicles in the visitation of

---

[1] *Volumes of Sufferings*, I, pp. 113–14.

[2] Henry Denne is supposed to have died in 1661. *Fenstanton Records*, p. xxii.

[3] Lyon Turner, *op. cit.* III, 299–300. W. T. Whitley included a note on the Cambridgeshire licences in 'The Baptist Licences of 1672', *Transactions of the Baptist Historical Society*, I (1908–9), pp. 162–3.

[4] If the identification of the 'Hawson' named in the Baptist records with 'Harston' rather than the more likely looking 'Hauxton' is correct. I have been able to discover no trace of Baptist affiliations in the latter.

[5] There is a brief note on the Wilbraham and Melbourn General Baptists in *The Baptist Quarterly*, n.s. III (1926–7), p. 107.

[6] Unless the licence for Edward Gardiner's house in Burwell in 1672 was in fact for a Baptist congregation (Lyon Turner, *op. cit.* p. 870, no. 25). See above, pp. 78–9.

[7] I have not been able to trace the site of this, which must have been the earliest chapel building in Cambridgeshire, and was early by any standards. Most meetings were licensed in houses or barns. The earlier Commonwealth meetings had also been in private houses, like the farm at Caxton Pastures.

1679. Despite the existence of a house set aside as a chapel in Fulbourn, the Wilbra-ham meeting alone obtained a licence in 1672. It was well attended by the people of the parish itself in 1679, when eleven Great Wilbraham people were presented for being Anabaptists, in the visitation that year. Amongst them was John Dennis, who had been the teacher of the Fulbourn meeting in 1669, and was then described by the bishop as a tailor.

Balsham was the main exception to the rule that the villages lying on the chalk ridge which carried the Icknield Way across south-eastern Cambridgeshire were almost entirely untouched by organized dissent. Balsham had had a history of separatism reaching back to the sixteenth century, when the Family of Love had adherents there. Baptists existed both in Balsham, and in the villages round Woodditton in 1654, but only survived in Balsham, where, as might be ex-pected from the previous history of the place, tiny conventicles of both Baptists and Quakers were found in 1669. Neither was large enough to apply for a licence in 1672.

The last true General Baptist meeting in Cambridgeshire lay amongst the other group of villages where dissent flourished, on the edge of the fens north-west of Cambridge. A great deal of the pastoral work of the Fenstanton church had been devoted to the difficulties of the Baptists in Over, who were much disturbed by the arrival of Quakerism there. In 1669, there were only four families of Baptists in the place, and, if Bishop Laney is to be trusted, they attended meetings elsewhere. But by 1672 the Baptists of Over had acquired their own licence. Here again, the work of the Caxton church had an influence which survived well into the period of persecution after the Restoration.

Apart from the General Baptists proper, the Open Baptists of Bedfordshire had meetings in Cambridgeshire also. The Bedford church, although it contained many members who were baptized as adults, had, since its foundation, made a principle of toleration in such matters. Baptism was not a prerequisite of admission to com-munion. Its first pastor left a letter as a testament to his church on his death in 1655, which ran:

Concerning separation from the Church about Baptisme, Lying on of hands, Anoynting with Oyls, Psalmes, or any externells; I charge every one of you respectively...that none of you be found guilty of this great eville: which whiles some have committed...through a zeale for God... yet they have erred from the Lawe of the Love of Christ.[1]

This principle of comprehension held through the 1660s, when 'Bro. holcroft' was amongst the preachers invited to address the church,[2] and the 1670s, when Bunyan applied for licences under the Acts of Toleration and styled them 'Congrega-tional', since he was at the time vigorously opposing making baptism a test of communion.[3] The Bedford meeting had had some influence as far into Cambridge-

---

[1] *The Church Book of Bunyan Meeting, 1650–1821*, ed. G. B. Harrison, f. 3.
[2] *Ibid.* f. 26.
[3] W. H. Whitley, 'The Baptist Licences of 1672', *Trans. Bapt. Hist. Soc.* I (1908–9), pp. 165–6.

shire as Toft as early as 1659. In that year, Thomas Smith, the Cambridge University Librarian, who was also rector of Caldecote[1] near Toft, wrote scoldingly to 'Mr E.' of Toft,[2] who had 'rebuked' Smith several times when he spoke at one of the meetings held in Toft in Daniel Angier's barn. Angier apparently invited Bunyan regularly to Toft, and 'Mr E.' had used him as a counsellor for one of his daughters, who was in spiritual distress. According to Smith, Bunyan had 'intruded into Pulpits in these parts' so Toft was not the only village accustomed to the presence of 'the Tinker' with whom Smith was 'angry... because he strives to mend Souls as well as Kettles and Pans'.[3] The implication of Smith's pamphlet is that he had been visited in his own parish and heckled there after a sermon, by Angier. Smith returned the compliment and invaded the Angier barn at Toft, where he was called a liar for his pains. The ordinary man behind the plough may have suffered from the curtailment of some of his amusements under the Commonwealth, but he seems to have gained some very lively free entertainment in exchange.

The small meeting held at Toft by John Wait, a yeoman of Toft, in 1669, must have been the direct descendant of the meeting in Angier's barn. John Wait started his career in the Cambridgeshire Congregational church. He was one of the four elders chosen at Eversden to minister to the church soon after Holcroft's ejection;[4] with Oddy, Corbin and Bard. They were all, with Holcroft, imprisoned shortly afterwards, but Wait

maid his escap from them into another counti, and mister Bard liekwise fell under sum surcomstance that he leaft the church too and this was a great greef to God's servants whoos harts was ficksed for crist...

God's servant, being as a good shepard zealos for God and ready to lay down his life for the sheep, was in great disstreas abowght mister Waits and mister Bards leafing the church in its aflickhon, and seant seaveroll admonishons to them to retorn to the church, wheirof they returned not and the church proceedid against them for theire not ansoerin their call and some other crims that was against them, and they was coot of from the church but som was dissatisfied.

This history explains the letter addressed to 'our elect sister' in Cambridge by the Bedford church in 1671, asking why Brother John Wait had been excommunicated. It inquired whether the sentence can have been just, since 'he is not [a] withered branch: he is still a fruitful bough by a well, whose branches run over the wall' to 'we who heare, see and observe him'. Holcroft replied that Wait, as an elder, had become a 'railer, and a blasphemer of God; who raised up amongst us strife and contention'. His answer was judged unsatisfactory and the Bedford congregation, 'witness of the power of God with our Brother, and of the success of his ministry', received Wait into fellowship just the same, in 1671.[5] The Bedford church seems to

[1] 'Cawcat'.
[2] Thomas Smith, 'A Letter in Defence of the Ministry, and Against Lay Preachers', printed in *The Quaker Disarm'd* (London, 1659).
[3] Henry Denne's description of Smith's case at the beginning of *The Quaker No Papist* (etc.) (London, 1659).
[4] See above, p. 81.
[5] *Church Book of Bunyan Meeting, 1650–1821*, ed. G. B. Harrison, ff. 32, 34, 36, 38–9, 47.

88

have had some justification, since Wait's ministry in Hitchin in Hertfordshire had been highly praised in 1669.[1] However, according to Richard Conder, writing in the 1690s, the action taken by Bedford 'maid such a breach of communion between thease churchis that to this day is not maid up'. It is possible that a doctrinal dispute lay at the back of this quarrel, as well as John Wait's defection under persecution. Wait had obviously adopted the principle of comprehension on which Bunyan's meeting was based. It is perhaps significant that in 1677, after the dismission of a brother from the Bedford meeting to the church at Hitchin, which Wait had earlier taught, a group of the Hitchin brethren sought their dismission to Holcroft's church on doctrinal grounds, and later formed a true Independent church in Hitchin.[2] Wait was licensed at Toft in 1672, but no permanent congregation seems to have been established there as a result of his ministry.[3]

The meeting of the Open Baptists of Gamlingay was much more important than that at Toft, and, indeed, one of the Gamlingay brethren was joint teacher of the Toft group, with John Wait. Gamlingay lies in the extreme west of the county, projecting into Bedfordshire. A couple of converts had been made there by the Caxton Baptist church in 1652 and 1653. By 1669 there were no less than forty hearers of a weekly conventicle there, taught by the schoolmaster, Samuel Smith; Oliver Scott, a maltster; Edward Dent, a brick-kiln master; and Luke Astwood, an oatmeal maker. The Gamlingay meeting does not appear to have been affiliated to Bedford until the following year, when the four men named in the bishop's returns as teachers at Gamlingay were received, with five more, at Bedford. The present Gamlingay Old Meeting certainly has a longer corporate existence than it claims, probably stretching back to the 1650s rather than to 1670. Almost at once, Gamlingay became one of the places where the Bedford General Meeting, which was still under heavy pressure, met.[4] According to the Compton Census, Gamlingay, which had forty-five dissenters in 1676, was the third largest nonconformist centre in the county after the Congregational villages of Orwell and Thriplow.

Twenty-three people were presented for absence from church in Gamlingay at the visitation of 1682, and this relatively high number is an indication of the continuing strength of the support for the Open Baptists in the parish. In 1685 the rough notes for the visitation mentioned disgustedly that there were thirty to forty 'unbaptized followers of Cummin ye Tinker' in the parish. The schoolmaster was both excommunicated and unlicensed. The Bedford General Meeting continued to meet occasionally in Gamlingay until 1710. In this year, the Gamlingay Open Baptists obtained their collective dismission from the Bedford church and established their

[1] W. Urwick, *Nonconformity in Hertfordshire* (1884), pp. 639–40.

[2] W. Urwick, *op. cit.* p. 645.

[3] John Wait's identity has been confused with that of Joseph Waite, who was ejected from Sprowton in Suffolk in 1662, but died in 1670. G. F. Nuttall, 'Northamptonshire and the Modern Question', *Journ. Theol. Stud.* n.s. XVI (1965), p. 112 n. 2. It is not clear whether John Wait was indeed the minister in London in 1681 whom Samuel Palmer, *Nonconformists' Memorial*, III, p. 287, took to be Joseph Waite. John was still alive in 1692, and acquainted with the situation in Cambridgeshire, for he wrote a letter in that year warning the members of Joseph Hussey's church against Antinomianism. G. F. Nuttall, *art. cit.* p. 112.

[4] *Church Book of Bunyan Meeting*, ff. 29, 31, 110.

own church with thirty founder members. The success of the church is indicated by Hussey's list of 1715–16, which ascribed two hundred and fifty 'hearers' to the Gamlingay Open Baptists. Hussey did not give estimates of the size of any other Baptist church in the county, and, while this may indicate his natural Congregational bias, it may also indicate that the General Baptists in Cambridgeshire continued to decline in the eighteenth century, as they had under persecution.[1] The Baptist cause faded out at Over for the time[2] but it retained a hold on its other old centres. Melbourn and Great Wilbraham, where there had been groups of Baptists since 1654, shared a preaching circuit in the eighteenth century with Fulbourn and Saffron Walden.[3] The entry for Wilbraham in Hussey's list was never filled in, however. The Melbourn Baptist chapel had recently been joined by a Congregational chapel in the village in 1717, and the older meeting could certainly not compete in drawing power with the newer, for the Baptists of Melbourn appeared only on Hussey's list as a crossed-out entry. However the church was still active in 1701, as was that of Great Wilbraham, which in this year took a stand against Socinianism in the General Assembly of General Baptists. In 1733 Melbourn and Fulbourn were amongst the churches of the reunited assembly.[4] Fulbourn had had a very early chapel building, and was the place at which converts from Cambridge were baptized in the later eighteenth century.[5] However, of all these Baptist centres, the chapel at Melbourn is the only one of the Baptist churches in Cambridgeshire known to Henry Denne which survives today. It is therefore the heir of the longest datable dissenting tradition in the county, reaching back to 1654.

QUAKERS

Much more information is available on the Quakers than any other dissenting body after the Restoration. The existence of their carefully kept Volumes of Sufferings means that a vivid picture of their tribulations can be built up for a period when only the brief factual records of non-sympathizers or would-be-persecutors exist for other churches.

The first Cambridgeshire items in the Volumes of Sufferings which record the persecution of villagers, as opposed to Quaker missionaries, for going to meetings and public testifying are for 1655 and 1656. They show that Quakerism had taken

[1] I owe much of my information on the Gamlingay open Baptists to the kindness and hospitality of the minister, Mr G. S. Tydeman, who not only arranged for me to inspect the first Church Book, but also for me to see the earliest trust deeds at Messrs E. T. Leeds, Smith and Co., in Sandy. Unfortunately, neither the trust deeds nor the Church Book give a date for the erection of the present chapel building. The meeting yard was first mentioned in 1722, and the meeting house itself in 1740.

[2] Although later in the eighteenth century the neighbouring Congregational church of Cottenham and Willingham itself became Baptist.

[3] *The Congregational Magazine, or London Christian Instructor*, II, pp. 503 and 696, and III, p. 168 (1818).

[4] Information taken from the list of general Baptist churches in Cambridgeshire compiled by W. T. Whitley (ed.), *Minutes of the General Assembly of the General Baptist Churches in England with Kindred Records*, I, 1654–1728 (1909), p. lvii, and II, 1731–1811 (1910), p. 12.

[5] R. Robinson, 'Historical Account'.

90

root both in the south and the north-east of the county. Men from Royston and Meldreth were imprisoned in Cambridge Castle in 1655 for meeting on the first day, so Royston meeting was under way. In the same year, Anne Norris of Swavesey was 'moved by the Lord to beare her testimony against the priest of Over in the Steeple-house' and went to prison for six months as a result. Her husband, who was nearly eighty, was fined in the same year for riding on the Sabbath, as he was caught on his way to a meeting two miles away from Swavesey. For refusing to pay, he also was imprisoned, and so they were both kept from their six children who were still 'not able to guide themselves'. A week after his release from prison, Boniface Norris died. So began the long series of painful family disruptions, and the imprisonments which sometimes led to martyrdom, which the village Quakers were to suffer over the next twenty years. Unlike most dissenters, who enjoyed relative freedom under the Commonwealth, the Quakers were persecuted from the time when the sect was formed. They had already suffered fines and imprisonments for several years when, in 1660, they and other nonconformists were hit by the first of the waves of persecution which were to continue until brought to an end in 1689 by the Declaration of Indulgence. For this reason, the Quakers' fortunes were a little different through the 1660s and 1670s from those of the other, orthodox sects. The sect had had no room for the half-hearted since its inception, since it was under constant pressure. The names in the Volumes of Sufferings therefore recurred, as often as not, again and again, as their possessors were gradually stripped of their goods over a decade or so and reduced to the state of John Smith of Over, who, by the end of 1670, had several charges of attending meetings against him, and eventually had two cows taken from him 'being all he then had'.[1]

The first period of persecution lasted from 1660, through the passing of the Act of Uniformity and the first Conventicle Act proscribing meetings, until the fall of Clarendon in 1667 and the adjournment of Parliament from 1667 to 1669 brought some relief. The Quakers were probably the worst sufferers. Even before the Restoration, they had been obvious scapegoats for communal feelings of superstition and xenophobia, as the credence given to charges of witchcraft brought against them in 1659 showed. These charges were linked with an unpleasant little tale of the defilement of an altar in Norwich, in a way well calculated to rouse feelings of disgust and hostility in the reader.[2]

The unpopularity of the Quakers brought mob violence down on them in Cambridge by April 1660, when the meeting in Jesus Lane was broken up, the house wrecked, two women stabbed in the street and blood drawn from another couple of dozen attenders. They wrote a letter of complaint to the king, quoting the Declaration of Breda against him and adding bitterly 'now heere all may see what muddy

---

[1] *Volumes of Sufferings*, I, p. 121.
[2] *Strange and Terrible Newes from Cambridge, being a true Relation of the Quakers bewitching Mary Philips*, etc. Anon. (London, 1659). Replied to by Alderman James Blackley et al. *A Lying Wonder Discovered and the strange and Terrible Newes from Cambridge proved false...and on answer to John Bunions Paper touching the said imagined witchcraft*, etc. (London, 1659).

waters this fountain of Cambridge streames forth'.[1] But by the beginning of the following year, their refusal to swear the Oath of Allegiance got them into worse trouble, and Cambridge gaol was filled with Quaker prisoners.[2] They were kept under evil conditions, which were described by John Aynslo, their spokesman:

Some of us are kept in and not suffered to go out at all to ease themselves but might doe it where they lye, and others of us shut up in dungeons and holes where they keepe their fellons and witches and Murderers and soe thronged y$^t$ they have but roome to stirr one by another and y$^e$ places doe smell soe nastily y$^t$ it were enough to poyson any creature but ye Lord is our preserver...

Worse still, these prisoners were of all ages, all conditions and both sexes, and their imprisonment had bitter consequences for their families. The worst-hit village was Swavesey, from which twenty-three people were taken, including men whose families were wholly dependent on their trade and who were now reduced to destitution. All adults were removed from some houses, leaving in one case two small children 'left as in ye streets without habitation'.[3]

Another particularly bad period for the Quakers followed the passing of the second Conventicle Act in 1670. The records show the same members of the same meetings distrained on again and again during 1670 for doggedly continuing their worship together. Proceedings were frequently taken under Elizabethan and Jacobean acts originally intended to cripple the Catholic gentry,[4] so the dissenting husbandman and yeoman of Cambridgeshire found their farm stock and household goods disappearing to satisfy demands for fines of £20 a month for not attending church.[5] John Smith of Over had already lost four cows worth £13 and three heifers worth £5. 10s. when his last two were taken from him.[6] Nine cows of John Aynslo's valued at £30, as well as household goods, were taken in 1670. At a time when the ordinary husbandman's goods at his death were worth £30 and the ordinary yeoman's goods £180[7] such repeated fines could be completely ruinous and it is perhaps no accident that, by 1674, John Aynslo only lost one brass pot and a pewter dish when he was caught at meeting. He may not have had much left to take. Under-sheriffs and informers grew fat on the proceeds of distraint, and a bitter note made in 1670 records that 'Edward Walls, of Cambridge, cobbler, one of the Informers...is now turned a grazier'.[8]

The Volumes of Sufferings and the Quaker register for Cambridgeshire, taken

---

[1] *Volume of Sufferings*, I, p. 107.

[2] Sir Thomas Sclater, one of the Cambridgeshire J.P.'s, made brief notes in his diary on this. They are printed as 'Commitments at Cambridge 1660–1', *Journ. of Friends Historical Soc.* XX (1923), p. 32.

[3] *Volume of Sufferings*, I, p. 109.

[4] A list of statutes under which Quakers were most frequently prosecuted is given in a letter of c. 1685 printed in J. Besse, *A Collection of the Sufferings of the People Called Quakers* (1753), I, pp. xl–xli.

[5] 23 Eliz. cap. 1.                    [6] See above, p. 90.

[7] H. M. Spufford, 'The Significance of the Cambridgeshire Hearth Tax', *Proc. C.A.S.* LV (1962), p. 54, n. 3.

[8] *Volumes of Sufferings*, I, p. 122. See also J. Besse, *op. cit.* p. 97, for the story of the under-sheriff deliberately taking household goods from the sufferers, since he was about to set up house himself.

[9] Public Record Office, R.G./6/1219.

together, give a very strong impression that Quakerism had got most hold in the group of villages round Over and Swavesey, where Anne Norris and her husband had been early pioneers, and where John Aynslo lived.[1] Almost all the identifiable Quakers taken in the mass arrests of 1661 came from this group of villages. It is perhaps no coincidence that George Whitehead, one of the more notable early Quaker missionaries, was visiting Cottenham in 1656.[2] By 1669, the Bishop recorded meetings in Willingham and Oakington, as well as Over and Swavesey. During 1670, meetings were broken up in all these villages except Willingham. They seem to have been held in rotation in this group of parishes, so that a meeting in any one of the villages drew in members from all of them. The register is preceded by a list of nine meetings in Cambridgeshire, and five of them—Swavesey, Over, Willingham, Oakington and Cottenham, lie close together in this area north-west of Cambridge. There are few entries in the register itself for the early period, from the 1650s to the temporary indulgence of 1672, and it does not seem to record most of the major events in the lives of those Quakers who are named in the Volume of Sufferings up to 1670. Many of those early entries which are included appear to be later insertions of some of the family affairs of the more notable Quakers of the conversion period, like the earliest births to be included in the register, of the children of Boniface and Ann Norris of Swavesey from 1648 on, and of the twelve children of John Aynslo. There is not much material from before 1665. However, for what it is worth, the register gives the same impression as the volumes of sufferings, that Quakerism was more strongly rooted in Over and Swavesey before 1672 than anywhere else. Even in Over the doings of only half-a-dozen families are recorded, however. After 1672 there were still more entries in the register for this area than for any other, although there were never more than six Quaker families in one village.

There were also Quakers in two other parts of the county, apart from Cambridge itself, but in most cases they were single, and isolated, individuals of strong conviction. John Prime of Little Wilbraham was one of these. In 1674 he was attending a strongly supported meeting in Fulbourn, together with Henry Bostock from Quy. Henry Bostock seems to have started his dissenting career as a Congregationalist, for he bore the same name as the man who had acted as host for a large Congregational conventicle in Stow-cum-Quy in 1669, which had since petered out.[3] John Prime was steadily mulcted of his household goods and farm stock for attending meetings and non-payment of tithes. He must have been a very substantial yeoman for, between 1673 and 1679, five horses, twenty cows, corn, pigs and household goods valued by

---

[1] Aynslo was not a Cambridgeshire man. According to the register, he came from Aynsley or Aynsley Hall in Northumberland. There was at least one gentry family of Aynsley in Northumberland (John Burke, *History of the Commoners*, 1 (1836), pp. 588–9) although it was not of Aynsley Hall but of Little Harle. The surname seems however to have been fairly common. One John Anesley was exempt from the Hearth Tax on the grounds of poverty, M. H. Dodds, *History of Northumberland*, XII (1926), p. 335. It is therefore difficult to know what social status John Aynslo was born to, before he married Tabitha Beadle of Bedfordshire in 1657 and settled in Over, when he was known to the bishop in 1669 as a 'farmer'.

[2] G. F. Nuttall, *Early Quaker Letters from the Swarthmore MSS, to 1660* (1952), no. 367.

[3] See above, p. 78.

the Quakers at over £100 in all were taken from him. In 1679 he was still being presented with his wife and two daughters for not attending church, and he was imprisoned in 1686. His influence must have drawn the meeting at Fulbourn to Little Wilbraham, when it was later listed in the Quaker register, for his was the only Quaker family there whose births, marriages and burials appeared in the register.

The meeting at Linton incorporated a handful of convinced Quakers from the parishes round about, most of whom had appeared in prosecutions since the 1650s, like Walter Crane of Horseheath, Richard Webb of West Wickham and John Webb of Balsham. John Webb's family were the only Quakers in Balsham, but he held meetings regularly in his house. Before 1670, the family of John Harvey, a grocer of Linton, seems to have been the only Quaker one in Linton, from the register, although as many as ten people were caught attending meetings there in that year. The movement obviously gained momentum after 1672, and half-a-dozen families in Linton town then had their family events recorded in the Quaker register. Linton Meeting grew into a sizeable and strong one and had its own meeting house by the early eighteenth century,[1] although it may have suffered a little from the arrival, relatively late on the scene, of Congregationalism in the place.

## CONCLUSION

The distribution of early dissent in Cambridgeshire shows that, on the whole, once a parish was touched by dissent, it was vulnerable to dissenting opinions in more than one form. Once nonconformist ideas were circulating at all, argument could easily develop, and the nonconformists of a single parish were liable to split their allegiance between the Baptist, Quaker, or Congregational churches. This did not always happen, but it happened in a significant number of places.[2] The Baptists of Over were of course early engaged in theological debate with the Quakers, and by 1669 Congregationalism had got a considerable hold there as well. The dissenters of Willingham were divided between Quakerism and Congregationalism and so were those of Oakington. Balsham had both early Baptists and early Quakers; and Meldreth, which was sending a couple of Quakers to meeting in Royston in 1655, was a Congregationalist stronghold by 1663. Doctrinal convictions not only divided villages, but even families within them. The uncommonly named Peacheys of Soham not only provided elders of the Quaker church, but also a member of Holcroft's church, listed in 1675, who was later admitted to the Rothwell congregational church. The process of fission and struggle amongst the denominations continued, not only in the period of the conversion under the Commonwealth, but under persecution, when Quakers first appeared in Little Wilbraham to challenge the Congregational family there. It also continued after Toleration. The Congregationalists then moved into the Baptist centre of Melbourn, and the Quaker centre of Linton.

[1] This was demolished after purchase by the Loyal Order of Ancient Shepherds in 1921. Cambridge University Library, W. M. Palmer Collection B4/1.

[2] See Map A (p. 70).

94

This pattern of the distribution of early dissent within Cambridgeshire, and its definite regional concentration, deserves further explanation. No doubt the simple process of discussion and argument was partly responsible. Once established in one village, nonconformist ideas tended to spread to the villages round about. But other factors must surely have been involved to explain the definite lines of demarcation which appear on the map between dissenting and conformist areas, and these would repay investigation.

NOTE ON THE COMPTON CENSUS

The degree of reliability of the Compton Census has been a matter of debate for some time (see the bibliography given by H. C. Johnson in his introduction to the *Warwick County Records*, VII (1946), pp. lxxviii–lxxx). One party feels that the number of dissenters was deliberately underestimated for political reasons in the return. C. W. Chalkin, in his article ('The Compton Census of 1676—the dioceses of Canterbury and Rochester', *A Seventeenth Century Miscellany*, Kent Archaeological Society Records Publication Committee, XVII, 1960, pp. 153–74), agrees that there was probably underestimation of nonconformists, although this may not have been intentional. The other side feels, from a comparison of the numbers of presentations in Act Books and Quarter Sessions minutes with the number of dissenters recorded in the census, that at least all *active* dissenters were probably numbered in it.

I have found that the census certainly records far more dissenters in the diocese of Ely than the visitation returns nearest to it in date. Whereas a group of ten or more dissenters stand out as a significant number in 1676, a group of only five presentations for dissent stand out in the same way in the episcopal visitations of the diocese in 1679 and 1682. Even where an impeccable nonconformist source of the right date provides evidence on the size of one particular dissenting group in various parishes, like the list of members of the Baptist congregation of Fenstanton and Caxton in 1676, or the names of those Quakers distrained on for meeting under the Conventicle Act of 1670 in the Volumes of Sufferings, the numbers given never approach the numbers given for the same parishes in Compton, which should, of course, have included dissenters from all groups, and which should therefore be larger. The only exception to this, which might cast doubt on the accuracy of the census rather than tending to confirm it, is provided by the Congregational church list of 1675, in which the total number of Congregationalists given, for instance, in the parishes within and around Cambridge exceed the total number of all dissenters for the area in Compton. However, the list is so corrupt (see above, p. 76, n. 1) that it cannot carry much weight. On the whole, therefore, the Ely section of the census seems to give a more complete record of the strength of dissent in the diocese than any other which is available.

On the other hand, I have also found that calculations based on the frequently made assumption that the census includes all adults aged 16 and over, give total population figures considerably below those based on, for instance, the 1664 Hearth

Tax. (Contrast C. W. Chalkin, *art. cit.*, who feels the chief use of the census is as a guide to the size and distribution of population.) Miss Anne Whiteman, of Lady Margaret Hall, Oxford, who is at present editing the census for the Staffordshire Historical Collections, has been good enough to tell me that those original parochial returns which survive for the census indicate that the figures were made up on all sorts of different bases: inhabitants over 16 including servants; inhabitants over 16 excluding servants; men only; families; and so on. In the circumstances, unless the original parochial return exists, it is impossible to be certain exactly what the figures entered in each column of the census represent. No original returns have been found for the diocese of Ely. This means that great caution must be employed in using the census, and that it is a difficult or impossible source on which to base estimates of total population, even if not of dissenters.

I am very grateful to Miss Whiteman for letting me have this information before the publication of her definitive edition of the census, and for sparing time to comment on an earlier draft of part of this paper. I am also much indebted to Mrs Dorothy Owen, the Ely diocesan archivist, as well as to those ministers and chapel secretaries and elders who have helped me at various times by producing their records, and to Mr Tibbutt, who lent me his transcripts of the Great Gransden Church Book and the Rothwell Church Book. I should particularly like to thank Mr Andrew Smith, of Emmanuel Congregational Church, Cambridge, who, with extreme generosity, lent me his own notes, and guided me to much material I would otherwise have missed.

# XIII

## *Puritanism and Social Control?*

One of the current received suppositions appears to be, put very crudely, that from the 1580s the group of more prosperous men who had always provided the officials to run village society, now labelled 'village puritan elites', were imposing a stricter moral code of behaviour, particularly on the poorer villagers. It is sometimes implied that this imposition was new. This tightening-up is reflected in the escalating number of cases of fornication, adultery, incontinence and, above all, illegitimacy, presented in the ecclesiastical courts. This essay is intended to examine this supposition and the assumptions about religious belief on which it rests for the late sixteenth and early seventeenth centuries and to compare this early modern period with the late thirteenth and early fourteenth centuries, which was in some ways demographically similar. The comparison should show whether the imposition of a stricter moral code of behaviour was indeed 'new'.

The main evidence for the escalating number of moral cases presented in the courts has been given by Keith Wrightson, who shows that nearly one-third of the cases of bastardy presented between 1570–1699 for Terling in Essex were brought between 1597 and 1607, and another notable group between 1613 and 1616. He calls this dramatic upswing 'an astonishing and, until recently, unsuspected aspect of the history of the period'.[1] Bastardy was very much an offence of the poor and obscure and even bridal pregnancy was increasingly presented for the poor. Martin Ingram, in his thesis on 'Ecclesiastical Justice in

---

[1] Wrightson and Levine, pp. 127–8. See also pp. 113–19, 132–3. This upswing was found elsewhere. P. Laslett and K. Oosterveen, 'Long Term Trends in Bastardy in England', reprinted and amended in P. Laslett, *Family Life and Illicit Love in Earlier Generations* (CUP, 1977), pp. 102 ff. See also D. Levine and K. Wrightson, 'The Nadir of English Illegitimacy in the Seventeenth Century' in P. Laslett, K. Oosterveen, R.M. Smith (eds.), *Bastardy and its Comparative History* (London, Edward Arnold, 1980), especially pp. 172–5.

42

Wiltshire, 1600–1640',[2] has done a very subtle analysis of presentments in the ecclesiastical courts. He shows that, in two parishes in the increasingly impoverished, populous and partly industrialised area of the county, 60 per cent and 75 per cent of the cases in which pre-nuptial pregnancy can be firmly deduced from the parish registers ended up by being presented in the ecclesiastical courts.

But in another pair of parishes where population pressure was far less great, on the sheep–corn uplands, either no cases or only 7 per cent of cases of pre-nuptial pregnancy were presented. He, too, demonstrates that presentment for fornication or conception out of wedlock was far more likely if the sinners were poor. The suggestion, very reasonably, is that at a time of increasing population pressure, immediately after the introduction of the new poor law, the village officials were afraid of the cost of bastards falling on the rates. This financial lever added, as it always so wonderfully does, an additional impetus to the moral fervour of these officials. This fervour stemmed naturally from their puritan beliefs, and their desire to impose godly discipline upon the unruly bottom of rural society, that mass of servants, vagrants and late Elizabethan poor which Peter Clark has christened the 'Third World' of the 1590s.[3] Peter Clark's 'Third World' appears to be approximately the same group as Peter Laslett's 'subsociety of the bastardy-prone'.[4] In the case of Terling, this moral fervour extended itself from the suppression of promiscuity into the suppression of alehouse keeping, always the recourse of the poor in times of great stress. The increase in alehouse cases there also ran between 1607 and 1625; again the initiative was taken by parish officers against the village poor, and the suppression was described as 'the very foundation of reformation'.[5]

Keith Wrightson suggests that we are witnessing a very important social change in the late sixteenth and early seventeenth centuries in which the increasing economic differentiation of village society was 'accompanied by a significant differentiation of attitudes and behaviour'. The manifestation of this was the willingness of the 'rich', the officeholders, of whom a high proportion happened also in Terling village to be the 'elect and chosen' of God, to present their lesser, and possibly also less regenerate, brethren in the courts. 'Custom', he writes, 'was on the retreat in Terling before changes in social attitudes which were to play a significant part in remoulding the pattern of social relationships in the village.'[6] This thesis is worrying for several reasons. The most important are

[2] M. Ingram, 'Ecclesiastical Justice in Wiltshire, 1600–1640, with Special Reference to Cases Concerning Sex and Marriage' (unpublished D.Phil. thesis, University of Oxford, 1976), particularly ch. 5 on 'Sexual Offences'.

[3] P. Clark, English Provincial Society from the Reformation to the Revolution: Religion, Politics and Society in Kent, 1500–1640 (Hassocks, Harvester Press, 1977), pp. 155–7, 175–7, 235–44.

[4] Laslett, Family Life and Illicit Love, p. 107.     [5] Wrightson and Levine, pp. 134–6.

[6] Wrightson and Levine, pp. 140–1. See also pp. 115–16, 133–6, 156, 161–3.

these. The unwary student draws from it the implications, which are not necessarily in the protagonists' minds, first, that puritanism always, or normally, spreads from above through the village, that is, that it is imposed by the group of yeomanry, 'the elite', who fill village office as bailiffs, reeves, churchwardens and so on. So religious belief becomes, to the student, a by-product of social and economic position. It then follows logically that it is either forced on, or foisted off onto, the poorer members of village society, who are not themselves interested in religious belief, or concerned with doctrinal change. If they do take an interest they are assumed, without much hard evidence, like Peter Clark's 'Third World', to be interested in magic, and probably reactionary catholics.[7] Secondly, the emphasis on 'puritanism' as an instrument of social control leads in no time at all into a simplified equation of puritanism with social control.[8] Too many students of social history asked to discuss religion in the later sixteenth and early seventeenth centuries produce a discussion of 'the mechanics of social control' in the period instead. This essay is both an attempt to discuss the distortions involved in this approach and also an attack on the central theses from which these distortions stem.

It sometimes appears that many social historians think that religious belief is primarily about moral behaviour and social attitudes, rather than the relationship of the individual with the being he thought to be exterior, whom he described as 'God'. From this relationship, of course, his relationship with his group of co-'believers' and his moral attitudes stemmed, so there is indeed a strong connection. But this is different from not comprehending the centrality to the believer of his or her relationship with 'God'. In other words, the first great commandment comes before the second.[9] Secondly, I do not believe that we know enough about the diffusion of puritan or 'the hotter sort of Protestant'[10] or indeed, separatist, beliefs socially, to state or even suggest as a maxim that puritan beliefs were the prerogative of the yeomanry, enforced on a reluctant and

---

[7] Clark, *English Provincial Society*, pp. 155–7.

[8] It is interesting to note that although 'this mounting initiative in the prosecuting of religious offences was undoubtedly aimed at persons low in the social scale for the most part', such persons naturally predominated numerically in the village of Terling. Therefore it is not significant that 53 per cent of those presented for failure to attend church were overwhelmingly drawn from Category IV, which in Wrightson and Levine's analysis is made up of those charged on, or excused, duty on one hearth in 1671, since 51 per cent of Terling people fell into that category in any case: Wrightson and Levine, pp. 156 and 35. Other figures which the authors quote of proportions of obdurates, excommunicates, evil-livers and so on are indeed significant, but these figures should always be checked against the proportion in the group on the key tables on pp. 34 and 35.

[9] 'Jesus said, "the first commandment is this: Hear, O Israel: the Lord our God is the only Lord. Love the Lord your God with all your heart, with all your soul, with all your mind, and with all your strength. The second is this: Love your neighbour as yourself. There is no other commandment greater than these" ' (St Mark, 12, vv. 29–31).

[10] P. Collinson, 'A Comment: Concerning the Name Puritan', *Journal of Ecclesiastical History*, XXXI (1980), 484.

44

possibly promiscuous mass of humbler villagers. Thirdly, I do not believe that the attempt to enforce 'godly discipline' was in any sense new, or unfamiliar, in the late sixteenth century.

I do not propose to discuss the first issue, about the nature of religious belief and the social attitudes flowing out of it, at all in this essay, although it is my most fundamental point. Evans-Pritchard, in his conclusion to *Theories of Primitive Religion*, wrote of anthropologists in a way that is not inapplicable to social historians.

As far as a study of religion as a factor in social life is concerned, it may make little difference whether the anthropologist is a theist or an atheist, since in either case he can only take into account what he can observe. But if either attempts to go further than this, each must pursue a different path. The non-believer seeks for some theory – biological, psychological, or sociological – which will explain the illusion; the believer seeks rather to understand the manner in which a people conceives of a reality and their relations to it. For both, religion is part of social life, but for the believer it has also another dimension. On this point I find myself in agreement with Schmidt in his confutation of Renan: 'If religion is essentially of the inner life, it follows that it can be truly grasped only from within. But beyond a doubt, this can be better done by one in whose inward consciousness an experience of religion plays a part. There is but too much danger that the other (the non-believer) will talk of religion as a blind man might of colours, or one totally devoid of ear, of a beautiful musical composition.'[11]

The social historian also can, and should, take into account only what he can deduce from ascertainable fact. But after that point, the non-believer's interpretations will vary from the believer's. Some current writing, ostensibly about religion, sometimes does indeed seem to talk of religion as a blind man might of colours.

My second point is that we need to know more about the social distribution of puritan, or separatist, beliefs at the parish level to state that they were the prerogative of one group of villagers over another. One or two, or even three or four, case studies will not do to establish the norm, if indeed there was such a thing. There are several types of argument to suggest that the 'poorer sort' may have had their own religious convictions. Much the most general evidence is to point out that in the sixteenth and early seventeenth centuries religion was 'news' at the alehouse level, as well as in the inn, and, as such, hotly discussed amongst mixed social groups. The earliest such case I have so far found is the delightful one in 1538 when a former friar was accused of heresy. He had been at a discussion at the 'Sign of the Bell' in Northampton at which the nature of the sacrament of the altar was hotly debated. A certain 'Sir' Thomas was there, who said it was 'only god his bodye', and when the ex-friar refuted this, a butcher of

[11] E.E. Evans-Pritchard, *Theories of Primitive Religion* (OUP, 1965) p. 121.

Northampton who was present said 'I saw this day the body of god present between a pristes hands.'[12]

Rather later, in 1553, an opposing line was taken by a lesser villager in Orwell in Cambridgeshire, who not only made an extremely rude gesture to explain his feelings about the reintroduction of the Mass, but also offered to hand round a ballad called 'maistres mass' in the alehouse.[13] Only a couple of years after that, in 1555, a half-yardlander, a 15-acre man of Willingham, walked to Colchester to refresh his soul with 'spiritual exercises'. In the inn overnight the husbandman of Willingham and a friend from St Ives tangled in debate on the divinity of Christ with a 'serving man' to a gentleman, two 'women gospellers' and a heretical joiner. The Willingham husbandman was so upset by his inability to argue his case in favour of Christ's divinity satisfactorily that he fully intended to walk to Oxford to seek council of Bishop Ridley and Mr Latimer, but, fortunately for his feet, met someone who satisfied his conscience in the 'mean season'. In the mid-seventeenth century, it was the regular habit of a group of men who marketed in Royston, and formed the seed-bed of a later congregationalist conventicle, to meet together and 'spend their penny in a private room, where without interruption, they might talk freely of the things of God'.[14] This was probably a more select and less argumentative group; but a whole range of cases has been found in which the alehouse formed a meeting-place at which anti-puritan songs could be sung, and anti-puritan feelings expressed or, alternatively, conventicles could be held. Some of the protagonists were very poor, like the Kentish tiler who rejoiced at the suspension of local puritan preachers.[15] So theological debate was very lively amongst the humble, not only the village oligarchs, in the sixteenth century. Women, tilers and husbandmen were involved. And cheap print was addressed to them, right from the opening of the *Stationers' Company Registers* in 1557.[16]

A much less general and more convincing proof is a monetary one. If humble people are prepared to put cash down in support of their beliefs, it seems likely that these beliefs mattered to them. And there is ample proof that the humble were indeed willing to put cash down. The involvement of individual smallholders, husbandmen, shopkeepers, craftsmen, artisans and their wives who all contributed in the 1470s to the building of the splendid new church at Walberswick in Suffolk has recently been demonstrated. At nearby Blythburgh, the contributors to the building of the church included both a small shopkeeper

[12] M. Bowker, *The Henrician Reformation: the Diocese of Lincoln under John Longland, 1521–1547* (CUP, 1981), p. 166.     [13] Spufford, p. 245.     [14] Spufford, pp. 244–5, 246–7.
[15] P. Clark, *The English Alehouse* (London, Longman, 1983), pp. 156–8. I am grateful to Mr Clark for letting me have access to this in page proof.
[16] M. Spufford, *Small Books and Pleasant Histories* (London, Methuen, 1981), p. 10.

46

and the madam of the brothel.[17] At Eye, the whole congregation passed the hat round in the early sixteenth century to make up the required sum for the foundation of a chantry.[18] Just as the people of the 1470s were willing to contribute substantial sums, in many cases worth a year's rent to them, so also two centuries later the Quakers were willing to pay the £20 fines originally designed to control Elizabethan recusants rather than to conform. In many cases, they faced total financial ruin. The case histories of individuals who were initially poor anyway can be traced through the Volumes of Sufferings, and the gradual distraint of their goods can be demonstrated until, as in one example, the final blow was struck and one man had two cows distrained, 'being all he then had'.[19]

The ultimate proof of religious involvement is surely the willingness to suffer martyrdom. No amount of external social pressure can account for a willingness to be burnt for one's beliefs. Therefore, the most striking piece of evidence in favour of the involvement of the humblest of the laity in the Reformation is the fact that over half the martyrs listed by Foxe whose social status was given were said to be agricultural labourers.[20] Of course these were the people most defenceless, and least likely to be able to retreat into exile.[21] In view of their martyrdoms, however, reformed beliefs do not appear to have been the prerogative of 'village elites'. Indeed, the distribution of reformed beliefs has not yet been adequately studied at the village level. No one, to my knowledge, has looked properly at the social backgrounds of the later Lollards, and this could be done with precision.[22] Meanwhile, it seems likely that Dr Bowker was right to characterise them as 'weavers and threshers'.[23] Nor have other, later groups of the 'hotter sort of protestant' been investigated sufficiently. I have found protestants of conviction throughout the strata of village structure in Cambridgeshire in the late sixteenth and early seventeenth centuries, but I have only worked in detail on five places.[24] This is not enough. I have also looked at the social distribution of post-Restoration dissent and have found that it certainly did not necessarily spread downwards. The deaf old fenwoman, a day-labourer

[17] C. Richmond, *John Hopton: a Fifteenth Century Suffolk Gentleman* (CUP, 1981), pp. 174–7.
[18] M. Cook, 'Eye (Suffolk) in the Years of Uncertainty, 1520–1590' (unpublished Ph.D. thesis, University of Keele, 1982), pp. 57–8.  [19] Spufford, p. 289.
[20] A.G. Dickens, *The English Reformation* (London, Batsford, 1964), pp. 266–7. The cases of a Suffolk agricultural labourer who would not receive the sacrament, and those of a husbandman and a linen-weaver who refused to hear Mass, all of whom were burnt, are discussed by Cook, 'Eye in the Years of Uncertainty', pp. 162–6.
[21] 'Nearly all of the 350 people known to have found refuge on the continent were gentlemen, merchants or clerics.' D.M. Palliser, 'Popular Reactions to the Reformation during the Years of Uncertainty, 1530–1570' in F. Heal and R. O'Day (eds.), *Church and Society in England: Henry VIII to James I* (London, Macmillan, 1977), pp. 43–4.
[22] J.A.F. Thomson, *The Later Lollards 1414–1520* (OUP, 1965), does not attempt this. Derek Plumb is doing so in a Cambridge Ph.D. now in progress.
[23] M. Bowker, *Henrician Reformation*, p, 146.
[24] Spufford, chs. 12 and 13, especially pp. 298–306, 320–44.

who was converted to Quakerism by the written word, was one proof of that. So also were the villages where dissent concentrated at the bottom of the social structure, or spread evenly through it. But there were other communities where dissent did make more appeal to the more prosperous. We simply do not know enough yet, and it would be unwise to generalise on the basis of less than a full examination of all the varieties of dissent across the whole of two contrasted counties of England. This has not yet been done.[25]

Individual case studies have, of course, been offered us. Terling, in Essex, with a living in the hands of the Mildmay family, provides one example of a village society which had an elite group of puritan officeholders in the 1620s.[26] On the other hand, the officeholders in the sixteenth century in the little Suffolk borough of Eye were divided between crypto-catholics, and those who tended towards protestantism.[27] Here are two conflicting examples; we will not know which is more 'normal' for different regions of the country until much more work has been done. Meanwhile, restraint seems highly necessary before religious belief of a particular bent is equated with any particular social or economic status at the top, or indeed, the bottom, of village society.

The hypothesis that the attempt to enforce 'godly discipline', particularly sexual discipline, on the poor was an innovation of the late sixteenth century suggests, reduced to the crudest possible form, that puritanism in the most practical terms equalled the greater enforcement of moral behaviour on the poorer villagers by the richer. It is demonstrated by an escalation of cases brought against the more humble in the ecclesiastical courts.

One way to test such a hypothesis is by removing one of the variables of the equation. Was puritanism a necessary condition for a greater enforcement of moral behaviour on the poor? The evidence for a catholic, post-Tridentine country would show whether there were similar developments in 'social control' at the end of the sixteenth century.[28] On the other hand, late thirteenth- and early

---

[25] Except by Vann, for the Quakers of Buckinghamshire and Norfolk, and for the initial leaders of the movement, 'the valiant sixty'. Amongst the latter, there were relatively large numbers of 'gentlemen' (11%) but over two-thirds (67%) were employed in agriculture and a quarter (24%) were 'husbandmen' as opposed to 'yeomen'. Amongst Quakers in general, the core of support seems to have been the yeoman and the wholesale traders, but, even so, early Quakers 'drew adherents from all classes of society except the very highest and the very lowest, ranging from the lesser gentry down to a few totally unskilled labourers'. R.H. Vann, *The Social Development of English Quakerism, 1655–1755* (Cambridge, Mass., Harvard University Press, 1969), pp. 47–87, especially pp. 55, 73, 74–5.

[26] Wrightson and Levine, pp. 154, 177–8.

[27] Cook, 'Eye in the Years of Uncertainty', pp. 275–6, and appendix E, pp. 290–1. The religious affiliation of about three-quarters of the officeholders is reasonably certain, and the occupational status of about half of them is known. 'Gentlemen' and 'yeomen', who were officeholders, tended to be catholic, whereas craftsmen who were officeholders tended to be protestant.

[28] F. Lebrun, *Histoire des Catholiques en France* (Toulouse, Privat, 1980), pp. 135–40, and bibliography, pp. 143–5, seems to provide an excellent point of departure for such an exercise.

48

fourteenth-century England is, in many ways, a period so parallel to sixteenth- and early seventeenth-century England that the inducement to see what happened then is high. This seems a much more possible exercise to an English economic historian. I have therefore chosen to look at English case studies for the late thirteenth and early fourteenth centuries.

Let me begin by underlining just how alike, in many ways, the sixteenth century and the thirteenth century were. Between 1550, when enough parish registers became usable, and 1650, the population of England rises very steeply indeed: it almost doubles, from a little over 3 million in 1550, to nearly 5.5 million in 1650, when it stabilises, or even sags. The very bad period of starvation in northern Europe from 1595–7 brought mortality crises in north and north-western England also.[29] The smaller farmers in the open, arable areas disappeared. The wage-labourers at the bottom of society saw a particularly disastrous fall in the purchasing power of their wages during the sixteenth century inflation: the wage-labourer's wages bought him less food in 1597 than at any other point recorded between the 1260s, when the records open, and 1950.[30] The distress was immense: this is the background to Peter Clark's 'Third World' of the 1590s and its vagrants. It is also, incidentally, the background to the boom in alehouse licensing that Wrightson observed, and that Peter Clark has worked on. To set up an alehouse one only needed a bench or two, and some ale. It was one of the additional ways for the very poor to try and make a living without taking to the roads. This is also the background to the wealthy yeomen of Terling and their puritanism, for it was the wealthy yeomen who made a profit out of scarcity, since the small surplus they did have for the market earned them much more. Moreover, and it is not a minor point, they could afford to marry off their daughters: a dowry for them was conceivable, whereas for the small husbandman and for the labourer, it was not. Wrightson, Levine and Martin Ingram are all scrupulous in pointing out the connection between the dowryless state of, for instance, daughters of the poor, girls in service and the greater sexual licence allowed them. So, indeed, are the sub-literary 'chapbooks' dealing with courtship in the 1680s, which treat the lack of dowry, and the greater freedom of individual choice it allowed servants, as a known fact of life.

Why is the thirteenth century so demographically like the sixteenth century? Between 1086 and 1377, dates for which we have information which will yield estimates of inhabitants, the population of England rose even more steeply than

[29] R.M. Smith, 'Population and its Geography in England, 1550–1730' in R.A. Dodgshon and R.A. Butlin (eds.), *An Historical Geography of England and Wales* (London, Academic Press, 1978), pp. 204, 207, 213–14.
[30] E.H. Phelps-Brown and S.V. Hopkins, 'Seven Centuries of the Prices of Consumables, Compared with Builders' Wage-Rates' in E. Carus Wilson (ed.), *Essays in Economic History* (London, Edward Arnold, 1962), vol. II, p. 186.

between the mid-sixteenth and the mid-seventeenth centuries. It tripled, and possibly quadrupled, between the end of the eleventh century and the second quarter of the fourteenth century.[31] The peak then was between 4 and 6 millions. In fact, population then was certainly as high as it was in the mid-seventeenth century, and was possibly even higher than at any time until the mid-eighteenth century.[32] This dramatic rise in population inevitably had its effect on the size of holdings: between 1275 and 1400, 85 per cent of the holdings of recorded size being conveyed in the manor of Hakeford Hall at Coltishall in Norfolk were of less than 5 acres, and the median was only 1 acre.[33] It is sinister, but not in the least surprising, that in, or after, the years of bad harvests between 1248 and 1309–19 on five manors of the Abbey of Winchester in counties as widespread as Somerset, South Hampshire and Berkshire, it was the poorer villagers, with fewest beasts and, by inference, little or no land, whose heirs paid the fines due on death.[34] So people were starving to death in the south of England, and not just the north-west, in the thirteenth century, even before the great series of harvest failures of 1315–22 which checked the population explosion, and have been described as 'a dividing line in the history of the medieval countryside'.[35] The landless, the wage-labourers, of course, suffered worse: the wage-labourer's wages bought him less food in 1316–17 than at any other date, except 1597, between the 1270s and 1950. The manor courts of the period were run by a village oligarchy. Dr Smith has convincingly demonstrated this for the two Suffolk manors of Rickinghall and Redgrave in the thirteenth century.[36] The tenants who then filled the local government and administration jobs, that is, the chief pledges, reeves, jurors, constables, bailiffs and ale-tasters, came from families with over ten acres. These do not sound large holdings, but they were, in terms of the sort of size of holdings in the east of England which the thirteenth-century population explosion had created. In fact, these officeholders were the exact equivalent of their sixteenth-century counterparts.

On the very extensive estate of the Abbey of Halesowen, in Worcestershire, recent investigation has again shown that the composition of the village oligarchy was exactly the same as on Dr Smith's Suffolk manors. Men from

[31] M.S. Campbell, 'Population Pressure, Inheritance and the Landmarket in a Fourteenth Century Peasant Community' in R.M. Smith (ed.), *Land, Kinship and Life-Cycle* (CUP, 1985), pp. 87–134, and E. Miller and J. Hatcher, *Medieval England: Rural Society and Economic Change, 1086–1348* (London, Longman, 1978), pp. 28–33, 57–8, 60–1.

[32] Smith in Dodgshon and Butlin (eds.), *An Historical Geography*, p. 207.

[33] M.S. Campbell in Smith (ed.), *Land, Kinship and Life-Cycle*, p. 106.

[34] Miller and Hatcher, *Medieval England*, pp. 57–8.

[35] Miller and Hatcher, *Medieval England*, pp. 60 ff.

[36] R.M. Smith, 'English Peasant Life-Cycles and Socio-Economic Networks: A Quantitative Geo-graphical Case Study' (University of Cambridge Ph.D. thesis, 1974), pp. 9, 392. See also Edward Miller, *The Abbey and Bishopric of Ely* (CUP, 1951), pp. 252–5, for a description of the election and responsibility of reeves, bailiffs, haywards and beadles in the thirteenth century.

50

poor families were never elected to public office between 1270 and 1400: the yardlanders, men with 25 to 30 acres, dominated the community, and Dr Zvi Razi writes, 'the major public offices in Halesowen were filled by members of a small group of families which dominated and led the village community for generations'.[37] So we may, I think, take it as firmly established that village officials in the sixteenth and seventeenth centuries, and in the thirteenth and fourteenth centuries also, were drawn from exactly the same groups of the more prosperous landholders and craftsmen in village society. This variable did not change over time.

On the two Suffolk manors of Rickinghall and Redgrave, between 1259 and 1319, or in a period economically comparable with the 1550s and 1620s, the manor courts were extending their interest to more and more people who had not previously come within their orbit. There was a dramatic increase in the volume of court business, presented, of course, by the village oligarchy.[38] But the motive was not financial. Although the number of cases increased over threefold, the level of fines sank with people's inability to pay, and more and more tiny fines reflected the poorest tenants attempt to make a living by baking bread and, just as in the late sixteenth century, by brewing ale. Exactly the same phenomena are found on yet three more Winchester manors in Wiltshire and Hampshire at the end of the thirteenth century.[39] So at the end of the thirteenth century, as at the end of the sixteenth century, running an alehouse was the way out for the poorest. Meanwhile, available land was increasingly concentrating in the hands of fewer people, just as in the late sixteenth century.[40] Also just as in the late sixteenth century, the thirteenth-century 'yeoman' could afford to give his daughter a dowry, so she could marry. The lesser man could not.

So when does religion, and the morality that should flow from it, come into this comparative picture? The thirteenth century, following the fourth Lateran Council of 1215 was, in some ways like the sixteenth century, a century of moral reform, although this is not a parallel I would want to push too far. Not only the morals and good behaviour of the parish clergy, but also those of the laity, were being tightened up. Indeed, in the diocese of Lincoln from 1253 onwards, there was considerable ecclesiastical pressure to see that Sunday was properly observed. By the mid-fourteenth century, Sabbatarianism was even extended

---

[37] Z. Razi, *Life, Marriage and Death in a Medieval Parish: Economy, Society and Demography in Halesowen, 1270–1400* (CUP, 1980), pp. 77–9, 122–3.

[38] R.M. Smith, 'English Peasant Life-Cycles', pp. 19, 43, 53. Dr Smith shows, for instance, that 66 fines worth 15s/4d were paid in 1262, but that 213 and 273 fines worth 15s/4d and 162/8d were paid in 1307 and 1309 at Rickinghall.

[39] A.N. May, 'An Index of Thirteenth Century Peasant Impoverishment? Manor Court Fines', *ECHR*, xxvi (1973), 389–402.

[40] R.M. Smith, 'English Peasant Life-Cycles', p. 175.

backwards into Saturday.[41] At the parish of Bardney in 1246, the nature of the faults enquired into on visitation were Sabbath and festival-breaking, wrestling and dancing, attendance at church – ales and playing at dice.[42] These all have a very familiar ring about them to the early modern historian.

The great difficulty in pursuing the parallels between the thirteenth century and the sixteenth century in a scholarly way is the absence of English archidiaconal records for exactly the period 1280–1320 which we need for a proper comparison with 1580–1620. The earliest surviving archidiaconal records are early fourteenth century.[43] There is indirect evidence on the effects of the archidiaconal courts and, indeed, the public dislike in which archdeacons were held. In 1215, one of the decrees of Lateran IV bothered to lay down the number of horses by which the archdeacon might suitably be accompanied on visitations.[44] In 1237, archdeacons were made responsible for 'overseeing the holy vessels and vestments' in the parishes.[45] A public debate was actually held in the University of Paris on the tricky, and obviously highly emotive, subject of whether an archdeacon could be saved. A metrical English satire of the late thirteenth century is a satire on the consistory courts. Its chief complaint is the particular severity shown towards poor men in the church courts. The only sins which are even mentioned in it are sexual ones, and the subject of grievance is the concentration by the courts on sexual behaviour. Furthermore, the author resented what he felt to be the way the clergy always took the part of women against men. He described the setting and personnel of the court, and wrote:

No ordinary man can lead his life [untroubled], however skilful a workman he may be, the clergy so lead us astray. If I happen to go with a girl, I must be brought up before them and learn their law, and I shall regret their advice . . . I wish to escape injury, and flee from my companion; they did not care what the offence was so long as they had it . . . If I am accused in their document, then I am slandered; for they make many men to blame for the misfortune of women . . . Moreover six or seven summoners sit there, misjudging men according to their natural ability, and bring out their register. Herdsmen and all men's servants hate them, for they put every parish in pain . . . A beadle rises, and proceeds with his rod, and shouts out loudly so that the whole court should hear, and calls Maggie and Moll. And they come, as covered with dirt as a moorhen, and shrink for shame, and are ashamed in men's presence, those unbeautiful ladies.[46] One of them begins to shriek, and soon screams out, 'if my lies have anything to do with it, it shall not happen so, everyone

[41] M. Gibbs and J. Lang, *Bishops and Reform, 1215–1272* (OUP, 1934), pp. 95–130, 143, 158–73.
[42] D. Owen, *Church and Society in Medieval Lincolnshire* (Lincoln, History of Lincolnshire Committee, 1971), pp. 110, 120.
[43] See Lincolnshire Archives Office, D. and C. A/2/24, *passim*. I am very grateful to Mrs Owen for this reference. [44] Gibbs and Lang, *Bishops and Reform*, p. 99.
[45] Owen, *Church and Society in Medieval Lincolnshire*, p. 117. The parishioners were to provide the holy vessels and vestments required.
[46] This phrase is a comic inversion of a formula meaning 'lovely ladies'.

52

shall bear witness that you must marry me and have me as your wife'. . . I am chased like a dog at church and through market, so that I would rather be dead than live like this, to the sorrow of all my relations. In the consistory court they teach us trouble and wish that things should go from bad to worse for us. Then a priest as proud as a peacock marries us both; they bring trouble to us far and wide because of women's doings.[47]

The archdeacon described by Chaucer at the beginning of the *Friar's Tale* seems to have shared the same preoccupations.

> there was dwelling in my contree
> An erchedekene, a man of heigh degree,
> That boldely dide execucioun
> In punishing of fornicacioun,
> Of wicchecraft, and eke of bawderye,
> of diffamacioun, and avoutrye,
> Of chirche-reves, and of testaments,
> Of contracts, and of lakke of sacraments,
> Of usure, and of symonye also,
> But certes, lechours dide he grettest wo;
> They sholde singen if that they were hent . . .[48]

At the end of the fourteenth century, the Dominican John Bromyard (fl. 1390) picked up the theme, and complained that even when wealthy fornicators and adulterers had been sentenced to bodily punishment in the ecclesiastical courts, they would come in and offer bribes to bishops, archdeacons and court officials, and get off without pain whereas, he wrote, 'the "simple" on the other hand, may be seen doing their penance naked in church and market-place, with other humiliations'.[49] From the beginning of medieval homiletics in English, meanwhile, preachers waxed as cloquent as any Nicholas Bownde against 'wowynges', 'kyssynges' (secret), 'syngnges', gay array, 'nice chere' and all such 'thynges that beth forbode as dawnsynge of women and other open syztes that draweth man to synne'.[50] 'Lechery' and 'taverns' form two of the biggest index

---

[47] Attributed to the reign of Edward I (d. 1307), although the manuscript from which it is taken, MS Harl. 2253, fol. 70v. is of the reign of Edward II. Thomas Wright (ed.), *The Political Songs of England* (Camden Society, vol. VI, 1839), pp. 156–9. The text of this poem has been re-edited in R.H. Robbins (ed.), *Historical Poems of the XIV and XV Centuries* (New York, Columbia University Press, 1959), pp. 25–7. The editor dated it very precisely to 1307. He did not retranslate it. Since the translation made in 1839 was unsatisfactory, Mr A.C. Spearing has very kindly spent time to make the present translation. He tells me that some phrases (which I have queried) are very obscure. He would also date the poem to the early fourteenth century, but says alliterated poetry of this kind is 'notoriously hard to date accurately'. MS Harl. 2253 is usually dated 1330–40, but most of the poems in it could have been written at any time in the previous eighty years. I am much indebted to Mr Spearing for his help.

[48] N.R. Haveley (ed.), *The Friar's, Summoner's and Pardoner's Tales* (University of London, 1975), pp. 57–8: 'avoutrye' is adultery. Again, I am very grateful to Mrs Owen for this reference.

[49] G.R. Owst, *Literature and Pulpit in Medieval England* (CUP, 1933), pp. 247, 251–4.

[50] Owst, *Literature and Pulpit*, p. 384.

entries in G.R. Owst's book on *Literature and Pulpit in Medieval England*, just as the harlot's door and the alehouse bench filled the thunderous warnings of the 'godly' chapbooks of the 1680s.

But all this, though suggestive, is not the kind of quantifiable proof we need of a parallel situation of escalating moral presentments in the late thirteenth and early fourteenth centuries with the late sixteenth and early seventeenth centuries, although we do have evidence of escalating presentments for all types of offence bringing in more and more people to the manor courts. The surviving ecclesiastical presentments of faults amongst the records of the Dean and Chapter of Lincoln for the 1330s and 1340s heavily emphasise, in a way most familiar to all sixteenth-century ecclesiastical historians, presentments for adultery and fornication, and even for harvest working on Sundays.[51] The dating is still too late for this purpose, however.

Yet even if the ecclesiastical records do not survive except in very small groups, there is still a possible way out. The manorial lord had a customary right to a fine on the marriage of a villein's daughter or, in lieu of this, a fine called 'leyrwite' or 'childwite' for her fornication or for her bearing of a bastard.[52] Whereas the ecclesiastical records do not survive, manorial records do. The relationship between the two sets of record is obscure. One suggestion is that when an active manorial lord was exacting fines for incontinence and bastardy, the local archdeacon might well concentrate on other villages, and vice versa. Certainly in an ecclesiastical peculiar, this jurisdiction seems to have been left to the lord of the manor. Occasionally, an unfortunate villein might fall into the, presumably inevitable, confusion between two jurisdictions and be fined twice for the same sin, as was the Cottenham man Henry Waveneys fined for wasting his lord's substance in the 'court Christian' in the manor court, after he had been presented for adultery with women in Dry Drayton and Cambridge in the archdeacon's court.[53]

Whatever the relationships between the two jurisdictions were, and presumably they may have varied from diocese to diocese, archdeaconry to archdeaconry and even manor to manor, it does not seem very likely that

[51] Owen, *Church and Society in Medieval Lincolnshire*, p. 121.
[52] There is a difference of opinion amongst medievalists about whether a leyrwite fine indicates the bearing of a bastard outside marriage, possibly even outside 'troth plight' or betrothal, or whether it is a fine on fornication only. For my purposes, this distinction does not matter, since early modernists are drawing attention to increasing prosecution of bridal pregnancy, bastardy and fornication. A count of leyrwite fines together with childwite, if they were separately taken, therefore gives a comparable figure of presentations for sexual misdemeanour, whether or not it resulted in the bearing of a child.
[53] J.R. Ravensdale, 'Deaths and Entries: the Reliability of the Figures of Mortality in the Black Death' in F.M. Page (ed.), *Estates of Crowland Abbey* (CUP, 1934), and 'Population Changes and the Transfer of Customary Land on a Cambridgeshire Manor in the Fourteenth Century', in R. M. Smith (ed.), *Land, Kinship and Life-Cycle*, pp. 197–226.

54

manorial lords were less exacting, when they had a right to dues, than ecclesiastical courts, since the rent-roll may be possibly as powerful an incentive as moral fervour. It therefore seems to me valid to look at the studies that have been made of fines taken for leyrwite and childwite in the late thirteenth and early fourteenth centuries, and see how these compare with the rising number of presentations for fornication, bastardy and pre-marital pregnancy[54] in the late sixteenth and early seventeenth century.

Richard Smith has analysed in detail the marriage patterns, and also the presentations for childwite of unmarried girls, on the manor of Rickinghall and Redgrave, but unfortunately only for the short period from 1260–93.[55] We know already that these girls were presented by jurors from the richest quarter of village society. Smith found thirty-five girls fined at Rickinghall in this period, and fifty-one at Redgrave. In both communities, the girls concerned commonly came from families who were landless or deficient in land. They also frequently came either from families presented for illegal brewing and baking, or were themselves illegal brewers or bakers. Both of these activities were also signs of poverty. The strongest link between these girls, however, was the number of them who came from much larger families than normal. That is, they came from families in which it was impossible, or nearly impossible, in a time of great economic pressure, to find a dowry. Furthermore, few of them were able to marry later.[56] At Redgrave, only a third of them eventually married; at Rickinghall, only a sixth did so, and they usually only married some years after their pregnancies. So we are entitled to say that in Suffolk in the thirteenth century, the richest amongst the villagers were not inhibited from presenting the poorest among the villagers for bearing illegitimate children, and that the pressures which led to these illegitimacies were economic ones. The 'sub-society of the bastardy-prone in English history' was not new to the sixteenth century.[57] And the age of marriage of the very poor was late, or non-existent. The jurors who presented these thirteenth-century girls were certainly aware that fornication was a sin, and one heavily punished by the ecclesiastical authorities, but they cannot have been motivated by any spirit of 'election'.

The fullest case study that has been made of medieval marriage and illegitimacy is the recent one by Zvi Razi of Halesowen on the border of Worcestershire

[54] Wrightson and Levine, p. 127.
[55] R.M. Smith, 'English Peasant Life-Cycles', appendix H, pp. 454ff, and ch. 4.
[56] See however, the caveat entered by Dr Smith in his unpublished paper 'Some Thoughts on the Social and Economic Content of Illegitimacy in English Rural Communities, in the Thirteenth and Fourteenth Centuries', p. 16, where he suggests that merchets, or marriage fines, may only be taken for girls with dowries, and therefore the marriage of dowerless girls may have gone unrecorded. I am grateful to Dr Smith for lending me the typescript of this paper.
[57] R.M. Smith, 'Some Thoughts on the Social and Economic Content of Illegitimacy in English Rural Communities', p. 20

and Shropshire.[58] Dr Razi shows that, on this huge manor of the Abbey of Halesowen, in the period from 1270 to 1348, before the Black Death, the numbers of women who paid leyrwite was very high indeed. For every two who married, almost one woman fornicated, or bore a child out of wedlock.[59] Again, there was an absolutely definitive connection between bastardy, or fornication, and poverty; 42 per cent of daughters from poor families were fined for fornication or conceiving out of wedlock, but only 10 per cent of daughters of rich families were fined for fornication or bearing bastards.[60] The reasons for fornication and the bearing of bastards were, as in Suffolk, not licentiousness, but poverty. Girls in Halesowen born to the families of yardlanders, 25- to 30-acre men, had dowries, married young and were at risk for only a short time. Girls born to poor families were often presented for stealing, gleaning and gathering firewood. They were dowryless, for fewer poor girls presented for sexual sins married than did the daughters of the better-off.[61] Some poor girls were even declared *persona non grata* and not allowed to stay in the village. Their families, in any case, were usually only there for one generation, unlike those of the landed.[62] A detailed breakdown of the figures for leyrwites for 1271 to 1348 shows that no significant attention was paid to the collection of leyrwites in the 1270s. From 1280 on, there was a general rise in the leyrwite rates up to the Great Famine, and then a decline and a rise again in the late 1320s and in the 1330s.[63]

But, as soon as the population pressure ended, and it became possible for girls with small, or no, dowries to marry in the second half of the fourteenth century, the number of leyrwites recorded in the court rolls fell sharply.[64] Truly, the medieval sermon writer was right in his analysis. In view of man's frailty, he says, God has permitted marriage, 'to lyve in Goddes law'

But mony wedd hem wyvys for her wordly goodes, for her grete kynne, other for ther fleschely lust: as, be a woman a pore wenche, and ther-wyth well condiciond, *abell of person, and have no wordly goodes and be come of sympell kynne the whiche may not avaunce here*, full fewe men covetyn suche on. Som had lever to take an old wedow, though sche be ful lothelyche and never schall have cheldren. And, fro the tyme that he hathe the mocke that he wedded her for, and felethe her breth foule stynkynge and her

---

[58] Razi, *Life, Marriage and Death*.
[59] See n. 52, above, on the dispute over the meaning of leyrwite fines. Dr Razi takes the leyrwite figures as indicating illegitimate births, p. 65.
[60] I have put together the figures for fornication and illegitimate births from Razi, *Life, Marriage and Death*, p. 66, in view of the doubt on terminology expressed in n. 52 above.
[61] See Razi's own reservation on figures for marriage drawn from merchet, p. 66, and n. 56 above.
[62] Razi, *Life, Marriage and Death*, pp. 66–9.
[63] Private communication from Dr Razi, breaking down the contents of his table 12, p. 67, by date.
[64] In the late 1340s, the collection of leyrwites again became insignificant. There was probably a high local rise in mortality amongst marriageable women in Halesowen in the period 1343–5, before the general mortality of 1348. This would have accounted for the fall in leyrwites before the Black Death. Razi, *Life, Marriage and Death*, pp. 41–2.

56

eyen blered, scabbed and febyll, as old wommen buthe, then they spend a-pon strompettes
that evyll-getyn goodes. And sche shall sytt at home wyth sorowe, hungry and thrusty.
And thus levythe they in a-vowtry, peraventure all her lif tyme. If a mayde be to wedde, the
furste thynge that a man woll aske-what her frendes woll yeve to mary here wyth: and but
they acorde ther in, . . . they kepe not of here. *It semeth, then, they wedden the goodes
more than the womman. For, had not the goodes be, sche schuld goo un-wedded, as all day
is seyne.*[65]

Although I cannot demonstrate with precision for more than one place that in
the late thirteenth and early fourteenth centuries the number of presentations for
sins of incontinence rose in the same pattern as the late sixteenth and early
seventeenth centuries, these initial figures from Halesowen are suggestive. It
would be highly unwise to suggest a strong correlation between population
pressure, poverty and leyrwite prosecutions on the basis of this one place. But it
certainly looks as if the topic, and its early modern parallels, deserves a further
search for evidence.

What can certainly be established is that there was no new social division in the
villages of late sixteenth-century England between officeholders and the poor
they were willing to present. Medieval evidence from several places has shown
that presentations for sexual immorality, whether to church or to manor court,
were traditionally made by the richest villagers who filled local offices.
They were presentations of the poorest families in village society, whose
daughters were not just an incontinent and lecherous group, but simply a
dowryless group. Late thirteenth- and early fourteenth-century society was
affected by the same stringent economic pressures as late sixteenth- and early
seventeenth-century society. Under them, the young behaved in the same way,
with the same results. But we are not dealing with a 'third world' of the immoral
poor, with the exception of girls who repeatedly bore bastards; nor are we
necessarily dealing with a 'subculture' untouched by religious scruple or moral
conviction. We are dealing with the poor and the dowryless girls, whose luckier
peers became pregnant too, but whose fathers were in a position to pay a portion.
The willingness of the 'rich', the officeholders, to present their poorer neighbours
for sexual offences in the courts was not, as Keith Wrightson thought, new to the
late sixteenth and early seventeenth centuries. Their 'ancestors' had done it all
before. In both societies, sins of the flesh were thought of as sins: but the fact that
the officeholders of Terling in the early seventeenth century also happened to
think of themselves as the 'elect and chosen of God' was probably not fundamental to their actions, although their actions may have been lent extra fervour by
their particular beliefs. I suggest that religion and religious belief are, in this

---

[65] My italics. This example is not dated by Owst, *Literature and Pulpit*, pp. 381–2, but it apparently
echoes a sermon as early as the first half of the thirteenth century, and Bromyard echoes it in his
*Matrimonium* of the late fourteenth century.

particular interpretation, a gigantic red herring. Puritanism was not necessary in the thirteenth century to bring about presentments like this: nor need it have been in the late sixteenth and early seventeenth centuries. The term 'puritan' has been removed from my hypothesis and yet without it, the rest of the equation does not collapse. May we not then question whether 'puritan' is a necessary term in the hypothesis?[66] I do not for one instant dispute that in any period, people of strong religious convictions will express these in rigidly held moral attitudes and actions, unless they happen to be antinomians. I do dispute that this situation was in any way peculiar to puritanism.

I have been arguing, in part, that there is a serious current danger of religious belief being equated with the practice of puritan 'godly discipline', and that it is very necessary to separate puritan beliefs, or the beliefs of the 'hotter sort of protestant' and, indeed, any other type of religious belief, from their moral application to everyday living. Religion cannot only, and solely, be equated with 'social control'. On the other hand, some social historians do not conceive of religion as primarily the recognition on man's part of an external and unseen power with whom he is in relationship, and who is entitled to obedience, reverence and worship, and secondarily with the moral attitudes stemming from this belief, and their effect on the community. I am, of course, perfectly prepared to agree that the moral attitudes of the believer have a profound effect on the community, and that they did so, in the late sixteenth century, in a way Wrightson and Ingram have demonstrated in the ecclesiastical courts. I would not be prepared to admit that this effect was in any way new, although we may, of course, be talking about one of those waves of reform and tightening-up that happen from time to time in both reformed and non-reformed countries in the history of the Christian church.

I have attempted to demonstrate that the lives of very humble people were affected in the late thirteenth century and that they were fined for adultery and fornication then, as in the late sixteenth century, more often if they were poorer. Finally may I extend the principle to its logical and possibly even risible conclusion. The Ten Commandments were themselves, regarded in this light, a prime instrument of social control. From the dating of the earliest version of them, possibly in the thirteenth century BC,[67] even the poorest Jews were liable, judging from *Deuteronomy*, to considerable and possibly unwanted interference in their lives if they coveted their neighbours' wives, or maidservants or actually committed adultery. To regard puritanism as exclusively to do with social control is to do it a gross injustice and to underestimate it. Further, to think or to imply that such social control was new shows a certain shortness of historical perspective on the part of the historians concerned.

---

[66] See above, pp. 42–3.     [67] J. Bright, *A History of Israel* (London, SCM, 1972), pp. 121–3.

**Bibliography**

Martin Ingram, *Church Courts, Sex and Marriage, 1570–1640* (Cambridge, 1987).
Derek J. Plumb, 'John Foxe and the Later Lollards of the Thames Valley', unpublished PhD thesis (Cambridge, 1987).
K. Wrightson and D. Levine, *Poverty and Piety in an English Village: Terling 1525–1700* (New York, 1979).

# XIV

# Can We Count the 'Godly' and the 'Conformable' in the Seventeenth Century?

*Aiacos*:      ...they're going to do
              Things you'd never believe.
              They're going to weigh poetry
              In the scales...
*Xanthias*:                    Tragedy
              Like meat?
*Aiacos*:                    And spirit-levels,
              And rulers for words, and oblong
              Moulds...
*Xanthias*:            Are they making bricks?
                    (Aristophanes, *Frogs*, trans. Patric
                    Dickinson, lines 796–802)

In 1966 Keith Thomas wrote an article in the *Times Literary Supplement* which laid down the axiom, 'All historical propositions relating to the behaviour of large groups, for example...religious activity, are susceptible of treatment in this [statistical] way, and indeed permit of no other.' Social historians have increasingly adopted this approach ever since. It has obviously great merits: I am sometimes afraid, indeed, that the principle is in some ways not being carried far enough, and that only the letter, and not the law, is being implemented. For instance, in my own field, individual village studies, often of high quality, are produced. But their authors frequently omit to indicate the nature of the agricultural and marketing region in which their community lies, and therefore fail to establish either its probable social structure or its 'normality' or 'abnormality' within its area. Quantified studies of great complexity and considerable value are therefore produced; but this value is diminished by the total ignorance of the reader, and sometimes it seems of the author, of the 'typicality' of the example.

I would like to thank Dr Gillian Sutherland for reading and commenting on this paper in draft.

COUNTING THE 'GODLY'?

In the religious field to which Mr Thomas was specifically referring in 1966, careful and illuminating work based on numerical analysis establishing 'normal' religious and devotional behaviour has indeed been done, and is of tremendous importance. But so far has the fashion gone, in a way which may be unfamiliar, indeed, to ecclesiastical historians, that it is sometimes assumed by social historians, who by now do not even question the original axiom, that all types of religious, devotional and spiritual activity can be quantified.

I was led to reflect on this current set of assumptions by a reviewer who made a passing remark, which was not important, within the context of a review[1] of my *Small Books and Pleasant Histories* (London 1981):

> Dr. Spufford confirms the existence of 'genuine popular devotion' (p. 194) in local communities, but is unable to provide any idea of its extent. Here is an instance where quantification would have been useful, since the weight of both qualitative and quantitative evidence continues to show mass apathy or even resistance to religion as defined by the reformers.

This was even more interesting as a passing remark since the page number, correctly cited, of my book led the reader to an attempted statement that quantification in the sense desired was impossible. Reflection led me to feel that, although in some ways I regret that social historians are not establishing their 'norms' with enough care, in others it seems to me that dangerous assumptions of the possibility of quantification are now being made without due consideration. This particular comment seemed to me to be seriously misleading to any historian not closely acquainted with the ecclesiastical sources of the period. It perpetuates an error which appears to be too common amongst social, and even occasionally, ecclesiastical, historians of the seventeenth century and is therefore worth correction. The deduction that would reasonably be made from the remark 'here is an instance in which quantification would have been useful' is not that it had been argued that this was not a possible exercise but that I had failed to perform it. Therefore it seemed that a survey of the available source-material of which I am aware which permits quantification of popular belief in the seventeenth century, together with a due consideration of its shortcomings and its innate bias, might be a useful exercise to both social and ecclesiastical historians. This would permit a safer and more reliable use of the material that does exist.

In 1981 I wrote:

> The degree of importance that religion held in the lives of non-gentle parishioners in the sixteenth and seventeenth centuries will never be established. The beliefs of such people were not normally of interest even to the ecclesiastical authorities, except in special circumstances, or in particularly idiosyncratic church courts. Genuine popular devotion of a humble kind leaves very little trace upon the records of any given time.

[1] Rab Houston in *Social History*, viii (1983), 385–7.

The believer, especially the conforming believer, makes less impact than the dissentient. At no period is it possible to distinguish the conforming believer from the apathetic church-goer who merely wished to stay out of trouble.

It is possible, therefore, for the historian to start from the very probable thesis that the 'hold of any kind of organized religion upon the mass of the population was never more than partial', add the complaints of puritan reforming ministers about their flocks' performance of their uncongenial duties, support these with figures of the considerable minority who were presented for absenteeism in the church courts, and point the case further with the disrespectful remarks of a further minority, which was also presented in the church courts. If it is set against this background, the importance of astrology and magic... then seems very great. Yet the negative picture that emerges is based on the silence of the majority of witnesses.[2]

An alternative picture, illustrating the religious convictions of the humble, also depends on the selection of examples which may be atypical. It runs from the demonstration of the bequests to the church lights, altar and fabric normally made by every parishioner who left a will before the Reformation, through the remarkably concrete fact that over half the Marian martyrs listed by Foxe whose social status is known were agricultural labourers. It continues by showing that the rural laity were actively involved in the complaints against scandalous ministers and in the anti-Laudian petitions of the 1640s. Analysis of the dedicatory clauses disposing of the soul in wills shows that throughout the sixteenth and seventeenth centuries a minority of will makers disposed of their most precious possession in idiosyncratic clauses that were not the normal ones used by the scribe who drew up the will. These idiosyncratic clauses probably therefore reflected the individual convictions of the testators. The records of the separatist churches under the Commonwealth and immediately after it show the very humble involved in religious debate. Examination of the social status of dissenters in their village shows that dissenting opinions were not confined to prosperous yeomen only.[3]

In so far as it is now possible to provide, as my reviewer wished, an idea of the extent of dissenting popular devotion, I have done so for the period after the Commonwealth (*Contrasting Communities*, London 1974, 300–6 especially table 18). But this picture of an involved group of non-gentle rural laity whose religious convictions were often sufficiently important to them for them to risk persecution after the Restoration is, of course, equally partial. It is based mainly, though not entirely, on the records of the separatist churches whose members made up 4 per cent of the adult population according to the Compton Census of 1676. It, like its alternative, is a picture that gives weight to a vocal minority of witnesses.

If both these pictures are partial and based on the records of a minority of witnesses, then they will serve the purposes of neither of the protagonists, since we are all concerned to get at the reality.

How can 'belief' be quantified? There are, of course, presentations in

---

[2] Furthermore, despite the great merits of *Religion and the Decline of Magic*, London 1971, Mr Thomas's findings in it did not, despite his *credo* of 1966, by any means rest firmly on a quantified base. He had presumably discovered the difficulties involved.

[3] See my *Small Books and Pleasant Histories*, London 1981, 194–5.

the church courts. The widest overall survey of these is still in R. A. Marchant, *The Church under the Law* (Cambridge 1969, table 32, p. 219), where he analyses presentments for 75 parishes in Yorkshire, 23 in Cheshire, 49 in Suffolk and 83 in Somerset for a number of years between 1590 and 1633. The overall number of presentations for non-attendance at Holy Communion was 108, or 4.25 per cent, out of 2,544 cases altogether. If non-attendance at church was added, the proportion of cases rose to 11.3 per cent. This figure was in fact slewed by the presentations for the deanery of Sudbury in Suffolk, which was atypical, in that 20 per cent of the cases there related to non-attendance at church or non-reception of Communion. Without these Suffolk parishes the proportion of cases of a 'devotional' kind presented before the church courts was nowhere higher than 10 per cent.

Even if we include Suffolk, it is frankly unbelievable that in the 230 parishes covered by Marchant there should have been only 287 people who failed to come to church or to receive Communion in those years of church court business he analysed. The odds that a parishioner would be presented for bearing a bastard, or for other sexual immorality were nearly three times as high. We cannot believe that we have here statistics for conformity, but only that we have evidence of the type of offence that caused most anxiety to churchwardens, incumbents and ecclesiastical court officials.[4] On the other hand, we do have a rough 'norm' established of the attention these various involved officials were prepared to give to 'devotional' cases. When the proportion rises to over ten or eleven per cent of cases, as in the deanery of Sudbury, we can reasonably guess that other special causes were at work. In the small village of Terling in Essex, which had a living in the Mildmay family's gift, the rate of presentation for failure to receive Communion was far higher than Marchant's 'norm'. Whereas Marchant found only 108 such presentations from 230 parishes, no fewer than 31 such presentations were made at Terling in the last thirty years of the sixteenth century. In the first thirty years of the seventeenth century such presentations were succeeded by prosecutions for failure to attend church. Drs Wrightson and Levine counted a total of 151 'religious offences' (unfortunately not broken down by type) among the presentations in the ecclesiastical courts between 1570 and 1639. Thirty-eight per cent of all offences presented came in this category. However, since the vicar between 1604 and 1625 was a puritan, followed between 1625 and 1631 by a separatist who would not use the Prayer Book, and since these incumbents had a band of five churchwardens of their own mind, this figure is almost impossible to interpret. It necessarily includes all presentments of the self-styled 'godly' against their fellow villagers, who either interpreted their religion differently, or not at all. However, it also included the presentations against the churchwardens who were in office

---

[4] For lack of space I have not included here figures from Ralph Houlbrooke, *Church Courts and the People during the English Reformation 1520–70*, London 1979, or from Martin Ingram's unpublished Oxford D.Phil. thesis (1976), 'Ecclesiastical justice in Wiltshire, 1600–1640'.

themselves in 1632, after the deprivation of the separatist vicar, for 'that they had neither divine service nor sermon in their church on Easter day last, nor on lowe sunday, nor on most of the holy daies in the yeare last past'. In other words, the wardens had made it impossible for any 'conformable' members of the laity to communicate, had they so desired.[5] Therefore, the figures on the whole reflect the activity of one religious group, which indeed in Terling became a sect, although for further confusion they also include the derelictions, according to the law of the Church, of that same group. In the single parish of Cranbrook in Kent, under a Protestant vicar who had three puritan curates, the rate of presentation for failure to receive Communion was even higher still. There were 114 such cases between 1560 and 1607. This was more than in all of Marchant's 230 parishes put together. It is likely that failure to attend church, or communicate, at Cranbrook was a response to the 'puritanism' of some of the curates.[6]

The high number of presentations cannot possibly be taken as reflecting general religious indifference, but only the lively activities of the 'godly'. Those who consider themselves 'elect' are the last to take as reliable witnesses on the spiritual state or beliefs of those they themselves considered 'unregenerate'. The same bias casts even more fundamental doubt on the often-quoted number of 34 communicants who were eventually admitted into fellowship by Ralph Josselin at Earl's Colne in 1651, after a gap in the celebration of Holy Communion, as Josselin wrote himself, of nearly nine years. Josselin, fortunately, described very fully his doubts and misgivings leading up to the Communion, including the occasion 'when divers came that wee could not comfortably joyne with...I spake as god enabled mee, that wee should search peoples knowledge and admonish them in point of scandall...then...bade our company to give in their names, *most went*, a few gave in their names' (my italics). Two days later, 'I admonisht divers, admitted others with consent, divers Christians hunge backe.' Even on the occasion of the celebration itself 'after the ordinance was done, and the collection for the poore, the rest withdrew we stayed'.[7] Thirty-four communicants, in these circumstances, is a meaningless figure. Of the non-communicants who had come to initial meetings, 'most went'. They had been subjected to intense social pressure to do so by their 'shepherd'. Yet it is altogether too easy now for the student to cite Terling or Earl's Colne as 'typical' examples of religious indifference by the laity, when due consideration shows they were probably highly abnormal. It is this lack of a statistical frame, and of an attempt to establish what is 'normal' that sometimes worries me about individual village studies.

The Laudians or 'proto-Laudians', of course, manipulated the church

[5] Keith Wrightson and David Levine, *Poverty and Piety in an English Village: Terling 1525–1700*, New York, San Francisco, London 1979, 119 (Table 5.2), 156, 158–60.

[6] Patrick Collinson, 'Cranbrook and the Fletchers', in *Godly People*, London 1983, 410 (Table I), 418–19.

[7] *The Diary of Ralph Josselin, 1616–1683*, ed. A. Macfarlane, London 1976, 77, 96, 234–7.

courts too. It is likely that some of the 39 men and women out of the 139 lay people presented in one of the deaneries of Bath and Wells in 1617[8] for not receiving Communion or attending church were puritans.

Furthermore, the petition of the freeholders of Hertfordshire to the Commons in 1640 may well have had Laudian incumbents in mind. They complained most precisely that they had of late years been overburdened

> by Innovations in matters of religion by some violent and indiscrete cleargy men, who in many Towns of this County under pretense of authority have boldly violated and audaciously attempted many things contrary to ye Canons of ye Church, ye Rubrick, and Book of Common Prayer, ye Proclamations of our religious Kings and Princes, and our most gracious Soveraigne King Charles and to ye acts of Parliament established, and in our Bibles imprinted. They daring to deny even ye holy sacrament, even for a yeare together, to hundreds in our Congregations, and *where they have found opposition* to reject great numbers which wee well know to be conformable persons and to give no offence in ther lives to ye Congregation. And where they have found opposition by ther Parishioners herein, ye course hath beene to cite great numbers of ye poorer sort of people to ye Ecclesiasticall Courts (wherein themselves are for ye most part ye Judges).[9]

Again 'comfortable persons', those rejected by Josselin also, were the sufferers. It is impossible that, in view of both puritan and Laudian activity in the church courts, the figures of presentments in them dealing with non-attendance and non-reception of Communion do not conceal very considerable local 'purges' made by one or another group. Where the percentage of court cases reflecting belief rises startlingly higher than Canon Marchant's 'norm' reflecting the attention of officials usually given to this type of case, as in the deanery of Sudbury, the parish of Terling, or the deanery of Cary in Bath and Wells, we may suspect the activity of a group of enthusiasts or zealots of either puritan or Laudian persuasion, debarring 'comfortable persons' from Communion in the way the freeholders of Hertfordshire complained. We may not, as social historians frequently do, assume that we have here statistics for apathy or indifference. That assumption is as ridiculous as its antithesis, the wholesale adoption of the 'normal' rate of presentation for devotional offences in the church courts, would be as an index of conformity. We may not, of course, assume that all those presented in one of these local purges were 'conformable persons' with any genuine interest in religion, who were the victims either of the 'godly' or the Laudians, but we may not assume either that they were not. We simply do not know. This was my original point in 1981.

It does not seem that the percentages drawn from the total number of cases in the church courts for absenteeism given above justify the original reviewer's deduction that 'qualitative and quantitative evidence shows mass apathy or even resistance to religion' *except* 'as defined by the

---

[8] Margaret Stieg, *Laud's Laboratory: The Diocese of Bath and Wells in the early Seventeenth Century*, Lewisburg 1982, Table 9:15.

[9] *Proceedings of the Short Parliament of 1640*, ed. Esther S. Cope with William H. Coates (Camden Society, 4th ser., xix, 1977), 277.

reformers'. Eleven per cent of cases do not constitute a 'mass'. My 'considerate minority' (*Small Books*, p. 194) seems to me nearer the mark. On the other hand, if we take the abnormal cases of Terling, or Earl's Colne, where religion was indeed 'defined by the reformers', the reviewer was, of course, absolutely right. I am not, naturally, denying the utility of those cases brought in the church courts on devotional or religious grounds to the historian of popular religion. On the contrary, these cases throw invaluable light not only on the attitudes of 'puritans' in office but also on the attitudes of 'conformists' who wanted services according to the Prayer Book, whose existence has been wholly neglected.[10] I only deny their validity as a basis for statistics.

The issue is, I believe, whether we are, like the reviewer, considering 'religion *as defined by the reformers*' (my italics) or, like me, considering the religion of the '*conforming believer*' (again my italics). The reviewer's definition is the one adopted by most social historians at present. Yet in this it seems to me there is an inbuilt error. The 'godly' were a self-styled group, as Professor Collinson so clearly points out. When a 'godly' man was beneficed, he would deny admission to the sacraments to those he considered unworthy, as Josselin did. If he was of greater importance, he would bemoan the lukewarmness of the 'unregenerate' in print. When a layman of stature in his own village was 'godly' he would frequently insert himself into office as a churchwarden. This did not only happen in Terling. Over a third of the wardens or questmen responsible for pre-sentments in nine Cambridgeshire parishes also signed a petition against episcopal government.[11] These office-holders therefore had an undue influence on the presentment of offences. We are therefore considering a whole set of biased records, some written with deliberate, if convinced, propagandist intent. Yet, with a naiveté that seems quite extraordinary, contemporary social historians swallow at their face value the judgements made by the 'godly' on those they themselves considered 'unreformed'. An initial recognition by an historian of the biased nature of the 'godly' man's comments on his own seventeenth-century society is usually followed by tacit acceptance of the judgements and values of the 'godly'. This acceptance is always signalled by the quiet dropping of quotation marks. For example, in a sensitive and splendid passage, Dr Wrightson uses Ralph Josselin's own distinctions between 'our society', 'my sleepy hearers' and 'the families that seldom heare'.[12] Dr Wrightson points out that 'the effective ministry of the pastor had become confined to a minority'. Yet, by the bottom of the same page, he is talking of the 'extent of the alienation of the mass of the unregenerate population from the Commonwealth Church', as well as 'the limited success of the enthusiastic preachers sent

[10] The latter are now under investigation by Miss Judith Maltby with a view to a Ph.D. dissertation at Cambridge. I am grateful to Miss Maltby for calling the Hertfordshire petition quoted above to my attention.

[11] My *Contrasting Communities*, 269.

[12] Keith Wrightson, *English Society, 1580–1680*, London 1982, 218.

out to win the people to godliness'. Neither 'unregenerate' nor 'godliness' appears in quotation marks. Thus is the contemporary judgement of a minority group which considered itself 'elect' taken over and received by social historians, who fail to remember the propagandist nature of the material. The mistake is a dangerous one, because no historian who is not closely acquainted with the material, let alone an undergraduate, can possibly be expected to identify or rectify it. It is somewhat as if only those who actually came forward as converts at a current meeting held by Billy Graham were acceptable as countable Christians.

Only two types of source seem to me to exist which may give us a more inclusive and less partial basis for counting Anglicans who took at least some active interest in their faith in the seventeenth century. The diocesan communicants' returns for 1603 have been used more or less frequently by demographers, but rarely by historians with popular religion in mind. Professor Dickens used the returns in this way in a glancing reference in 1948[13]. The figures he used have recently been corrected by Professor Wrigley and Dr Schofield, who arrive at a figure of 2,091,000 persons for England and add a quarter to adjust for omitted adults, giving a total of 2,700,000 persons able to receive Communion.[14] I suggest that the number of communicants amongst the two million persons listed could well be used to give a blanket estimate of those with a surviving interest in religion. There is, however, almost inevitably, a major difficulty here. Most returns are recorded in summarised form only, and although those for some dioceses do so in a manner which may indicate non-communicants, as well as both communicants and recusants, the returns for only two dioceses are completely unambiguous. The two dioceses, Ely and London, are fortunately from areas of almost totally different settlement pattern, economy and social structure. Ely returned 30,569 persons who received, did not receive, or were recusant. Of these 668 were non-communicants and 19 were recusant. The two together amounted to just over 2 per cent of the total. Amazingly enough, the diocese of London, with its total of 148,747 possible communicants returned, had an even lower percentage of recusants and non-receivers together. They amounted to a bare 1.3 per cent of dissident opinion. Figures for a further two archdeaconries may probably also be trusted. For the two archdeaconries of Bedford and

[13] A. G. Dickens, 'The extent and character of recusancy in Yorkshire, 1604', *Yorkshire Archaeological Journal*, xxxvii (1948), 32. Dr David Palliser kindly supplied me with this reference. He has himself listed, with L. J. Jones, the surviving returns for 1563 and 1603 in *Local Population Studies*, xxx (1983), 55–8. He has also used them for both England and Wales, in the form uncorrected by Wrigley and Schofield, in *The Age of Elizabeth: England under the later Tudors, 1547–1603*, London 1983, 331. I am also particularly grateful to Dr Palliser for supplying me with the detailed figures for Ely and London, referred to later in this paragraph, from his own files, as well as much general information. The 1563 and 1603 returns are currently being investigated in detail by him.
[14] E. A. Wrigley and R. Schofield, *The Population History of England 1541–1871*, London 1981, 569. I have, of course, omitted the 35 per cent that they added to represent those under sixteen, who were also mainly non-communicants.

Buckingham, in the diocese of Lincoln, for which apparently full figures of communicants, non-communicants and recusants exist, only one-half of one per cent failed to receive Communion out of a total of 29,050 able to do so.[15] These figures are really very low indeed, and suggest a large turnout of active conformists. Certainly nothing like mass apathy is in question here.

One of the few historians who has used the Communicants' Returns in a manner related to their original purpose is Peter Burke, who used a figure of 75 per cent of communicants in the diocese of Lincoln in 1603 as evidence for limited popular support of the Church. Whether three-quarters of the population returned as communicants would have constituted a low level of conformity is debatable, but at least the material for a genuine debate appeared to exist. Unfortunately the figures used by Mr Burke turn out to be wrong, but surely he was on the right lines to think of using the 1603 returns.[16] Possibly future work will discover original and full returns for more than two dioceses and two archdeaconries.[17] Meanwhile, we do at least have figures for just over 200,000 people, or around a tenth of the adult population returned. These figures represent a better base for argument than any parochial work can possibly do, since, whatever pressure the communicants were under, Marchant's figures show that these pressures were very much less than those involved in the intense local purges by puritans, as in Earl's Colne, or by Laudians, as in Hertfordshire.

From these we may be clear that a very low percentage of non-receivers of Communion existed in 1603 in the two dioceses of Ely and London and in two of the archdeaconries of Lincoln, at least as far as the ecclesiastical officials were concerned. We may also note in passing that, although they could undoubtedly do with as much testing and checking from other sources as possible, the figures for both dioceses and both archdeaconries are convincingly odd ones, in no way made up of round numbers for ease of addition, or for ecclesiastical comfort. However, the major difficulty of how to treat the rest of the returns which either contain communicants and recusants only, or an ambiguous category which might be non-

[15] *The State of the Church in the Reigns of Elizabeth and James I as Illustrated by Documents Relating to the Diocese of Lincoln*, ed. C. W. Foster (Lincoln Record Society, xxiii, 1926), i. 443-5.

[16] Peter Burke, 'Religion and secularisation', in Peter Burke (ed.), *New Cambridge Modern History*, xiii (Companion Volume), Cambridge 1979, 309. Burke took his figures from A. D. Gilbert, *Religion and Society in Industrial England*, London 1976, who based them in turn on a note in Canon Foster's introduction to his Lincoln diocesan documents, op. cit., p. lviii. The actual number of communicants given in the bishop of Lincoln's return of 1603 was 196,926. There were forty non-communicants listed for two archdeaconries only, but the relevant columns for the other archdeaconries were left blank; Foster, ibid., pp. 444-5. The archbishop's summary of figures of communicants for Lincoln shot them up to 242,550, and, reasonably in the circumstances, he added 'quere'. As Canon Foster wrote, rather dryly, 'most of the figures in this summary have been altered, and their appearance does not inspire confidence' (p. lv).

[17] Some of these may appear in the course of Dr Palliser's research, and others may indeed be already in print, since my investigations for this communication have necessarily been of the briefest kind.

receivers, remains. It is compounded by Wrigley and Schofield's suggestion that the overall total of adults able to receive Communion should be raised by a quarter, to cover omissions. It might be most proper, however, to estimate that those under-enumerated contained a similar ratio of communicants to non-communicants as that contained in the two million who were enumerated. However, if all those added to compensate for under-registration are counted as non-communicants, certainly no one could accuse the historian with an interest in conformity of over-optimism. Neither way do we end up with numbers which indicate mass apathy or mass indifference to the point which will face even minor ecclesiastical penalties for non-reception.[18]

Professor Wrigley and Dr Schofield's work on the Compton Census of 1676 suggests that the sections of it which refer to communicants may well be more reliable than has been previously supposed.[19] If so, it may also give some quantifiable guide to conformity in the later seventeenth century. To anyone who dismisses the material completely on the grounds that the communicants of 1603 or 1676 were 'subject to social pressure', I can only say that they, as a whole group, cannot all have been subject to the kind of extreme distorting pressure exerted by Ralph Josselin in Earl's Colne. So large a spread of material, although it must include, of course, many parishes where particular pressures from either puritan or 'proto-Laudians' were at work, probably cancels out any such distortions. It might well be objected that the payment of a shilling fine, to which noncommunicants were liable, did indeed constitute 'social pressure'. However, the loss of a single day's wages was arguably much less extreme a pressure than the emotional soul-searching with which Josselin, for instance blackmailed his flock.

The second source which may bear on popular religion more precisely, and may actually give us some detail, are the practically unknown 'Easter Books' or 'Token Books' which survive for a few urban areas for the late sixteenth and early seventeenth century and sometimes list communicants street by street. Those for Southwark have been worked on by Dr Jeremy Boulton, and those for Salisbury and elsewhere by Dr S. J. Wright. If these were used to explore the purposes for which they were initially drawn up, rather than as demographic sources, we might have some hard facts about religious practice, at least in towns.[20] Until then, I continue to feel that religious belief is not quantifiable. I am prepared to admit that the 1603 communicants' returns and the Compton Census may give us an index of conformity of the most general kind, and that the Easter Books may give us a more precise index, relating only to urban areas. But the first

[18] Foster, n. 15 above, shows from the ecclesiastical court records that non-communicants were usually admonished and were willing to conform.

[19] Wrigley and Schofield, *Population History*, 570 and ch. 2.

[20] It is just possible that Miss Maltby's current work on the few petitions in favour of the Prayer Book which bear original signatures may reveal another source for a few rural areas. They, however, will only permit the historian to count the 'conformable', not the 'godly'.

two are only acceptable because they are all-inclusive enough for individual parochial distortions to be cancelled out, at least to some extent. They are also large-scale enough to provide a sample. I am not prepared to concede that the 'godly' were the only members of the laity to hold religious beliefs in seventeenth-century England. If anyone has new sources to add to those I have listed above I should be delighted. I have been searching for sources which permit me to quantify genuine religious conviction of all types for some fifteen years. Until I find more, I shall continue to feel that although measurement and its instruments, spirit-levels, rulers and moulds, should all be used to their fullest sensible limit, and that quantification must always establish the 'norm' where possible, there are areas beyond its reach. Aristophanes failed to see the utility of weighing tragedy. Can we weigh souls, or count them?

# XV

## THE IMPORTANCE OF THE LORD'S SUPPER TO SEVENTEENTH-CENTURY DISSENTERS[1]

I am a social historian interested in the practice of religion, and involved in a debate with other social historians of the seventeenth-century about the importance of religious practice. This paper concentrates on the sacramental content of seventeenth-century religion, which to the Dissenters was so inextricably connected with the Word.[2] Quite apart from the intrinsic vital importance of the subject, I am, as a social historian, interested in habitual, repeated experiences of a ritual kind. It seems to me that the importance of the experience of the dominical sacraments (and I would like to concentrate only on the Lord's Supper) is severely underestimated amongst social historians. Nor is their potential importance to the participants understood. For this reason I have been led from considering what contemporary social historians think of seventeenth-century religion, to what sacramental actions were regularly performed in the seventeenth-century: from there, very dangerously, since I am

1.  This piece was given as the Annual Lecture to the United Reformed Church History Society in September 1988. The serious illness and death of my daughter precluded publication until now. I would particularly like to thank Dr. Clyde Binfield, the Editor, for his kindness and forbearance and the members of the audience, including Dr. David Thompson and the Revd. Ronald Bocking, for their warmth and helpful suggestions. Parts of the text will be included in the 'Introduction' to my forthcoming book, *The World of Rural Dissenters, 1520-1725* (Cambridge, 1993). I should like to thank the Netherlands Institute for Advanced Study, which has given me the opportunity to revise it now.
2.  I owe the original remark which stimulated me to write this paper and to the exegesis of "Fat Things" to Dr. Eamon Duffy. He is in no way responsible, however, for any errors into which I have fallen.

neither an ecclesiastical historian, nor a theologian, to the significance of those actions, and the possible meaning to those participants who are actively rather than passively involved.[3]

I was much struck by an essay of Natalie Davis's[4] in which she suggests that one of the defects of historians of popular religion is a propensity to proceed as if their important task is to separate the grain from the chaff, to distinguish between beliefs and practices that are "truly" religious, and those which are "superstitious" or "magical". This, she suggests, is to do a serious injury to the complexity of the network of beliefs and practices to be found, for instance, in late seventeenth-century France. There the people made their required Easter Communion; the parish Mass was the centre of religious life: and yet the peasantry were also polytheistic, deflecting Christian Sacraments to this-worldly ends, or making use of pagan rites. If, says Natalie Davis, we stamp as "superstition" peasant ceremonial dancing, or the fires and leaping on the Feast of St John the Baptist, will we be able to see how these things were intended to protect the biological and agricultural life of the village, and comprehend how they perpetuated, in sacred celebration, moods of festivity and joyful ecstasy which were sorely lacking in the post-Tridentine Church?

It seems to me that Natalie Davis is right: that the separation of the investigation of "religious" beliefs and "magical" ones creates an artificial division which did not exist to the uneducated, and perhaps still does not. The *Oxford English Dictionary* definition of "religion" is "the human recognition of supernatural controlling power, and especially of a personal God" whereas the definition of "magic" is "the pretended act of influencing the course of events by occult control of nature, or of spirit, witchcraft". The two are very close. If Natalie Davis is right, then I, for one, stand convicted of error because in the 1970s I studied religious beliefs amongst Cambridgeshire villagers, and only investigated the spread of beliefs which theologians would have recognised as "religious".[5] But I am in good company: Keith Thomas makes no distinctions between the truth or authenticity of the Catholic, Protestant, astrological and witchcraft beliefs he studies, but he does, on the other hand, make distinctions between the functions of magic and religion. Magic to Keith Thomas comprises the methods and practices intended to tap supernatural power for solving concrete problems and misfortunes; religion, to him, has functions of explanation and consolation, supplies a moral code, and has important connections with the social order, reinforcing it, suppressing it and sometimes criticising it.[6] It seems to have little or nothing to do with the believer's creed that

3.  Professor Patrick Collinson in his presidential address to the Ecclesiastical History Society in June 1988 drew attention to the fact that historians, unlike anthropologists, do not evaluate routine which he felt might be a useful thing to do.
4.  "Some Tasks and Themes in the Study of Popular Religion" in *The Pursuit of Holiness in Late Medieval and Renaissance Religion*, ed. C. Trinkhaus and H.A. Oberman (Leiden, 1974).
5.  *Contrasting Communities* (PB, 1979, Part III).
6.  Keith Thomas, *Religion and the Decline of Magic* (1971), pp. 26-8, 46-7, 73-77, 151-54.

he or she is establishing a relationship with a supernatural controlling power. Religion is "rational", magic is not.

Now I would like in this paper to question this assumption amongst social historians that religion is "rational", and primarily concerned with morals, social order, and even, at the Holy Communion, with social bonding, for according to Sir Keith "Communion symbolises the unity of believers". The symbols involved in the participation of the Lord's Supper are surely much deeper and much richer than that: so I want initially to consider the proportion of the seventeenth-century population regularly involved in the celebration of Holy Communion, the breaking of bread, or the Lord's Supper, and what it might have meant to them.

"Statistics" of religious practice, in the very limited sense that they exist for the seventeenth-century, are necessary, for they give an overall impression of the proportion of the community exposed to religious experience. They are important in establishing what is "normal" in seventeenth-century religious practice. But they are also misleading, for they include a whole spectrum of belief, ranging from those who are merely induced by social pressure and the fear of a 12d fine to conform, right through to people for whom the practice of religion was a conscious and important act of belief and, ultimately, to those who could, and did, face martyrdom for their beliefs. They are misleading in a deeper sense too: casual use by the historian implies the passivity of the subject, and this implies a flaw in the historian's relation to the people who are the object of study, a lack of respect for the human beings involved which was splendidly objected to by Richard Cobb in 1971:

> I do not care to learn that members of the upper bourgeoisie of Elbeuf possessed from 6-20 servants, but members of the middle bourgeoisie of Elbeuf possessed from 2-6 servants, and the members of the lower bourgeoisie of Elbeuf possessed from 0-2 servants. I do not know what sort of a non-person a 0 servant can be: and I even find it distasteful thus to equate the number of servants to visible signs of wealth and status, along with knives and forks and silver teapots, pairs of sheets and household linen, even if this may in fact be a useful measurement for the assessment of relative wealth. Perhaps I am being sentimental, but it disturbs me to see ... country girls sweating it out below stairs, or freezing in the attic, the object of the lust of the Master and his sons, being further humiliated, long after their death, by being forced into graphs in the galleyships of ... doctoral candidates.

> These girls after all, however poor, possess their own identity, and faces, sometimes pretty ones, though generally pock-marked, often a generous and open disposition, a great deal of naivete, a

proneness to revere and obey their fathers and to love and slave for their brothers, even if their intellectual baggage was as limited as their wardrobe.[7]

What Cobb is objecting to, with a force for which "passion" is not too strong a word, is not the use of numbers, but the degree of depersonalisation that may go with them, the loss of the "wealth and variety of human motivations ... the myriad variations of human lives". Despite this, statistics are still indispensable to establish the experience to which seventeenth-century society was normally exposed, so long as we go further after establishing them. So I shall be using the figures for communicants in 1603, and the Compton Census of 1676, to establish this statistical "frame". But I shall try to take the exploration further: I want to end by considering, the words of Isaac Watts at the very end of the seventeenth century, and Philip Doddridge, in the early eighteenth century, what these routine sacramental actions might have symbolised to the tiny minority of Dissenters to whom, we may be quite sure, the practice of their religion was indeed a conscious and important act of belief.

There were, I have no doubt, equally convinced conformists: but it far more difficult to get at the meaning of the beliefs of conformists, who were not singled out, or persecuted, for the practice of their faith.

The great faith of the French school of religious sociology founded by Le Bras in the 1930s seems to me that its members are Catholics, who comprehend the tradition in which they are working, as well as, in Le Bras' own words "desiring to see things as they are" and therefore examining religious behaviour with scrupulous detached statistical exactitude. A splendid example is Toussaert's work on *Religious Belief in Late Medieval Flanders.*[8] Jacques Toussaert was an Abbé, and his book was originally a doctoral thesis, of which he wrote

> This work is not only put in front of my examiners, it is also in the presence of an invisible multitude of bishops, priests, religious and the medieval laity themselves: they know, at this present time, what was their strength and what was their weakness: they have already seen their terrestrial history in the light of the Divine Presence and their eternal end is ruled by the sole True Judge who knows all ... and also will judge these lines.[9]

This is not exactly the normal phraseology to be found in an English PhD thesis. It would certainly startle the examiners considerably to be put so firmly in their place in the hierarchy of judgement. Moreover the comprehension of the whole passage depends on the comprehension of the doctrine of the Communion of Saints, which might not be the first intellectual framework to

---

7.  Richard Cobb, "Historians in White Coats", *Times Literary Supplement,* Dec. 3, 1971, pp. 1528-7.
8.  J. Toussaert, *Le Sentiment réligieux en Flandre à la fin du Moyen Age* (1963).
9.  *Ibid,* p. 487.

come to the minds of most English social historians. Because Abbé Toussaert works from inside the tradition, he is able to write of the Mass:

> On each Easter Day, each Sunday, and every other day of obligation imposed by the Church, each Christian ... to affirm his faith in the Resurrected Church in an external gesture, by which he unites himself to Christ, and to His redemptive sacrifice, the Cross, the Resurrection and the Ascension. At the holy table, if the Christian wishes to unite himself more fully with the Person of Christ, he feeds on the Son of God himself.[10]

From these beginnings, anchored in a tradition, he understands he writes an exact, and in the French sense of the word "scientific" thesis, which concludes that the Flemish laity were largely indifferent to communion and confession in the fifteenth century; naive, excited and sensationalistic in matters of faith, timing their sporadic religious activity to occasions defined by family needs, natural catastrophes, and folk-tradition. There was a general religiosity, an extraordinary stress on peripheral details of piety and observance, a calendar marked off in the rhythm of the liturgical seasons and feasts, but an absence of what a theologian would recognise as genuine informal devotion.[11] Toussaert thus understates the importance of the "general religiosity" he finds, which to Natalie Davis would be of extreme importance. Yet it seems to me to be a great strength of his that he does understand what was supposed to be going on a fifteenth-century Mass, even if he feels that the ignorant Flemish laity probably did not understand it.

By comparison Keith Thomas ends his consideration of religion by writing:

> Stoicism had become the basic religious message for those in misfortune ... it was the general social importance of religion which enabled it to outlive magic. For magic had no Church, *no Communion symbolising the unity of believers* [my italics] it remains an interesting question as to how religion's social functions made it possible to survive when magic had been found redundant. But it would be a question *mal posée* if it were not remembered that the official religion of industrial England was one from which the primitive 'magical' elements had been very largely shorn.[12]

I suggest that an interpretation of religion is not adequately full if it describes as "rational" and "socially cohesive" a set of ritual practices that involved at their heart, even for Dissenters who had no set form of service,[13] consecrating the

---

10. *Ibid,* pp. 122-3.
11. *Ibid,* p. 499.
12. *Religion and the Decline of Magic,* p. 766.
13. Stephen Mayor, *The Lord's Supper in Early English Dissent,* (1972) pp. 154, 155-6, 157.

elements with Christ's words of institution at the Last Supper "take, eat: this is my body, which is broken for you: do this in remembrance of me... This cup is the new testament in my blood: this do ye, as oft ye drink it in remembrance of me."[14] These are surely not words shorn of primitive significance; nor are they words which express merely a comfortable social cohesion between those who say them, however they are interpreted. They express a belief in, and a search for, an exterior being who is supposed to be in some relationship with the participant; and their meaning could no more be expressed in purely "rational" terms than can the desire of Bishop Cooper in Lincoln in the 1580s that his parishioners might "eat the body and blood of Christ more effectually and fruitfully".[15]

It is no part of my general design, or competence, to trace the development of Anglican or Dissenting doctrine on the Eucharist or Lord's Supper and its application through the sixteenth and seventeenth centuries. It is only my design to consider the actions in which common people were routinely involved in those centuries, before considering the possible significance of those actions for them.

The laity were, as William Harrison wrote in his *Description of England* in 1577[16] expected regularly to be at Morning and Evening Prayer on Sundays:[17] Morning Prayer included the Epistle, Gospel, and Nicene Creed followed by a sermon or homily, unless there was to be a Communion. Cranmer, like Calvin, started off with the idea of a weekly, corporate Communion in English[18] but this idea was never realised. According to the rubrics of the Book of Common Prayer in 1559 "every Parishioner shall communicate at the least three times in a year: of which Easter to be one".[19] One of my unresolved problems is to work out whether the common English parishioner in the sixteenth century, asked to communicate at a Holy Communion in a tongue he could understand, three times a year, compared with attending a Mass he could not understand every Sunday, suffered a diminution, or an increase, in the sacramental content of his life. Certainly the Easter Eucharist of obligation continued to be well attended. A.G. Dickens calculated there were 2.25 million communicants in England and Wales in 1603, which was probably something like seventy-five per cent of the

---

14. I Corinthians 11, vv. 24-5 (Authorised Version).
15. Thomas Cooper *A briefe homily wherein the most comfortable and right use of the Lords Supper is very plainly opened and delivered, even to the understanding of the unlearned and ignorant* (London 1580), A ii (a) – B i (a), *cit* John E Booty, "Preparation for the Lord's Supper in Elizabethan England". *Anglican Theological Review* XLIX (1967), p. 132.
16. William Harrison, *Description of England,* ed. G.Edelen (1968), p. 34.
17. Professor Collinson in his presidential address to the Ecclesiastical History Society in 1988 estimated that 500 hours were spent annually at the reading of Morning and Evening Prayer.
18. John E. Booty, *art cit.,* p. 144.
19. *Ibid,* p. 144.

adult population, that is the population over sixteen.[20] There are certain difficulties about this, in view of Dr. Wrigley's and Dr. Schofield's population figures for 1603, which suggest that the communicants' returns omitted something like a quarter or a fifth of the adult population. Nevertheless, even if all those omitted were non-communicants, which is the most pessimistic reading, and therefore the most suitable for our purposes, the figures still suggest that the laity cared about its Easter Communion despite the undoubted undermining of habit and continuity so vital to religious practice, which was precipitated by the constant upheavals in the clergy, in language and in the arrangement of church interiors symbolising the rearrangements of theological attitudes caused by the Reformation. In the Diocese of Ely, for instance, the altar was removed from chancels in 1550 and replaced by a "decent table suitable for the administration of the sacrament of bread and wine" in the nave: it was carried back up again with the reintroduction of the Mass in 1553, and carried down again on its reabolition in 1559. The constant disturbances in the position of the altar led churchwardens to fail to repave the place where the altar had stood, obviously uncertain of its lasting position. There was then acute disturbance over the repositioning of the altar in the 1630s.[21]

Until recently demographers have been the chief users of the returns of communicants made by the bishops in 1603. Peter Burke first used them in 1979 as they were originally composed, as a kind of census of religious conformists, and religious behaviour at the beginning of James's reign,[22] for the Diocese of Lincoln, where in Easter Week 1603, seventy-five per cent of those eligible to receive the sacrament had actually done so. Again, whether this indicates a low or a high attendance is not my concern, although three-quarters of those eligible seems to me not bad after a period of such great upheaval.

More recently, in an important article, Jeremy Boulton has examined the administration of Communion in two rapidly-growing London parishes, St.

---

20.   A.G. Dickens, "Extent and Character of Recusancy in Yorkshire, 1604", *Yorks. Arch. Jo.*, XXXVII, Part I (1948), p. 32. I owe this reference to the kindness of Professor D.M. Palliser. Dickens relies on the figures of B. Magee, *The English Recusants*, who calculates a total of 2,250,765 communicants in England and Wales. He says elsewhere that Dr. Magee's figures should be regarded with reserve (*art cit*, p. 28, n. 3). E.A. Wrigley and R.S. Schofield, *The Population History of England, 1541-1871* (1981), p. 569 arrive at a total of 2.091 million adult communicants, non-conmunicants and recusants in 1603 for England, excluding Wales. They suggest adding thirty-five per cent to these figures for the proportion of the population under sixteen, which would bring the population total for England to 3.217 million. They then suggest that the total should have been 4.156 million, so that the communicants' survey missed between a quarter and a fifth of the adult population. There is no way of reconciling Professor Dickens's figure with those of Dr. Wrigley and Dr. Schofield, because of the inclusion in one case, and exclusion in the other, of Wales.
21.   *Contrasting Communities*, pp. 242-3, 268.
22.   Lincolnshire Record Society, XXIII, p. lviii. Cited A.D. Gilbert, *Religion and Society in Industrial England: Church, Chapel and Social Change, 1740-1914* (Longman, 1976), p. 6. Peter Burke, "Religion and Secularisation" in Peter Burke (ed) *New Cambridge Modern History*, XIII (Companion Volume) Cambridge 1979, p. 309.

Botolph's-without-Aldgate and St. Saviour's, Southwark, on the south bank of the Thames.[23] St. Saviour's had a series of token books which was unique for London, although they exist for other large towns and cities, which recorded both tokens delivered out to intended communicants, and those received back again. This issue of tokens was not to exclude the "ungodly" from Communion, which was "open" to St. Saviour's, but was simply to pay for the expense of delivering Communion in both kinds, which included at St. Saviour's, for instance, the purchase of seventy gallons of wine in 1613. Dr. Boulton's examination of the issue and receipt of these tokens demonstrates that in this parish in late Elizabethan and Jacobean London between eighty and ninety-eight per cent of potential communicants made an annual Communion. This mass attendance, as he writes, "cannot be written off solely as a form of social control", although, as he adds,

> Admittedly, there were the constraints of ecclesiastical penalties on parishioners to attend Holy Communion and the payment of 6d made for the communion tokens by a poor householder and his wife after 1620, representing nearly half a day's wages, might also have been a significant inducement to attend communion following the delivery of tokens.

Yet it was perfectly possible to receive a token, and not attend Communion, so the high proportion of tokens probably does, in Dr. Boulton's opinion, represent "an element of popular demand for the communion service".[24]

In 1981, I wrote:

> The degree of importance that religion held in the lives of non-gentle parishioners will never be established... genuine popular devotion of a humble kind leaves very little trace on the records of any given time. The believer, especially the comforting believer, makes less impact than the dissentient. At no period is it possible to distinguish the conforming believer from the apathetic church-goer who merely wished to stay out of trouble.[25]

By that cautious judgement I stand. But I think that Dr. Burke's seventy-five per cent of communicants in 1603 in the Diocese of Lincoln, and Dr. Boulton's eighty to ninety-eight per cent of potential communicants in the late-sixteenth and early-seventeenth-century in Southwark demonstrate that the mass of the population were still participating in the major rituals of the Elizabethan

---

23. J.P. Boulton, "The Limits of Formal Religion: The Administration of Holy Communion in Late Elizabethan and Early Stuart London", *The London Journal*, 10 (1984), pp. 135-153, especially 137 and 149. I believe that Dr. Susan Wright has a major piece of work in hand on the token books of other cities, although it may be more demographically focussed.
24. *Art cit.*, p. 149.
25. *Small Books and Pleasant Histories* (London, 1981), pp. 194-5.

church, and that the weight of the evidence points to a participating mass, not to the "mass apathy" cited by some social historians. This participating mass was at least familiar with the Communion Service. Some of the people who made up this mass, even a majority perhaps, may have been the kind of people who, in their behaviour or beliefs, were the despair of the Elizabethan Reformers. In 1618, at St Saviour's in Southwark, communion tokens were delivered to Jane Toby, a single woman living in the churchyard, who had two bastard children living in her household. A third bastard child of hers was baptised in 1621.[26] So members of what Peter Laslett has described as the "bastardly prone sub-society" were, or could be, receiving Communion. And this is not at all unimportant considering the current belief amongst social historians that the poor were "hostile, or resistant, or at best indifferent to Protestant Christianity",[27] or that sections of the population "below a certain economic level" managed without religion altogether.[28] Some of the contemporary comments of the Reformers, meant only to condemn the ignorant rabble who made up their flocks, demonstrated incidentally the strength of popular religious practice among that same rabble. The Vicar of Redbourn in Hertfordshire complained in 1585 "at the verie time when I should minister the said Sacramente ... they comme thronginge and pressinge in great numbre commonly without all good order". Richard Leake, preaching in Westmorland in 1599, suggested the appalling harvest and epidemics of the 1590s were a consequence of the north-country people's behaviour at Communion, thronging and pressing forward to receive their "rightings" and making no better than "a common banket of it".[29] In both these instances, the common people were accused of too much eagerness to receive the Sacrament, along with ignorance. The picture fits with a need for reform, but the condemnation of the Reformers is not of apathy.

Amongst this possibly non-apathetic and ignorant mass there must have been a proportion, we shall never know how large or how small, to whom their participation was important, to whom their belief in practice mattered in a fashion even a theologian would admit to be "religious". I am strengthened in this belief by the work of Dr. Judith Maltby,[30] who has found in the ecclesiastical courts of the dioceses of Lincoln and Chester evidence of groups of active

---

26.  Jeremy Boulton, *art cit.,* p. 143 and p. 153, n. 65.
27.  Eamon Duffy, *Seventeenth Century Journal,* I, no. 1 (Durham, Jan 1986), p. 31.
28.  Patrick Collinson, quoting Keith Thomas, in the *Religion of Protestants* (1982), p. 198.
29.  Both quoted by Patrick Collinson, *ibid,* pp. 211-12 and 213-214.
30.  Judith Maltby, "Religious Conformity in Late Elizabethan and Early Stuart England" (unpublished Cambridge Ph.D. 1992). This thesis is being revised for print in the Cambridge Studies in Early Modern British History. The diary of William Coe, a yeoman of Mildenhall after the Restoration, which is being edited for publication along with the *Diary of Isaac Archer,* his own incumbent, for the Suffolk Records Society by Mathew Storey, illustrates the life of the type of conformist the reformers would not have approved, very well. William Coe spent much of his time tippling, much repenting, and much on receiving the Sacrament, which was very important to him.

conformists, who attempted to prosecute their non-conforming ministers for failing to provide services according to the Book of Common Prayer, on Wednesday, Fridays and Saints' and Holy Days, and also for failing to celebrate Holy Communion. The churchwardens of Thurleigh, in Lincoln, for instance, complained in 1608 that their vicar had failed to administer the Sacrament at least three times a year in the last two years. In Cheshire, Dr. Maltby has been able to identify the social and economic status of some of the parishioners who signed a petition in the late 1630s in favour of the Prayer Book. She has demonstrated that these parishioners crossed all economic groups in some parishes, and, most notably, included those on poor relief, even when one of the overseers of the poor failed to sign the petition. The poor did not necessarily therefore sign as a result of social pressure. So committed conformists practising their religion according to the Elizabethan settlement were to be found at all social levels, even amongst those on poor relief.

What was then the meaning of their participation in Holy Communion to the committed amongst the mass of participants at Easter Communion in the diocese of Lincoln in 1603? Again, we can never know, but Bishop Cooper of Lincoln in 1580 composed a homily on the "right use of the Lord's Supper" to be read "before everie celebration of the Lord's Supper, in all such Churches and Parishes as have not a sufficiently hable preacher" so his words were probably heard by a considerable number of people in the Diocese. He wanted his people, even the "unlearned and ignorant" to understand the benefit of the sacrament, and particularly how the eating of the outward elements "quickeneth, stirreth, strengtheneth and increaseth our faith, that we may eat the body and blood of Christ more effectually and fruitfully".[31] These are strong words, even possibly shocking in their purport to someone outside the eucharistic tradition. There was a drop-off in attendance in Brussels amongst nominal Catholics exposed to the Mass in the vernacular after Vatican II. These words cannot have been less startling, surely, to the Elizabethan peasant? Bishop Cooper would have his worshippers in the Diocese of Lincoln in the 1580s say to themselves:

> even as certainly as my taste feeleth the sweetness of bread and wine... even so the taste of my faith and sense of my heart doth feel the sweetness of Christ his body and blood broken and shed for me and all mankind upon the cross.[32]

Ian Green traced over 280 different catechisms published between 1549 and 1646, excluding the longest forms.[33] The most popular of these went through as many as fifty-six editions. One of the four elements expounded in the majority of these catechisms was the doctrine of the sacraments, which only appeared in the official Prayer Book catechism from 1604 onwards. Until then, the

---

31.  John E. Booty, *art cit.,* pp. 131-48.
32.  Booty, *ibid,* p. 146.
33.  Ian Green, " 'For Children in Yeeres and Children in Understanding': The Emergence of the English Catechism under Elizabeth and the Early Stuarts", *Journal of Ecclesiastical History,* xxxvii, 3 (July 1986), pp. 399–400, 402, 405, 410–11.

importance of the omitted subject had been the motive behind the appearance
of many of the alternative catechisms, which had preparation for Communion
as one of their major objectives. They emphasised the "understanding of the
precise nature and purpose of the sacrament, and the need for a rigorous self-
examination before each Communion."[34]

Cranmer and Calvin had wanted a weekly Communion or Lord's Supper:
Calvin wrote that the custom of communicating once a year was "a veritable
invention of the devil".[35] The Anglican church did not manage to avoid this
condemnation: although there are some hints that a monthly celebration was
held by at least some Elizabethan and Stuart reformers. The vicar who
grumbled at Redbourn in Hertfordshire in 1585 of his flock's unseemly
eagerness to receive, himself celebrated once a month, after divine service and
his sermon.[36] George Herbert in the early 1630s wished for a monthly
celebration, but if this was not possible, "at least five or six times in a year: as at
Easter, Christmas, Whitsuntide, afore and after Harvest, and at the beginning of
Lent".[37] If we move away from parochial Communions to the conventicles of the
godly, in which the separatist churches may often have been rooted, we find that
some of the puritan exercises, like the "eager and vast crowds ... flocking to
perform their practices" under the jaundiced eye of an imprisoned Jesuit in
Wisbech Castle in 1588, ended with a Communion. He estimated the number
involved, no doubt wrongly, as high as 1000.[38] In the same way the very different
minister at Denton Chapel in the 1630s, John Angier, held monthly communions,
which attracted "hundreds" of "godly folk", some of whom travelled thirty miles
to attend. Patrick Collinson writes that "monthly sacraments" seem to have
been a special feature of life in the north west.[39] Only local research would show
whether this was rooted in earlier popular belief. When Richard Baxter
established his monthly communions which "gather the faithful from a wide
catchment area" in Kidderminster in the 1650s[40] he seems to have been building
on long-established puritan practice.

---

34.  George Herbert laid down "the time of every one's first receiving is not so much by
     yeers, as by understanding: particularly, the rule may be this: When anyone can
     distinguish the Sacramentall from common bread, knowing the Institution and the
     difference hee ought to receive, of what age soever. Children and youths are usually
     deferred too long, under pretence of devotion to the Sacrament, but it is for want of
     instruction: ... Parents and Masters should make hast in this... which while they
     deferr, both sides suffer. *A Priest to the Temple, or, The Country Parson His Character,
     and Rule of Holy Life* (Printed 1662) in *The Works of George Herbert* ed. F.E.
     Hutchinson (Oxford, 1941), pp. 258-9.
35.  Stephen Mayor, *The Lord's Supper in Early English Dissent* pp. xiv-xv and x.
36.  Patrick Collinson, *ibid*, pp. 211-12.
37.  George Herbert, *ibid.*
38.  Quoted *in extenso*, in my *Contrasting Communities* pp. 262-3.
39.  Patrick Collinson, *ibid*, pp. 263-64.
40.  Patrick Collinson, "Towards a Broader Understanding of the Early Dissenting
     Tradition" (1975), reprinted in *Godly People* (London 1983), p. 537.

The next great religious census of the seventeenth century after 1603 is the Compton Census of 1676[41] which lists "Conformists", "non-Conformists" and "Papists" by parish. If we consider only the four per cent of the population in 1676 who were counted as Dissenters, then we shall be moving away from a consideration of a proportion of the population who had at least a general acquaintance with popular religion and religious practice, to a tiny minority, who, we can be quite sure, held beliefs a theologian would recognise. For the Dissenters in 1676 were a hunted and persecuted people. Their genuine religious convictions can never be in doubt. For them it was very costly to practice, whereas in 1603 it had been costly, albeit in a very minor way, not to conform.

Just as we found from Dr. Maltby's work in Cheshire that the active conformists desiring the continuance of the Prayer Book in the late 1630s crossed all social groups including those on poor relief, so also do we find that the Dissenters of the 1670s crossed all groups taxed in the Hearth Taxes of that decade, even including those exempt from taxation on the grounds of poverty. William Stevenson has worked on the social and economic status of Dissenters in the late-seventeenth-century. He has come up with a massive group of more than 750 non-conformists of all denominations identified in the relevant Hearth Taxes of 1674 for Bedfordshire, Cambridgeshire and Huntingdonshire. He collected enough members of the Quakers, Congregationalists, Baptists and Open Baptists to form satisfyingly large samples for each sect. The results are therefore the most thorough examination that we have or are likely to have of the status of Dissenters immediately after the Restoration. "It is the very 'ordinariness' of sectaries which is so striking" he writes.

> They were not confined to any particular social rank or subgroup...
> they ranged from lowly servants and labourers to humble craftsmen
> and husbandmen, small retailers, prosperous wholesalers, yeoman,
> professionals and gentlemen.

The contemporary slur so often used by the Bishops in 1669 against them, that the congregations consisted simply of "mean mechanicks" and the "vulgar sort" was wrong.[42]

Post-Restoration Dissenters seem, in general, excluding the Quakers of course, to have lived a much richer sacramental life than their Anglican counterparts, although they still did not achieve the weekly Communion desired by both Calvin and Cranmer.[43] This is a change that has been missed.

---

41. Anne Whiteman (ed.), *The Compton census of 1676: a critical edition*, Records of social and economic history, N.S. x (British Academy, 1986).

42. W. Stevenson, "The Economic and Social Status of Protestant Sectaries in Huntingdonshire, Cambridgeshire and Bedfordshire, 1650-1725" (Cambridge Ph.D, 1990), pp. 251, 343-44. Dr. Stevenson is contributing two chapters to my forthcoming book *The World of Rural Dissenters, 1520-1725.*

43. Patrick Collinson, "Towards a Broader Understanding of the Early Dissenting Tradition" (1975), reprinted in *Godly People* p. 537.

Stephen Mayor in the *Lord's Supper in Early English Dissent* writes, indeed,

> it is of course true that the early Dissenters gave a smaller place to
> the Eucharist than many Christians have done... for those who
> believe it to be absolutely central to the Christian Faith, the place
> they gave it was inadequate.[44]

The magnitude of the change, to a Lord's Supper not three times a year but
monthly, or at least six-weekly, on Baxter's model, may have been missed
because of the format of the surviving seventeenth-century Church Books. They
place very little emphasis on the substance of the routine meetings of which they
record the dates: they hardly ever describe the "normal" events, which are
assumed. The bulk of the business recorded is dealing with the errant and the
aberrant, not the normal. Yet careful reading seems to show that groups of
Dissenters, separated in doctrine from Arminian to Calvinist, and in geography
from Cambridgeshire and Bedfordshire to Yorkshire, celebrated monthly and
sometimes even more frequently. This was true of the Open Baptists of
Fenstanton and of Huntingdonshire in the 1650s[45] and of Bunyan's Open
Baptist Church on the Bedfordshire border where the members agreed in 1659
"to entreat our brother Wheeler, brother Donne, brother Gibbs and brother
Breedon to give their assistance in the worke of God in preaching and breaking
of breade once every moneth or 3 weeks, one after another on the Lordes
Dayes".[46] It also seems to be true of the strict Calvinist Church of Guyhirn and
Isleham in north east Cambridgeshire, which covenanted in 1687,[47] and the

---

44.  *Ibid*, pp. 158-9.
45.  *Records of the Churches of Christ gathered at Fenstanton, Warboys and Hexham, 1644-
     1720* ed. E.B. Underhill (Hanserd Knollys Soc., London, 1854). Up to the beginning
     of 1654 the Church Book only gives details of disciplinary disputes. In 1655 it
     becomes evident that every general meeting opens with prayer, supplication and an
     exhortation, before the discipline, and business. (See for instance pp. 127, 135).
     During that year, the minutes also record that the meeting closes with praise, and a
     dismissal (p. 147). Soon afterwards, the "observation of some ordinances of God" or
     "the Most High" were recorded after the business, before the praise and the dismissal
     (p. 179). Once, the standard description varied helpfully, "after which praise was
     rendered to God: then we broke bread together", before the dismissal (p. 200). One
     explanatory clause was sometimes added "And so (the day being spent) the assembly
     were dismissed" (e.g. p. 201). This is interesting in view of the stress in the church that
     the "breaking of bread" should, scripturally, follow supper (pp. 36-7, 61, 67-70, 188).
     The general meetings were held monthly. It is impossible to say whether the change
     in recording in 1655, and the regular monthly "observation of some ordinances of
     God" represents simply a change in the detail of the minutes, or a genuine change in
     church practice. Anyway, by 1655, the breaking of bread, one of the "ordinances of
     the Lord", took place monthly.
46.  *The Minutes of the First Independent Church at Bedford* (now Bunyan Meeting), p.
     35.
47.  *The Church Book of the Independent Church (*now Pound Lane Baptist) *Isleham, 1693-
     1805*, ed. Kenneth A.C. Parsons, *Cambridge Antiquarian Records Society*, 6 (Cambridge,
     1984), p. 29-30 (1693/4 Covenant, nos. 5, 6 and 12) and pp. 62, 1756 Covenant, nos. 4,
     16 and 63.

church of the non-conforming Presbyterian, Oliver Heywood, based in the West Riding of Yorkshire in the 1680s and 90s.[48] The magnitude of the change involved in the lives of the Dissenters of 1676 by the routine of the constantly repeated practice of breaking bread together in the sacrament of the body and blood of the Lord seems very important indeed. It is a change that does not seem to have been stressed in the literature. It was of course theologically possible because the "gathered" churches were a people set apart, or in Isaac Watt's words:

> A Garden wall'd around,
> Chosen and made peculiar Ground.[49]

They thus no longer faced the problems of discipline and the barring of unworthy recipients of Communion, whilst still collecting the essential tithes on which the incumbent lived, which had caused Ralph Josselin not to celebrate for nearly nine years in Earls Colne,[50] or Richard Baxter during his whole time in Bridgenorth.[51] On the contrary, for the members of these churches "preaching the Gospell and breaking of bread" were inextricably interlinked[52] or, as the same Church Book put it, "the nature of fellowship [is] the Word, prayer, and breaking of bread".[53] Withdrawal from this sacrament ordained by Christ was therefore an offence, as a long letter of rebuke written by Bunyan's Church to one of its members in 1669 shows. One of the chief accusations was:

> In your so long neglecting to be conscionably found in the godly practise of the Lord's Supper, concerning which, had you bene tender, had not the table of the Lord bene too meene in your thoughtes, how could you for years have absented your self. And if by that bread and that cup, we show to our selves and each other the Lord's death, we had seen it by that but seldom had we therein taken you for example. In considering that appointment is such that is oft to be put into practise, and that for the help of our faith, both as to our remembering the Lord, and discerning of his body and blood, we cannot but judge you guilty.[54]

---

48.  J. Horsfall Turner (ed.) *Autobiography, diaries anecdotes and eventbooks of Oliver Heywood,* (Brighouse, 1881), pp. 1, 32-3 and 35-6.
49.  Considered in Donald Davie, *A Gathered Church: the Literature of the English Dissenting Interest, 1700-1930* (London, 1978), pp. 28-30.
50.  *The Diary of Ralph Josselin, 1616-1683,* ed. A. Macfarlane (London, 1976), pp. 77, 96, 234-7.
51.  *The Autobiography of Richard Baxter,* ed. N.H. Keeble (London, 1974), p. 18.
52.  *Minutes of the First Independent Church at Bedford,* p. 35.
53.  *Ibid,* p. 20.
54.  *Ibid,* p. 43.

The rules promulgated by Soham Church in the 1690s laid down that

> abstaining from any instituted ordinance which the Lord may call
> us to... is also a breach of covenant.[55]

At a later renewal of the covenant in the same church, the point was emphasised.
There was no acceptable excuse for

> forsaking the assembling of ourselves together... to worship God...
> when we break bread in the Lord's Supper, for there all ought to
> assemble with the church let what gospel man soever preach.[56]

What then did this increased frequency of celebration of the Lord's Supper,
which I suggest is a very significant change, mean to these post-Restoration
Dissenters? The Savoy Declaration of 1658, drawn up by delegates from
Independent Churches[57] was orthodoxly Calvinist in its doctrine:

> Sacraments are holy Signs and Seals of the Covenant of Grace,
> immediately instituted by Christ to represent him and his benefit,
> and confirm our interest in him... Our Lord Jesus Christ in the night
> wherein he was betrayed, instituted the Sacrament of his Body and
> Blood, called the Lord's Supper... for the perpetual remembrance
> and shewing forth of the Sacrifice of Himself in his death, the
> sealing of all benefits thereof unto true believers... and to be bond
> and pledge their communion with him, and with each other.[58]

Richard Baxter wrote a programme of meditation for the communicant in his
*Christian Directory* and emphasised the presence of Christ

> When you behold the consecrated bread and wine, discern the
> Lord's body, and reverence it as the representative body and blood
> of Jesus Christ; and take heed of profaning it, by looking on it as
> common bread and wine; though it be not transubstantiate, but still
> is very bread and wine in its natural being, yet it is Christ's body and
> blood in representation and effect. Look on it as the consecrated
> bread of life, which with the quickening Spirit must nourish you to
> life eternal... Even as in delivering the possession of house or lands,
> the deliverer giveth you a key, and a twig[59] and a turf, and saith "I

---

55. *The Church Book of the Independent Church* (now Pound Lane Baptist) *Isleham, 1693-
    1805,* p. 29.
56. *Ibid,* pp. 62-3.
57. Fully laid out and discussed in Stephen Mayor, *op. cit.,* pp. 79-85.
58. *Ibid,* pp. 79 and 81.
59. This reference must have been extremely familiar to all copyholders who were given
    entry to their lands "by the rod, at the will of the Lord".

deliver you this house, and I deliver you this land": so doth the minister by Christ's authority deliver you Christ, and pardon, and title to eternal life.[60]

But the theology of the Savoy Declaration, and the devotional directives of Baxter still do not tell us of the relative importance of the Lord's Supper in the lives of ordinary seventeenth-century Dissenters, and what they made of this increasing sacramental activity. Was Keith Thomas right after all in postulating that seventeenth-century religion was really increasingly rational and socially cohesive? Was the religion of Dissenters, at least, as it emerged into the industrial eighteenth century, one "from which the primitive 'magical' elements had been very largely shorn"?[61]

To examine what seventeenth-century Dissenters made of the sacramental activity of the Lord's Supper, I turn to the literature. John Bunyan is writing for the same rural audience whose doings are recorded in *The Minutes of the First Independent Church of Bedford,* and whom we now know from Dr. Stephenson's work to be even poorer than the rural average. His verse disappoints us: his poem written in *A Book for Boys and Girls or Country Rhimes for Children,* printed in 1686, on the Sacrament is more concerned to warn against the dangers, than to stress the benefits of reception.

> Two sacraments I do believe there be,
> Ev'n baptism and the Supper of the Lord:
> Both mysteries divine, which do to me,
> By God's appointment, benefit afford:
>
> But shall they be my God, or shall I have
> Of them so foul and impious afford,
> To think that from the curse they can me save?
> Bread, wine, nor water me no ransom bought.[62]

Bunyan's prose is more revealing however.

> Christian in the Palace Beautiful sat down, when supper was ready, to... a Table... furnished with fat things, and with Wine that was well refined; and all their talk at the Table, was about the Lord of the Hill.[63]

In turn, Mr. Greatheart brings a token from the Lord to Christiana which is a "Bottle of Wine". And at supper in the inn where Christiana stays, which is a forerunner of the "Supper of the great King in his Kingdom" is a "Bottle of Wine,

---

60. Richard Baxter, *Christian Directory, Works,* IV, pp. 337-8, quoted Stephen Mayor, *op. cit.,* p. 137.
61. Keith Thomas, *Religion and the Decline of Magic,* pp. 760-6.
62. *A Book for Girls and Boys,* p. 26.
63. John Bunyan, *Pilgrims Progress,* (OUP ed. 1904, reprinted 1945), p. 65.

red as Blood", which is the "juice of the true Vine, that makes glad the Heart of God and Man".[64]

But for more extensive and real insight into the importance of the Lord's Supper to the late seventeenth- and early eighteenth-century Dissenters, we have to turn to the two great hymn writers of the Old Dissent, Philip Doddridge and Isaac Watts. Philip Doddridge was born as late as 1702, and ministered to the very important Dissenting congregation in Northampton.[65] We owe to him a hymn still regularly sung at the Eucharist in Anglican churches.

> My God, and is thy table spread,
> and doth thy cup with love o'erflow?
> thither be all thy children lead,
> and let them all thy sweetness know.
>
> Hail, sacred feast which Jesus makes,
> rich banquet of his flesh and blood!
> thrice happy he who here partakes
> that sacred stream, that heavenly food.
>
> O let thy table honoured be,
> and furnished well with joyful guests;
> and may each soul salvation see,
> that here its sacred pledges taste.[66]

As well as his own work, he also gives us a glimpse which is even more important, since it is in the correct period, into the rôle and importance in the lives of rural people who formed the sort of congregations in Bedfordshire and Cambridgeshire we have been talking about, of the hymns of his senior, Isaac Watts. In 1731, he wrote to Dr. Watts, who was then aged 57,

> When preaching in a barn to a pretty large assembley of plain
> country people, at a village a few miles off... we sung one of your

64.  *Ibid*, pp. 279 and 311.
65.  *Calendar of the Correspondence of Philip Doddridge. DD. 1705-1751*, ed. Geoffrey F. Nuttall, H.M.S.O. joint publication 26 and Northants. Rec. Soc. XXIX (1979). I am particularly grateful to the Revd. Ronald Bocking who spent some time after my lecture searching for, and sending me, references to the observance of the Communion Service in the Castle Hill Church of Northampton while Doddridge was minister there. The tradition was a monthly evening celebration. The date varied according to the phase of the moon, so that the worshippers could get safely home by moonlight. Malcolm Deacon, *Philip Doddridge of Northampton* (1980), p. 72; C. Stanford, *Philip Doddridge* (1880), p. 127; John Stoughton, *History of Religion in England*, Vol. VI, p. 94.
66.  *Hymns Ancient and Modern, New Standard* (1983) no. 259. Professor Alan Everitt points out to me (personal communication) that I should not properly use Doddridge's work to illustrate this paper, in view of the great shift in sensibility and taste that took place in just this period. See Alan Everitt, "Springs of Sensibility: Philip Doddridge of Northampton and the Evangelical Tradition", in Alan Everitt, *Landscape and Community in England*, (London, 1985), pp. 209-245.

Hymns... these were most of them poor people who work for their living. On the mention of your name, I found they had read several of your books with great delight, and that your Hymns and Psalms were almost their daily entertainment. And when one of the company said, "What if Dr. Watts should come down to Northampton?", another replied with a remarkable warmth "The very sight of him would be like an ordinance [i.e. the Lord's Supper] to me".[67]

Isaac Watts had been born in 1674, and may properly be regarded as a seventeenth-century author: his hymns were published in 1707[68] and were already being sung from manuscript in the Dissenting Chapel in Southampton in 1694 and 1695.[69] He himself wrote that he had "just permitted [his] verse to rise above a flat and indolent style" and was "sensible that [he had] often subdued it below" the esteem of the critics, "and because I would neither *indulge* any bold metaphors, nor admit of hard words, nor *tempt the ignorant worshipper to sing without his understanding*".[70] So Isaac Watts had deliberately pitched his words and their meaning at the type of congregation worshipping in a barn, "plain country people... poor people who work for their living" whom Philip Doddridge later observed singing them with such enthusiasm. Isaac Watts wanted them to understand the words. And what words, and what meaning, they were. If the Holy Communion, or the Lord's Supper was "instituted by Christ to represent Him and His benefits" in the words of the Savoy Confession of 1658, then the Dissenters singing in Southampton in the 1690s and in barns in Northamptonshire in the 1730s, were certainly not practising a religion from which the primitive magical elements had been shorn. For the Lord's Supper represented more than bonding between believers: it represented bonding and union with God. The last section of Isaac Watts's *Hymns* were those "prepared

---

67.  *Calendar of the Correspondence of Philip Doddridge*, p. 62. Professor Davie in *A Gathered Church* drew attention to Leslie Stephen writing on Isaac Watts's hymns. Stephen wrote that for many years 50,000 copies of Watts's psalms and hymns were printed annually. And Davie comments: "We a century after Leslie Stephen have no way of dealing with such phenomena, no method by which to translate the quantitative facts of so many copies printed and sold year after year, into the qualitative consideration of how they conditioned the sensibility of the English-speaking peoples. But what we can, and should do... is to confess and insist... just what a vast lacuna this reveals in our pretensions to chart cultural history". *Small Books and Pleasant Histories*, p. 8. The Doddridge/Watts correspondence suggests that Watts's influence was indeed enormously widespread and should not be under-estimated amongst the common people. At the end of the eighteenth-century, James Raines's grandmother, who was blind and had lived in an almshouse, taught him the whole of Watts's *Hymns* from memory. *A Raine Miscellany*, ed. Angela Marsden, Surtees Society CC (1991), p. 17.
68.  Bernard Manning, *The Hymns of Wesley and Watts: Five Informal Papers* (Epworth, 1942), p. 81.
69.  Donald Davie, *op. cit.*, p. 30.
70.  Quoted Donald Davie, *op. cit.*, p. 24.

for the Holy Ordinance of the Lord's Supper".[71] And to Isaac Watts, in accordance with the doctrine of the Savoy Declaration, the Lord's Supper was more than a memorial.[72] These late seventeenth- and early eighteenth-century Dissenters do not seem to have been condemned to mere stoicism, for in Watt's own "flat and indolent style"

> This holy bread and wine
> Maintains our fainting breath
> By union with our living Lord
> And interest in His death.

> Here have we seen Thy face, O Lord
> And view'd salvation with our eyes;
> Tasted and felt the Living Word,
> The bread descending from the skies.

---

71.  Bernard Manning, *ibid,* p. 80.
72.  Bernard Manning, *ibid,* p. 104.

# Index

Capp, Bernard, study of almanacs by 198
Carleton, Thomas, education of 229–30
Carlton, heath in 103
carrier services 6
Carrington, Roger, of Lincoln 54
Carter, John, bibles bequeathed by 38
cartography, growth of 207–10
catechisms, Elizabethan and early Stuart
    333–4
Caxton
    Baptist church at 271, 284, 286
    Baptists at 265, 282
    Open Baptists at 270
    persons of 271
Cecil, William, set of routes owned by
    207–8
chapbooks 307
    collected by Samuel Pepys 198
    courtship 302
    purchasers of 165, 166, 200
    readership of 212–13
    as sources of some of Bunyan's
        imagery 232
chapmen
    almanac for 208
    gross and net values of estates of
        58–9
chapwoman, stock in trade of 211–12
Charity School movement 249, 250
Charles II, complaint by Cambridge
    Quakers to 288–9
Chartier, Roger 202, 205
Chartres, Professor John 6
Chatterton, Richard, of Snitterby 70, 71
Chaucer, Geoffrey, archdeacon described
    by 306
cheap print
    availability of 197, 198–9, 299
    content of 216
    rarely listed in inventories 55
    vendors of 200–1
Cheesewright family, of Chippenham 181
Cheshire
    conformists in 335
    Macclesfield in 48–9

presentments in church courts from
    316
Chester, diocese of, active conformists in
    332–3
Chew, Edward, of Lancaster 50
Chicksands, Gilbertine house at 104, 106,
    111, 112
children, expenses of keeping 65–6
children, under-age, influence on will
        making 157–9
childwite fines 308–9
Chippenham 2, 10, 24, 26, 97–149
    10th-century land acquisitions in
        101–2
    in 1544 149
    in the 15th century 123–30
    1544 survey of 105–6, 130–36, 179
    1712 map of 97, 139, 141, 143–4
    alehouses at 153
    ancient roads at 99
    annotations to 1544 rental 137
    Badlingham hamlet in 136
    bordars in 103
    bronze age barrows at 99
    changes in open fields at in 18th
        century 143–4
    changing size of population 97–8
    Clericus family of 111, 113–14,
        117–18
    community of in Hundred Rolls
        120–23
    consolidation of copyhold holdings at
        129–30
    conversion to leasehold at 137, 138
    cottars in 122, 125
    de Camera family of 111, 113, 114,
        116–17
    decline of free peasants at 119–20
    demesne in 121, 122, 130–31
    deserted house sites in 123–4
    disappearance of smallholdings at 143
    dissenters at 177–8
    Ditch Way in 99
    in Domesday Book 103–4, 116
    early setlement at 98–100

20                                    INDEX